Patent Cultures

This book explores how dissimilar patent systems remain distinctive despite international efforts toward harmonization. The dominant historical account describes harmonization as ever-growing, with familiar milestones such as the Paris Convention (1883), the World Intellectual Property Organization's founding (1967), and the formation of current global institutions of patent governance. Yet throughout the modern period, countries fashioned their own mechanisms for fostering technological invention. Notwithstanding the harmonization project, diversity in patent cultures remains stubbornly persistent. No single comprehensive volume describes the comparative historical development of patent practices. *Patent Cultures: Diversity and Harmonization in Historical Perspective* seeks to fill this gap. Tracing national patenting from imperial expansion in the early nineteenth century to our time, this work asks fundamental questions about the limits of globalization, innovation's cultural dimension, and how historical context shapes patent policy. It is essential reading for anyone seeking to understand the contested role of patents in the modern world.

GRAEME GOODAY is Professor of the History of Science and Technology in the University of Leeds School of Philosophy, Religion and History of Science. From 2007 to 2010 he led the Arts & Humanities Research Council-funded project "Owning and Disowning Invention," which produced the prize-winning *Patently Contestable* (2013) with coauthor Stathis Arapostathis. He was also coleader with Claire L. Jones of the international research network "Rethinking Patent Cultures" (2014), the first workshop of which generated this *Patent Cultures* volume.

STEVEN WILF is the Anthony J. Smits Professor of Global Commerce at the University of Connecticut Law School where he founded the Intellectual Property program. He has served as Microsoft Fellow at Princeton University and Abraham L. Kaminstein Scholar in Residence at the United States Copyright Office. He is the author of *The Law before the Law* (2008), *Law's Imagined Republic: Popular Politics and Criminal Justice in Revolutionary America* (Cambridge University Press, 2010), and numerous articles.

Cambridge Intellectual Property and Information Law

As its economic potential has rapidly expanded, intellectual property has become a subject of front-rank legal importance. Cambridge Intellectual Property and Information Law is a series of monograph studies of major current issues in intellectual property. Each volume contains a mix of international, European, comparative and national law, making this a highly significant series for practitioners, judges and academic researchers in many countries.

Series Editors

Lionel Bently
Herchel Smith Professor of Intellectual Property Law, University of Cambridge

Graeme Dinwoodie
Global Professor of Intellectual Property Law, Chicago-Kent College of Law, Illinois Institute of Technology

Advisory Editors

William R. Cornish, Emeritus Herchel Smith Professor of Intellectual Property Law, University of Cambridge

François Dessemontet, Professor of Law, University of Lausanne

Jane C. Ginsburg, Morton L. Janklow Professor of Literary and Artistic Property Law, Columbia Law School

Paul Goldstein, Professor of Law, Stanford University

The Rt Hon. Sir Robin Jacob, Hugh Laddie Professor of Intellectual Property, University College London

Ansgar Ohly, Professor of Intellectual Property Law, Ludwig-Maximilian University of Munich

A list of books in the series can be found at the end of this volume.

Patent Cultures

Diversity and Harmonization in Historical Perspective

Edited by

Graeme Gooday

University of Leeds

Steven Wilf

University of Connecticut

CAMBRIDGE
UNIVERSITY PRESS

CAMBRIDGE
UNIVERSITY PRESS

University Printing House, Cambridge CB2 8BS, United Kingdom

One Liberty Plaza, 20th Floor, New York, NY 10006, USA

477 Williamstown Road, Port Melbourne, VIC 3207, Australia

314-321, 3rd Floor, Plot 3, Splendor Forum, Jasola District Centre, New Delhi - 110025, India

103 Penang Road, #05-06/07, Visioncrest Commercial, Singapore 238467

Cambridge University Press is part of the University of Cambridge.

It furthers the University's mission by disseminating knowledge in the pursuit of education, learning and research at the highest international levels of excellence.

www.cambridge.org
Information on this title: www.cambridge.org/9781108468886
DOI: 10.1017/9781108654333

First published 2020
First paperback edition 2022

A catalogue record for this publication is available from the British Library

Library of Congress Cataloging in Publication data
Names: Gooday, Graeme, 1965– editor. | Wilf, Steven Robert, editor.
Title: Patent cultures : diversity and harmonization in historical perspective /
  [edited by] Graeme Gooday, Steven Wilf.
Description: 1. | New York : Cambridge University Press, 2019. |
  Series: Cambridge intellectual property and information law |
  Includes bibliographical references and index.
Identifiers: LCCN 2019038200 (print) | LCCN 2019038201 (ebook) |
  ISBN 9781108475761 (hardback) | ISBN 9781108468886 (paperback) |
  ISBN 9781108654333 (epub)
Subjects: LCSH: Patent laws and legislation. | Intellectual property.
Classification: LCC K1505 .P373 2019 (print) | LCC K1505 (ebook) |
  DDC 346.04/86–dc23
LC record available at https://lccn.loc.gov/2019038200
LC ebook record available at https://lccn.loc.gov/2019038201

ISBN 978-1-108-47576-1 Hardback
ISBN 978-1-108-46888-6 Paperback

Contents

Part VI   Epilogue   341

Figures

Tables

Contributors

Stathis Arapostathis is Assistant Professor of History of Science and Technology in the Department of History and Philosophy of Science at the National and Kapodistrian University of Athens. In addition to coauthoring, with Graeme Gooday, *Patently Contestable: Electrical Technologies and Inventor Identities on Trial in Britain* (MIT Press, 2013), he coedited with Graham Dutfield *Knowledge Management and Intellectual Property: Concepts, Actors and Practices from the Past to the Present* (Edward Elgar, 2013).

Edward Beatty is Professor of History and Faculty Fellow at the Kellogg Institute for International Affairs at the University of Notre Dame, USA. A historian specializing in economic development in nineteenth- and twentieth-century Latin America and especially in Mexico, he has published *Institutions and Investment: The Political Basis of Industrialization in Mexico before 1911* (Stanford University Press, 2001) and *Technology and the Search for Progress in Modern Mexico* (University of California Press, 2015), which won the 2016 Friedrich Katz Prize for the best book on Latin American and Caribbean history from the American Historical Association.

Kjell Ericson is a Program-Specific Assistant Professor in the Center for the Promotion of Interdisciplinary Education and Research at Kyoto University, Japan. He writes about environmental and legal history in Japan, with a focus on marine issues. He is now completing a book manuscript on the history of pearl cultivation.

Bernardita Escobar Andrae is an Economist and Economic historian in the Department of Political Science and Public Administration at the Faculty of Law and Social Sciences, University of Talca, Chile. She has written numerous articles on the economic and business history of Chile, focusing on issues of intellectual property and gender.

Courtney Fullilove is an Associate Professor of History and affiliated faculty in the Science in Society Program at Wesleyan University,

USA. She researches the history of sustainability, biodiversity, intellectual property law, traditional knowledge, and cultural heritage. She is the author of *The Profit of the Earth: The Global Seeds of American Agriculture* (University of Chicago Press, 2017).

Gabriel Galvez-Behar is a Professor in contemporary history at the University of Lille, France, specializing in economic history, history of science and technology, and the history of innovation in France. His first monograph was *La République des Inventeurs: Proprieté et organisation de l'innovation en France, 1791–1922* (PU Rennes, 2008).

Graeme Gooday is Professor of the History of Science and Technology at the University of Leeds. He led the Arts & Humanities Research Council (AHRC)-funded project "Owning and Disowning Invention" from which he produced with coauthor Stathis Arapostathis the prize-winning *Patently Contestable: Electrical Technologies and Inventor Identities on Trial in Britain* (MIT Press, 2013); this is currently being translated into Mandarin. Gooday was also the principal investigator for the international AHRC network "Rethinking Patent Cultures" in which he and coauthor Karen Sayer extended patents research to the history of hearing aids.

Karl Hall is Associate Professor in the Department of History at the Central European University, Hungary. Training as a historian of Soviet physics, he now specializes in Central and East European intellectual history, with research on industrial laboratories, intellectual property, and tacit knowledge. He was the coeditor with Michael Gordin and Alexei Kojevnikov of *Intelligentsia Science: The Russian Century, 1860–1960* special issue of *Osiris* (2008).

B. Zorina Khan is Professor of Economics at Bowdoin College, USA. Her research examines issues in law and economic history, including intellectual property rights, technological progress in Europe and the United States, antitrust, litigation and legal systems, and corporate governance. Her first book, *The Democratization of Invention: Patents and Copyrights in American Economic Development, 1790–1920* (Cambridge University Press, 2005), received the Alice Hanson Jones Biennial Prize for outstanding work in North American economic history.

Alessandro Nuvolari is Professor of Economic History at Sant'Anna School of Advanced Studies, Pisa, Italy, specializing in the economics of innovation, especially the roles of science and technology in "modern economic growth" and has published extensively on the relationship between patent systems and economic performance both in historical and contemporary contexts.

Ana Romero de Pablos is a Research Fellow at the Institute of Philosophy in the Department of Science, Technology and Society at the Spanish National Research Council in Madrid, Spain. As Historian of Science and Technology, she has published extensively on the history of physics and nuclear energy in Spain, female scientists in physics, and on patents and on the circulation of knowledge and scientific objects. In addition to her co-authored volume with María Jesús Santesmases *Cien años de Política Científica en España* (Fundación BBVA, 2008), her most recent book is *Las primeras centrales nucleares españolas. Actores, políticas y tecnologías* (Sociedad Nuclear española, 2019).

Rajesh Sagar is a qualified solicitor advocate in England and Wales and a member of the Bar Council of Delhi in India. He regularly advises clients on intellectual property and ancillary matters and has extensive experience of co-ordinating high value, multi-jurisdictional patent litigations across the Life Sciences and TMT sectors. He was recently instrumental in enforcing the current European data and marketing exclusivity regime for the very first time. Within the TMT sector, Rajesh has a particular focus on issues of FRAND royalty terms and the enforceability of standard essential patents. He is regularly published on these subjects, and has worked on several intellectual property projects funded by organisations such as the European Commission and UK Research Councils. His PhD thesis is entitled "The evolution of patent policy in India from 1856 – 2005", and he has regularly published and spoken about his research at conferences.

Tania Sebastian is Assistant Professor of Law at School of Law, Vellore Institute of Technology, Chennai, India (previously she was an assistant professor at the Gujarat National Law University in Gandhinagar, India). Currently pursuing her PhD, she has published on patent and healthcare law in India.

Michelangelo Vasta is Professor of Economic History in the Department of Economics and Statistics at the University of Siena, Italy. His main fields of interest are economics of innovation in the long-run perspective, institutions and economic performance, the economic history of living standards, entrepreneurship, and trade. He has published extensively in the major economic history and business history journals.

Steven Wilf is the Anthony J. Smits Professor of Global Commerce, Law School, University of Connecticut, USA. His research focuses on intellectual property law and legal history, and he is the author of *The Law before the Law* (Rowman & Littlefield, 2008), *Law's Imagined Republic: Popular Politics and Criminal Justice in Revolutionary America* (Cambridge University Press, 2010), and numerous articles. In 2016 and 2018 he was a visiting professor at Yale Law School.

Preface

This collective volume arises from the workshop "International Diversity in Patent Cultures – a Historical Perspective" that was held May 15–16, 2014 at the University of Leeds. This was funded by the UK's Arts & Humanities Research Council grant "Rethinking Patent Cultures" AH/L009803/1. Like the edited chapters that have come together here, there was no direct aspiration then to achieve any "global" conclusions: that would have required a much larger event than we could achieve with an open call for papers at a two-day workshop. After an international open call for contributors, we received participants from Europe, North America, South America, and Asia; that international representation is matched in the chapters of this book. Overall we draw from the work of contributors some provisional claims about the diversity and commonalities of patent cultures in sixteen countries in those four continents, with comments on the recent roles of Africa and China. This is therefore definitely not the last word on the topic, only (we humbly think) a starting point. We very much hope that other scholars will be able to take this topic further to achieve a broader geographical and cultural reach in discussing patent cultures than can be achieved in one volume.

Acknowledgments

We are grateful to the Arts & Humanities Research Council for supporting the Research Network project "Rethinking Patent Cultures" that funded the workshop that generated this book, also the principal investigator, Graeme Gooday, co-investigator, Claire L. Jones, and the network administrator, Carl Warom.

We thank commentators at the May 2014 workshop, especially Lionel Bently, Mario Biagioli, Graham Dutfield, and Steven Wilf, and all the participants, including Jose Bellido and Patricio Sáiz. Also three anonymous reviewers for Cambridge University Press whose comments helped us to refine the book considerably in the latter stages of its development.

Versions of papers were presented at the Society of History of Technology Round Table at the National University of Singapore on June 24, 2016.

Graeme Gooday would particularly like to thank Gregory Radick, Jamie Stark, and other colleagues and PhD students in the Centre for History and Philosophy of Science, School of Philosophy, Religion and History of Science at the University of Leeds, and of course Christine "Chris" MacLeod for her unfailing wisdom and moral support for our exploration of the history of patents.

Steven Wilf would particularly like to thank the Law School of the University of Connecticut for its support. The many students who have served as interlocutors over the years have been a special source of encouragement. As always, this book would not have been possible without Guita and our family.

In preparing the manuscript of this book we thank our three dedicated proofreaders: Lewis Hodges, Hannah Hunt, and Callum Duguid, and Debbie Foy for her final assistance in assembling the script.

At Cambridge University Press we thank Matt Gallaway and his team for making the publication process so smooth. This has been a global project, and one of the benefits of the conferences, conversations, and the production of this volume has been the opportunity to exchange ideas with such a talented cohort. The coeditors are especially fortunate to have enjoyed the process of collaboration – even if it has meant the juggling of two busy academic schedules. Our conversations in person over three continents and across two disciplines has been a pleasure. We may have had the only conversation about patent sovereignty and harmonization that has taken place at Raffles Long Bar in Singapore with (naturally) the assistance of a few Singapore Slings. And we hope this book is better for such convivial moments.

Note on the Cover Image

This volume's cover image comes from the front of a 1948 Japanese children's book entitled *Two Inventions That Will Lift Up the Nation: The Pearl and the Automatic Loom*, written by an elected Diet member named Toyosawa Toyoo and illustrated by artist Kinoshita Shigeru. Toyosawa's book consists of hagiographic accounts of two individual inventors, the pearl cultivator Mikimoto Kōkichi and the loom maker Toyoda Sakichi. Heroic inventor narratives (and illustrations) of British industrial figures like James Watt circulated widely in the late nineteenth-century world. Meiji Japan (1868–1912) was no exception. Tales of Japanese invention, centering on figures including Mikimoto and Toyoda, appeared with regularity from the first decade of the twentieth century onward. In one sense, *Two Inventions That Will Lift Up the Nation* reflected the ongoing resonance of the heroic inventor genre in mid-twentieth-century Japan. Toyosawa's book can also be read as part of broader efforts to promote "national" invention in the aftermath of the imperial Japanese state's wartime suspension of industrial property protections, the post-1945 collapse of the Japanese empire, and proposals for patent reform then circulating amid the American-led occupation of Japan. As Kinoshita's illustration shows, invention encompassed not only wood-and-metal machines, but living shellfish, too. Further discussion of this front cover image can be found in Chapter 15.

Part I

Introductory

1   Diversity versus Harmonization in Patent History
An Overview

Graeme Gooday and Steven Wilf

1.1   Introduction

If intellectual property is a universally recognized category for ordering creative rights, why does every country still have its own distinct patent system?[1] This lack of commonality is not so surprising if we consider that no single system of any kind is generally adopted as a standard across the globe. There are many diverse monetary currencies, units of measurement, and standards of power supply. Certainly, we do not share a common spoken language. Yet amongst this resilient and multifaceted pluralism we have flourished, trading between diverse systems around the world as our ancestors did for millennia.[2] More to the point, those whose living depends upon expertly translating between these systems have well-entrenched interests in maintaining the diversity of the status quo. Having professionally invested in the nonconvergence of their economic, technological, and linguistic systems, we can surely expect their sustained collective heterogeneity to continue.[3]

Why do so many therefore believe the situation for national patent systems is different – that their unification would be both natural and indeed anticipated? Could this be as much an ideal vision as a prediction about where we are heading? One common supposition is that the

---

[1] World Intellectual Property Office, *Guidelines and Manuals of National/Regional Patent Offices*, www.wipo.int/patents/en/guidelines.html, last accessed August 12, 2019.
[2] For the case of historical pluralism in schemes of measurement see Graeme Gooday, *The Morals of Measurement: Accuracy, Irony and Trust in Late Victorian Practice* (Cambridge: Cambridge University Press, 2004), 13–16.
[3] James Sumner and Graeme Gooday, eds., "By Whose Standards? Standardization, Stability and Uniformity in the History of Information and Electrical Technologies," a special themed issue of *History of Technology*, vol. 28 (London: Continuum, 2008). An excellent collection on the diverse histories of patents and attempts at internationalization can be found in a dedicated special issue on patent history, Ian Inkster and Anna Guagnini, eds., *History of Technology*, vol. 24 (New York/London: Thoemmes Continuum, 2002).

integration of national patent systems into a single coherent international framework is desirable because it would promote the enhancement of global welfare.[4] To the extent that critics of globalized patent agreements such as the Agreement on Trade-Related Aspects of Intellectual Property Rights (TRIPS) of 1995 have associated such overarching treaties with *injustice* to the poorer developing nations, it is not necessarily clear that recent moves to international harmonization are heading in the direction of global welfare.[5] Another stronger view, chiefly emanating from the World Intellectual Property Organization (WIPO), is that such unification is the expected outcome of certain harmonization processes that have been operating for well over a century.[6] However, this view has been contested by Graham Dutfield who argues that there are political limits to complete harmonization. Less developed "follower" nations have little to gain from acquiescing in the specific forms of strong patent protection demanded by powerful innovator countries.[7] In a cognate vein, recent research on the geographies of intellectual property highlights the global variety of intellectual property in the face of pressure toward harmonization.[8] Our contributors continue and extend that interest in the global mapping of the many varieties of patent systems, and place the narrative of harmonization within the broader framework of patent diversity.

In this volume our global historical approach suggests a further reason for suspending teleological assumptions about the long-term prospect of global patent law harmonization. We look at how the legal governance of invention has long embodied a resilient cultural-national element that leads nation-states to resist complete harmonization. It is this key feature that underscores how any *complete* long-term transnational unification of

[4] Alexander James Stack, *International Patent Law: Cooperation, Harmonization and an Institutional Analysis of WIPO and the WTO* (Cheltenham: Edward Elgar, 2006).
[5] Peter K. Yu, "The Global Intellectual Property Order and Its Undetermined Future," *The WIPO Journal* 1 (2009): 1–15.
[6] WIPO's manifesto statement specifies that its "mission is to lead the development of a balanced and effective international intellectual property (IP) system that enables innovation and creativity for the benefit of all." www.wipo.int/about-wipo/en/, last accessed August 12, 2019; James Boyle, "A Manifesto on WIPO and the Future of Intellectual Property," *Duke Law & Technology Review* 9 (2004): 1–12.
[7] See especially Graham Dutfield, "The Limits of Substantive Patent Law Harmonization," in *Patent Law in Global Perspective*, ed. Ruth L. Okediji and Margo A. Bagley (New York: Oxford University Press, 2014), 127–46. For a broader deconstructive perspective, see Mario Biagioli, Peter Jaszi, and Martha Woodmansee, eds., *Making and Unmaking Intellectual Property: Creative Production in Legal and Cultural Perspective* (Chicago: University of Chicago Press, 2011).
[8] Peter Yu, "Intellectual Property Geographies," *The WIPO Journal* 6.1 (2014): 1–15; Margaret Chon, "Notes on a Geography of Global Intellectual Property," *The WIPO Journal* 6.1 (2014): 16–25.

patent law would be a fraught project that demands overcoming long-entrenched cultural disparities. In any case such unification remains far from being accomplished – whether as the natural course of events or by fiat – and conceivably might never be so. By examining historically the diverse roots and evolutionary patterns of patent systems around the world over the last two centuries, we establish how deeply an entrenched heterogeneity lies at the roots of patent systems – and that it remains a persistent and underestimated challenge to any project of unification.[9]

1.2   The Limits of Harmonization

According to one popular view, of course, all patent systems are expected to be alike in one key sense. This is in respect of the benefits to be reaped through the patent "bargain" or social contract. In exchange for their disclosure of know-how through publication of a patent specification, patentees have typically secured from the state (time-limited) exclusive rights over their technological innovations.[10] Nevertheless we would emphasize that even if each patent system is in that respect like every other, each is like others in its own distinctive ways. We emphasize how diversity of patent cultures emerges from their interrelated yet nevertheless contingent origins and socioeconomic contexts. Most of our contributors show how patent systems across their regions were developed, not from one single fundamental template, but by borrowing from and *adapting* other countries' systems to specific national needs, each retaining some particularities. This is one obvious historical reason why there is still such diversity among national patent systems.

Modern patent systems are an early modern invention that transforms feudal privileges into general legal rules. The English Statute of Monopolies (1624) evolved from an earlier practice of letters of patent whereby monopolies were granted by the monarch as a matter of crown favor. It regularized the assignment and provided patents for new inventions during a term of fourteen years when the patent met the requirements of novelty and not causing harm to the public.[11] Japanese patent

---

[9] For perspectives on the role of property rights in economic development see Douglass North, "Institutions," *Journal of Economic Perspectives* 5.1 (1991): 97–112; Heino Heinrich Nau, "Institutional, Evolutionary and Cultural Aspects in Max Weber's Social Economics," *Cahiers d'économie Politique / Papers in Political Economy* 49.2 (2005): 127–42.

[10] For a European perspective on this, see Dominique Guellec and Bruno van Pottelsberghe de la Potterie, *The Economics of the European Patent System: IP Policy for Innovation and Competition* (Oxford: Oxford University Press, 2007).

[11] Stathis Arapostathis and Graeme Gooday, *Patently Contestable: Electrical Technologies and Inventor Identities on Trial in Britain* (Cambridge, MA: MIT Press, 2013), 13.

regulation similarly commenced with a shift from a more feudal governance to an emerging modern state. With the opening of the country
during the Meiji period, an imperial decree of 1871 permitted the introduction of a modern form of patent system. This became operational
when the national Patent Office at Tokyo was inaugurated in 1888.[12]
The differences between these two systems might be explained by the fact
that England was a progenitor of Western patent systems while Japanese
patent emerged with numerous institutional models in the form of various patent offices around the globe. Global patent diversity partly reflects
transplantation – and alteration – of model patent systems created in one
place and adopted in another, whether autonomously or under (neo)
colonial conditions.

The essays in this volume are the first attempt in over a half century to
survey the history of how patent frameworks have developed across the
globe and by a variety of mechanisms.[13] Although patent law has become
increasingly important economically and thus a subject of substantial
attention for a significant number of scholarly disciplines from the sciences to the humanities, there is no single, comprehensive volume
describing comparative patent practices in historical perspective. *Patent
Cultures* fills this gap by tracing the emergence of different modes of
national patenting from the period of imperial expansion in the early
nineteenth century through two world wars. Much of the writing covers
the period before WIPO was launched in 1967 in an ongoing attempt to
harmonize patent law in a unified international framework under the
rubric (hitherto not globally adopted) of "intellectual property." Nevertheless, even while becoming an institutional entity in 1970 and notwithstanding its many achievements such as facilitating multinational treaties
such as TRIPS,[14] WIPO has not resolved all key issues in a single global
framework. In this volume, for example, Tania Sebastian's chapter
emphasizes India's role in pioneering a differential approach to the costs
of proprietary drugs among "developing" nations. In patented health-
care, national welfare needs can thus override commercial claims to
global intellectual property rights.

To illustrate the scope and drama of the topic, let us consider the very
limited success of WIPO's attempts in the five years up to 2000 to

---

[12] Hu, *International Patent Rights*, 139–42.
[13] Guellec and van Pottelsberghe de la Potterie give a brief overview in *The Economics of the
European Patent System*, 15–45. The most recent comparable volume is Jan Vojáček,
A Survey of the Principal National Patent Systems (New York: Prentice-Hall, 1936).
[14] Uruguay Round Agreement: TRIPS (Trade-Related Aspects of Intellectual Property
Rights), www.wipo.int/treaties/en/text.jsp?file_id=305907, last accessed August
12, 2019.

negotiate an international Patent Law Treaty. This aimed to "harmonize and streamline formal procedures in respect of national and regional patent applications and patents," and thus to make such procedures more "user-friendly."[15] Yet even this relatively modest ambition to regularize the formalities of patent applications did not meet with global compliance. To date only thirty-five nations have signed up to this minimal treaty, with large swathes of Latin America, Africa, Asia, and even substantial parts of the industrial Northern hemisphere declining to ratify it. The dissonance becomes even more evident when we look at WIPO's next stage of attempted harmonization of what constituted a legitimate patent specification. This second Treaty addressed six issues of "direct relevance to the grant of patents" on which a common transnational approach was necessary to achieve patent harmonization:

i.   the definition of prior art,
ii. novelty,
iii. inventive step/non-obviousness,
iv. industrial applicability/utility,
v.   the drafting and interpretation of claims,
vi. the requirement of sufficient disclosure of the invention.[16]

Yet after six unsuccessful years of negotiations from 2000, this broad-ranging approach to complete unification of patent systems came to a halt. Evidently, the deeply entrenched and profound national differences on interpreting and applying these central facets of patenting practice led to irreconcilable difficulties in achieving agreement. As a result, plans for a full Treaty were put on hold, and less ambitious discussions have since continued (until at least 2010) on limited aspects of patenting unification, again without resolution.[17] Such are the divergences in practice between national patenting practices, it is unclear whether any resolution could be achieved; accordingly the framework for agreed patenting practices remains at the subglobal level: the nation-state, federal treaty, or economic treaty – just as it did in the period 1830–1967 covered by the main part of this book.

In fact, recently the legitimacy of patent law itself has come under attack once again, for backlogs and insufficient gatekeeping at patent offices, creating barriers to market entry, patent thickets and trolls, and

---

[15] WIPO, *Summary of the Patent Law Treaty (PLT) (2000)*, www.wipo.int/treaties/en/ip/plt/summary_plt.html, last accessed March 10, 2014.
[16] WIPO, *Draft Substantive Patent Law Treaty*, www.wipo.int/patent-law/en/draft_splt.htm, last accessed March 10, 2014.
[17] WIPO, *Standing Committee on the Law of Patents*, www.wipo.int/policy/en/scp/, last accessed August 12, 2019.

uncertain litigation. Nongovernmental organizations (NGOs), grassroots citizen groups, and corporations promoting new technologies increasingly spar over the balance between patent protection and user rights. Public policy advocates, for example, believe that international patent cooperation immunizes patent offices from public-directed goals such as introducing green technologies to counter climate change or ensuring affordable access to pharmaceuticals. Moreover, the recent resurgence of economic nationalism has reopened the question of how nation-states can best utilize the patent system to maximize economic benefits. There is a concern that countries absent a robust international patent framework might utilize their patent laws in anticompetitive fashion to shield domestic industries from foreign competition. However, it is also the case that ceding control over the design of patent systems to international agencies under the rubric of harmonization has entailed a loss of creativity in designing patent governance. This is even more of a challenge as the introduction of new technologies recurrently demands a rethinking of the terms of the patent bargain.[18]

1.3   Competing Patent Historiographies: Social Contracts and Property Rights

One historiographical tradition in patent history starts with the first international agreement that is widely treated as the originating source for WIPO: the "Paris Convention for the Protection of Industrial Property" in 1883.[19] Passing over the shift in terminology from "industrial" to "intellectual" property, accounts in this tradition tend to project backwards into the late nineteenth century an inevitable trajectory toward unification. In prescriptive teleological accounts, the inception of WIPO is thus a natural outcome of integrative processes, not (as one might contrarily infer) that the additional creation of WIPO was motivated by the failure of such spontaneous processes to accomplish integration. The assumption has been that a variety of unifying agreements under the auspices of a United Nations Agency, WIPO, has forged common global substantive and procedural rules for patent protection under the universal rubric of intellectual property. Indeed, this historiography largely traces a broad narrative arc that explains how nations shifted from particular territorial patent laws to embracing the pursuit of a global patent system. In a world of ever-increasing technological exchange,

---

[18] See discussion in Oekdiji and Bagley, *Patent Law in Global Perspective.*
[19] "Paris Convention for the Protection of Industrial Property of March 20, 1883," www.wipo.int/treaties/en/text.jsp?file_id=288514, last accessed August 12, 2019.

where international borders seem porous, patent law appears like simply another example of the master narrative of globalization.[20] There have, of course, been many critiques of globalization as both conceptually and politically problematic, and our account adds to those who claim that patents are no more amenable to globalization than other socioeconomic enterprises.

A second, older historiographic tradition starts from a rather different point. In a more geographically descriptive vein, it tells the story of particular national patent systems notably as seen in the work of the international patent agent Jan Vojáček (1937)[21] and Edith Penrose (1951)[22] who conducted wide-ranging surveys of national regimes. Focusing on the contrasts between patent regimes, national systems are described as isolated, cabined illustrations of how countries grappled with the problem of crafting incentives for technological development. More recently, Eda Kranakis has shown how patents might be tools of power deployed by European countries in the sphere of international relations, with differentials between patent systems a key feature of those power relationships. For the most part, however, most national patent historiographies are not in conversation with each other, apparently reflecting disparate political and social negotiations within a given polity.[23] And until now, no contemporary historian has offered historical analysis of the *diversity* of approaches to patenting.

Accordingly, this volume argues that harmonization and resilient diversity remain in dynamic tension with each other. It therefore both synthesizes and departs from the prevailing historiographic traditions described. Looking at the history of modern patent law across the globe, it is impossible to embrace either a triumphalist historical narrative of intellectual property harmonization or a willingness to view national patent histories as unrelated to each other. The issues raised are very much part of the new critical global history. How do we explain the surprising tenacity of patent diversity despite pressure to establish a seamless unified international patent system? What economic and political strategies impel nations to adopt alternative ways of protecting

---

[20] Among many critiques of globalization on access to knowledge, see for example Ruth Rikowski, *Globalisation, Information and Libraries: The Implications of the World Trade Organisation's GATS and TRIPS Agreements* (Oxford: Chandos, 2005).

[21] Vojáček, *Principal National Patent Systems.*

[22] Edith Penrose, *The Economics of the International Patent System* (Baltimore: Johns Hopkins Press, 1951).

[23] Eda Kranakis, "Patents and Power: European Patent-System Integration in the Context of Globalization," *Technology and Culture* 48.4 (2007): 689–72. A valuable recent collection is Ian Inkster, ed., "Patent Agency in History: Intellectual Property and Technological Change," *History of Technology* 31 (2012).

innovation? These questions of the balance between the local and the global are at the frontier of many debates in the history of technology as well as law. Hence any attempt at a history of intellectual property globalization must address the substantial resistance to international norms in much the same way as the history of intellectual property protection needs to encompass the long-standing subversive role of piracy.[24]

But beyond the historiographic significance of resurfacing the abundance of different patent cultures in a comparative perspective, there is a compelling policy reason to rethink patent diversity in historical perspective. If we ask what patents are supposed to accomplish and for whose benefit, we find that a revealing assortment of answers is available. Mario Biagioli has shown that patents for invention evolved independently in many different trading and market cultures at different times around the world.[25] Letters of patent in the early modern period were often awarded by monarchs, emperors, or other heads of state for reasons of patronage or favoritism and did not necessarily reflect any novelty in the invention. Biagioli's account shows compellingly a *longue durée* transformation from monarchical privileges to global patent rights based upon some form of objectified criteria. However, the lingering diversity of these criteria has often been somewhat understated, not least in explaining how patent systems came to be so diverse in the first place.

As Fritz Machlup and Edith Penrose pointed out in their classic 1950 paper, four entirely independent arguments generally have long been used to defend the legitimacy and utility of patents for inventions. These arguments served to fend off the many critics who have, at different times, disputed the moral and economic credentials of the patenting enterprise. These arguments are:

(1) A natural and exclusive property right exists in intellectual creations;
(2) Adequate reward for useful inventions is a matter of social justice;
(3) Patents provide the framework for the risk-taking that is necessary for industrial progress;
(4) Patents provide the incentives necessary for the sharing of innovation.

---

[24] Steven Wilf, "Intellectual Property," in *The Blackwell Companion to American Legal History*, ed. Al Brophy and Sally Hadden (Chichester: Blackwell, 2013), 441–60; Adrian Johns, *Piracy: The Intellectual Property Wars from Gutenberg to Gates* (Chicago: Chicago University Press, 2009).

[25] Mario Biagioli, "Patent Republic: Specifying Inventions, Constructing Authors and Rights," *Social Research* 73 (2006): 1129–72.

Whereas the first two are grounded in claims to the moral rights of the inventor and thus characteristically deployed by patentees and their legal counsel, the latter two presuppose utilitarian motives to achieve industrial "progress" for society at large, and thus more commonly are used by politicians and others claiming to speak for public interest. Evidently then, these four principles are not equivalent – all have been contested – and indeed can run into direct conflict when used by different parties in attempts to resolve the basis of a patent system. Each of these notions of patenting leads to different priorities in the kind of social contract required to reward patentees for their inventions. Different sorts of interest groups selectively promoted these arguments. And, not surprisingly, the choice of intellectual grounding for patent law can determine outcomes in patent disputes. According to Machlup and Penrose, many defenders of patenting have opportunistically shifted between these defenses when responding to critiques of their particular patent system.[26]

The first of these principles now is most popular under the notion of "intellectual property" – with a long pedigree in France and the United States. In those countries especially, this term displaced long usage of older terms such as "privilege," "protection," and "monopoly" to describe the sociopolitical status of patents under a new conception of "ownership" of intangible creations. Traditionally it has been much easier to accord property-like status to copyright than to patents, as copyright is accorded largely unconditionally for an author's whole lifetime and with minimal or no cost; this is in stark contrast to patents that are only temporary (rarely more than two decades) and rights for which are only secured with significant bureaucratic effort and expenditure. The pressure for patents to be granted property-like status seemingly comes from legal commentators, keen to secure for their patentee clients the greater protection that "property" law can bring – a form of protection characteristically more robust than the conditional and readily revoked powers for monopoly or privilege. It is only since the 1967 advent of WIPO that "intellectual property" has acquired a popular transnational vogue in matters of patenting.

The second argument for patents is that they offer the inventor a just reward for sharing an invention by publication as a specification, without conferring ownership rights. This "social contract" defense was adopted in countries such as the United Kingdom in the nineteenth century in which technically all patents were temporary monopolies awarded by appeal to a sovereign (as they had been since the 1620s). The need for

---

[26] Fritz Machlup and Edith Penrose, "The Patent Controversy in the Nineteenth Century," *Journal of Economic History* 10 (1950): 1–29.

a reward was commonly invoked by patentees that sought compensation for their investment in the labor of making, developing, trialling – and also patenting – an invention, as well as the potential costs of litigation to defend it against alleged infringers. From this point of view, the key economic consideration was the individual patentee's overall accounts book. Following this underpinning for patents, the aim was to secure a patent system of lowest cost to patentees, highest remuneration, and simplest defense against challenges. Britain's inventor-friendly 1883 Patent Act and the United States' Leahy-Smith Patent Act of 2011 are examples of statutes premised on such a claim.[27]

The third of these arguments, providing the sinews for technological risk-taking, was adopted more by those interested in direct wealth-creation from patenting, namely investors. In the guise of exclusive rights to make and/or manufacture for a limited period, patents were a crucial way of securing investment from those seeking a guarantee that rival inventions would not prevail. As the Patent Agent, William Phillips Thompson noted in several editions of his *Handbook of Patent Laws of All Nations* from 1874 to 1920 (see further discussion below), potentially much more money was to be made from investing in the patented inventions of others than that which could be secured by patent royalties alone. Capitalist investors therefore have a strong interest in patenting as a source of secondary profit from this state protection of risk-taking invention. We can see here one reason why developing nations initiate patent systems in the immediate aftermath of decolonization: the scope of foreign investment in a newly independent nation's industries would be premised on a secure patent system to protect the inward investments made by foreign companies.

Incentive for the exchange of knowledge, the fourth of these arguments, was adopted by state regimes determined to prevent inventions remaining secretly with the inventor: such inventions could only be subject to government taxation (or appropriation) if they were public. Indeed, for new patenting regimes, the taxation opportunities on incoming companies were a potential major source of revenue for the state. Since an alternative – trade secrets – long existed alongside patenting as an often less costly system of proprietary knowledge management, securing the patent grant had to provide sufficiently robust advantages over that rival for the patent option to be worth pursuing. We see in this state-centred system the origins of the German system introduced in 1877. As Vojáček notes, it combined the formal inspection for novelty that the US

---

[27] Arapostathis and Gooday, *Patently Contestable*.

Patent Office adopted in 1836 with the public opposition proceedings adopted by Britain's new Patent Office in 1852. Between them these combined bureaucratic forces provided a powerful double set of challenges to any prospective patentee. Indeed, such was the contrast with the French system, in which neither of these regulatory principles applied, that special advice was needed for inventors in France to rewrite their patent specifications to enable them to survive this level of scrutiny at the Kaiserliches Patentamt Berlin from 1877 onwards.[28]

Overall, then, a key driving force for diversity in patent systems was the tension between the different alleged beneficiaries of patenting. Who was the patent system in general, or any patent specification in particular, supposed to benefit? Was it primarily the patentee, the public, the manufacturer, the government, or investors, or others still, such as the legal profession? Not all could benefit equally, and as intranational lobbying took place for changes to patent law, the balance of influence between different groups resulted in an idiosyncratically specific form of patent laws in particular countries. As Christine MacLeod has shown, the balance of power in Britain in the 1852 Patent Act moved away from the interest of the state and large-scale capitalist toward the interest of inventors, liberalizing their access to patent protection.[29]

Moureen Coulter and Adrian Johns have argued that the 1860s campaigns to abolish patent law revealed how manufacturers were exasperated by this new generation of patentees who persisted in extracting payments from them for alleged infringements – this often being cheaper than entering into litigation.[30] The new British patent law of 1883 lowered the cost of both patents and of litigation, so that a huge wave of litigation began that seemed to bring the greatest benefit to the legal profession, specifically patent agents and specialist patent counsel. Only when the sheer amount of litigation was such as to embarrass the government in 1902 was the British Patent Office granted powers (from 1905) to examine for priority; thus it could at last prevent multiple similar patents being granted in ways that benefited only successful litigants and their legal counsel.[31]

---

[28] Vojáček, *Principle National Patent Systems*, 166–7; Guillaume Pataky wrote for a French audience in *Les Lois sur les brevets d'invention et marques de fabrique des principaux pays, et la procédure allemande en matière de contestations relatives aux brevets d'invention* [The Patent and Invention Laws of the Principal Countries and the German Patent Dispute Procedure] (Paris, 1907).

[29] Christine MacLeod, *Inventing the Industrial Revolution: The English Patent System, 1660–1800* (Cambridge: Cambridge University Press, 1988).

[30] See Moureen Coulter, *Property in Ideas: The Patent Question in Mid-Victorian Britain* (Kirkville, MI: Thomas Jefferson University Press, 1991); Johns, *Piracy*.

[31] Arapostathis and Gooday, *Patently Contestable*, 59–85.

Conversely, where implementing a patent law was not in the interests of the powerful, there were no patent laws. As pointed out by patent abolitionists in the mid-nineteenth century, the levels of infringement litigation, patent trolling, monopolistic bullying, and bureaucratic vexation brought many to see patenting practice as undesirable, leading to its temporary abolition in the Netherlands.[32] And when we consider that many countries, especially in Asia, did not implement patent laws – or like Thailand allowed instead an ad hoc pluralist approach – we see not "backwardness," but instead that patent laws were apparently not relevant to solving the key political or economic questions of such cultures. Above all, it must be noted that patents could be meaningless or illegitimate in political cultures that did not recognize the rights of individuals to monopolize inventions – a situation that might be found in many noncapitalist nations.

1.4   The Contingent Status of Patents

In the English language, at least, the term "patent" has mutated over five centuries from being an adjective into a concrete noun. As Christine MacLeod documented, the premodern "letters patent" – an open letter awarding a royal exclusive privilege to import – evolved in the eighteenth and nineteenth centuries to become a state-sanctioned monopoly for innovation, and then apparently reified in the twentieth century to emerge as a contested notion of "intellectual property."[33] All of these diverse modalities of patent systems can more generally be understood as a malleable and geographically contingent *social contract* between state and patentee. Known as the patent bargain, there has been a broad spectrum of social contracts for patents in which states have sought to advantage their own economic and strategic interests by seeking disclosure of an invention in exchange for a monopoly, with the interests of patentees balanced in a variety of ways and to different degrees.

The patent bargain might vary in its terms – for example in the extent of the monopoly powers or the term of protection for an inventor. Given

---

[32] See Christine MacLeod, *Heroes of Invention: Technology, Liberalism and British Identity, 1750–1914* (Cambridge: Cambridge University Press, 2007); Coulter, *Property in Ideas*; Johns, *Piracy*. For historical discussion of patent-free political cultures, see Eric Schiff, *Industrialisation without National Patents: The Netherlands, 1869–1912, Switzerland, 1850–1907* (Princeton, NJ: Princeton University Press, 1971).

[33] MacLeod, *Inventing the Industrial Revolution*; Michele Boldrin and David K. Levine, *Against Intellectual Monopoly* (Cambridge: Cambridge University Press, 2005); Alain Pottage and Brad Sherman, *Figures of Invention: A History of Modern Patent Law* (Oxford: Oxford University Press, 2010).

the shifting terms of the patent bargain, it is not surprising that it reflects changes in culture, economic pressure to innovate, and the overarching sense of the transformative role of science and technology in societies. Given such a broad array of variables, and the fact that as a monopoly patents can be used to exercise considerable economic power, the patent bargain has been a major source of contention through much of the period covered by this book.

The very contingent constitution of the nation-specific patent bargain thus undermines the idea of a patent as a fixed, universal right, naturally granted to inventors that can readily be unified across all nations. Patents are remarkably indeterminate, constructed categories. After all, it has long been clear to many critics of patents that eligibility to patent was not a universal right derived simply from the raw empirical facts of an individual's inventive activity. Instead, virtually every patent system covered by our contributors had inventions excluded from patent. Many European patent systems in the nineteenth century precluded the patenting of medicines and other commodities where monopolies under the control of a private patentee might adversely affect public welfare. At the other extreme, the United States' exceptionally liberal regime of patents in the first half of the nineteenth century excluded only patents for methods of assassination and gambling.[34]

Second, the process of becoming a patentee was typically collaborative – not just an individual inventor transmuting naturally into an individual patentee by their own efforts. Patent agents, draftsmen, patent model builders, and lawyers were some of the many collaborators who worked as intermediaries to fashion the patent itself. The patent agent did at least as much work as the patentee to codify a material invention into the text of a patent specification. How should the rewards of technological invention be distributed when the patent itself is an act of invention? Should patent agents, who were particularly important when navigating the obstacles of filing multinational patents, also be considered the joint-holder of the patent?[35]

The question "who can patent?" was explicitly or implicitly raised in patent handbooks and differed significantly between nations because clearly patentee status was not a global right. A number of these followed the language of the earliest modern patent statute, Great Britain's

---

[34] Steven Wilf, "The Moral Lives of Intellectual Properties," in *Transformations in American Legal History: Essays in Honour of Professor Morton Horwitz*, ed. Daniel W. Hamilton and Alfred L. Brophy (Cambridge, MA: Harvard University Press/Harvard Law School, 2009).

[35] Arapostathis and Gooday, *Patently Contestable*, 60–8.

1624 Status of Monopolies, which vested prima facie rights in the "true and first" inventor along with collaborators in the invention or patenting process, or heirs or assignees from the first and true inventor. Some national systems granted patents to the first to introduce an invention to a territory. Under this approach, it was sufficient to be the initial importer. Other countries set citizenship requirements to be eligible to hold a patent. In the nineteenth century, the United States was often considered the most liberal state for patentees' rights. Zorina Khan has characterized the United States of America as epitomizing the most inclusive and permissive patent regime in the world for the period 1790–1920. Contrasted to the British and French oligarchical systems, she shows how the United States' patent system provided opportunities even for relatively disadvantaged groups – especially women and impoverished artisans – to secure patentee status.[36] Yet the situation for those suffering the condition of slavery was different. While US patent law served to prevent at least some slave-owners appropriating inventions by their slaves, nevertheless, in stark terms of sociopolitical opportunity, nobody in the political condition of slavery had any real prospect of securing a patent.[37]

1.5   The International Patent Agent's Handbook: A Guide to Diversity

To navigate the stark differences of patent rights that emerged across the nineteenth-century world, one important analytical source was the numerous handbooks produced by numerous international patent agents/attorneys.[38] These handbooks emerged apparently in response to the rise of international trade as markets became increasingly global in scope. For the novice inventor, many were the financial and strategic pitfalls if they either left it too late to secure additional patents for their inventions in countries other than their own, or whose limited knowledge of the patent regulations of other countries led to unsuccessful patent applications. To enable them to navigate such difficult territory,

---

[36] Zorina Khan, *The Democratization of Invention: Patents and Copyrights in American Economic Development, 1790–1920* (Cambridge: Cambridge University Press, 2005).

[37] Portia James, "'To Collect Proof of Coloured Talent and Ingenuity': African-American Invention and Innovation," in *Technology and the African-American Experience*, ed. Bruce Sinclair (Cambridge, MA: MIT Press, 2004), 49–70; Patricia Maria Sluby, *The Inventive Spirit of African Americans: Patented Ingenuity* (Westport, CT: Praeger, 2011), 11.

[38] For a broader discussion of patent agents, see Arapostathis and Gooday, *Patently Contestable*, chapter 3; and David Pretel, "Patent Agents in the European Periphery: Spain (1826–1902)," in Inkster, "Patent Agency in History," 97–113.

international patent agents offered inexpensive advice in their handbooks, thereby also accomplishing a genteel form of advertising for their more direct (and more expensive) legal services. One very widely used volume was the *Handbook of Patent Law of All Countries* by the international Liverpool-based patent agent William Phillips Thompson: this was published in no fewer than eighteen editions between 1874 and 1920.[39]

In the transnational analysis of such handbooks, we can see not only a range of principles operating upon who could legitimately be a patentee (for example, in restrictive regimes only adult national citizens) but also considerable variation in what could be patentable matter. In Britain and the USA, there were very few limits on what could be patented, with much discretion allowed to the patentee. In the case of the USA, the focus was liberality: any "new and useful" product or process could be patented, with no explicit exclusions, so long as it showed a significant degree of utility.[40] A more autocratic political culture, such as postunification Germany and (prerevolutionary) Russia, provided not only very robust patent examining procedures (that in Russia could take up to two years) but also extensive restrictions on what could be patented. In Germany, only bona fide citizens could take out patents, but the patentee did not have to be the true inventor, merely the first to file (unless a crime was involved), although patent rights could be deployed against those who have used that invention before the patent was taken out. Inventions could be patented if capable of "industrial exploitation," but with the crucial exceptions of food, drinks, medicine, and chemical products (although chemical *processes* could be patented). Patents could also be annulled if subsequently found contrary to the public interest. Infringers of patents were treated not according to civil law (as in the USA and

---

[39] William Phillips Thompson, *Handbook of Patent Law of All Nations* (London: Steven and Sons, 1874). Discussion below is from the fourteenth edition, 1908; the final, eighteenth, edition was published in 1920. For other examples: Alexandre Tolhausen, *A Synopsis of the Patent Laws of Various Countries...* (London: Taylor and Francis, 1857); 2nd ed. (London: Trübner & Co., 1868); James Johnson, *An Epitome of the Law and Practice Connected with Patents for Inventions, with a Reprint of the Patent Acts of 1883, 1885, and 1886, and Rules, and a Summary of the Patent Laws of Foreign Countries and British Colonies* (London: Longmans & Co., 1887); 2nd ed. (1894); W. Lloyd Wise, *Gleanings from Patent Laws of All Countries: With Information As to Points of Practice, Area, Populations, Productions, etc.* (London; Paris; Melbourne: Cassell and Company, Limited, 1895); Reginald Haddan, *The Inventor's Adviser and Manufacturer's Handbook to Patents, Designs & Trademarks: Being an Instructional Guide to the Commercial Development of Inventions, Their Protection by Patents at Home and Abroad etc.* (London: Harrison & Sons, 1894); 9th ed. (1913); 12th ed. (1924).

[40] Notwithstanding Thompson's claims, US patent law prohibited the patenting of equipment for gambling and assassination.

Britain) but accused as criminals, subject to fines or imprisonment if found guilty.[41]

Russian law was even more autocratic than German, imperial rule allowing no patenting of anything "dangerous to the state or public morals," munitions being reserved as a matter of government proprietorial control. While the prerevolutionary Russian government allowed the patenting of firearms for "sporting purposes" (for example, by the Russian aristocracy) these inventions were subject to expropriation by the government. Other countries' exclusions from patentability were also interestingly particular, pointing to prohibitions stemming from troubling past episodes. In France, patents for finance or banking systems were explicitly banned, and in Turkey, patents were not only banned for any warlike banking or finance-related inventions, but the Sultan had personally banned all patents on electrical products. As in most European countries (but unlike the USA and Britain), there were strict "compulsory working" requirements for patents to be worked within a prescribed time period, or annulled. This was a standard approach to preventing indigenous or foreign companies repressing innovation against the national interest of host countries.[42]

Looking further afield to Southern and Eastern Europe, patenting was not universally established until the twentieth century. In 1908 Bulgaria, Poland, and Serbia had no patent systems, allowing only trademarks on inventions, though Serbia was then reportedly planning to introduce such a system. Despite the fact that Greece had joined the international Union for the Protection of Industrial Property, there was no patent law, only an ad hoc procedure to obtain a patent by a "special Act of Legislature." As Thompson noted of these special patent requests, "Very few are applied for." After World War I, however, this situation changed: Poland secured a patent system in 1919, and Greece (also Palestine) introduced patent systems in 1920. This raises the question of whether the spread of military conflict across Europe, North Africa, and the Middle East in the "Great War" brought postwar reconstruction linked to external demands for patent systems to be set up before infrastructural investment would be offered by the United States and other industrial nations.[43]

Turning to Asia in the early twentieth century we see that the institution of an indigenous patent law was far from being a cultural norm, especially where property and creativity were subject to strong religious

[41] Thompson, "Germany and Colonies," in *Handbook of Patent Law*, 14th ed. (1908), 134–41; "Russia,"ibid., 181–5.
[42] Thompson, "France and Colonies," ibid., 117–33; "Turkey," ibid., 201–2.
[43] Thompson, "Greece," ibid., 142.

or monarchical control that problematized the very notion of personal inventor rights. For example, Buddhist Siam/Thailand had no patent law of its own, but would allow noncitizens to apply their own national species of patent law in litigation pursued through Siamese courts. For example, infringements in British patent law in Siam could be redressed by application to Siamese courts without compromising Siam's disinclination to allow patents to be secured within its territory. China had no patent system extant, but had at least submitted plans to major European trading nations for their consideration; these were not, however, implemented until 1964.[44]

According to Thompson, no patent systems existed circa 1908 in other Asian and Middle Eastern sovereign countries, apart from colonies of industrial powers and the rising industrial power of Japan. The patent system of Japan was in part modelled on the Anglo-American notion of the "true and first inventor" as the only legitimate claimant to patents, but with restrictions akin to those of continental Europe on medicine, food, drink, and luxury items – as well as patents for purposes "contrary to public order or morality." While an impending accession to the International Union on Industrial Property would allow widespread international business patenting, at the time of Thompson's writing only Japanese citizens of agents of favored trading nations were permitted that right: Austria, Belgium, Denmark, Germany, Britain, Holland, Norway, Sweden, Spain, France, and the USA.[45]

By contrast, if we look to Latin America we see a rather earlier phenomenon: in the wake of the Spanish and Portuguese imperial withdrawal, many countries adopted patent laws early in their period of postcolonial growth. Brazil enacted its own patent law in 1809, while still part of the Portuguese Empire, and six decades after independence was one of the founding members of the Paris Convention for the Protection of Industrial Property in 1883. According to Thompson, Brazil's patent law was very liberal, allowing "any new industrial product, or new process, or new application of old process for obtaining and industrial product, or improvement on an existing invention." Formal examination of the patent addressed questions of public health, security, law, and morality rather than any consideration of novelty. In the early twentieth century Brazil was evidently open for business with any prudently managed foreign trading company, especially gold and diamond

---

[44] Thompson, "Siam," ibid., 188; "China Including Manchuria," ibid., 110.
[45] Thompson, "Japan," ibid., 157–60.

mining concerns, and associated patentees with any plausible if not necessarily original claims.[46]

Elsewhere in Latin America, patenting rapidly developed in the fading days of Spanish imperial rule. For example, Mexico's first law on "property rights for inventors" dated from 1832, four years before formal independence, and apparently with some borrowing from preceding imperial Spanish law.[47] It too was relatively liberal in allowing patents within the broad scope permitted by British and American law, although with criminal sanctions against infringers and compulsory working requirements very much akin to those of continental Europe. The first full patent law for Chile dated from 1840, the year that Spain formally recognized the independence of its former colony. Chile operated this new patent approval system not with a US-style Patent Office, but with a "scientific commission" that evaluated applications for patents for inventions on grounds of both novelty and utility. Most strikingly, like European rather than US law, Chilean patent law prescribed the annulment of patents that were not worked within two years.[48] By contrast such a requirement for the compulsory working of patents has never been part of the US patent system: that enabled what we now call patent "trolls" to build up a stock of unworked patents and then lie in wait for unwitting infringers, providing thereby plenty of lucrative opportunities for payoffs or even litigation.

Finally, in understanding the historical geography of patent systems, we need to recognize that changes of patent law over time were not always a matter of free choice by nation-states. Colonies occupied by imperial forces, of course, had little freedom to resist imposition of the patent systems of their "mother" country, with industry and commerce there subordinated to imperial projects. Indeed, Thompson tells us, the patent systems of Germany, Belgium, Spain, France, Denmark, and Italy were apparently imposed upon their colonies quite directly without variation: any patent taken out in an imperial capital also had automatic validity in all colonies associated with the relevant regime. In Thompson's *Handbook* these nations are thus listed clearly with their colonies or "possessions" explicitly included in all patent regulations; no further comment about these colonies is made. It was a different story after imperial rule ended. As suggested above for the case of both

---

[46] Thompson, "Brazil," ibid., 99–101; Iran F. Machado and Silvia F. de M. Figueiroa, "500 Years of Mining in Brazil: A Brief Review," *Resources Policy* 27 (2001), 9–24.

[47] See Manuel Márquez, "The Oldest Patent Granted in Mexico and Latin America," in Inkster, "Patent Agency in History," 163–7.

[48] Thompson, "Mexico," in *Handbook of Patent Law*, 14th ed. (1908), 164–76; "Chili [*sic*]," ibid., 109–10.

the independent United States of America and some of the large and diverse nations of Latin America, once Britain, Spain, and Portugal had withdrawn, former colonies in the Americas adapted and reinvented their patent regulations to the new circumstances of independent development. As Lionel Bently has pointed out, however, although imperial Britain was highly prescriptive in the way that copyright law extended to its colonies, it was very unusual in allowing those same colonies considerable autonomy in deciding how to formulate and implement patent law.[49]

1.6   Harmonization versus Diversity in Historical Perspective

Given all that we have just said about the contingent and diverse origins and purposes of patenting, how then did we arrive at the point where expectation of patent harmonization became the global legal norm? As a historical project launched in the late nineteenth century, harmonization – the convergence of international patent systems – has a complicated trajectory. The Paris Union for the Protection of Industrial Property of 1883 and its close copyright counterpart, the Berne Union for the Protection of Literary and Artistic Works (1886), were established at the urging of inventors and writers. As such, these two agreements are often considered a first step in the shaping of a global knowledge economy framework, especially as their leaders sought to unite their common goals in 1893 under an umbrella organization, the International Bureaux for the Protection of Intellectual Property (Bureaux Internationaux réunis pour la protection de la propriété intellectual; BIRPI).

World War I ushered in a new era for the international regulation of what was by then more commonly known as industrial property. In the wake of the Great War, industrial property became an important lever of economic relations for the world's leading industrial powers. During World War I, various countries, including Great Britain and the United States, passed statutes permitting the seizure of patents held by enemy nationals. Such confiscations underscored the fragility of patent protection without international legal underpinnings. The various conferences held during the interwar period testify to a newly emerging global industrial property regime. The Paris Union became one of a constellation of international associations where a variety of countries jostled to shape industrial policy, international politics, and legal frameworks for

---

[49] Lionel Bently, "The 'Extraordinary Multiplicity' of Intellectual Property Laws in the British Colonies in the Nineteenth Century," *Theoretical Inquiries in Law* 12 (2011): 161–200.

technological innovation. These debates often focused on the idea of competing models of patenting.

In the 1967 Stockholm Conference, the decision was made to transform BIRPI into a specialized agency of the United Nations by establishing WIPO headquartered in Geneva. The founding of WIPO meant that developing nations had a more prominent role while the link to the United Nations placed it within the orbit of larger international political trends. Yet even as BIRPI and its successor WIPO promoted harmonization across the globe, internal dissension often challenged such efforts – just as during the nineteenth century, antipatent political movements and mercantilist economic policies had sought to fashion dissimilar domestic patent regimes.

WIPO attempts at patent law harmonization have not entirely accomplished harmony because they have been seen by some critics in developing nations and elsewhere as the imposition of a western regime of intellectual property rights.[50] It has been difficult to follow up the major achievements of harmonization such as the Patent Cooperation Treaty (1970) that simplified patent filing. While harmonization over formal rules such as registration was comparatively straightforward, deeper harmonization concerning the operating of patent offices and courts, remedies, and the divergent policy agenda of different industrial economies often proved elusive. Political gridlock in Geneva increasingly prompted the emergence of alternative routes to harmonization such as multilateral treaties. The 1995 Agreement on Trade-Related Aspects of Intellectual Property Rights (TRIPS) set minimum standards for national patent systems. Significantly, it linked enforcement to trade and provided for a compliance mechanism through the World Trade Organization (WTO). WIPO imposed legal norms from the outside that often proved disadvantageous to developing economies. Following the broader trends in postcolonial political mobilization, academics and activists articulated a broad critique of harmonization.

The threat of potential trade sanctions contracted the policy space allotted to signatory nations, and reduced their flexibility in shaping national patent systems that reflected domestic needs. At the urging of developing nations, the WTO in 2001 launched a round of talks that resulted in the Doha Declaration that declared that TRIPS' patent provisions should be interpreted with the goal of providing access to medicine. At the urging of non-Northern hemisphere countries such as Argentina, Brazil, and South Africa, and after three years of rancorous

---

[50] Ana Agostino and Glenn Ashton, *A Patented World?: Privatisation of Life and Knowledge* (Johannesburg: Jacana Media, 2006).

debate, WIPO adopted in 2007 the Development Agenda that specified that promotion of intellectual property must accord with the wider aims of improving the conditions of less developed economies.

More generally, it would be simplistic to reduce the history of intellectual property to a single and linear process of harmonization under the aegis of Occidental capitalism. Over a century after the launching of harmonization initiatives, a wide variety of national patent regimes continue to emerge. Such persistent diversity arises partly from differential responses to the introduction of new technologies, and partly as a result of corporations and nations deploying multiple competitive strategies in different areas. Harmonization, in whatever form it is planned, is characteristically an uneven process. It occurs at manifold levels, and must be understood as both historically contingent and continuously dynamic.

An examination of harmonization processes entails noting both its political economy context and the relevant governmental institutions. Countries with a weak administrative apparatus and difficulties in enforcing regulation often struggled to protect patentees against infringers, whether domestic or overseas. In these countries, a patent system was as much aspirational as it was an instrument for promoting invention. It was proof of membership in the community of nations, a gesture toward modernization, and a promise of someday launching future innovative technologies as a core element of the economy. It was the increasing international exchange of products, industrializing countries fostering international trade networks that first prompted awareness of a struggle with the diversity of patent law. Harmonization was at the epicenter of debates about the implementation of free trade, industrial knowledge, and monopoly.

Harmonization was discussed not simply within international congresses, but also in other sites such as universal exhibitions and mechanic associations. Examining various institutional settings allows us to view the ideological underpinnings of harmonization that comprise the core of the Paris Union Agreement, and the difficult negotiations to forge shared patent norms. Attempts at harmonization were politically contested. Initially only a very few states adopted the Paris Union, and its extension was gradual. The periodic updating conferences show how difficult – and sometimes unsuccessful – the process of harmonization proved. At least the concurrent creation of the *Bureaux réunis* (1893) in Berne to manage the two Unions of copyright and patent did establish a permanent international organization devoted to intellectual property.

Yet even with the creation of WIPO in 1967 and the adoption of the Patent Cooperation Treaty in 1970, significant proponents for diversity appeared. Less developed countries promoted a development agenda, traditional knowledge, and implementation of protection for biodiversity, thereby constructing a patent system much more favorable to such aspirations – typically with legislation for compulsory working of patents. Regional groups and patent blocs emerged: in 1962, the African Industrial Property Organization was founded, and the European Patent Convention was created in 1973. Yet multinational companies – many of which contended with differences in legislation – promoted an emerging global patent framework.

WIPO sought to oversee the entire gamut of harmonization under its aegis. Yet the task of negotiating common patent rules among a diverse array of developed and developing economies has proved increasingly difficult. As a result, alternative routes to harmonization emerged beyond WIPO. These include the turn toward incorporating intellectual property protection in trade agreements, such as TRIPS, and various treaties to promote policing patent infringement. Can the traditional paradigm of patent harmonization – especially the classic model of relying upon a unitary governing body – still function? How might harmonization continue as countries recognize the role patents play in varying trajectories of economic development? Is harmonization at a regional scale still at work, as suggested by the creation of the European unitary patent? And if so, is it a challenge to broader harmonization or does it reflect recognition that common patent systems must share common economic values?

More recently, advanced industrial nations have promoted patent harmonization through trade-related agreements rather than focusing on overarching global institutions such as WIPO and the Paris Convention. Yet, here too, the future of harmonization seems uncertain. The United States recently abandoned the Transpacific Partnership (TPP) that included intellectual property provisions in a trade treaty. Although it appears that some of the TPP patent standards will survive through adaptation by a segment of the global community, the linking of trade and intellectual property – that provided enforcement mechanisms undergirding harmonization – might be unravelling. The ongoing contention between harmonization – in all its forms – and national diversity continues to be the core narrative of international patent law, and the historical account this volume interrogates is the prelude to contemporary ever-evolving forms of harmonization.

A major overarching point that emerges from this volume's essays is that while the idea of imposing a universal unifying framework has always been difficult, the history of patent law is marked by extensive borrowing between different models. In mapping out the international patent treaties and conventions for the 1870s to the 1920s, Gabriel Galvez-Behar's chapter emphasizes the enormous cultural and practical difficulties of establishing a single unifying framework for patents that was acceptable to all participating nations. Acknowledging such challenges, Zorina Khan's chapter instead emphasizes the role of the US patent system – in her view the most democratic of all – as the most obvious candidate model for universality.

Outside of the imposition of the British governance in its colonies, many countries preferred not to adopt what was seen as a troubled patent system. Rajesh Sagar discusses the fraught legacy of imperial patenting. The United States had what Khan has characterized as a more democratic structure without working requirements or compulsory licenses. Moreover, the United States was committed to keeping the fees for filing low so as to encourage invention among ordinary citizens. Other countries borrowed bits and pieces of these two Anglo-American patent offices. As noted above, Germany forged a combination where there was both a rigorous examination system as in the United States and high fees such as were found in Britain, and Japan forged a system combining elements of both Anglo-American and German laws.

Patent cultures often followed the contours of political and legal cultures. Central and Eastern Europe emerged as part of a new Europe after the breakup of empires in the wake of World War I. Yet, as Karl Hall shows, these new states were heirs to legal pluralism. Not surprisingly, then, Central and Eastern European countries created chimeric patent systems combining elements from both French and US intellectual property law. Ana Romero de Pablos describes how a fragmented Spain, deeply divided between regions, looked for unifying touchstones. Liberals interested in industrial development and conservatives concerned with national unity combined to shape the Spanish patent system. Italian unification was a discrete political process largely welcomed across the political spectrum. Nevertheless, as Alessandro Nuvolari and Michelangelo Vasta discuss, unification highlighted class differences. Italy adopted an open, more democratic patent system modelled on the United States.

The newly independent states of Latin America had to grapple with the legacy of Iberian colonialism and the economic neocolonialism of the United States. Chile was self-consciously postcolonial. Concerned about patents due to its mining sector at the core of a colonial extraction economy, Chile saw its own patent system as an assertion of independence. Bernardita Escobar Andrae points out that Chile mirrored the United States by taking the unusual step of incorporating an intellectual property clause in its 1833 constitution. As for Mexico, Edward Beatty writes how late nineteenth-century robust protection for foreign patent

holders reflected a patent system constructed in the shadow of its powerful northern neighbor, the United States.

Describing the significance of cultural norms, Kjell Ericson underscores the importance of protecting natural production, such as was
the case for pearl cultivation, even though other patent systems eschew
extending patent to products of nature. Modernization – or, at least, the
pretence of modernization – motivated many countries to design patent
systems. A particular technological elite in Greece, for example, intended
to signal that while the country was a latecomer to patenting, there was an
abiding concern with industrial advancement. As Stathis Arapostathis
shows, Greeks in particular wanted to contrast themselves with what they
considered a less enlightened, backward Turkey.

Nevertheless, Courtney Fullilove writes, even an early patent adopter
such as the United States had a need to reinvent itself. The use of patent
models served as a bridge to an increasingly abstract understanding of
patent. Patent was simply the legal representation of invention. Standing
at the crossroads of a complex political history and legal culture, it
operated as a utilitarian legal technology to foster scientific technology;
created the preconditions for industrialization and economic independence; emerged as a legacy of imperial governance; signalled modernization; and was a touchstone of democratization and membership in the
community of nations for new states.

But it is not merely such historical contingencies or origins that lie at
the heart of diversity in the foundations and practices of patenting, There
are philosophical, political, economic, and cultural reasons for difference
as well. Given the diverse views of why we have patenting systems, and
why they matter, different kinds of social contract have emerged concerning the kind of bargain enacted between states and inventors in
agreeing on the terms on which patent rights have been granted. At one
end of the spectrum, some systems are very much focused on the individual rights of the inventor, whereas at the other end, there are those
that emphasize the needs of modern states to generate economic growth
(whether for welfare states or warfare states). It is therefore unsurprising
that nationally distinctive patent systems can emerge, with associated
persistent differences between them.

While it is too early to identify this next stage as one of postharmoniza-
tion, patent sovereignty provides the possibility of greater leverage for
harnessing invention to a broader political agenda that includes human
rights, environmental, and democratizing concerns. Yet, of course, the
outcome might be just the opposite, as Arapostathis and Gooday showed
of the 1883 Patent Act in Britain. The aims of its founder (Joseph
Chamberlain) to favor the small-scale inventor were hardly borne out

in practice.[51] We cannot understand the possibilities of patent law without reference to the historical fashioning of patent cultures.

In the chapters that follow, the structural organization of this book reflects the operations of the main international patent systems operative before WIPO: Anglo-American, French, and German. Although identified (approximately) as such in Vojáček's prize-winning 1937 study, these politically differentiated systems are nowadays invisible within WIPO's globalizing narrative of patent harmonization. Following further analytical discussion of harmonization of patent systems by Galvez-Behar and Khan, we cover the Americas: the USA, Mexico, and Chile, which largely operated on – or responded to – versions of the relatively liberal examination-based Anglo-American system. By contrast much of Southern Europe – Greece, Italy, and Spain – adopted the French system as a very simple and easy approach for newly industrializing nations to adopt. Then again, Central and Eastern Europe followed the stringently implemented and relatively state-centred German system in Austro-Hungary and Russia. We conclude with a section on Asia, particularly in the context of imperialist strategies and postcolonial appropriation in the contrasting cases of India and Japan.

We have organized the chapters in terms of specific national or imperial patent jurisdictions since that is how the expertise of our contributors is configured. While acknowledging that this is a limiting framework, most of the chapters point beyond their own territorially specific analyses to show that most countries' patent laws and cultures of deployment changed by responding to shifting patterns elsewhere in the world. In the spirit of global history we do not assume a center-periphery model of patent trendsetters and follower nations; rather we work with the assumption of fluidity in the making and evolution of hybrid and transplant varieties of patent systems, with emergent patterns both of integration and of difference.[52] This is all the more important in writing for a twenty-first-century audience in which nation-states are clearly no longer the main actors in the story of intellectual property since we are witnessing a turn toward private ordering to protect technologies and shifting international coalitions of global stakeholders.

In this discussion of cross-border borrowing from a heterogeneous array of patent systems, the meaning of our term "patent cultures" should become clearer. Insofar as they resisted homogenization, it was not simply national legal systems of patenting that proved to be

---

[51] Arapostathis and Gooday, *Patently Contestable*, 46–7.
[52] A. G. Hopkins (ed.) *Global History: Interactions between the Universal and the Local* (Basingstoke: Palgrave Macmillan, 2006).

distinctive. We will see that the specific concerns that molded both the principles and practices of patenting included the balance of contractual power between the state and its population of patentees; the cultural status of inventors as valorized or instrumentalized individuals; the trade relations between nations and their neighbors or former colonial associations, and indeed the processes of nation-making that focused upon individual inventions as constitutive of state identity. Given all of the multiple factors at play, it should be no surprise that patent cultures were neither obviously unified nor converging on a common single form.

1.7   The Structure of this Book

Having covered the overlapping themes of this book shared between the writing of our contributors, let us now turn to outlining its overall organization. True to the purpose of introducing the topic's dynamics, the remaining two chapters in this first section offer contrasting perspectives on both the foundation and prospects of the project to harmonize patent systems around the world.

In "The 1883 Paris Convention and the Impossible Unification of Industrial Property," Gabriel Galvez-Behar suggests that the problems within early attempts at harmonization arose largely from the tensions between the very different requirements of the French and German types of patent system. He contends that attempts at transnational harmonization, such as epitomized in the Paris Convention of 1883, served to exacerbate rather than mitigate the apparent incompatibility of such systems. Demonstrating that this rivalry persisted into the interwar period, Galvez-Behar's broad narrative shows how resilient cultural divergences such as these have motivated skepticism about prospects for reconciling the lingering heterogeneity of patent laws.

Without contradicting Galvez-Behar's argument, B. Zorina Khan's discussion takes the debate in a somewhat different direction. Her piece, "One for All? The American Patent System and Harmonization of International Intellectual Property Laws," proposes that the US patent system has served at least as a possible model for unification, albeit not one that has been universally accepted. Indeed, she shows how there was resistance to this model among "follower" countries to the economic imperialism of presumed deference to the US patent system. Even nations in Asia that did elect to borrow from the US system did so in a selective fashion, adopting strategically chosen elements of French and German systems too. It hardly seems likely now that the US model of patent law could ever become universally adopted as a means of resolving the tension delineated by Galvez-Behar.

The second part of this volume takes both a broader and more detailed look at the management of patents across the two American continents, North and South. Courtney Fullilove's chapter, "Technical Imaginaries: US Patent Models as Specimen and Specification," offers a contrasting perspective to Khan's. Contrary to the thesis that the nineteenth-century US patent system helped to democratize invention, Fullilove argues that its requirements for inventors to present working models of their inventions to secure their patent rights actually imposed two barriers on them. Not only did this object-based approach implicitly preclude the patenting of physical processes and new (chemical) substances, the requirement presupposed access to highly skilled model-making: whether possessed by aspirant patentees or secured by hiring professional model-makers, such skills were not equally accessible to all inventors. Rather than being a world leader in this regard, the United States eventually dropped this prohibitive element from its system after other countries did so. We therefore see that one of the original distinctive features of the US patent system never became part of any process of harmonization, nor did it feature in any discussions at the Paris Convention for the Protection of Industrial Property in 1883.

Edward Beatty's chapter, "Mexico and the Puzzle of Partial Harmonization: Nineteenth-Century Patent Law Reconsidered," shows how a former colony of Spain inherited a patent system in its first patent law of 1832 based on a traditional regime of "patents-as-privileges" (without examination for novelty). While much of its patent legislation and patenting activity followed this pattern until 1890, Beatty emphasizes that after much lobbying for more progressive and transparent approaches, Mexico thereafter adopted new laws designed to be more attractive to foreign patent applicants. The overall aim was to secure greater investment in the Mexican economy and specifically to attract new technologies, such as transportation and manufacturing, with overseas applicants, while also aligning its patent system with that of its immediate northern neighbor, the USA – that Beatty himself characterizes as a "global outlier." Beatty argues that the evolution of Mexican patent law epitomizes the various factors that have driven global attempts at coordinating patent laws and also the forces for retaining specific nationally expedient priorities. He thereby offers an explanation of the limited "partial" harmonization of Mexican patent law with international initiatives.

Bernadita Escobar Andrae's chapter, "An Early Patent System in Latin America: The Chilean Case, 1840s 1910s," illustrates a different set of dynamics of how patent systems evolved in a postcolonial environment. Like Mexico, the newly independent Chile of 1818 inherited elements of the old Spanish system, itself based on the simple examination-free French system of the 1790s, but made the radical move in 1840 of adopting a formal expert-based examination system, just four years after the US Patent Office was set up in 1836. She shows, however, that some other traditions were long retained, noting that Chilean patent law was shaped in part by old colonial mining regulations and its "ancient regime" of privileges maintaining the continental European tradition of permitting a separate category patents of "introduction" (inventions already established abroad) until the 1870s. Nevertheless, through a detailed analysis of activities across all sectors of the economy, Escobar Andrae demonstrates how within half a century, Chile had acquired a vigorous patenting culture that contrasted starkly with that of its former colonial master Spain and indeed of some other neighboring countries.

In the third part of this volume we turn to the first of our sections on Europe, looking initially at a few nations in Southern Europe. In Alessandro Nuvolari and Michelangelo Vasta's piece, "The Italian Patent System during the Long Nineteenth Century: From Privileges to Property Rights in a Latecomer Industrializing Country," we see another adoption of the French patent system based on inventors' claims to "natural rights" (hence low fees) rather than on any formal examination for novelty. Such was the 1864 resolution of the multiplicity of diverse systems that operated in the preunification Italian states. Indeed, this remained largely in place up to the years of Mussolini's rule, with only some adaptations to accommodate the terms of the 1883 Paris Union. Overall Nuvolari and Vasta analyze the comparative benefits of this system for the modernizing Italian state, and conclude that it probably benefited foreign patentees and their technology-transfer enterprises rather more than domestic cultures of innovation in Italy.

In "Industrial 'Property,' Law, and the Politics of Invention in Greece, 1900–1940," Stathis Arapostathis examines a Southern European state that adapted its traditional system of privileges to a widely working civic patent law based loosely on the traditional French model. He shows that Greece only set up a Patent Office in Athens in 1920 sometime after other European nations had done so, and under pressure both externally from those same European nations and internally from Greek innovators and engineers to secure greater transparency and accessibility to patents. This chapter examines the symbiotic development of Greek patent law and its associated emerging technocratic culture of invention up to World War II with international treaties demanding ever stronger protection measures for patents. Interwar Greece moved toward new technocratic goals with state-defined roles for industrial scientists and engineers.

Finally, in the European section, Ana Romero de Pablos looks at another early national adopter of the French patent system. Her chapter, "Mediation and Harmonization: Construction of the Spanish Patent System in the Twentieth Century," focuses on a recent episode of imported biomedical patents – a phenomenon barely permissible given the prior broad European prohibition on intellectual property in health-care matters. Taking a chronological-comparative approach she examines first the reception of know-how patented first in the USA, and then received in Spain under its patent laws of 1929 – a patent to protect penicillin production processes. When the patent was granted in 1948, she shows that the original patent for the substance could not be accepted under Spanish law, so had to be reconstituted as a patent for the *process* of producing penicillin. A further challenge was the requirement for all foreign and domestic patents to be published in Castilian Spanish, which raised linguistic and terminological frictions that had the potential to inhibit full international harmonization. As a result, when Spanish researchers in 1988 wished to take out a patent for a DNA polymerase, they sought legal protection for their invention in the United States before doing so in Spain. The politics of harmonization were thus somewhat asymmetrical in a period when US patent law was the dominant force.

In a trio of chapters that looks at the development of some patent systems in Central and Eastern Europe, Karl Hall examines how the politics of managing knowledge was somewhat more attentive to the state's interests in managing inventive activity than to the rights of the inventor epitomized in earlier developments in Southern European (and indeed South American) countries. To a significant extent the starting point was the recently unified state of Germany, which in 1877 implemented a Patent Office that implemented both a US-style rigorous examination for novelty and a British Patent Office allowance for Opposition proceedings from rival inventors before any patent claim could be authenticated. While this double-system of checking was designed on the face of it to limit the bolder claims of patentees in Germany, in "The Struggle over 'the Social Function of Intellectual Work in the Economy of Nations': Engineers, Patent Law, and Enterprise Inventions in Germany and Their European Significance," Hall shows that this nation had the most extensive debates and published literature.

There was considerable nuance in the metaphysical debates among German scholars of patent law, and in fact – not unrelatedly – considerable practical discretion was permissible for patent examiners in the German state's handling of any specific inventor's claim to state-sanctioned monopoly rights. Against this background, Hall shows how

German engineers and chemists fought hard to secure greater involvement in the adjudication of patent claims. Even as German debates on patent law continued to the interwar years, with the rights of the "inventor" increasing in priority by the 1930s, other neighboring regions had already drawn upon versions of the state-centered German patent law.

Hall's next chapter, "Multiple Loyalties: Hybrid Patent Regimes in the Habsburg Empire and Its Successor States," explores the complex significance of the evolving German patent system for the multiple legal debates across the broad Austro-Hungarian region. While older Austrian patent law exhibited stronger French influences than had ever been manifest in the German states, the terms of the German system came to matter greatly by the latter decades of the nineteenth century, owing to Germany's dominant economic power. Noting considerable tensions in patent priorities law between the several parts of the empire, he shows how Austrian, Hungarian, and Czech regions were gradually permitted to devolve from the imperial patent system, eventually crystallizing into their own national statutes when the Habsburg Empire collapsed at the end of World War I. Nevertheless, all of these newly distinct countries pragmatically continued to seek ways to ensure mutual recognition with German patent law. Such regional imperative was of considerably greater importance than ambitions fostered elsewhere for global patent law harmonization.

In his third and final chapter, "Patent Debates on Invention from Tsarist Russia to the Soviet Union," Hall probes the results of Imperial Russia in 1896 adopting a revised patent system for inventions with close links to the German model enacted two decades earlier. However, this adoption of patent law from Berlin by no means entailed a parallel development of a thriving industrial economy, as was manifest in Russia's collapse into revolution in 1917. Hall argues that a common thread uniting the enactment of the first Russian patent law in 1812 and its Soviet successor was that there was resistance to granting the institutional bureaucracy of a patent office the definitive power over creativity in invention. Instead collaborative processes of invention seemed to predominate until finally the matter was resolved in the Soviet era with a new priority attached to "worker inventiveness." As Hall observes, while the Soviet patent law of 1924 had been a pragmatic concession to trade with industrial European neighbors, the statue of 1931 reaffirmed – at least in official terms – the state's preeminent rights over patented know-how.

In the final section of this book we look at some contrasting episodes of how imperial and postcolonial power relations shaped the evolution of patent law in India and Japan, two of the earliest Asian regions to acquire patent regulations – sooner indeed than some areas of Europe. Just four years after the British Isles secured its own formal national bureaucracy and London Patent Office in 1852, an Act for "granting exclusive privileges to inventors" was extended to regions of the Indian subcontinent governed by the British Empire. However, as Rajesh Sagar argues in "Patent Policy in India under the British Raj: A Bittersweet Story of Empire and Innovation," the introduction of British patent law to India in 1856 was not intended for the benefit of indigenous inventors. To make clear that this law served the purposes of colonizing forces, a revised law of 1859 clarified that any aspirant Indian patentee would need to secure patent rights in London first before a secondary patent could be secured in India. Even where indigenous inventors could obtain such "privileges" as were allowed them under this Anglo-centric legislation, Sagar shows that it was very difficult for native Indian patentees to operationalize their patent rights to any significant extent against competitors that copied their novel technologies without permission. Since the leading forces of the British Empire saw India as little more than as a supplier of raw material for its industries, it was not until Independence in 1947 that the newly formed Indian state could formulate new patent legislation, university training courses, and career structures that would enable it to develop a robust independent industrial base.

By contrast, Tania Sebastian's chapter, "The India Twist to Patent Culture: Investigating Its History," argues that, especially since the early twenty-first century, independent India has been able to assert the interest of its population on the international stage. This has been most apparent in the emergence of international patent rights for medicines – a controversial development that has raised major questions of equity of access. The issue arises particularly in relation to the 1995 Agreement on TRIPS. Sebastian shows how India has been a leading player among emerging (formerly "developing") nations in effecting flexibilities in TRIPS regulations in order to challenge the hegemony of large multinationals in charging unaffordably high prices for antiretroviral drugs for treating HIV patients. This was especially manifest in the 1996 Doha Declaration that asserted that the TRIPS Agreement should not impede any signatory nation's adoption of public health measures. Sebastian's key claim is that, whereas Brazil and South Africa were unable to break the demands of the pharmaceutical giants in this regard, it was India that succeeded in this task in the 2012 case *Natco Pharma Limited* v. *Bayer Corporation*. The Supreme Court of India in 2014 upheld against an appeal by Bayer a decision that the drug Sorafenib, for treating advanced liver and kidney cancer, should be

produced under compulsory license in sufficient quantities to be supplied free of charge to 600 Indian patients a year.

Finally, Kjell Ericson's chapter, "The Life and Times of Patent
No. 2,670: Industrial Property and Public Knowledge in Early
Twentieth-Century Japan," illustrates a story not only about active
patent management by an imperial Asian state, but also one of the first
ever patents relating to enhanced living matter. The Meiji government's
synthesis of patent laws from European and US sources in the 1880s
(including the 1888 examining Patent Office) was geared at first to
protecting indigenous industries. One of the most important among
these industries was the cultivation of spherical "culture pearls" inside
living shellfish; yet by the time that Japan became actively engaged in
patent law this industry was in decline with decreasing pearl yields.
Ericson characterizes the coevolution of Japanese patenting practices
and innovative technology through the extraordinary story of Mikimoto
Kōkichi's 1896 patent for artificially generating pearl depositions.
Although very similar methods had been developed in Chinese territory
and published openly, Mikimoto's patent was safe from invalidation from
"prior disclosure" in the public since the Japanese courts decreed (extraordinarily) that the only relevant public domain was the territory of
Japan's empire – nothing disclosed beyond was relevant for the purposes
of the Tokyo Patent Office. Thus, we see that even the more refined
modernizing patent systems could be adapted locally to serve imperial-
national purposes, very far from the goals of international harmonization.

1.8   The Roles of Africa and China

Our volume covers the emergence of patent law through the long nineteenth century to the launching of international patent governance under
the auspices of WIPO in 1967. Hence we did not include extensive
discussions of two important global actors – Africa and China – that
emerge later. Fortunately, two excellent recent studies on patent cultures
in these world regions can helpfully frame and inform our analysis.[53]

Several sets of pan-African alliances have since the 1960s become
an important international force in the shaping of world intellectual
property rights (IPR) debates. Tshimanga Kongolo shows how in the
1960–70s a significant number of newly independent African nations
were determined to escape the historical patent regimes imposed upon
them while they were colonies of British or French empires. Faced,

---

[53] For WIPO's origins see Christopher May, "The Pre-history and Establishment of the
WIPO," *The WIPO Journal* 1 (2009): 16–26.

moreover, with a new threat from old industrialized nations under WIPO rules to claim patent rights on traditional forms of African knowledge, the African Regional Intellectual Property Organisation (ARIPO) and the African Intellectual Property Organisation (Organisation Africaine de la Propriété Intellectuelle; OAPI) emerged in the 1970s. These represented the collective voices of nations seeking protection against uniform and uncongenial world patent systems, not (primarily) to promote their broader harmonization.[54]

During the 1990s, Kongolo tells us, most African nations assumed these challenges in developing their own postindependence patent laws. Far from acquiescing in global harmonization, these groupings defiantly carved a different path for African nations in managing their own indigenous knowledge, public health plans, protected life forms, research exemptions, and so forth. Kongolo in fact credits African nations with coordinating demands that the 1995 TRIPS Agreement allow first in 2001 local compulsory licensing arrangements for drug manufacture and then in 2011 persuaded WIPO to adopt a broader working program on the relationship between patents and health. While crediting African nations with shaping a more comprehensive international policy on such matters beyond their continent, Kongolo does not represent this as a form of globalization or harmonization – words in fact never used in his study. Instead, his is a clear characterization of such developments emerging from African defiance of corporate initiatives for strong patent rights on anything patentable under WIPO rules. Embodied in Euro-American patent laws, such hostile claims under WIPO regulations were tantamount to a second wave of imperialism, and were to be resisted as such.[55]

By contrast, Weinian Hu's study of China is explicitly premised on the desirability and even inevitability of the harmonization of patent law; she articulates a certain sense of puzzlement at China's persistent reluctance to recognize the strong intellectual property claims of Western industrial nations.[56] After many decades of shunning any individualist claims to patent rights in favor of state or collectivist ownership of invention (whether under imperial or communist rule) it was only in the 1980s that industrializing post-Maoist China began to engage with the wider international range of protection for intellectual property. Hu's account

---

[54] Tshimanga Kongolo, *African Contributions in Shaping the Worldwide Intellectual Property System* (London: Routledge, 2013).
[55] Kongolo, *African Contributions*, 285–6.
[56] Weinian Hu, *International Patent Rights Harmonisation: The Case of China* (New York: Routledge, 2017).

documents a series of patent laws introduced by the Chinese government from 1984, at which point she argues Chinese culture first began to acknowledge infringements of individually owned IPR as a form of theft punishable under law. Further developments in intellectual property law came in 2002 to comply with WTO agreements as China sought to increase its world trade portfolio. China now matches other industrialized nations in production of the new technologies of 3D printing, nanotechnology, and robotics, and being a leading nation in terms of the sheer number of patents granted.[57]

Yet, as Hu observes, even as it accepted TRIPS, China operates its patents system in a somewhat different fashion to the EU and US, refusing – for example – to allow the patenting of medical techniques, animal or plant varieties, products of nuclear transformation, designs for patterns, and color of prints. Indeed, China has followed the pattern of India and Japan in moving from being at first a "norm taker" to becoming a "norm shaker," disrupting moves to global harmonization. China's reluctance to enforce patent rights against putative infringers is thus described by Hu unsentimentally as China's "Achilles Heel": its foundational 1984 Patent Act had made no explicit provision for measures to punish infringers – Chinese law did not prioritize the individualist property rights claims of patentees. Indeed, given the resilient Chinese traditional valorization of altruism, Hu sagely observes that it is not easy for China to "depart from its ideological origins" to enforce IPR rights: a branch of private property law hitherto "unheard of in Chinese Society." No wonder then that Hu can only express optimism that China will change its patent culture to embrace the economic advantages of strong patent enforcement. With this, the world's fastest-growing patenting nation, declining to align its patent culture with the WTO, what prospect can there be in the near future of any global harmonization?[58]

Although not within the chronological purview of this volume, the African and Chinese cases highlight the key issue that culturally specific needs and values in implementing patent law are at least as important as any countervailing moves toward global harmonization. Our contributors look at these themes in countries spread across four continents: Europe, North America, South America, and Asia. They adopt a variety of interpretive perspectives on the diverse ways that patent law around the world developed prior to the founding of WIPO.

Inevitably a single volume cannot cover the patent system of all countries in the world. We hope at least that this volume will resurface the

---

[57] Ibid., 11, 219.   [58] Ibid., table 9.1 (206), 213, 228.

varieties of national patent systems, trace their historical trajectories, and show how they are linked to broader historical themes. Against the narrative of relentless harmonization, this book shows how patent diversity and compatibility can exist in a dynamic equilibrium. It is too early to identify the next stage as one of post-harmonization. Patent sovereignty provides the possibility of greater leverage for harnessing invention to a broader political agenda that includes human rights, environmental, and democratizing concerns, but – of course – the outcome might be just the opposite. We cannot understand the possibilities of patent law without reference to the historical fashioning of patent cultures. The past is patent's prologue.

2 The 1883 Paris Convention and the Impossible Unification of Industrial Property

Gabriel Galvez-Behar

2.1 Introduction

The International Union for the Protection of Industrial Property (Paris Union) was one of the first international multilateral organizations to provide a framework for the development of trade on a global scale. Its creation in 1883 followed that of the International Telegraph Union (1865), the Universal Postal Union (1874), and the International Bureau of Weights and Measures (1875). The Paris Union thus emerged in a triple context: the decline of the controversies on patents that had characterized the first two-thirds of the nineteenth century, a period of reaffirmation of protectionist tariffs, and a period of colonial European expansion symbolized by the Berlin Conference (1885). This concomitance of processes might suggest that the Paris Union was one of the important elements of the wave of globalization from the 1870s to World War I. The global nature of its ambitions indeed echoes the role played today by intellectual property rights in the more recent form of the globalization process that has been developing since the 1980s.[1]

Yet the late nineteenth-century trend towards globalization went hand in hand with an affirmation or even confrontation of nations on a global scale. That contradiction, which, from a Marxist perspective, is an essential feature of imperialism, can be also found in patent law, as discussed by Graeme Gooday and Steven Wilf in their Introduction. This chapter thus aims to show that the Paris Union was part of such tension: while the

I want to thank Clare Tame for the translation of the first version of this text and Graeme Gooday for his helpful comments.
[1] Vandana Shiva, *Protect or Plunder? Understanding Intellectual Property Rights* (Brooklyn, NY: Zed Books, 2002); Susan K. Sell, *Private Power, Public Law: The Globalization of Intellectual Property Rights* (Cambridge: Cambridge University Press, 2003); Carolyn Deere, *The Implementation Game: The TRIPS Agreement and Global Politics of Intellectual Property Reform in Developing Countries* (Oxford: Oxford University Press, 2008); Dan Gorman, "Globalization, Intellectual Property Rights and the Emergence of New Property Types," in *Property, Territory, Globalization: Struggles over Autonomy*, ed. William D. Coleman (Vancouver/Toronto: UBC Press, 2011), 122–47.

1883 Convention partly responded to the desire to harmonize patent rules at the international level, it was also the place where national specificities continue to emerge and even confront each other.[2] To this end, we adopt two complementary points of view. As Sam Ricketson points out, "Paris has always been a forum for contest between diverging national interests."[3] This chapter analyzes these divergences and the balance of power characterizing the patent law from the creation of the Paris Union up to the eve of World War II.

First, we return to the international nature of the development of patents in the world before the creation of the Paris Union. While patents were undeniably booming, legislation was characterized by strong heterogeneity. This diversity was an essential argument against patents during the controversies of the mid-nineteenth century: the search for harmonization was thus a means of responding to critics of patents. Second, we analyze the negotiation of the 1883 Convention to show that it can only be understood in the context of a strong rivalry between the French and German models. In a final section, we show how these divergences continued to characterize the Paris Union even in the interwar period.

2.2   The Internationalization of Patent Rights in the Nineteenth Century: A Multilevel Game

In the nineteenth century, patent laws were developed in a large number of countries around the world. The internal debates in each country were always informed by external references. For example, when a special committee of the British House of Commons investigated patent legislation in 1829, discussions on France were frequent.[4] Moreover, these discussions were then taking place in new arenas such as international conferences or associations. Despite this obvious transnational dimension, the expansion of patent systems was carried out in very different ways and led to heterogeneous legislation in both homeland areas and colonies.

---

[2] Introduction, 8–9.
[3] Sam Ricketson, *The Paris Convention for the Protection of Industrial Property: A Commentary* (Oxford: Oxford University Press, 2015), liv. In addition, Ricketson highlights how European colonies were integrated into the Union in order to better understand the links often suggested between the development of intellectual property, globalization, and imperialism.
[4] *Report from the Select Committee on the Law Relative to Patents for Inventions* (London: House of Commons, 1829).

2.2.1 *The Contrasting Expansion of the Patent Regime*

Whilst many historians trace the history of the patents to the introduction of the Venetian Patent Statutes in 1474, it is the nineteenth century that can be considered the century of the patent.[5] Three periods are prominent in this process.[6] Initially, in the first half of the nineteenth century, several European and American countries drafted patent legislation. The first three countries involved in formulating patent laws (Great Britain, the United States, and France) were subsequently joined by Italy, Germany, and Russia (1812), the Netherlands (1817), and Spain (1810–26).[7] This process was based on technological but also cultural transfers, which generated a transnational dimension of the patent regime.[8] At the end of the eighteenth century Great Britain had been a generally recognized standard for the legal embodiment of an inventor's rights and the British model inspired American and French revolutionaries.[9] In France, for example, Stanislas de Boufflers stressed the English exemplar in his *Rapport sur la propriété des auteurs de nouvelles découvertes et inventions en tout genre d'industrie* presented to the Constituent Assembly. For him, the law on patents had made England "a great corporation of arts and trades: a fearful association, where the most skilled craftsmen and the best manufacturers and above all the most inventive geniuses of all nations [rushed] to join."[10] As both competitor and model, Britain

---

[5] Yves Plasseraud and François Savignon, *L'État et l'invention, histoire des brevets* (Paris: Le Seuil, 1982); Alain Beltran, Sophie Chauveau, and Gabriel Galvez-Behar, *Des brevets et des marques. Une histoire de la propriété industrielle* (Paris: Fayard, 2001).

[6] Bureau international de l'Union pour la protection de la propriété industrielle, *Recueil général de la législation et des traités concernant la propriété industrielle*, 7 vols. (Berne, 1896–1912).

[7] G. Galvez-Behar, "Controverses et paradoxes dans l'Europe des brevets au XIXe siècle," in *Innovations et transferts de technologie en Europe du Nord-Ouest aux XIXe et XXe siècles*, ed. Jean-François Eck and Pierre Tilly (Brussels: Peter Lang, 35–51); G. Galvez-Behar, "Les empires et leurs brevets," in *Les techniques et la globalisation au XXe siècle*, ed. Liliane Hilaire-Pérez and Larissa Zakharova (Rennes: Presses universitaires de Rennes, 281–96).

[8] On cultural transfers, see W. Schmale, "Cultural Transfer," *European History Online (EGO)* (2012), www.ieg-ego.eu/schmalew-2012-en, last accessed August 2, 2019.

[9] G. Galvez-Behar, "Genèse des droits de l'inventeur et promotion de l'invention sous la Révolution française" (April 2006), http://halshs.archives-ouvertes.fr/halshs-00010474/en/, last accessed February 21, 2014; C. Demeulanaere-Douyère, "Inventeurs en Révolution: la Société des inventions et découvertes," *Documents pour l'histoire des techniques*, 17.1(2009): 19–56; Jérôme Baudry, "Une histoire de la propriété intellectuelle: les brevets d'invention en France, 1791–1844" (unpublished PhD in History, École des hautes études en sciences sociales, 2014); Jérôme Baudry, "Examining Inventions, Shaping Property: The Savants and the French Patent System," *History of Science* (2018), https://doi.org/10.1177/0073275318767233, last accessed September 15, 2018.

[10] Galvez-Behar, "Genèse des droits"; Demeulanaere-Douyère, "Inventeurs en Révolution."

promoted its industry by attracting foreign inventors to take out patents there. In order to compete, France would have to follow suit in drafting its own patent law to protect inventors and their inventions.

Notwithstanding the strength of the British model, the French patent law of 1791 became the default format of patent rights in nineteenth-century continental Europe and Latin America. The Napoleonic wars imposed the French model de facto in the territories annexed to the Republic, and then across the Empire. In occupied countries French influence was also strong: thus in Spain, a Royal Decree on patents in 1811 was largely based on the French law. Even if a return to the ancient system of royal privileges was tried in 1820, a new law adopted the liberal and French model six years later.[11] The situation was much the same in the Kingdom of Naples in 1810 where a Royal Decree formed in March based the main part of its content on the French law. In 1817 the Netherlands adopted legislation largely based on the French 1791 law.

The situation in the Germanic Confederation was more varied. Rhenish Bavaria remained subject to French law of 1791, whereas in Prussia the rights of inventors were governed by an 1815 *publicandum*. The rest of Bavaria adopted a law on industry in 1825 authorizing the granting of patents. However, the progressive emergence of the *Zollverein* imposed the implementation of an agreement in 1842 to avoid all exchange barriers while protecting the invention of machines (see Karl Hall's chapter on Germany in this volume).[12] We should also note the emergence of patent law in South American countries such as Brazil (1806–24), Argentina (1826), and Mexico (1832), among others. For some of these former Spanish and Portuguese colonies, recognition of inventors' rights was written into the constitution of the country itself (Brazil 1824; Chile 1833). These developments took models not only from the French 1791 law: the recognition of inventors' rights in the Peruvian (1828) and Chilean constitutions (1833) embodied characteristics of the United States constitution. Other countries in Latin America, such as Uruguay (1853) and Venezuela (1878) continued to draft their own patent laws. Although the development of patent laws worldwide resulted from a process of hybridization between different models, it was also based on national particularities. The national level

---

[11] Patricio Sáiz-González, *Invención, patentes e innovación en la España contemporánea* (Madrid: Oficina Española de Patentes y Marcas, 1999).

[12] Alfred Müller, *Die Entwicklung des Erfindungsschutzes und seiner Gesetzgebung in Deutschland* (Munich: Lindauer, 1898); Alfred Heggen, *Erfindungsschutz und Industrialisierung in Preußen, 1793–1887* (Göttingen: Vandenhœck & Ruprecht, 1975); Margrit Secklemann, *Industrialisierung, Internationalisierung und Patentrecht im Deutschen Reich 1871–1914* (Frankfurt a.M.: Vittorio Klostermann, 2006).

remained fundamental because the patent legislation was one of the attributes of national sovereignty.

The second period of patent innovation ran from the 1850s to the early 1880s with two complementary processes: the development of bilateral treaties and agreements and the introduction of patent law in the British and French colonies. As noted by Stephen P. Ladas, there were sixty-nine bipartite international acts in 1883.[13] Although all of them dealt only with trademarks, their existence had an impact on patents. In the Swiss case, Nicolas Chachereau has shown that the negotiation and renegotiation of the treaty of commerce with France contributed to the emergence of a patent law movement in Switzerland.[14] During this period the colonial powers used also a number of methods to develop legal devices to protect inventions in their colonies. It was in New South Wales (1852), Jamaica (1857), and the Cape that British patents really became recognizable. Sometimes they exported their own model like France, or they inspired the law passed in the Ottoman Empire in 1879.[15]

Beginning in the 1880s, the final period is marked by a clear acceleration in the spread of patent legislation. Some European states such as Switzerland and Denmark ended up adopting a law on patents during this period, but it is primarily the colonial powers that account for this acceleration: Great Britain and France in particular at this time were consolidating their carve-up of Africa. In 1901, half the territories with patent laws had passed them between 1880 and 1900. So, in the early twentieth century, most industrialized countries in the world granted inventors legally recognized rights, even if some countries still remained without legislation. In Europe, the Netherlands abolished its patent law in 1869, whereas Bulgaria, Greece, Romania, and Serbia had none. In Egypt, Madagascar, and Morocco there was no specific law on patents, although in Egypt the courts governing relations between Egyptians and foreigners, or among foreigners, managed the registration of inventions. Yet, importantly, at the start of the twentieth century there were still numerous states in Asia, most notably China and Persia, which had no patent law.

---

[13] Stephen P. Ladas, *Patents, Trademarks and Related Rights: National and International Protection*, vol. 1 (Cambridge, MA: Harvard University Press, 1975), 43.

[14] Nicolas Cachereau, "Introduire des brevets pour qui? Seconde révolution industrielle en Suisse et mondialisation de la propriété intellectuelle (1873–1914)." (unpublished PhD, University of Lausanne, 2018), 71.

[15] H. Raclot, *Brevets d'invention. Aperçu général et droit comparé* (Brussels: E. Bruylant; Paris: A. Pédone, 1905), 614.

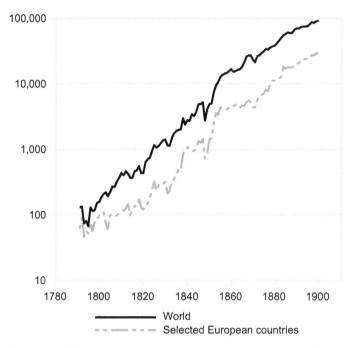

Figure 2.1 Number of patents issued in the world and some European countries, 1791–1900.
Note: European countries are Germany, Belgium, France, the Netherlands, and the United Kingdom.
Source: P. J. Federico, "Historical Patent Statistics," *The Journal of the Patent Office Society* 46.2 (1964): 89–171

The extension of patent law led to a quantitative expansion in the number of patents both on European and global levels. It was reflected in a number of statistical observations, the limits of which are well-known.[16] However, we can detect some trends and draw some lessons from this data on the condition that we take it for what it is: a measure of the use of a legal mechanism to protect inventors' rights. The data points to three types of characteristics: a globally exponential trend, national

---

[16] François Caron, *Les brevets. Leur utilisation en histoire des techniques et en économie* (Paris: CNRS, 1984); Zvi Griliches, "Patents Statistics As Economic Indicators: A Survey," *Journal of Economic Literature* 38 (December 1990): 1661–707. Moreover, the statistical sources are sometimes contradictory. Data collected in 1964 by Pasquale Joseph Federico, then in charge of the American Patent Office, reveal contradictions when compared with national sources. P. J. Federico, "Historical Patent Statistics," *The Journal of the Patent Office Society* 46.2 (1964): 89–171.

differences, and differential timing. Starting in the early nineteenth century the number of patents multiplied by almost 600 at both the world and European levels. Several phenomena explain this trend: the "innovatory dynamic" specific to the period; the extension of legislation on patents; and the reforms of patent law. The French reform of 1844 lowered the real cost of patents and thus allowed a rapid increase in the number of applications. The same applied to the Belgian laws of the 1850s, and the British reform of 1852. However, this growth was not constant. If political crises had a strong impact, as the development of the number of patents after the 1848 revolutions seems to suggest, we can nevertheless delineate distinctive periods. In the period 1800–40 the increase was slow due to the small number of countries with patent legislation, the sheer cost involved, and the relatively slow pace of industrialization. The years 1840–50 mark a new phase: the number of patents increased at the same time as countries undertake reforms facilitating the issue of patents. In the period from 1850 to the 1870s the number of patents issued in the main countries in Northwest Europe (Great Britain, France, the German states, Belgium, and the Netherlands) stagnated. After the Franco-Prussian war of 1870, the number of patents again rose rapidly whilst a new technical system was taking shape.

Combined with the rise of patent laws, this exponential growth of patent systems themselves might give the impression of an irresistible affirmation of intellectual property in the nineteenth century. However, the movement was far from being coherent and homogeneous. Legislation across nations proved to be diverse due to very localized dynamics.

2.2.2 *Heterogeneous Legislation, Localized Dynamics*

In spite of the general trend to general expansion, patent law systems conserved marked differences on a practical level. The operation or otherwise of a process of prior examination is one key measure of the philosophy underlying each national patent system. France stands out for its original refusal of such a procedure that commentators likened to a censure worthy of the *Ancien Régime*. With some exceptions, protection of the inventor's property was considered a natural right that government should not deter a priori. Only the courts could void a patent or deprive the holder of their rights. The patent was thus issued *Sans Garantie du Gouvernement* (without government guarantee) – the famous SGDG – to risks and dangers of the applicant. The same was true for Belgium. In Great Britain, on the other hand, even after the reform, a system of objections theoretically allowed the patent to be challenged by rival claims before a decision was made on its definitive issue. Lastly, in

Prussia patents were issued subject to an examination to evaluate the innovatory nature of the invention. The patent was still seen as a privilege conferred by the state, and thus not inherently the property of the inventor.

It was not only a question of different principles. There were other key disparities. In the early 1860s, the maximum duration of protection varied from fifteen to twenty years in most of Northwestern Europe. The status of the foreign inventor also varied. In Great Britain, France, and Belgium, foreigners had the right to be patent holders, whereas in Prussia this was limited to Prussian citizens. Lastly, the cost of patents differed from one country to another. Faced with such disparities, entrepreneurs needed a thorough knowledge of the regulations that intermediaries, starting with patent agents, guaranteed. Besides variations in the cost-effectiveness of patents, there was the question of the socially differentiated access to the protection of inventors' rights and their impact on economic performance: not everyone was capable of describing a technology and of managing industrial property.

In addition to these disparities between different national legislative regimes there was also a marked spatial concentration of patent holders. For example, in Great Britain around 60 percent of patents were concentrated in the London area from the early nineteenth century onwards. The same applied to France where Paris accounted for up to two-thirds of patents issued in France in the entire nineteenth century, far exceeding other industrial areas such as the Rhône or Bouches-du-Rhône. From a legal perspective and in regard to usage, the distribution of the patent mechanism was far from homogeneous.

2.2.3   The Question of Colonies

The same phenomenon occurred in the colonies. Contrary to a generally accepted idea, patent law was not always imposed by the colonial powers on their colonies.[17] It was more complex since the patent was both a property right and a mode of regulating economic competition between the colonies and their parent states. The distance often separating the colonies from their parent states favored the adoption of local law to regulate technical exchanges within colonial economies, and even in more extensive spaces, straddling several colonies within the same geographical area. While we cannot launch here into a detailed analysis of

---

[17] Deere, *The Implementation Game*, 34.

the use of patents in colonial spaces, we will mention some illustrations from the French, British, and Spanish colonial empires.

French legislation adopted under the Revolution did not take colonies into account and the laws of 1791 had not been promulgated there. "Thenceforth, the right to use any new discovery or invention, made in the parent state, far from belonging exclusively to its author, had fallen within the colonial public domain."[18] In fact, between 1791 and 1844, only 6 patents were issued to colonials that were resident overseas out of a total of 17,007 patents issued in the period.[19] However, some colonies felt the need to benefit from legal measures on patents. In 1831, the governor of the île Bourbon, Étienne-Henri Mengin du Val d'Ailly, issued an order allowing inventors to obtain a temporary title from the colonial government until they could obtain a patent from the royal government. This was clearly motivated by the governor's desire to promote local industry, as evidenced by the creation of a Trade Council on his arrival, but perhaps also by the importance of local sugar production.[20] Four years later, Mengin du Val d'Ailly vainly drew the royal government's attention to the gaps in the legislation on intellectual property in the île Bourbon and took the initiative to grant local patents.[21]

The situation changed gradually in the 1840s. The adoption of the new patent law on July 5, 1844 was a first milestone since Article 51 stated that royal orders could regulate patent applications in the colonies. The advent of the Second Republic and its assimilationist spirit accelerated the process: in 1848 an order of the Council of Ministers of October 21 extended the application of the 1844 law to all the colonies, on the condition that it be decreed in situ.[22] This order was then decreed in Martinique (February 3, 1849), Guadeloupe (January 26, 1849), Réunion (April 20, 1849), Guyana (March 7, 1849), and India (February 10, 1849).[23] We must wait until 1880 for a ruling of the

---

[18] Delabarre de Nanteuil, *Législation de l'île de la Réunion*, vol. 1 (Paris: E. Donnaud, 1861), 203–4.

[19] Database analysis XIXe INPI. Five of the six patents were issued between 1841 and 1844.

[20] Jean-François Géraud, "Joseph Martiel Wetzell (1793–1857)," *Revue historique des Mascareignes* 1 (1998): 1–38.

[21] De Nanteuil, *Législation de l'île de la Réunion*, 204.

[22] Myriam Cottias, "Esclavage, assimilation et dépendance," *Les Cahiers du Centre de Recherches Historiques* 40 (2007), DOI: 10.4000/ccrh.3394, last accessed April 27, 2013.

[23] Édouard Sauvel, *La propriété industrielle das les colonies françaises* (Paris: Marchal Billard et Cie, 1881), 10.

Table 2.1 *Some characteristics of patents in 1859*

	Great Britain	France	Belgium	Prussia
Maximum duration	14 years (7-year extension possible)	15 years	20 years	15 years
Prior examination	System of opposition	No	No	Yes
Minimum cost	5£ (125 F.)	100 F.	10 F.	Administrative
Maximum cost	175£ (4,375 F)	1,500 F	2,110 F	registration fees
Right of foreigner	Yes	Yes	Yes	No

Source: Charles Renouard, "Brevets d'invention," in *Dictionnaire universel, théorique et pratique du commerce et de la navigation*, vol. 1 (A–G) (Paris: Guillaumin, 1859), 410–11.

Supreme Court to consider the promulgation in the colonies that had not promulgated (in particular Senegal) as acquired.

The United Kingdom differed from the French case in that it was more inclined to retain local legislation.[24] Before the reform of the patent law in 1852, the United Kingdom had two coexisting modes of issuing patents, in the parent state, where patents could be issued in England – but also in Ireland or Scotland – and in the colonies. The parliamentary debates of 1851 highlight the issue of colonial patents. The draft law, which tended to homogenize the right of patents to the British standard, did not deal with the colonies. This sparked stiff opposition from parent-state sugar refiners who feared that their colonial competitors would profit free of charge from techniques invented by them. On the other hand, colonial plantation owners were keen to use these techniques gratis to offset competition from Cuban and Brazilian plantation owners. Parent-state sugar refiners managed to have colonies included in the 1852 law, but on the condition that patents issued in the parent state should not be invalidated with regard to the domestic regulations in place in colonies already with patent law.[25]

In 1853, the British government launched a survey with the governors of around forty colonies and British possessions, asking them to describe the state of industrial property in situ and to consider the wisdom of extending British law. This consultation ended mostly with the rejection of any extension. The colonies without patent law, like the governor of

---

[24] Lionel Bently, "The 'Extraordinary Multiplicity' of Intellectual Property Laws in the British Colonies in the Nineteenth Century," *Theoretical Inquiries in Law* 12.1 (2011): 161–200.

[25] Thomas Webster, *The New Patent Law* (London: Chapman and Hall; F. Elsworth, 1854), 37.

Table 2.2 *The patent in the British colonies, 1853*

	With legislation	Without legislation
Colonies and possessions	Cape of Good Hope, Canada and other North American countries Jamaica, Barbados, British Guinea the East Indies, Australian territories	African colonies, Falkland Islands Hong Kong, the West Indies, New Zealand

Source: Moureen Coulter, *Property in Ideas: The Patent Question in Mid-Victorian Britain* (Kirksville MO; Lanham, MD: Thomas Jefferson University Press), 168.

the Gold Coast, considered it of no use in their territories, whereas colonies already with a legal framework for patents did not want to see it replaced. Besides, some plantation owners pointed out that the planned extension carried the risk of reducing their competitive edge over competitors, particularly when it came to preventing them from using patented material produced abroad.[26]

The particular situation of sugar-producing colonies also applied to Spanish colonies.[27] In 1833, a Royal Charter extended the 1826 Decree, reforming the right of patents to three overseas territories: Cuba, Puerto Rico, and the Philippines. However, Article 2 of the Royal Charter stipulated one notable exception:

Given the particular state of the Island of Cuba, it is not necessary to stimulate the development of the agricultural industry, mainly in sugar manufacturing, since both planters and institutions pay a great attention to foreign advances, taking and adopting machines, instruments, artefacts, scientific processes and methods, thus privileges are limited in Cuba to inventors and improvers.[28]

The case of entrepreneurs introducing foreign techniques, who could benefit from an importation patent in the parent state, was left to the discretion of the Governor General, after consultation with the various Cuban intermediary bodies.

These colonial patenting processes might be marginal from a quantitative point of view. If the sets of data on patents issued in the parent state are relatively easy to obtain, they do not necessarily give a breakdown by

---

[26] Moureen Coulter, *Property in Ideas: The Patent Question in Mid-Victorian Britain* (Kirksville, MO; Lanham, MD: Thomas Jefferson University Press), 168.

[27] Nadia Fernández de Pinedo, David Pretel, and Patricio Sáiz, "Patents, Sugar Technology and Sub-imperial Institutions in Nineteenth-Century Cuba," *History of Technology* 30 (2010): 46–62; David Pretel, *Institutionalising Patents in Nineteenth-Century Spain* (Basingstoke: Palgrave-Macmillan, 2018).

[28] *Collection legislativa en Espana*, LXVI (Madrid: Imprenta nacional, primer cuatrimestre 1849), 107.

Table 2.3 *British patent applications by country of origin, 1884*

Country of origin	No. of patent applications		%
England	12,356		
Scotland	901	13,511	79.0
Ireland	254		
The Indies	40		
[Australia]	38	113	0.66
New Zealand	16		
[South Africa]	10		
West Indies	6		
Birma	2		
British Guyana	1		
United States of America	1,181	1,181	6.90
European countries, excluding Great Britain	2,211	2,211	12.92
Other non-European countries	94	94	0.55
Total	17,110	17,110	100.00

Source: La Propriété industrielle (Jan. 1, 1888), 5.

the applicant's country of origin. It is also difficult to have reliable figures on patents issued in the colonies. The nineteenth-century database of the French Patent Office reports only six patents issued to residents of French colonies until 1844. This figure is risible in relation to the 17,007 patents (invention, importation, improvement) issued during the same period, yet we cannot estimate the number of colonial patents that could be issued on the initiative of governor generals, as in La Réunion.

It seems to be difficult to obtain figures for the United Kingdom and its colonies for the nineteenth century, but we do have data for the 1880s.

In Spain between 1850 and 1880, patents applied for by resident Cubans accounted for no more than 1 percent of all patents applied for by Spanish subjects. Yet according to Nadia Fernández de Pinedo, David Pretel, and Patricio Sàiz, around 4,000 patents were registered in Cuba between 1830 and 1880, accounting for 40 percent of all patents granted in the Spanish Empire.[29] As already suggested, with the example of La Réunion prior to 1848 and the British case, it was as if there were two coexisting regimes of intellectual property rights: a parent-state regime and a colonial regime more adapted to local industry and to the circulation of techniques in transnational spaces.

Overall then, we see that the expansion of patent systems worldwide in the nineteenth century was far from homogeneous. Despite the power of

[29] Fernández de Pinedo et al., "Patents, Sugar Technology."

the American, English, and French models, the rise of such legislations was marked by strong differences between countries and even in their own areas of influence. These differences can be explained by the fact that the use of patents was most often concentrated in certain places and in certain industries. The establishment of legislation had to strike a balance between the interests of stakeholders who were certainly in favor of patents but who needed different rules depending on the nature of their industries. However, throughout the nineteenth century, patents remained also under pressure from those who challenged their legitimacy.

2.3   From the Patent Controversy to the Paris Union

This heterogeneity of patent law posed acute practical problems for those who wanted to protect inventions worldwide. It consequently served as one of the arguments for the abolition of patents. Paradoxically, however, the idea of harmonizing patent legislation was put forward by some abolitionists. This is why the controversy over patents and the emergence of the Paris Union cannot be studied separately. Both were built in a transnational framework characterized by the importance of universal exhibitions – that also required specific measures to protect the exhibited inventions – and by the international associations that then emerged. The latter were both the place where harmonization was sought and the place where various patent law models were displayed or even confronted. The Paris Union did not erase this tension: it only framed it anew.

2.3.1   *The Patent Controversy: A Transnational Debate*

Far from being limited to national disputes, the debate on patents even took place very early at an international level. The emergence of the free trade movement in Europe helped to structure the abolitionist current, which was, paradoxically, one of the motors of the internationalization of patents. In 1856, at the time of the international congress for customs reform in Brussels, Jan Akersdyck, professor of Economics at the University of Utrecht and representative of the Dutch Society for the Development of Industry, demanded the suppression of patents as he considered them to be an unacceptable obstacle to free enterprise.[30] Free traders were far from unanimous on the idea of abolition, however, as borne out by the divisions among liberal French economists.

---

[30] *Congrès international des réformes douanières, réuni à Bruxelles: 22–25 septembre 1856* (Brussels: Weissenbruch, 1857), 119.

The London Universal Exhibition in 1862 was a great moment of mobilization of supporters of the abolition of patents. On this occasion, the French economist Michel Chevalier, who was one of the architects of the free trade agreement between France and Great Britain, spoke out strongly against the abusive monopoly granted by patents.[31] However, some abolitionists were more pragmatic and put forward other measures to mitigate the dysfunctions of the patent system, particularly at the international level. For example, there is the role played in Great Britain by the industrialist, sugar refiner, free trader, and president of the Liverpool Chamber of Commerce, Robert Macfie. Faced with competition from colonial and continental competitors, Macfie became an advocate of the abolition of patents or, at least, in favor of homogeneous legislation on an imperial scale, in order to prevent uneven competition. In 1862, he proposed a plan for a patent union to help standardize the legislation in different countries and to expropriate all patents after a deadline of three years in return for compensation paid to inventors.[32] This plan was discussed in Ghent the following year at the congress of the International Association for the Development of the Social Sciences.

Some abolitionists then supported similar compromise solutions. Although opposed to patents in principle, the famous British inventor and arms manufacturer William Armstrong proposed their extension to all countries:

However great the advantages of uniform legislation in the countries which have approved patent systems, they would not be less in countries that do not recognize patents. In reality, it is irrefutable that they are the first to pay patents that the latter exploit. It is sometimes the case that the exoneration of countries that have no patents allows them to use the invention beyond a fair share. Without the chance to extend patents, free trade is an injustice, a contradiction in terms, only tolerable due to the great benefits generated by free trade.[33]

Free traders opposed to patents thus ended up defending a paradoxical position. The patent was certainly harmful since it created monopolies and hindered freedom of enterprise, but above all it was harmful because it was a handicap for countries *with* patent legislation in relation to those *without*. The distortion of the protection of inventor's rights disturbed

---

[31] Michel Chevalier, ed., *Rapports des membres de la section française du jury international sur l'ensemble de l'exposition internationale*, tome 1 (Paris: Imprimerie et librairie centrale des chemins de fer, 1862), CLXI–CLXVIII.

[32] *Annales de l'Association internationale pour le progrès des sciences sociales. Première session, Congrès de Bruxelles* (Brussels/Leipzig: Lacroix et Verboeckhoven; Paris: Guillaumin, 1863), 690–7.

[33] *Annales de l'Association internationale pour le progrès des sciences sociales. Deuxième session, Congrès de Gand* (Brussels: Lacroix et Verboeckhoven; Paris: Guillaumin, 1864), 747.

competition. To correct this imbalance the alternatives were either a total suppression of patents or their adoption by all countries.

The British debate on the future of the patent fed into the debate for the standardization of national legislations. In 1872, the Parliamentary Select Committee on Patents declared itself in favor of an assimilation of national laws.[34] Following a delegation requesting Lord Granville to take measures to this end, the next year Thomas Webster was sent to the Congress of Vienna as a delegate of the British government.[35] The history of the Vienna Congress of 1873 on patent is well-known; it was a strong moment for the supporters of industrial property rights.[36] The origin of this congress rested on the United States' refusal to take part in the Great Exhibition in Vienna due to a lack of protection for foreign exhibitors. Stung by their participation in earlier exhibitions, the Americans blamed the Austrian authorities for their vexatious behavior in respect of their industrialists.[37] Faced with the threat of an American boycott, the Viennese authorities took all measures to avoid frustration on the part of foreign participants, and also agreed to convene a congress on patents suggested to them by the Americans.

The main aim of the congress was to find a way to regulate the question of patents, more or less definitively. In Vienna the German delegation was large thanks to the efforts of the Verein Deutscher Ingenieure (Union of German Engineers), directed by Werner von Siemens, who was also vice president of the congress.[38] His brother, William, presided over the meetings, and Carl Pieper, a Dresden patent agent, was in charge of the secretariat at this meeting, now in the hands of ardent supporters of patent law. Thus, it is not surprising to see that the Congress of Vienna consecrated patent rights. Although some critical voices could be heard, all resolutions adopted crowned the rights of the inventor. In regard to the internationalization of the patent, the congress remained extremely modest, despite the law on patents being considered

[34] *Report from the Select Committee on Letters Patent* (The House of Commons, 1872), V.
[35] Coulter, *Property in Ideas*, 174.
[36] On the Vienna Congress see Thomas Webster, *Congrès international des brevets d'invention tenu à l'exposition universelle de Vienne en 1873* (Paris: Marchal, Billard et Cie, 1877); Yves Plasseraud and François Savignon, *Paris 1883. Genèse du droit unioniste des brevets*, chapter II; Ricketson, *The Paris Convention for the Protection of Industrial Property*.
[37] See the article in the *Scientific American* of December 23, 1872: "Constructors and patentees who have introduced their inventions in European countries have suffered grievous ill-treatment at the hands of the Austrian authorities, whose regulations on the subject of patents are, to say at least, not formed for the protection and reward of foreign talent and ingenuity," cited in Plasseraud and Savignon, *Paris 1883*, 126.
[38] Johannes Bähr, *Werner von Siemens. 1816–1892: A Biography* (München: C.H. Beck, 2017), chapter 10.

a civilizing element. Indeed, if the same treatment was demanded for foreigners as for nationals, the question of an international understanding was handled in a rather rapid and superficial way, leading to the adoption of a simple resolution.[39] As for the question of the colonies, it did not feature in any of the resolutions.

The Congress of Vienna allowed the controversy to be closed on patents and it provided a precise framework to improve these laws, taking English, American, and Belgian law as well as the plan of the Verein Deutscher Ingenieure as reference points. France, which was not represented by a single delegate, was effectively left on the sidelines. For a majority of delegates the French law of 1844 was not suitable as a model.[40] In a sense, the congress reaffirmed the legitimacy of patents and called for their convergence, but simultaneously stressed the heterogeneity of national models.

The Austrian government did not seem inclined to follow up the work of the Congress of Vienna. In the International Law Association (ILA) set up in 1873 in Brussels under the name of the Association for the Reform and Codification of the Law of Nations the debate continued. Thanks to the British patent agent Lloyd Wise, debate was initiated, as his communication to the Congress of The Hague in 1875 brought up key talking points.[41] During the congress in Bremen in 1876, the ILA decided to take the resolutions of the Congress of Vienna as a working basis and it created a committee to draw up a draft for an international law.[42] The latter was faced with the examination of the proposed amendment of the British Patent Act and, above all, the adoption of the German law on patents in May 1877.

As Hall's chapter in this volume demonstrates, the theoretical foundations of the German law contrasted with their French counterparts. To resolve the deadlock posed by the issue of patent rights for inventions, as some jurists by the 1870s proposed the idea of a right to immaterial goods as distinct from a personal right or a real right.[43] From this

---

[39] *Revue de droit international et de législation comparée* (1874), 507.

[40] No French figure appears in the list of members published in Thomas Webster's work, *Congrès international des brevets;* Charles Lyon-Caen, "Brevets d'invention. Congrès international de Vienne. Compte rendu de ses travaux," *Annales de la propriété industrielle, artistique et littéraire* (1873): 377.

[41] W. Lloyd Wise, "Assimilation of the Laws and Practice of Various Nations, in Relation to the Protection of Invention," *The Law Journal* (December 11, 1875): 730–2.

[42] Association for the Reform and Codification of the Law of Nations, *Report of the Fourth Annual Conference Held at Bremen, September 25th 28th 1876* (London: William Clowes & Sons, 1880), 77.

[43] The idea is defended by Josef Kohler, "Aus der Praxis," *Annalen der badischen Gerichte* 41 (1875): 100–4. In Belgium, the jurist Edmond Picard defends similar ideas; see also

perspective the right of the inventor did not arise from their person, or
from a contract between the inventor and society, but from the immaterial character of the invention. According to this opinion, the invention
comes from an intangible idea that as soon as it becomes "part of our
conceptions and our customs, become, as air and light, *res communis
omnium*" banishes by the same token, "the domination of the individual."[44] Instead, if the genesis of the invention had an undeniably
individual aspect, it also had a deeply collective character and the right
of patents had to take into account both the claims of the inventor and
those of society.[45]

The German conception of patent rights thus expressed a will to
construct a legal system not so much to protect the inventor but the
community in general, concerned above all with the rights of industry.
This imperative was all the stronger since, far from being eternal, the
justification of the inventor's right must answer to social and historical
constraints. The expectations of big industry and capital, which allow
society to spread the benefits of invention, also had to be met. In contrast
to the French tradition that tends to base the rights of the inventor on
immutable principles, the German model was basically pragmatic and
dynamic.

In its work the ILA resumed the perspective of the congress of
industrial property convened in Paris in September 1878. During the
Congress of Frankfurt in 1878, the patent committee, which included
influential French jurists such as Bozérian, Gide, Lyon-Caen, Pataille,
Huart, and Pouillet, adopted twenty-one resolutions. These contrasted
with the resolutions adopted five years earlier in Vienna. The questions of
principle were dealt with less forcefully. Patent legislation was no longer
considered a feature of civilization even if under a "liberal law" that
would benefit both individual inventors and achieve commercial and
industrial progress as a whole. More concretely, the legislative priority
was to establish a temporary patent together with an oppositional procedure. Moreover, the congress's resolutions specified arguments in
favor of prior examination of patent specification and conditions for

Gustave Huard, "De l'évolution du droit en matière de propriété intellectuelle," *Annales
de droit commercial* 14 (1900): 206–7.
[44] Josef Kohler, *Forschungen aus dem Patentrecht* (Mannheim: Bensheimer, 1888), 117.
[45] Josef Kohler, *Handbuch des deutschen Patentrechts in rechtsvergleicher Darstellung*
(Mannheim: Bensheimer, 1900), 6: "Die Erfindung ist nach ihrer Anlage wesentlich
individualistisch; allein sie hat einen tief genossenschaftlichen Zug. Und so auch das
Patentrecht."

establishing priority of invention. On the other hand, no resolution dealt with the colonies.[46]

So, despite the participation of French jurists, the work of the ILA drew up criteria opposed to the basic features of the French law: prior examination and the end of the exploitation clause. The drive for such a rapprochement of patent legislation proved contradictory. As the risk of a victory for patent abolition diminished, it turned out to be a "conversation among the deaf" between different models of industrial property. It was up to the Congress of Paris to overcome this contradiction.

2.3.2 The 1878 Congress, a Foundational Moment

The 1878 Congress dedicated to patents, trademarks, and industrial designs and models, was unquestionably a key step in the legitimation of industrial property and the search for a unitary right. At the same time it aspired to harmonization of patent law by emphasizing the disparities among the various national models for the protection of inventions. Such disparities were perceptible through the diverse importance of the delegations and the domination of the French representatives. Almost 490 members took part in the congress, yet effective participation was uneven, especially as the participants had to pay twenty francs for the right to vote. For instance, only eighty-six delegates took part in the vote debate on the patentability of chemical products. Even the international nature of the meeting was rather limited since only seventy-seven members registered were foreign nationals (under 16 percent of members). However, around ten governments were represented, in particular those of Germany and the United States. The British government did not send a delegation.

The organizers of the Congress of Paris decided to put back on the agenda some theoretical issues, which had been already discussed in Vienna.[47] It was a good way to contain the influence of a strictly utilitarian patent law model such as the German one. Furthermore, such theoretical discussions provided an indirect answer to the new challenges of French abolitionists led by Michel Chevalier, then professor at the Collège de France.[48] So the first debate focused primarily on the

---

[46] Association for the Reform and Codification of the Law of Nations, *Report of the Sixth Annual Conference Held at Frankfurt-on-the-Main, August 20–23rd 1876* (London: William Clowes & Sons, 1879), 79–84.

[47] *Congrès international de la propriété industrielle tenu à Paris du 5 au 17 septembre 1878* (Paris: Imprimerie nationale, 1879), 36.

[48] Michel Chevalier, *Les brevets d'invention dans leurs relations avec le principe de la liberté du travail et avec le principe de l'égalité des citoyens* (Paris: Guillaumin et Cie, 1878).

problem of the basis for inventors' rights. The recurring question of assimilating industrial property to property under common law again raised its head, but the lines of division on this issue did not align with the nationality of those taking part in the debate. While the Parisian lawyer Claude Couhin refused to assimilate the rights of the inventor to property, the British delegate Jasper Henry Selwyn was not against it. For those who wished to avoid dealing with the "metaphysical" question of inventors' rights, the famous French lawyer Eugène Pouillet, although at first reluctant to deal with the issue, forced the congress to adopt a position of principle that turned out to be a monument to caution:[49] "The right of industrial inventors and authors to their works, or of manufacturers and traders on their trademarks is a property right; civil law did not create it: it only regulates it."[50] The right of the inventor was thus considered to be a positive right, even if all explicit reference to natural law, initially planned, was suppressed.[51]

The "metaphysical" questions touching on the definition of rights were rapidly scrapped, in fear that the Congress would get bogged down debating the issue. However, they reappeared during more concrete discussions. Debate on prior examination gave rise to tense discussion and the fear that the Congress would turn out to be a resounding failure. Even before the Congress started, several contradictory opinions had been expressed. Several reports submitted to the Congress organizers favored such a procedure. However, a good number of reports by patent agents in particular opposed this idea.[52] A priori, on the eve of the congress, the debate was still open.

Discussions were nevertheless subject to pressure from opponents of prior examination. Thus, denouncing the lack of probity of some American examiners, Pouillet declared prior examination useless: it subjected the inventor to the arbitrary power of uncertain administrators and conferred no definite guarantee for the patent holder.[53] This position was considered mistaken and offensive by some foreign delegates. Several French agents and jurists voiced their fears of seeing inventors faced with examiners who while honest might not be sufficiently clear-sighted to judge new and unexpected inventions.

The debate soon turned to the disagreement between French delegates and those of countries, such as Germany, that had opted for prior

---

[49] *Congrès international de la propriété industrielle tenu à Paris du 5 au 17 septembre 1878*, 128.
[50] Ibid., 130.
[51] The draft resolution stipulated that inventors' rights were "based on natural law," ibid.
[52] In particular, E. Barrault, A. Cahen, and D.-A. Casalonga. Casalonga proposed the implementation of a system of prior opposition.
[53] *Congrès international de la propriété industrielle tenu à Paris du 5 au 17 septembre 1878*, 190.

examination. The famous German jurist Klostermann defended the principle of prior examination, arguing that a government had the duty to validate the truth of a right that it would then have to recognize. Schmidt, the Austrian delegate, voiced his concern that no international agreement could be reached if France and Belgium did not adopt this principle.[54] Given the numerical superiority of the French delegates, the principle was rejected.[55]

At this point the congress needed a compromise so that the idea of international conciliation, which was the aim of the meeting, did not disintegrate. For purely tactical reasons, the demand for a prior and secret opinion was made and defended by the most determined opponents of prior examination. In this way the congress adopted a conciliatory motion, accepting that the applicant be granted "a prior and secret opinion, so that he can maintain, amend or abandon his application, as he pleases."[56] Thanks to an optional opinion, the liberal character of the protection granted to inventors was safeguarded and a mechanism was planned to reinforce trust in the patent's validity. Plans for an international agreement remained, despite the tensions and intense differences that had appeared.

The overall tone of the Congress of Paris was conciliatory. The participants were aware of the difficulty posed by the notable differences between each national patent law but tried to build the base of an international agreement, which could facilitate the use of patents at the international levels. The Paris Conference also provided the opportunity to expand the patents within the colonies, even though this issue was not a major one. A resolution defended by Admiral Selwyn demanded a common legislation for "the mother country and its colonies":

It is desirable that in matters of industrial property the same unique legislation govern a State and its colonies, as well as the different parts of the same State. It is also desirable that the conventions of reciprocal guarantee for industrial property concluded between two States be applicable to their respective colonies.[57]

This statement was contested by the US delegate, Pollock, who considered that such a claim was only relevant for the British Empire. The fear was certainly to have another patent law adopted by Canada.

As for other countries, the proposal made by the French lawyer resident in Egypt stipulated that:

---

[54] On Klostermann's position, see *Congrès international de la propriété industrielle tenu à Paris du 5 au 17 septembre 1878*, 188; on that of Schmidt, see ibid., 202.
[55] *Congrès international de la propriété industrielle tenu à Paris du 5 au 17 septembre 1878*, 206. The breakdown of the vote is not given.
[56] Ibid., 216.   [57] Ibid., 165.

The international congress on industrial property expressed the wish that, with regard to non-Western countries that had not provided laws for the protection of industrial property, particularly with regard to Egypt, where there was a mixed international jurisdiction, diplomatic action should intervene so that the governments of these countries take effective measures to guarantee industrial inventors and authors respect for their property.[58]

When the congress came to an end on September 17, 1878, its president, the senator Jules Bozérian, was pleased to see the emergence of "an international commitment, that is, one which does not confine itself to any particular principle specific to any one country or another."[59] Keen to safeguard the *acquis* of the Congress of Vienna and the ILA Congress, and determined to find the necessary consensus to preserve the international character of their initiative, the members of the Congress of Paris did not hesitate to make "reciprocal sacrifices." A break had well and truly been made.

One of the most striking aspects of this outcome is the fact that industrial property was then constituted as a set of various branches dealt with from an international angle regarding patents, trademarks, designs and models, and even industrial rewards. On the level of principles, industrial property was not entirely identified with a positive right. Nor was it broadly attributed the status of a natural right. The tones and nuances had changed. While the utilitarian and positive position was affirmed on the banks of the Danube, on the banks of the Seine, supporters of natural right had received a better hearing without questioning the basic consensus.

The contrast between the resolutions passed in Vienna and Paris was even more perceptible: the obligation of prior examination disappeared in favor of secret notification, the exploitation clause was kept, and the principle of compulsory licenses was rejected.

2.3.3   The Negotiation of the Paris Union

The resolutions of the Congress of Paris still had to be realized on a diplomatic level. Here we need to examine the period from the end of the congress to the signing of the Treaty of Union on March 20, 1883. In fact, this five-year period witnessed a significant reduction of initial ambitions. From the end of the congress in 1878, the French minister for trade had been calling for the permanent commission appointed to implement the resolutions to ditch any points stressing disparities between different national laws.

[58] Ibid., 244.   [59] Ibid., 423.

When the international conference for the protection of industrial property met in November 1880, the draft drawn up by the French diplomat Charles Jagerschmidt turned out to be much narrower than the conclusions of the 1878 Congress.[60] The latter had adopted sixty resolutions, whereas the new draft could be summed up in around fifteen articles. As regards patents, all areas of possible disagreement had been omitted whether this was prior examination, or the obligation to exploit a patent or compulsory licenses. In addition, the topic of the harmonization of legislation between parent states and colonies was not mentioned by Jagerschmidt's draft, just like the laws to adopt in Eastern countries. On November 20, twenty states – including the United States and Great Britain – agreed to the draft convention and final protocol, leaving the French government to convene a final conference.

On March 6, 1883 the delegates of around twenty states met in Paris. If Germany and Austria-Hungry were absent, other states, such as Spain, Luxembourg, Romania, and Serbia were represented. Right from the start nine states were ready to sign the proposed plan. Conference discussions were limited to the amendment of the final protocol in order not to delay the signing of the text itself. This took place on March 20, 1883, bringing together the delegates of eleven states: Belgium, Brazil, Spain, France, Guatemala, Italy, the Netherlands, Portugal, El Salvador, Serbia, and Switzerland. Great Britain, then reforming its own legislation, waited until 1884 to join the Paris Union and the United States waited until 1887.

The aim of the Paris Union was twofold: to reinforce national regimes of intellectual property – in ensuring, for example, that each signatory state had a specific administration in the subject; and to promote the harmonization of national legislation. To meet the second objective, two principles were ratified: actors under the jurisdiction of signatory states were to be treated in the same way as national actors under the same jurisdiction and the institution of a priority right allowing an actor under the jurisdiction of the Union having filed a patent in his own country to file in another country of the Union.

Beyond these legal devices, the Paris Convention created an International Bureau of the Union for the Protection of Industrial Property under the aegis of the Swiss Confederation. The closing protocol of the Convention provides that:

---

[60] Ministère des affaires étrangères, *Conférence internationale pour la protection de la propriété industrielle* (Paris: Imprimerie nationale, 1880), 26–9.

The International Bureau will centralize information of all kinds on the protection of industrial property and unite this in a general statistic that will be distributed to all governments. It will proceed to studies of common utility of interest to the Union and will draft, with the help of documents which will be provided by the various governments, a periodic publication, in French, on questions regarding the purpose of the Union.[61]

The adoption of the Berne Convention for the Protection of Literary and Artistic Works in 1886 led to the setting up of an analogous bureau. In 1893, the two bureaux merged to become the United International Bureau for the Protection of Intellectual Property (BIRPI), which the historian Christopher May did not hesitate to call an "early precursor to contemporary global governance."[62]

The history of the genesis of the Paris Union allows us to better appreciate its impact. In comparison with the initial inspiration to obtain a convergence of national legislation in an almost cosmopolitan perspective, the Paris Union appears as a timid compromise, unable to deal with irreconcilable national models, and even as a renunciation. It nevertheless laid the foundation for an organization covering all domains of industrial property whose legitimacy it strengthens by granting it legal status under international law. In this debate among industrialized countries, the question of colonies was not the chief concern of the day – except, perhaps, for the question of trademarks. The Paris Union would deal with this problem gradually as it developed.

2.4   The Paris Union, a Global Mechanism?

We should note that the international regulation of intellectual property was not done in a day and that its extension was not immediately actualized. If we only examine the domain of industrial property, we must note that the Paris Union underwent many series of revisions. There were different revision conferences before World War I: Rome (1886), Madrid (1890), Brussels (1897–1900), Washington (1911). Besides, a number of countries, starting with the Netherlands, were members of the Union without even having a complete law on industrial property. The harmonization of the international patent law was all the

---

[61] *La Propriété industrielle*, 1.1 (January 1, 1885): 4.
[62] Christopher May, "The Pre-history and Establishment of the WIPO," *WIPO Journal* 1 (2009): 19; for a different view on the early years of *Bureaux réunis*, see Justin Hughes, "A Short History of 'Intellectual Property' in Relation to Copyright," *Cardozo Law Review* 4 (2012): 1293–340.

more difficult given the wide variation in patent systems. Furthermore, the question of assimilating colonies into the new mode of regulating industrial property was dealt with very gradually.

2.4.1   A Fragmented Union

The development of the Paris Union up to World War I might be described as conflicted and even chaotic.[63] The number of patents granted in Europe and worldwide increased exponentially. In addition, several large countries joined the Paris Union, Great Britain in 1884, the United States in 1887, Japan in 1899, Germany and Austria-Hungary in 1903. All these successes must not hide the deep uncertainties at the beginnings of the Paris Union. Three states, Ecuador, Guatemala, and El Salvador, did not ratify the treaty. In addition, the Union was the subject of very strong protests in some countries, such as France, where a protectionist and nationalist current considered it to be the Trojan horse of free trade. Review conferences produced mixed results: for example, the 1886 Rome Conference was the subject of strong opposition between France and other countries on the nature of the exploitation clause. The only way out of the impasse was a provision leaving it to each country to interpret what could be said to be exploited. While the Union was supposed to harmonize practices, the confrontation of models and interests made it necessary to preserve or even create differences. Moreover, the failure to ratify the conclusions of the Rome Conference made it completely vain.

The following conferences were more fruitful. The Madrid Conference of 1890 had been prepared a year earlier thanks to a congress devoted to industrial property on the occasion of the Universal Exposition in Paris. However, the results in terms of patents were quite poor. The same confrontation took place over the exploitation clause, accentuated by the presence of the United States. The main contribution of the Madrid Conference was the Agreement on the International Registration of Marks adopted in its wake in April 1891. The Brussels Conference in December 1897 and again in December 1900 was more successful with regard to patents. It was preceded by the creation of the International Association for the Protection of Industrial Property in May 1897. This

---

[63] Pascal Griset et al., *The European Patent. A European Success Story for Innovation* (Munich: European Patent Office, 2013); Ladas, *Patents, Trademarks, and Related Rights*, chapter 4; Ricketson, *The Paris Convention for the Protection of Industrial Property*, chapter 4.

association brought together engineers, businessmen, and lawyers. One of the purposes of the new Association was in particular to "study and compare existing legislation with a view to preparing for its improvement and unification."[64] For Pouillet, "the inventor protected everywhere and protected everywhere in the same way [was] a beautiful dream!"[65] Despite this support, however, the Brussels Conference achieved a more limited result with the extension of the duration of the right of priority.

Finally, the Washington Conference of 1911 made some progress in the formalities for applying the right of priority and in affirming the absolute independence of patents taken in different countries for the same invention. This provision thus reaffirmed the specificity of each patent system since the invalidation of a patent in one country could not justify its invalidation in another. Far from moving toward a unification of legislation on patents for inventions, the Paris Union proved to be an institution that recognized their differences. Such a contradiction undoubtedly explains why calls for greater harmonization remained valid. By the end of the 1900s, several patent agents were in favor of an international patent, following the example of the German Emil du Bois-Reymond.[66]

This contradiction is in fact explained by the antagonism of patent laws accentuated by the imbalances in terms of technological flows between the main industrial powers. On the eve of World War I, Germany was clearly an exporter of patents, while Great Britain and France were on the defensive. This situation explains the recriminations in these two countries against the German Patent Office, whose rejections of applications were considered arbitrary. The new patent law adopted in Great Britain in 1907 can be interpreted as a response to the effectiveness of the German model. Moreover, even for some scholars within the International Association for the Protection of Industrial Property, the patent laws of each country seem difficult to reconcile because of economic, legal, and even psychological differences.[67] On the eve of World War I, the unification of patent law remained a dream.

---

[64] *Annuaire de l'Association internationale pour la protection de la propriété industrielle* (Paris: H. Le Soudier, 1897), 27.

[65] Ibid., 25.

[66] A. du Bois-Reymond, "Das Weltpatent," in *Studien zur Förderung des gewerblichen Rechtsschutzes: Josef Kohler als Festgabe zum 60. Geburtstage zugeeignet von deutschen Praktikern* (Berlin: C. Heymanns Verlag, 1909), 465–91; "La question du brevet international," *La Propriété industrielle* (juin 30, 1919): 65–9, (juillet 31, 1919): 81–4.

[67] Albert Osterrieth, "Das Problem der einheitlichen Gestaltung der Patentgesetzgebung," *Zeitschrift für das gesamte Handelsrecht und Wirtschaftsrecht* 68 (1910): 1–29.

Table 2.4 *Number of patents taken out in Germany, the United States, France, and Great Britain by foreigners between 1905 and 1915*

		Place of residence of the holder			
		Germany	United States	France	United Kingdom
Patent	Germany		10,730	6,127	6,893
taken	United States	11,666		3,298	9,387
out in	France	27,502	15,651		11,465
	United Kingdom	30,892	29,331	10,599	

Source: Gabriel Galvez-Behar, "Des brevets en guerre: science, propriété industrielle et coopération interalliée pendant la Première Guerre mondiale," in *L'industrie dans la Grande Guerre*, ed. Patrick Fridenson and Pascal Griset (Paris: Institut de la gestion publique et du développement économique, Comité pour l'histoire économique et financière de la France, 2018), 176–85.

2.4.2 Return to the Question of Colonies

At the Rome Conference in 1886 the question of colonies in the Union was raised again. The regulatory project for the revision of the Paris Convention planned two measures in this regard. The first dealt with the accession of colonies to the Convention of Union.[68] In this case, the implicit issue was the weight of the imperial powers within the Paris Union but this point was adjourned following a discussion among French and British delegates. The second mechanism tended to make the national members of the Union aware of "those of their possessions which are part of the Union by the mere fact of the accession of the homeland."[69] This proposal was adopted, despite the reticence of the Spanish delegate on the use of the term "possessions," but here, too, the nonratification of the 1886 agreements left the issue pending.

It was taken up again in 1890 at the Madrid Conference. The International Bureau and the Spanish government hosting the Conference tackled the topic of colonies and foreign possessions, and proposed a double perspective in Arts. 10–11:

Colonies and foreign possessions
10. When one of the signatory States wishes one of its colonies or foreign possessions to be considered as belonging to the Union by the fact of the accession of the parent state, it must notify the government of the Swiss Confederation, that will give notice to all the others.

---

[68] Ministère de l'agriculture, de l'industrie et du commerce, *Conférence internationale de l'Union pour la protection de la propriété industrielle. Rome 1886* (Rome: Botta), 129.
[69] Ibid., 130.

11. If, then the accession to the Union of a colony or foreign possession belonging to one of the signatory states, is requested for this colony or possession a deliberative voice in the conferences of Union delegates, this demand will be the first subject on the agenda of the next conference.[70]

Article 10 was adopted unanimously and allowed the inclusion of colonial territories in the Union. By contrast, Article 11, which gave colonies an opportunity to influence the future of the Union, was rejected following the French and British interventions.[71] This Interpretative Protocol of the 1883 Convention of Union was only ratified by four countries.

The question of the role of colonies in the Paris Union was not taken for granted. Some colonial powers feared that the inclusion of their colonies in the jurisdiction of the Union might be interpreted as a recognition of sovereignty. They exercised caution at the Brussels Conference of December 1897, where the Spanish delegate was careful to specify that the colonies of Cuba, Puerto Rico, and the Philippines did not come within the jurisdiction of the Union.[72] In 1900, the British representative stipulated that only the United Kingdom of Great Britain and Ireland were covered.[73] In 1911 things developed at the Washington Conference. This adopted, without much debate, an article opening up membership to the colonies, under the control of the colonies themselves or that of their parent states:

Art. 16*bis*. The contracting countries have the right to accede to the present Convention at any time for their colonies, possessions, dependencies and protectorates, ... or any of them.

For this purpose they may either make a general declaration, including all their colonies, possessions, dependencies or protectorates ... in the accession, or expressly name those included, or confine themselves to indicating those which are excluded.

Under the same conditions the contracting countries may denounce the Convention on behalf of their colonies, possessions, dependencies, protectorates, or some of them. ...

This declaration shall be notified in writing to the Government of the Swiss Confederation, and by the latter to all other Governments.[74]

[70] *Procès-verbaux de la Conférence de Madrid de 1890 de l'Union pour la protection de la propriété industrielle* (Berne: Jent and Reinert, 1892), 141–2.
[71] Ibid., 142.
[72] *Actes de la Conférence réunie à Bruxelles du 1er au 14 décembre 1897 et du 11 au 14 décembre 1900* (Berne: Bureau international de l'Union, 1901), 202.
[73] Ibid., 391.
[74] Union internationale pour la protection de la propriété industrielle, *Actes de la conférence réunie à Washington du 15 mai au 2 juin 1911* (Berne: Bureau international de l'Union), 255.

This measure took up Article 19 of the Berne Convention in regards to the creation of an International Union for the Protection of Literary and Artistic Works, except that the formulation adopted at the Washington Conference was slightly different.[75] It included protectorates and "dependencies" to satisfy a British request anxious to integrate its dominions under the Paris Union.[76] The consideration of colonies in the Paris Union was thus progressive and prudent on the part of countries that did not necessarily wish to question the specific regulations that had developed in their colonies. The Paris Union was not so much a means of achieving unified legislation as an institution for maintaining differences while adopting coordination measures as a necessary compromise.

2.4.3   World War I and the Emergence of a New Intellectual Property Regime

World War I ushered in a new era for the international regulation of industrial property. From 1916, while the bases for the interallied economic cooperation were being put in place, patent issues were the focus of discussions to weaken the German patent system that had become the point of reference in the prewar period. Among the many measures discussed, and which cannot be listed here, the plan, subsequently aborted, for an international central office to register patents was clearly one of the most significant. In the wake of the Great War industrial property had become one of the levers of antagonism and economic cooperation for the great powers.

The Paris Union could have suffered from the conflict since all the prewar treaties linking the warring parties had to be annulled. Nevertheless, its multilateral character and the presence of neutral countries made the Paris Union sustainable. In a preliminary note to the international conference that met to create an international central office of patent registration in 1919, the French Ministry of Trade affirmed that:

It was thus necessary to proclaim that this Convention which France is proud to have initiated, constitutes an evident sign of progress in international relations based on justice and equity, [one which] it is desirable to see increasingly

---

[75] *Actes de la 3ᵉ conférence internationale pour la protection des œuvres littéraires et artistiques réunie à Berne du 6 septembre au 9 septembre 1886* (Berne: K.-J. Wyss, 1886), 34.
[76] The British delegation also hoped that the term "dominion" would figure clearly in the text but this was not the case. The International Union for the Protection of Industrial Property, *Actes de la conférence réunie à Washington*, 221.

established, [thus] consecrating the international recognition of industrial property rights in a definitive fashion.[77]

It was not a question of challenging the existence of the Paris Union, but a question of going further down the road toward the unification of legislation. The unknown author of a note asserts that:

The new Union thus formed would complement and improve the large and rather basic Union created by the Paris Convention in 1883. Its realization was a new step on the road towards the unification of legislation that the French promoters of the Paris Convention had placed at the top of their agenda as the ideal goal to be reached and which would allow ..., in the future, the recognition of a unique international patent in all countries, guaranteeing definitively the international protection of inventors' rights in the most efficient way possible.[78]

In actual fact, the double movement of convergence and divergence was present right from the outset of discussions on the central office of registration, which in turn ended up being abandoned by its own promoters.

The congress of amendment in The Hague in 1925 testifies to this new industrial property regime.[79] New international organizations came into play in the Paris Union: alongside the Bureaux in Berne, the League of Nations and, more importantly, its economic committee took part in the work of the conference, just as the International Chamber of Commerce (ICC) created in 1919. Moreover, the United States put great pressure on the Union to make it develop according to its own ideas. Together with Great Britain, it demanded the use of English as the official language and the introduction of the notion of reciprocity in the treatment of nonnationals so that the Union, under construction since 1883, would be based on the principle of simple assimilation. Lastly, the United States pushed for the abolition of the obligation to exploit in the countries that practiced it. If France was ready to do this, the principle was fiercely defended by Poland and other European countries on the grounds of their less developed industrial status. In The Hague, the influence exercised on the international regulation of industrial property was seen as a way to increase or reduce comparative economic advantage.

---

[77] "Avant-projet d'arrangement pour la création d'un Bureau central international d'enregistrement et d'examen des brevets d'invention" (s.d. November 1919), Archives du Ministère des Affaires étrangères, 429 QO/311.

[78] Ibid.

[79] Union internationale pour la protection de la propriété industrielle, *Actes de la conférence réunie à la Haye du 8 octobre au 6 novembre 1925* (Berne: Bureau international de l'Union, 1926).

This was not an overwhelmingly important issue for the colonies, but they did start to become an issue, albeit a minor one, in the functioning of the Union. Territories under a League of Nations mandate were integrated to the Union thanks to a British proposal to amend Article 16*bis* of the Convention. Yet the director of the United Bureaux opposed the participation of nonsovereign states in the Union and proposed that Syria's involvement as a linked territory under a French mandate be refused.[80] When asked to explain this behavior, the French ambassador in Berne stated that: "[M. Röthlisberger] expresses the concerns of the federal council, always keen not to allow the influence of the great powers in possession of world empires to increase in international organizations to the detriment of smaller states."[81]

In addition to such shows of concern we should add the initiatives of the United Bureaux to communicate directly with the industrial property offices of states under protectorate. For example, the Moroccan Office was contacted directly by the Berne Office to prepare for the upcoming Hague Conference, and to defend amendments without any prior negotiation with France.

What was at stake for a colonial power such as France was the control of the presence of its colonies in this international arena. The French state did so by firmly reasserting its privileges, particularly in regard to sovereignty, but also by involving the colonies and the dependant states under its control in decision-making. Syria and Lebanon refused to take part in the drive for an international registration of trademarks for fear of seeing the Office of Industrial Property in Beirut lose key financial resources.

2.5   Conclusion

The rise of patent legislation in the nineteenth century involved processes toward encouraging diversity. A common purpose – providing a monopoly of rights for inventions – did not prevent important differences arising between national patent systems. These dissimilar laws were characterized by strong particularities that distinguish them beyond their distinct similarities: the complexity of the application procedures; the existence or otherwise of a preliminary examination; the cost of patents; the publication of the specification; and the judgment of piracy were all elements

---

[80] Letter from French ambassador in The Hague to the French Ministry of Foreign Affairs (November 14, 1925), Archives du Ministère des Affaires étrangères, 429QO/37.
[81] Letter from French ambassador in Bern to the French Ministry of Foreign Affairs (December 9, 1925), Archives du Ministère des Affaires étrangères, 429QO/37.

on which national legislations differed greatly. Moreover, their connection to different legal systems contributed to widening the gaps between the different patent systems. Finally, the heterogeneous practices within each national patent law added yet further to the diversity. At the local level – and more particularly in the colonies – or within particular industries, patents were used in a specific way. All of these factors led to patents worldwide developing in a highly differentiated institutional framework.

Nevertheless, several transnational processes also introduced a kind of homogenization between national patent systems. The growth of international trade encouraged the use of patents for the same inventions in several countries, although inventors still had to face the difficulties caused by the international diversity of patent laws. In addition, the implementation and later reforms of national patent statutes were typically drawn from a comparison with other national patent systems. After all, the invention of a particular patent system was never undertaken in an autarkic process but instead based on a set of borrowings and hybridizations from other nations; this helped to maintain diversity even while maintaining a common background of legislative resources. Finally, the abolitionist campaign of the 1860s reinforced the transnational character of patent systems, paradoxically by contributing to the emergence of a new international institution in 1883. By criticizing the disparity of legislation and calling for its unification, abolitionists themselves laid the foundations for the survival of patents in an international context.

The appearance of the Paris Union stemmed from all these seeming contradictions. It did not make them disappear, however, but instead gave them a new form. If the complete unification of patent law appears to be a rhetorical topic or, at best, a regulatory ideal, the promoters of the Paris Union were rather aware of the unrealistic nature of such an objective. In fact, we must bear in mind the narrowness and even fragility of the Union in its early years. It did not then bring together all the industrial countries, since it was opposed by the supporters of protectionism and indeed challenged by its own internal contradictions. The essential point, however, is that the Union was becoming one of the areas in which the various industrial property models could be confronted. Industrial countries, especially the most important ones, have thus long had an interest in maintaining or even promoting their comparative institutional advantage in patent systems that others, on the contrary, sought to contain. The Paris Union thus became one of the key sites where a strong diversity of patent systems was built into international competition.

3 One for All? The American Patent System and Harmonization of International Intellectual Property Laws

B. Zorina Khan

Strictly nationalistic conceptions prevailed against the extremely liberal propositions of the United States, which one could only recognize as approaching the ideal of the future.[1]

3.1   Introduction

The movement for the harmonization of laws toward patents and copyrights affects the entire global community of producers and users, but such policies were not compiled from equal and representative contributions by all countries. Instead, policies toward patented inventions today have been disproportionately affected by the central role of US intellectual property institutions in the nineteenth century. Patent harmonization was largely motivated by the American model of strong protection and enforcement of property rights in inventions, an influence that was almost entirely in one direction until the end of the twentieth century.

The United States became one of the world's foremost economic powers during the nineteenth century, and many attributed its undoubted success to its technological prowess, concluding that US intellectual property policies comprised "the ideal of the future." Bolstered by their advances in technological innovations that dramatically improved productivity and consumer well-being, American patentees turned to the multinational market. After the mid-century mark, many of the industrializers in Europe, including Britain, voluntarily started to

I've benefited from discussions and comments by Stanley Engerman, Graeme Gooday, Adam Mossoff, and Steven Wilf. The chapter was written while a National Fellow at the Hoover Institution. I am also grateful for funding from the National Science Foundation. Liability for errors is limited to the author.
[1] Casimir Akerman, *L'obligation d'exploiter et la licence obligatoire en matiére de brevets d'invention* (Paris: Sirey, 1935), 91, cited in Edith Penrose, *Economics of the International Patent System* (Baltimore: Johns Hopkins Press, 1951), 81.

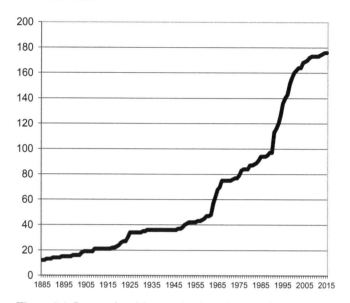

Figure 3.1 International harmonization of patent laws.
Note: The data comprise the cumulative number of signatories by year to the Paris Convention on Patents.
Source: World Intellectual Property Organization (www.wipo.org//treaties)

emulate American rules and standards because they realized that secure property rights in inventions were necessary for attempting to maintain their comparative advantage in the domestic and international arenas. The United States also began to use its growing political leverage to influence other countries who exhibited greater reluctance to introduce and enforce equally strong patent rights, in order to protect American patent-holders who were competing in overseas markets. By the twentieth century, countries that significantly deviated from patent policies that the US regarded as desirable risked the imposition of sanctions on both trade and aid.

Developing countries today are encouraged to adopt policies to ensure that intellectual property rights are effectively protected. Figure 3.1 shows the cumulative number of countries that have joined the primary international patent treaties, and indicates that the most recent decades stand out as a period of high enrolment, with a convergence toward at least de jure uniformity among intellectual property laws. Membership of the World Intellectual Property Organization (WIPO) now includes almost all countries, and in the past three decades the number of parties to international treaties has almost doubled. Of these, 168 have acceded

to the Berne Convention for literary and artistic works, and 176 adhere to
the Paris Convention for industrial property. In 2000 alone, there were
sixty new signatories to WIPO treaties, 56 percent of which comprised
developing countries. Nevertheless, de facto enforcement and actual
practice vary greatly, and the US "Special 301 Report" for 2014 identified
some thirty-seven countries that had engaged in unsatisfactory policies
toward intellectual property.

Adherence to such treaties, as the editors of this volume point out in
their introductory chapter, comprises a blanket that covers a more multifaceted reality. Within this aggregate multilateral movement toward
stronger patents and copyrights, considerable diversity is evident, in part
driven by the variation in costs and benefits to different interest groups. It
is worth noting that the United States itself was not immune to self-
interested resistance to harmonization in the global market for intellectual property rights, as was clear from its experience in the realm of
copyright policies. The US Constitution united in one clause protections
for authors and inventions, but tensions between access to ideas and
rights of exclusion were especially evident in markedly different treatment for the rights for authors and patented inventions. Throughout its
history, American copyrights were among the weakest in the world. The
US failure to recognize the rights of foreign authors was unique among
the major industrial nations, and Americans were justly accused of
widespread international piracy of copyrightable products until the end
of the nineteenth century.[2]

By the 1890s, the balance of trade in cultural goods was moving in
favor of US producers, creating an incentive for their recognition of
copyrights in other countries, in order to ensure reciprocal treatment.
US legislators explicitly justified the passage of the Chace Act (the
International Copyright Act of 1891 [26 Stat. 1106, March 3, 1891])
by arguing that the "balance on the ledger" was shifting in favor of
American authors (broadly defined). Despite such advances, at the
national level, copyrights remained significantly different from patents,
and protectionist measures were undertaken to shelter the domestic
printing industry. In marked contrast to its leadership in patent conventions, the United States declined an invitation to a pivotal copyright
conference in Berne in 1883, and failed to qualify for membership until
1988. In a parallel fashion to the status of the United States in patent
matters, France led and shepherded the movement toward multilateral

[2] B. Zorina Khan, *The Democratization of Invention: Patents and Copyrights in American Economic Development* (Cambridge: NBER and Cambridge University Press, 2005), 222–87.

negotiations, and its influence was evident in the subsequent evolution of international copyright laws.

The divergences documented by other authors in these chapters are not surprising, since both theory and empirical research fail to reach definitive conclusions about whether the optimal policy for all countries is to import intellectual property legislation and institutions from developed societies. The usual rationale for granting such rights is to provide incentives for inventive activity and creativity, to enhance access and diffusion of information, as well as to support well-functioning markets in innovation. It is further possible that stronger patents and copyrights might benefit a society even if local residents were unlikely to possess the human capital to contribute to making new discoveries or technological change. Multinational corporations that were at risk of costly imitation or counterfeiting might expand their overseas activities and employment if the target country were to strengthen their enforcement of intellectual property rights. Stronger patent rights could lead to increases in knowledge-intensive industries, in particular, and transfers of technology might facilitate the growth of a domestic market on both the demand and supply side.

By contrast, empirical estimates of current proposals for international harmonization of patent and copyright laws suggest that the net effect was likely to result in a net welfare loss for developing economies, and even some mid-level developed countries, paired with large net benefits to the United States and a few other advanced developed countries. Network models imply that weak enforcement of intellectual property rights might not harm technology producers, and might even benefit them if more extensive unauthorized use of the product increased the total value of legitimate use. Also in this vein, price discrimination or market segmentation across pirates and nonpirates can result in net welfare benefits for society and also for the legitimate patent owner. In the absence of royalties, firms may be able to appropriate returns through ancillary means, such as the sale of complementary items, or higher income through an enhanced reputation. Piracy could theoretically increase the demand for products by ensuring that producers credibly commit to uniform prices over time. If the cost of imitation increases with quality, infringement can also benefit society if it causes firms to adopt a strategy of producing higher-quality commodities, or matching differentiated products to consumer tastes.

At a more aggregate level, endogenous growth models suggest that the voluntary adoption and enforcement of intellectual property rights by such "follower countries" as China and India might help to explain their rapid convergence toward the growth paths of early industrializers.

Neoclassical growth models regard inventive activity and innovations to be exogenous, and dependent on forces beyond the control of such nations. Rather than viewing themselves as passive consumers of Western innovations, such countries are grappling with ideas about the sources of economic progress, and about the most appropriate types of institutions and economic arrangements that would allow them to become serious contenders in the global competition for leadership in new technological discoveries.[3]

This chapter discusses the historical experience among key players in the global economy in order to shed light on the current debate about the harmonization of intellectual property laws. Some might argue that international harmonization of intellectual property laws is the natural result of autonomous economic processes that tend toward efficient outcomes, but such a view is only partially supported by the evidence. Historical analysis reveals a complex and variable latticework of strategies that contrasts significantly with the current monolithic tendencies toward uniformly strong enforcement of patents and copyrights. Indeed, the current international system of strong patent and copyright laws based on natural or moral rights was never spontaneously adopted by any single country in the world. Rather than resulting from a coherent underlying economic rationale, the policies espoused by the WIPO were somewhat serendipitously created by a political economy of self-interest among the world's industrial and economic leaders.

3.2   Leaders in Patenting and Patent Institutions

Patent institutions have a long history, although their specific objectives and outcomes have varied significantly over time. The primary goals of early patent institutions typically were to raise revenues for the state, to promote commercialization, and to achieve import substitution or the domestic manufacturing of formerly imported products. Britain stands out for a patent system that has been in continuous operation for a longer period than any other in the world, but its features were typical of most nations at the time. In particular, some have argued that such approaches to inventive rights reflected social contracts for government-sanctioned monopolies, rather than intellectual property rights per se.[4] British

---

[3] Paul M. Romer, "The Origins of Endogenous Growth," *Journal of Economic Perspectives* 8 (1)(1994): 3–22.
[4] See Stathis Arapostathis and Graeme Gooday, *Patently Contestable: Electrical Technologies and Inventor Identities on Trial in Britain* (Cambridge, MA: MIT Press, 2013).

patents were granted through a registration system, in which patent fees were exceedingly high, and were deliberately kept well out of reach of the ordinary artisan. Exclusive rights were offered to wealthy importers of inventions that had been created abroad, and patent agents frequently applied for patents under their own names on behalf of inventors from overseas. The legal system and the common law regarding patents were unpredictable, and property rights to inventions could not be regarded as settled unless the patent had been contested in court with a favorable outcome. When coupled with the uncertainties inherent in a registration system, the purchase of a patent right involved a substantive amount of risk and high transactions costs. The market for inventions was consequently hampered by unpropitious rules and practices, and both assignments and licenses tended to be quite limited.[5]

The continual dissatisfaction of participants in the British patent system led to numerous calls for institutional reform. Debates about patent rights were repeated in other countries, and centered on contentious questions about trade, comparative advantage, and conflicting rights of users and producers. European proposals to replace patents systems ranged from the creation of a national fund to reward inventors through the complete abolition of any property rights in inventions. The Crystal Palace Exhibition in 1851 finally precipitated an official recognition in Britain of the need for legislative action to meet some of these long-standing criticisms. The British were threatened by industrial and technological advances in the United States, and the reforms that were introduced in 1852 and 1883 were explicitly motivated by the American practices of accessible property rights. However, policies that emerged from this era of activism were far from optimal. Legal advances in the nineteenth century were inevitably piecemeal and incomplete, consisting as they did of compromises between those with vested interests in maintaining rents under the former system, inventors (especially those of limited means) who stood to benefit from reforms, and protectionist manufacturers and politicians who wished to deter short-run foreign competition even if at the risk of high costs in the long run.

Despite their rhetoric of natural rights, the patent systems of other European countries such as France were similarly primarily motivated by mercantilist objectives and an emphasis on commercialization, rather than the intent to create incentives for new discoveries. French patentees

---

[5] B. Zorina Khan, "Selling Ideas: An International Perspective on Patenting and Markets for Technology, 1790–1930," *Business History Review* 87 (Spring 2013): 39–68.

could file through a simple registration system without any need to specify what was new about their claim, and could persist in obtaining the grant even if notified that the patent was likely to be invalid. Accordingly, the government warned the public that these rights were entirely free of any state backing. The inventor could obtain a patent for a period of five, ten, or fifteen years, and protection extended to all methods and manufactured articles with the exception of theoretical or scientific discoveries without practical application, financial methods, medicines, and items that could be covered by copyright. The first introducer of an invention covered by a foreign patent would enjoy the same "natural rights" as the patentee of an original invention or improvement. The statutes placed another limit on the rights of inventors in the form of working requirements, which could be avoided but only after significant monetary and transactions costs.

As a new republic, the United States rejected these European precedents, and established a system that ultimately would have the most significant impact on patent laws around the globe. The United States created the world's first modern patent institution, a system whose foremost objective was to create incentives for inventive activity through strong enforcement of property rights in new discoveries. Affordable fees and low transactions costs help to ensure universal access to the benefits of property rights in inventions.[6] The canonical "American system" was first established in 1836, with the primary feature that all applications were subject to an examination for conformity with the laws and for novelty by technically trained patent examiners. In addition, American legislators were concerned with ensuring that information about the stock of patented knowledge was readily available and diffused rapidly. The laws were enforced by a judiciary that was willing to grapple with difficult questions such as the extent to which a democratic and market-oriented political economy was consistent with exclusive rights. The rights of inventors, however, were typically viewed as compatible with the rights of society, and trade-offs were regarded as inevitable but of secondary concern. Throughout its history, the United States emphatically rejected restrictions on the rights of American inventors. Working requirements and compulsory licenses were dismissed as unwarranted infringements of the rights of "meritorious inventors," and incompatible with the philosophy of US patent grants. There were no opposition proceedings and, once granted, a patent could not be revoked unless there were evidence of fraud. Americans could not obtain protection for

---

[6] Khan, *The Democratization of Invention*, 106–27.

imported discoveries and, after 1861, patents were available to all applicants on the same basis without regard to nationality.[7]

A notable characteristic of the American system comprised its focus on
promoting markets for inventions, and the adoption of measures that
facilitated trade and contractual exchange. These extensive markets
enabled a specialization and division of labor that benefited inventors,
intermediaries, and consumers alike. By the 1870s the average annual
number of assignments reached over 9,000 per year, and this increased in
the next decade to over 12,000 contracts.[8] The market for patented
inventions provided an incentive for further inventive activity because
inventors were able to appropriate the returns from their efforts, and
trade linked patents and productivity growth. Patentees were not allowed
to extend their rights of exclusion to establish monopoly privileges,
however, since ex-post antitrust policies restricted unfair exploitation
and ensured a competitive environment in current and future markets
for products and innovation.

3.3   Follower Nations: Europe

Britain, France, and the United States accounted for the vast majority of
patents granted throughout the world in the next two centuries, and
subsequent follower countries were influenced by their intellectual property laws, both directly and indirectly. British institutions toward intellectual property were largely adopted by Britain's colonies and
dependencies such as the West Indies, Malta, and New Zealand, New
South Wales, and other Australian colonies. However, it is important to
note that the followers were able to make adjustments that suited their
own circumstances, resulting in an inherent diversity in specific rules and
standards. French patent laws similarly influenced the intellectual property institutions in France's own colonies, such as Tunis and Algeria.
Moreover, French policies also diffused to other countries through
France's impact on Spain's intellectual property system, and the French
model thus also affected the Spanish colonial jurisdictions.

---

[7] This liberality was noted as one of its essential features: "Our law gives to all men of all
nations the same privileges, and recognizes to the fullest extent the international character
of property in inventions. In this respect ... the United States may claim to have led the
world and to be leading it still." F. A. Seely, "International Protection of Industrial
Property," in *Proceedings and Addresses: Celebration of the Beginning of the Second Century
of the American Patent System* (Washington, DC: Gedney & Roberts, 1892), 205.
[8] See Naomi Lamoreaux and Kenneth L. Sokoloff, "Long-Term Change in the
Organization of Inventive Activity," (NAS Colloquium) *Science, Technology and the
Economy* 93 (Nov. 1996): 1286–92.

The transfer of technology was a major concern in the political economy of Spain, because of the prevalence of foreign inventors and expertise in its economic development.[9] Between 1759 and 1878, roughly one-half of all patent grants in Spain were to citizens of other countries, notably France and (to a lesser extent) Britain. This dependence on foreign technologies was reflected in the structure of the Spanish patent system, which permitted patents of introduction as well as patents for invention. Patents of introduction were granted to entrepreneurs who wished to produce foreign technologies that were new to Spain, with no requirement of claims to being the true inventor. Thus, the sole objective of these instruments was to promote import substitution and to enhance innovation and production in Spain. The owners of introduction patents could not prevent third parties from importing similar machines from abroad, so they also had an incentive to maintain reasonable pricing structures. Patentees were required to work the patent within one year, and about a quarter of patents granted between 1826 and 1878 were actually implemented. Since patents of introduction had a brief term, they encouraged the production of items with high expected profits and a quick payback period, after which monopoly rights expired, and the country could theoretically benefit from its diffusion.

The "patent controversy" of the nineteenth century about the merits of intellectual property protection was reflected in debates among the states that comprised the German alliance. Germany forged a hybrid of the American and British systems that later influenced legislation in a number of countries, including that of Argentina, Austria, Brazil, Denmark, Finland, Holland, Norway, Poland, Russia, and Sweden, and also Japan and China. Germany passed a unified national Patent Act in 1877 that created a centralized administration for the grant of a federal patent for original inventions. This included an American-style examination system, and applications were initially examined by consultants to the Patent Office who were expert in their field. German patent fees, like the British, were deliberately set high to eliminate protection for trivial inventions. During the eight weeks before the grant patent applications were open to the public and an opposition could be filed denying the validity of the patent.

The German state also introduced innovations in patent rules that were suited to its particular circumstances. After 1891 a parallel and weaker version of patent protection could be obtained through a utility or petty patent, which was granted through a registration system.

---

[9] See Patricio Sáiz, "Did Patents of Introduction Encourage Technology Transfer? Long-Term Evidence from the Spanish Innovation System," *Cliometrica* 8(1) (2014): 49–78.

Protection in the form of utility patents was available for inventions that could be represented by drawings or models with only a slight degree of novelty, and for a limited term of three years (renewable once for a total life of six years). Patent protection based on coexisting systems of registration and examination appear to have served distinct but complementary purposes. In particular, it was likely that the more extensive rights were initially secured by foreign inventors, whereas the petty patent encouraged experimentation and inventive activity by domestic independent inventors. The German patent system also facilitated the use of inventions by firms with laws that allowed enterprises access to the rights and benefits of inventions of employees. In another significant departure from American policies, German patents were subjected to working requirements and compulsory licenses. The grant of a patent could be revoked after the first three years if the patent was not worked, if the owner refused to grant licenses for the use of an invention that was deemed in the public interest, or if the invention was primarily being exploited outside of Germany.

German patent policies encouraged diffusion, innovation, and growth in specific industries, in order to encourage a desired or existing comparative advantage. The lack of restrictions on the use of innovations and the incentives to patent around existing processes arguably spurred productivity and diffusion in these industries, and the authorities further ensured the diffusion of patent information by publishing claims and specification before they were granted. In the United States, the courts adopted an extremely liberal attitude in interpreting and enforcing existing patent rights, regardless of the identities and nationality of the patent owner. By contrast, researchers claim that the Germans administered their patent system in ways that protected indigenous innovation and discriminated against foreign applicants.[10]

According to some observers, such differences in patent laws across countries led to asymmetries that benefited foreigners in the US market, and disadvantaged American firms overseas. A number of American policymakers attributed these divergences in patent rules to the increasing dominance of German firms in the chemical industry and production of dyes within the United States.[11] In Britain, lobbyists for the domestic chemical industry succeeded in getting patent legislation passed, which

[10] See Ralf Richter and Jochen Streb, "Catching-Up and Falling Behind: Knowledge Spillover from American to German Machine Toolmakers," *Journal of Economic History* 71 (Dec. 2011): 1006–31.
[11] United States Congressional Report: H.R. No. 326, 62d Congress 2d Session, Report on Schedule A: Chemicals, Oils and Paints (Washington, DC: GPO, 1912), 362.

provided for working requirements that reduced such asymmetries. American legislators, however, refused to revise the patent laws along the same lines as the German legislation because those measures were not in keeping with the fundamental principles of the American patent system. Thus, German enterprises were able to successfully arbitrage the differences across countries in patent institutions to dominate both the domestic and foreign markets for such industries.

3.4   Follower Nations: Japan and China

In the last third of the nineteenth century, Meiji Japan was a "follower" nation that deliberately designed its institutions to emulate those of the most advanced industrial countries of that era. After 1860, discussions of the role of patents in Japanese economic development led to visits to foreign intellectual property offices, and then to preliminary attempts to introduce patent legislation in Japan. The most influential of these envoys, Takahashi Korekiyo, was sent on a mission in 1886 to examine patent systems in Europe and the United States. The Japanese emissary was not favorably impressed with the European countries; instead, he reported: "we have looked about us to see what nations are the greatest, so that we could be like them; ... and we said, 'What is it that makes the United States such a great nation?' and we investigated and we found it was patents, and we will have patents." As a result of his efforts, the first significant national patent statute in Japan was passed in 1888.[12]

The Japanese patent institution replicated many features of the US system, including the examination procedures, low fees, and the grant of patents to the first and true inventor. In Japan, as in the United States, the objective of the grant was not to raise revenues for the state, but to promote domestic ingenuity. As in the United States, novelty was initially interpreted as new to the world, implying that inventions that had been created overseas could not be patented in Japan, but this stringent interpretation was subsequently changed when it was found to be too costly to implement. A key element of the success of the American system of patents was arguably due to its exceptional examination procedures. A centralized examination process with relatively low fees and a registration system with high fees both provide a filter, but the former was more likely to favor the encouragement of domestic ingenuity. Thus, it is a measure of Japan's desire to promote indigenous enterprise that it

---

[12] Cited in Story B. Ladd, "Patents in Relation to Manufactures," *12th Census of the United States*, vol. X(IV): 751–66. For further discussion of the history of patent law in Japan, see Chapter 16 in this volume.

devoted scarce human capital toward the administration of patent examinations.

However, Meiji technology policy was formulated in accordance with an ideology of achieving economic growth within the boundaries that were consistent with Japanese cultural norms and national interests. For instance, conflicts between competitors (interferences) were discouraged, and inventors who wished to patent improvements on an existing invention had to get the permission of the original inventor, who was entitled to some compensation. The early regime focused on encouragement for Japanese discoveries, and foreigners were not allowed to obtain patent rights. Not only were foreign residents denied intellectual property rights, patents were not granted for any invention that had previously been patented overseas. As in Germany, certain industries were exempt from patents, and protection was not extended to military inventions, fashion, food products, or medicines. Inventors were able to obtain patent protection for a period of five, ten, or fifteen years, as in the French system. Patents that were not worked within three years could be revoked, and severe criminal remedies were imposed for infringement, including penal servitude. If patented inventions were imported from abroad and sold in Japan, the patent right was also overturned.

After Japan signed the Paris Convention treaty a new patent law was passed in 1899, which amended existing legislation to accord with the agreements of the Convention. Most notably, it extended patent protection to foreigners (despite manifest obstacles because the patent rules and standards were not translated, applications had to be filed in Japanese, and some claimed that examiners favored Japanese applicants). The influence of the German laws was again evident in subsequent reforms in 1909 (petty or utility patents were protected) and 1921 (protection was removed from chemical products, work for hire doctrines were adopted, and an opposition procedure was introduced). The Act of 1921 also permitted the state to revoke a patent grant on payment of appropriate compensation if it was deemed to be in the public interest.

The modern patent system in Japan remains an intriguing amalgam of features drawn from the major patent institutions in the world, but modified to accord with Japanese priorities. Patent applications are filed, and the applicants then have seven years within which they can request an examination. Before 1996, examined patents were published prior to the actual grant, and could be opposed before the final grant; but at present, opposition can only occur in the first six months after the initial grant. Patents are also given for utility models or incremental inventions that are required to satisfy a lower standard of novelty and nonobviousness, and can be more quickly commercialized. The Japanese system favors the filing of a plethora of narrowly defined claims for utility models that build on the more substantive contributions of patent grants, potentially leading to the prospect of an anticommons. Others argue that utility models aid the dissemination of information and innovation in the early stages of the patent term, and that the pre-grant publication of patent specifications also promotes the diffusion of knowledge.

The Meiji government certainly focused on policies that would circulate ideas and information, and this was achieved through a variety of measures, both within and outside the patent system. The Home Ministry encouraged participation in industrial fairs at the domestic and international levels to "expand people's knowledge and [encourage] the search for technical improvement."[13] Foreign specialists and technologists were invited for training sessions and to work at technical institutes and colleges to benefit local artisans. Moreover, numerous Japanese representatives traveled overseas on fact-finding missions, and to obtain formal education in science and technology. At the firm level, parties with access to new ideas about products or processes often shared information with competitors, in a horizontal process of cooperative innovation.

The patent data in Figure 3.2 support the notion that the acquisition of technological capabilities in Japan occurred in three stages. During the nineteenth century there was little familiarity with intellectual property rights, and this in part explains the lack of success of the 1871 statute. The time series of patent applications and grants climbed steadily after the first decade of the twentieth century, in accordance with the expansion in the domestic market, as Figure 3.2(a) illustrates. Over this period, Japanese innovators were acquiring more skill and experience, and a few became world-class inventors of new and original discoveries that would be patented in other countries, including the United States. Kjell Ericsson's fascinating contribution in this volume highlights some of the complexities of melding domestic norms with patent grants, in a case study of Kokichi Mikimoto, who was granted four US patents between 1911 and 1938 for the culture of pearls.[14]

---

[13] P. F. Kornicki, "Public Display and Changing Values: Early Meiji Exhibitions and Their Precursors," *Monumenta Nipponica* 49(2) (1994): 167–96, at 185.

[14] Suyeoto Fujiki, a citizen of Japan, residing at Tokyo, seems to have been the first Japanese national to obtain a patent in the United States. Kantaro Nobuhara patented in 1923 improvements in rotary electric machines, and Isumu Iwamoto of Osaka obtained protection in the United States for his improvement in the process of malting charcoal. See Chapter 16 for further discussion of the patenting of artificial pearls by Japanese inventors.

(a)   **Patent applications and GDP per capita in Japan, 1885–2000**

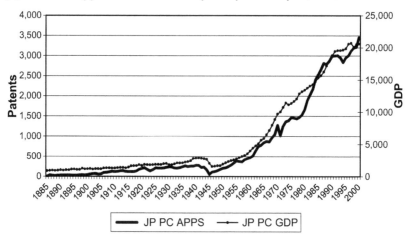

(b)   **Patenting in Japan and the United States:
percent granted to foreign residents, 1885–2010**

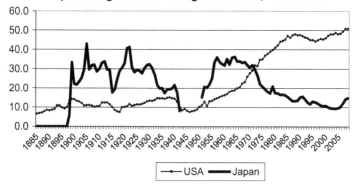

Figure 3.2 Patenting in Japan, 1885–2010.
Source: WIPO and World Bank, 2014 (www3.wipo.int/ipstats/)

Although a few such men were world-class inventors, in the early period this was atypical among Japanese technologists. The path of per capita patent grants in the two countries highlights the third stage, which occurred in the 1970s, when the Japanese caught up and became competitive with American technology. This claim is consistent with the data on the percent of total patents granted that accrued to foreign residents (Figure 3.2[b]). The majority of follower countries had very high rates of foreign penetration in their patent system and, indeed, may have assessed costly fees because the authorities did not expect much domestic participation in patenting. Even if many of these domestic Japanese patents were actually granted to foreigners who were resident in the country, Japan's rate of patenting by locals is unusually high. This may have occurred because of such "natural rights of exclusion" to foreign applications as language barriers, or the size and distance of the domestic market.

The patterns of patenting show that the Japanese innovation system had attained convergence by the 1970s, and was on the way to itself becoming a world leader in technology markets. The Meiji administration introduced an eclectic approach to industrialization that emphasized competence in each of the stages of technological change: education, adoption, invention, adaptation, diffusion, and commercialization. Policies were far-ranging, and included subsidies, the award of prizes, as well as the protection of inventive output through strongly enforced property rights in patents. Causation is difficult to determine, but the data are at least suggestive that technological change through patenting was associated with the rapid growth in income that Japan was soon to achieve. At that point, strong patent enforcement accompanied policies that also promoted investments in other forms of intellectual property.

Like Japan in the twentieth century, China illustrates the evolution of intellectual property laws that today's developing countries are experiencing in the twenty-first century. Initially, such economies perceive benefits from low enforcement because the opportunity cost of resources for patent systems and enforcement is high. In addition, emerging countries tend to view strong global enforcement of patent laws with some hostility, because they typically lack domestic technological capabilities, and regard intellectual property rights primarily as a means of transferring income to foreign producers. The growth of foreign direct investment in China was associated with lobbying by the United States and other source nations of multinational corporations to strengthen patent enforcement. However, it is not clear that exogenous attempts at imposing uniform laws were successful, apart from the enactment of pro forma statutes. Instead, as Figure 3.3(a) indicates, as more Chinese residents have entered into competition with foreigners in these product markets, firms within China have increased their filings of patent applications. And, as domestic capabilities altered within the domestic economy, the incentives and self-interest correspondingly shifted in China in a direction that aligned with international laws. Under these circumstances, harmonization became part of an endogenous process, whereby institutions adjusted to changes in underlying fundamentals.

(a)

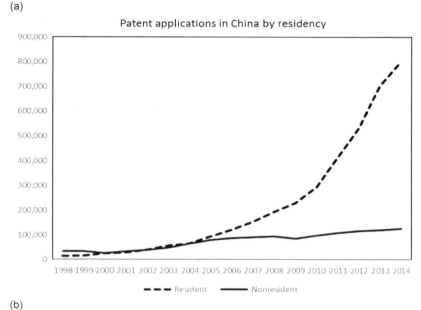

(b)

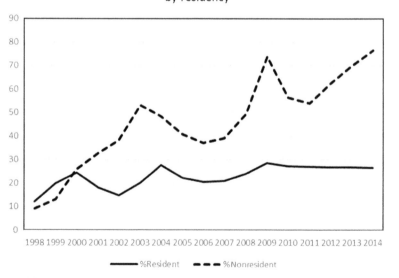

Figure 3.3 Patenting in China, 1998–2014.
Source: WIPO, 2014 (www3.wipo.int/ipstats/)

Patent laws at the national level have been amended several times in China, since its first modern patent law of 1984, in the direction of enhancing the value of property rights and the functioning of markets in those rights. Nevertheless, it is not surprising that this process has still not resulted in a significant reduction in "piracy" and the disregard of intellectual property rights in China. Figure 3.3(b) shows the percentage of applications that are granted, which sheds partial light on the quality of technological capabilities. These patterns correspond to evidence from patent renewals and other indicators of patent quality, which show that domestic patenting in China continues to be of lower quality than patents filed by foreigners.[15] Moreover, the balance of trade is still strongly unfavorable in the markets for cultural products that are covered by copyrights and trademarks. As economic history shows, this gap signals the existence of self-interested incentives for lower protection of intellectual property rights.

3.5 Harmonization of Intellectual Property Laws

At the beginning of the twentieth century, significant diversity was evident in the policies that individual countries pursued in the realm of patents and copyrights. However, efforts were increasingly being directed to attaining uniformity among intellectual property rights regimes. Part of the impetus for change occurred because the costs of divergent national rules became more burdensome as the volume of international trade in patents and patented industrial products grew over time. The United States comprised the most prominent actor in the movement for harmonization of patent laws, primarily because American patentees were launching multinational enterprises to penetrate international markets, and wished to secure the same level of protection that they enjoyed at home. Americans were also concerned about the potential for intellectual piracy of their exhibits at the World's Fairs that were an important venue for commercialization of innovations. Indeed, the first international patent convention was held in the Austro-Hungarian Empire in 1873, at the suggestion of US policymakers who wanted to be certain that American technologies would be adequately protected at the International Exposition in Vienna that year.[16]

---

[15] See Albert G. Z. Hu and Gary H. Jefferson, "A Great Wall of Patents: What Is behind China's Recent Patent Explosion?" *Journal of Development Economics* 90(1) (2009): 57–68.

[16] See Penrose, *Economics of the International Patent System*, 45 and Chapter 2 of this volume for further discussion of the significance of the 1873 Vienna Congress.

International conventions did not propose compromise solutions that would reflect the needs and wishes of all participants, but rather were directed toward the monolithic end of securing strong enforcement of patent laws. However, even though the overarching declared goal among member countries was to pursue uniform international patent laws, there was little agreement about the finer points of these laws. Complete uniformity of rules toward inventive property was never practicable, given the different objectives, ideologies, and economic circumstances of participants. Harmonization was not entirely driven by the size of a country's economy or by political power; instead, outcomes were catalyzed by the interaction of self-interest, the relative strength of domestic laws and institutions, and economic prowess. Nevertheless, in 1884 the International Union for the Protection of Industrial Property was signed by Belgium, Portugal, France, Guatemala, Italy, the Netherlands, San Salvador, Serbia, Spain, and Switzerland. The United States became a member in 1887, and a significant number of developing countries followed suit.

The United States was the most prolific patenting nation in the world, and many of the American enterprises that dominated international markets owed their standing to their patent portfolios. Even hostile participants acknowledged that the US patent system was the most successful, and that patent harmonization would eventually imply convergence toward the American model, despite resistance from many other nations. Countries such as Germany were initially averse to extending equal protection to foreigners because they feared that their domestic industry would be overwhelmed by American patents. Ironically, because its patent laws were the most liberal toward patentees, the United States found itself with weaker bargaining abilities than nations who could obtain concessions by offering to change their provisions.

The movement to create an international patent system elucidated the fact that intellectual property laws comprise part of a bundle of rights that are affected by other laws, institutions, and policies. Stipulations about trade, protectionism, domestic rules regarding contracts, torts, and crimes, and international laws regarding intellectual property were closely linked. For instance, the Paris Convention in 1880 considered remedies in the context of compulsory working requirements and provisions to allow imports by the patentee, and explicitly ruled out forfeiture of the patent or confiscation of products, which led some commentators to argue that restrictive tariffs were needed as a counterbalance. Frustrated by the resistance of other countries to harmonization, the United States increasingly used its leverage in bilateral trade negotiations and imposed tariff sanctions to force reforms in international patent policies.

3.6   Conclusion

Economic efficiency as an abstract concept depends on well-defined property rights, markets that feature low transactions costs, and an appropriate dynamic balance between access and incentives. These features were recognized and incorporated in early American policies toward inventions and inventors, which resulted in patent institutions that were unique to the world. Such patent policies were certainly appropriate for a developing economy that was endowed with high stocks of human and inventive capital, an effective and extraordinary judiciary and court system, transparent political and economic institutions, and a relatively equal distribution of income that promoted the rapid growth of a mass market. However, the rest of the world was not characterized by the endowments of the United States, including factor inputs and institutions. As such, even modernizing European nations like Germany and Spain found that the most effective policies to suit their specific circumstances required adjustments and deviations away from the American model.

Harmonization therefore can be assessed from two complementary perspectives. First, certain endogenous forces propel countries to voluntarily adopt stronger intellectual property protection in the course of their development, whereas exogenous pressure toward uniformity might redistribute global income toward the already developed economies and risk lowering global welfare. The second interpretation is that perhaps one can regard current approaches to harmonization as a form of "policy discrimination" that is analogous to price discrimination, which favors a strategy that sets the highest rules and standards as the global norm, and subsequently offers discounts or exemptions to each country according to its income (a proxy for willingness to pay). Just as in the model of price discrimination, we might speculate that this form of policy discrimination would likely increase overall welfare for all participants.

Criticisms have been levied against today's developing countries for not adhering to the rules of multilateral patent conventions, in a way that overlooks the practices of the developing countries of the nineteenth century. For instance, at present India, Thailand, and Brazil have been condemned for not offering patent protection for such products as drugs, chemicals, and some foodstuffs, whereas the majority of developed countries previously exempted these industries from protection. Unequal treatments of various sorts are also today subject to disapproval even though dual systems in Japan and Germany and introduction patents in Spain succeeded in allowing residents to participate in a patent system that was dominated by foreign inventors, created an incentive for the transfer of technology, and encouraged the commercialization of follow-on inventions.

As several other chapters in this volume illustrate, harmonization and resistance to uniformity have played equal roles in the global experience of international property protection at both the individual and national levels. The current emphasis on increasing the level of protection accorded to the owners of intellectual property further tends to distract attention from other means of appropriation and rewards, including reputation, lead time, or first-mover advantages.[17] Widespread copyright piracy of digital music and products has markedly increased the potential for disproportionate social costs from enforcement of producers' rights. The international community has also become more sensitive to the redistribution that might occur when rights of exclusion are introduced in indigenous communities at the expense of access to traditional knowledge and the public domain.

In sum, a number of the changes in the US and European intellectual property regimes – such as the introduction of the examination of patent applications – achieved what might be thought of as technical improvements. However, others such as process exceptions and cheaper patents for local residents involved adaptations that seem appropriate to the stage of economic development. Today's developed economies and even those of many developing countries undoubtedly benefit from the strong enforcement of secure property rights in inventions. At the same time, developing economies exhibit great heterogeneity in key dimensions, including domestic technological capabilities, absorptive capacity, the scarcity of human capital and other inputs, and net trade flows in innovations. Such variation warrants adjustments and exemptions to the policy of one rule for all, at least in the short term. This analysis of the evolution of intellectual property regimes in Europe and the United States raises questions about the desirability of applying the same rules and standards in all places at all times. Indeed, the major lesson from the economic history of the leading industrial countries is that intellectual property rights best promoted the progress of science and arts when such institutions were calibrated to serve the needs and interests of social and economic development in each nation.

---

[17] The reputational effect may partly explain why foreign pharmaceutical firms in Brazil increased their share of the domestic market even in the absence of patent protection. See C. R. Frischtak, "The Protection of Intellectual Property Rights and Industrial Technology Development in Brazil," in *Intellectual Property Rights in Science, Technology, and Economic Performance*, ed. F. W. Rushing and C. G. Brown (Boulder, CO: Westview Press, 1990), 61–98.

Part II

Americas

4 Technical Imaginaries
US Patent Models as Specimen and Specification

Courtney Fullilove

4.1 Introduction

In December 1835, shortly after Congress passed an act establishing a federal system of patent examination, a fire consumed the headquarters of the US Patent Office in Washington, DC. Every patent model perished. "I trust you will never meet such an awful catastrophe?" the commissioner of patents, Henry Ellsworth, wrote to his successor twenty years later. "I had to lose every model and drawing. I felt at times as though I should not effect a restoration."[1] Ellsworth spent his remaining ten years as commissioner trying to replace the lost models. For this task, Congress appropriated $100,000, reserving it for the 3,000 most important models, which it hoped would form "a very interesting and valuable collection." Thus, it was left to the commissioner of patents to reconstruct the material evidence of American inventiveness based on his judgment and available resources, applying standards of utility and representation quite different from those in which the original models had been produced.

This chapter examines concepts of invention illuminated by the proliferation of models as "legal specifications" in the examination system, and as "specimens of ingenuity" within the restoration project. The examination system made scale models, long customarily submitted by patent applicants, into required application components for assessment by examiners and in courts of law. The model requirement implicitly restricted the possible scope of patents by shifting the locus of invention to mechanical operation, excluding patents on pure processes and other concepts of origination. For these and other reasons, inventors' lobbies vehemently opposed it. Their efforts contributed to Congressional abolition of the requirement in 1870. Meanwhile, the restoration project

---

[1] Henry Ellsworth to Commissioner Charles Mason, requesting seeds from Patent Office, Records of the Agricultural Division of the Patent Office, 1839–60, RG 16.1, VI.862, National Archives and Records Administration, Washington, DC.

shored up a myth of heroic invention based on models of mechanical reproduction, in contradiction to the broadening of patentable material to include process and chemical compounds.

While at first blush legal and exhibitory modes of representation seem opposed, they were actually complementary forms. In industry as in natural history, a specimen is the thing itself, which can stand in for others of its kind and serve as a reference point for them. Specifications, instead, describe how something works: the operational principle of a thing. In practice, these categories overlapped, with specimen and specification mingling into a fetish of claims to inventiveness as a right of property and a proof of national greatness. Patent models were functional and symbolic: technical imaginaries bound up with the republic's aspirations to territorial expansion and economic development. The requirement to represent invention in three dimensions hastened problems of classification and justified an apparatus of bureaucracy and law to adjudicate them. Meanwhile the display of patent models in Washington became a prominent tourist attraction, figuratively linking nation, invention, and property rights in knowledge.[2] Each form shaped a bureaucratic and legal culture of property rights in knowledge that celebrated heroic invention and remained tethered to mechanical concepts.

The US patent system was unusual in requiring models, which it did from the inception of the examination system in 1835 until 1880, when the Patent Office acceded to the 1870 Congressional resolution nullifying the provision. Countries without examination systems, such as France and Great Britain, had no requirement for models. Some countries with examination systems, which were generally modelled on that of the United States, adopted the model requirement in less rigid form. Germany, Russia, Sweden, Canada, Newfoundland, Guatemala, Chile, and Uruguay each required models if the case admitted, generally as determined by the examiner. In Germany, for example, the patent act of 1877 unified the policies of its states, which had been operating independently since the formation of the empire in 1871. The statute strongly resembled that of the United States in form, pursuing innovation and growth through the establishment of an examination system to verify an invention's novelty, nonobviousness, and potential for increased efficiency. As a form of specification, however, models were required only occasionally. The 1888 Swiss statute, adopted in response to anxieties

---

[2] On museums as legitimating national or imperial governance, see e.g., Benedict Anderson, *Imagined Communities* (New York: Verso, 1983); Bernard S. Cohn, *Colonialism and Its Forms of Knowledge: The British in India* (Princeton, NJ: Princeton University Press, 1996).

about competitiveness with American manufacturers in mass production, provides an exception. The statute included a strict requirement for mechanical models from its inception in 1888 to 1907 to the exclusion of patents on pure processes. Thereafter reforms extended the scope of patentable material.[3]

Whereas the US system provided a template for the formation of many other national patent systems, such as Germany's and Japan's, by the time it became an example, the model requirement was already destined for the scrap heap. Countries that did require models, such as Switzerland, had patent cultures that were comparatively restrictive and/or insignificant in the context of the domestic economy.[4] By the time of the Paris Convention for the Protection of Industrial Property in 1883, the prior tradition of making and examining models was virtually irrelevant.

The US patenting requirement for models is worth studying in spite of its exceptionality, for this historical anomaly sheds light on shifting concepts of invention and the function of models as an instrument of international publicity for the US patent system. The sheer number of models amassed legitimated the creation of a physical space and a bureaucracy to manage them, underwriting federal investment in the patent system. However cumbersome and restrictive, the models requirement elevated a culture of invention populated by professional model makers and lawyers clustered in the nation's capital, a public museum in the Patent Office building, and a postal system that conveyed unwieldy creations to its halls.

Contrary to the thesis that the US patent system democratized invention, the models requirement introduced new barriers to patentees by increasing the role of model makers and lawyers as experts and translators in the patent process. Rather than facilitating access, these intermediaries acted as bottlenecks and added costs in patent applications, stimulating what H. I. Dutton dubbed "an active trade in invention."[5]

---

[3] For comparisons of the national patent systems and their requirements for models, see multiple editions of William Phillips Thompson, *Handbook of Patent Law of All Countries* (London: Stevens & Sons, 1920). For information on the context of the German and Swiss patent acts, see B. Khan, "An Economic History of Patent Institutions," EH.Net Encyclopedia, ed. Robert Whaples (March 16, 2008), http://eh.net/encyclopedia/an-economic-history-of-patent-institutions/, last accessed August 2, 2018.

[4] William Phillips Thompson, *Handbook of Patent Law of All Countries* (London: Stevens & Sons; New York: D. Van Nostrand, 1882); Alexander Melville, William Clark, and William Phillips Thompson, *Analytical Summaries of the Patents, Designs, and Trade Marks' Act, 1883, and of the Patent Laws of All Foreign Countries and British Colonies* (London: Stevens & Sons, 1884).

[5] On US patents as democratizers, see Chapter 3 of this volume and B. Zhorina Khan, *The Democratization of Invention: Patents and Copyrights in American Economic Development, 1790–1920* (New York: Cambridge University Press, 2005). On the growth of a patenting

Presented as proof of the patent system's democracy, in fact the new infrastructure of specification facilitated the appropriation of patents as tools of business by a select group of entrepreneurs who turned the patent system to their advantage. Models functioned as fetishes, obscuring trends toward industrial control of the patent system, while the enormous scale of the Patent Office building represented the republic's commitment to economic development. Ellsworth's collection of restored models, celebrating individual ingenuity, obscured the increasing complexity of the patent application process and its orientation toward process and chemical patents. They nevertheless cast the history of the US patent system as a success story for the world stage by linking liberal provision of property rights in invention with the promise of economic growth.

4.2   Exhibition

The prominence of patent models in the US patent system was an artifact of the system's administrative autonomy, with the Constitutional provision for patents and acts of Congress delegating substantial authority to administrative officials.[6] The first superintendent of patents, William Thornton, and his successors enjoyed substantial latitude in defining and justifying requirements for patent applications. (Thornton, a member of the American Philosophical Society and architect of the US Capitol building, wanly noted in his guidelines on patents that no applications for perpetual motion machines would be received without a working scale model.)[7] Congress's 1793 statute required a model only "if the machine be complex," but models nevertheless became a standard test of a patent's validity in courts. The statute also specified that the dimensions and style of models were also specified: "not more than twelve inches square," they were to be "neatly made, the name of the inventor should be printed or engraved upon, or affixed to it, in a durable manner."[8] According to proponents, models had a trifold purpose. First, they allowed for the testing of the nature and extent of the invention,

---

industry, H. I. Dutton, *The Patent System and Inventive Activity during the Industrial Revolution, 1750–1852* (Dover, NH: Manchester University Press, 1985).

[6] Jerry L. Mashaw, *Creating the Administrative Constitution: The Lost One Hundred Years of American Administrative Law* (New Haven, CT: Yale University Press, 2012); W. J. Novak, "The Myth of the 'Weak' American State," *American Historical Review* 113 (2008): 752–72.

[7] William Thornton, *Patents: Patent-office, March 5, 1811* (Washington, DC: J. Elliott, printer, 1811).

[8] Kendall Dood, "Why Models?" in *American Enterprise: Nineteenth-Century Patent Models* (Washington, DC: Cooper-Hewitt Museum – Smithsonian Institution, 1984), 65.

especially when the courts became involved in patent litigation. Second, they enabled the public to enjoy the invention after the patent had expired. Finally, they protected the patentee by providing a material record of the invention.[9] While patent models remained optional supplements to application until the passage of the Patent Act of 1835, applicants customarily provided them.

The 1835 statute's specific provisions for models were in large part the work of Charles Keller, the Patent Office's custodian of models. Keller, who had inherited the post from his father, was one of the chief members of the committee led by Senator John Ruggles to draft the report preliminary to the Patent Act of 1835. Keller prepared his portions of the report based on his personal assessment of the Office's dysfunction, which he attributed, in part, to the shortage of space to arrange the models. In this, Keller echoed the complaints of earlier administrators.[10]

Indeed, want of display space for models justified the construction of the Patent Office building. Even partially completed, in 1841, the Patent Office was the largest building itself in Washington, an indication of just how important visual representation was to the imagination of technology in the early republic. The very "object in establishing the Patent Office," the 1823 Committee on Expenditures reported to the State Department, "was the preservation of the models of the inventions, which may be deemed of sufficient importance to merit preservation."[11] The exhibition of models was a testament to American ingenuity, quickly becoming a popular attraction in Washington. Foreign visitors were invited to admire the specimens of American ingenuity, if not to study them too closely.

The Hall of Models nested claims to education and enlightenment within an ideology of national competitiveness and commercial might. In the new Patent Office building, the models shared space with a popular

---

[9] Many including Thornton worried instead that the display of models invited piracy, although there was little evidence that formal exhibition provided novel opportunities for espionage. On diffusion and piracy, Christine Macleod, "Paradoxes of Patenting: Invention and Diffusion in Eighteenth and Nineteenth-Century Britain, France, and North America," *Technology and Culture* 32 (1991): 885–910.

[10] On the Ruggles report and the reforms of the Patent Office, Daniel Preston, "The Administration and Reform of the U.S. Patent Office, 1790–1836," *Journal of the Early Republic* 5 (1985): 331–53 and B. Zorina Khan, "Property Rights and Patent Litigation in Early Nineteenth-Century America," *The Journal of Economic History* 55 (1995): 58–97. On the crisis in the courts, see Steven Lubar, "The Transformation of Antebellum Patent Law," *Technology and Culture* 32 (1991): 932–59.

[11] "The Committee on the expenditures of the Department of State, to which was referred the letter of the Secretary, of Dec. 3, 1822, accompanied by one addressed to him by the Superintendent of the Patent Office," Report on the Patent Office for 1823, from vol. 1 of the Annual Report of the Commissioner of Patents 1790–1836, copy in the commissioner's private official library, 783–7.

museum housing the spoils of government science expeditions and treaties of commerce. Nature specimens abutted Native American artifacts and donations from American manufacturers and agriculturalists, symbolizing territorial mastery over the continental West in support of national economic development.[12]

The Patent Office museum followed the pattern of early national museums in Europe, many of which derived from private collections and cabinets of curiosity enlarged through colonial expansion, imperial acquisition, scientific exchange, and public and private patronage. Many eighteenth-century scientific societies and early museums maintained cabinets of mechanic models as adjuncts to their natural history collections, including the Royal Society of the Arts in London, the French Academy of the Sciences, and the Conservatoire des Arts et Métiers. These mechanical cabinets were descendants of the previous century's private collections, elevated by the Baconian contention that science should have practical utility. In the United States, the American Philosophical Society maintained a significant collection of devices and improvements reflecting its concern with the promotion of the useful arts. These comingled with the collections of the Lewis and Clark expedition to the West and many private donations of objects.[13]

The Hall of Models in Washington was the successor to these early scientific societies, and more immediately to the collection of patent models in Blodgett's Hotel made under William Thornton's charge. Models had been displayed there since 1810, when their quantity required the superintendent to move from an office in the Department of State to more capacious quarters. Public display satisfied the disclosure requirement of patent applications: patents were granted in exchange for making the operations of an invention open to the public. But Thornton also envisioned the exhibition as a great museum of models and scientific instruments consistent with enlightenment projects of

---

[12] On the museum in the Patent Office building, Douglas Evelyn, "The National Gallery at the Patent Office," in *Magnificent Voyagers: The U.S. Exploring Expedition, 1838–1842*, ed. Herman Viola and Carolyn Margolis (Washington, DC: Smithsonian Institution Press, 1985), 227–54. On collections as representations of expansionism, Curtis Hinsley, *Savages and Scientists: The Smithsonian Institution and the Development of American Anthropology, 1846–1910* (Washington, DC: Smithsonian Institution Press, 1981); William H. Goetzmann, *Exploration and Empire: The Explorer and the Scientist in the Winning of the American West* (Austin: Texas State Historical Association, 1993).

[13] Robert P. Multhauf, *Catalogue of Instruments and Models in the Possession of the American Philosophical Society* (Philadelphia: The American Philosophical Society, 1961); Eugene S. Ferguson, "Technical Museums and International Exhibitions," *Technology and Culture* 6 (1965): 30–46; Charles R. Richards, *The Industrial Museum* (New York: The Macmillan Company, 1925).

public edification. The models were a popular attraction. One patron applauded the collection of models as "900 singular specimens of genius," while another derided them as "a singular assemblage of knick-knacks." A notice urged visitors not to touch the models in consequence of many having been "shamefully broken and deranged by handling," providing some indication of the popularity of the museum.[14]

Thornton's museum, however modest and overcrowded, established the Patent Office as a site of tourism and an instrument of public education, a program he considered well within the Office's constitutional mandate to promote the progress of science and useful arts. If his greatest aspirations were not realized, he nevertheless took the charge of the patent models seriously. As the British burned Washington in 1814, Thornton rode from Georgetown on horseback to save Blodgett's Hotel from ruin. As the British army approached the building, Thornton reportedly pleaded with the commanding officer that its destruction "would be as barbarous as formerly to burn the Alexandrian Library for which the Turks have since been condemned by all enlightened nations." Allegedly balking at such infamy, the officer had his troops let it alone. Thornton watched the Capitol building burn, while Blodgett's Hotel survived.[15]

Politicians and journalists styled the Patent Office alternately as a cabinet of curiosities, a national gallery, a temple of invention, and a rational place of amusement. These competing characterizations reflected the indeterminacy of its mandate to promote science and useful arts. The exact functions of collections remained as imprecise, with botanical specimens and models functioning simultaneously as working collections and objects of exhibition.[16] Until 1874, when the commissioner barred the public from the model halls for reasons of practicability, patent examiners shared quarters with the public, who came to view the models for information or entertainment.

---

[14] Bernhard Karl, Duke of Saxe-Weimar Eisenbach, *Travels through North America during the Years 1825 and 1826*, vol. 1 (Philadelphia: Carey, Lea & Carey, 1828), 175; Henry Bradshaw Fearon, *Sketches of America: A Narrative of a Journey of Five Thousand Miles through the Eastern and Western States*, 2nd ed. (London: Longman, Hurst, Rees, Orme and Brown, 1818), described in C. M. Harris, "Specimens of Genius and Knickknacks: The Early Patent Office and Its Museum," *Prologue: The Journal of the National Archives* 23 (1991): 406–17; on manufacturers studying models to improve machinery, David J. Jeremy, *Transatlantic Industrial Revolution: The Diffusion of Textile Technologies between Britain and America, 1790–1830s* (Oxford: Basil Blackwell, 1981).

[15] Harris, "Specimens of Genius and Knickknacks."

[16] On the Patent Office's sponsorship of plant introduction and the sharing of horticultural specimens, Courtney Fullilove, *The Profit of the Earth: The Global Seeds of American Agriculture* (Chicago: University of Chicago Press, 2017), chapters 1–2.

4.3   Examination and Classification

While models were symbolic of American ingenuity, they also had a utilitarian function in the new examination system, inaugurated in 1836. Models, with written specifications and drawings, enabled examiners to assess the practicability of a proposed invention. Examiners and judges frequently consulted models in matters of infringement and reissue of faulty patents. At times, the commissioner would withhold judgment on unresolved cases until he could examine the model in question.[17]

If models encouraged precision on certain fronts, they also suggested limits on the scope of patentable material. Chiefly, the notion that technical knowledge could be materialized privileged certain kinds of improvements, tilting the early patent system toward the protection of mechanical devices. Although samples of textiles and the products of chemical processes were also required by the 1835 Act, the early patent system told the tale of a nation built on sowers, mowers, and reapers. In 1823, one-half of patents were mechanical, with agricultural machinery, manufactures, and navigational improvements predominating.[18]

As Alain Pottage and Brad Sherman have emphasized, this paradigm of industrial manufacture supported a style of "mechanical jurisprudence" in which the choreographed demonstration of scale models provided the means for examiners, lawyers, and judges to figure invention as the "principle of the machine." Anatomizing models revealed the parts and operations essential to a machine's operation. The principle of mechanical reproduction, in turn, supposed a division between labor and knowledge, providing the conceptual basis for property in the latter.[19] This disassociation of knowledge from the material object itself created a regime of representation rather than presentation, as Mario Biagioli has characterized it: rather than being demonstrated by an artisan or importer, patentable knowledge was described in textual, pictorial, and three-dimensional forms. These representational forms, and the concepts of property in knowledge they supported, distinguished modern patent systems from early modern grants of privilege.[20]

---

[17] Charles Mason, for example, noted in his diary in reference to one application that he could not understand it without an examination of the model. He postponed the matter until Monday when he could go see the model with the examiner. Journals of Charles Mason (1829–82), February 2, 1878, Charles Mason Remy Family Papers, Box 18, Library of Congress, Washington, DC.
[18] Committee on Expenditures, State Dept., 1823.
[19] Alain Pottage and Brad Sherman, *Figures of Invention: A History of Modern Patent Law* (Oxford: Oxford University Press, 2010).
[20] Mario Biagioli, "Patent Republic: Representing Inventions, Constructing Rights and Authors," *Social Research* 73 (2006): 1129–72 and Mario Biagioli, "From Print to

The proliferation of models hastened problems of classification by obliging officials to systematize arrangement. Early classification of patents was patchwork, mixing function, class, or industry, with limited cross-references and no division between a process and a product patent. In the first years of the patent system, the number of patents issued was modest enough that a simple listing sufficed. Even as patent issuance proliferated during the years of registration, redundancy, overlap, and searchability posed few problems since no search for prior art was required. Yet by 1830, Superintendent John D. Craig prefaced his organization of patents into sixteen classes by noting that art rivalled nature in its defiance of easy classification. Craig directed a clerk to list all the models, including 95 nail cutters, 66 pumps, and 65 ploughs, etc. Thus, having recorded 635 models, the clerk sufficed to categorize the other 1,184 for "various other purposes" for a total of 1,819 models in all. For the most part, this classification retained Thomas Jefferson's early organization by trade, but the schema imperfectly contained even the 6,170 patents to date.[21]

Craig did not intend for his arrangement of models to support a systematic search or classification, and the new cadre of examiners in the 1840s struggled to conduct searches for prior art and categorize inventions within the existing framework. Classifying models in a single category led to inevitable problems with omission and inconsistency. Groupings based on industry and trade overlapped with ones based on principles of mechanics and chemistry. After 1836, patent officials expanded and reshuffled the Office's classification schemes to reflect new categories of research and experimentation. For example, a category in the 1830 classification for "chemical compositions" with subheading "tanning, patent medicines, cements, dyes, etc." expanded repeatedly between 1836 and 1866 to include various processes and products before being disaggregated into twelve related categories in 1872. In 1880, a formal classification division was established. The proliferation of models justified a bureaucracy to arrange them, with every commissioner after

---

Patents: Living on Instruments in Early Modern Europe," *History of Science* 44 (2006): 139–86.

[21] Report on the Patent Office for 1830, from vol. 1 of the Annual Report of the Commissioner of Patents 1790–1836, copy in commissioner's private official library, 789–802, 31st Congress [Doc No. 38] House of Representatives, 1st Session State Dept. Patent Office, Jan. 27, 1830. On patent classification, see Kendall J. Dood, Irving J. Rotkin, and Matthew A. Thexton, *A History of Patent Classification in the United States Patent and Trademark Office* (Arlington, VA: Patent Documentation Society, 1999); M. F. Bailey, "History of the Classification of Patents," *Journal of the Patent Office Society* 28 (1946): 468.

Ellsworth lobbying for more space and more examiners to support the rapidly increasing business of the Patent Office.

4.4   The Rapid Increase of Business

The requirement for models as legal specifications precipitated the growth of an industry in technical imaginaries. Whereas early US patentees typically prepared their own specifications, the scrutiny of the examining corps called for more exact hands. A growing body of model-making manuals advised patentees that under no circumstances should their models appear amateur, cheap, or crudely made. As advertisements to prospective manufacturers, models ought to convey the inventor's acumen and professionalism.

Model makers clustered near the Patent Office building, many of them staffed by skilled German immigrants. Firms like Daniel Ballauf Company, at 619 H St., dominated the trade with a half-dozen model workers and offices crowded with inventors overseeing the construction and adjustment of their models for submission. Model makers and draftsmen aided in the production of patent applications, often working in conjunction with the growing body of patent solicitors stationed near the Patent Office building. The institution of the examination system hastened this trend.[22]

Models and drawings required mechanical literacy that bridged the material world and a culture of print, crafting new styles of professional documentation. As natural history illustration became standardized in the 1830s, so too did technical documentation. As type specimen supplanted landscape painting in systematics, professionally drafted diagrams of technologies in isolation replaced hand-colored illustrations depicting machines with human operators. Whereas once patentees would prepare their own drawings and specifications freehand, patent solicitors and professional draftsmen prepared documentation according to new standards of descriptive geometry and technical illustration. Mechanics' institutes provided courses in descriptive geometry, as did textbooks and treatises on model making.[23] These styles of representation supported systems of mechanized production prioritizing standardization, uniformity, and interchangeability. As Steven Lubar has argued,

---

[22] William Ray and Marlys Ray, *The Art of Invention: Patent Models and Their Makers* (Princeton, NJ: Pyne Press, 1974), 14–27.
[23] Edward W. Stevens, Jr., *The Grammar of the Machine: Technical Literacy and Early Industrial Expansion in the United States* (New Haven, CT: Yale University Press, 1995).

models were instruments of managerial control: specifications for technical rationality enabling the division of labor.[24]

Inventors of lesser means nevertheless continued to construct their own models for submission. As a young Congressman in 1848, Abraham Lincoln devised an improved method for buoying river vessels over shoals and whittled an eighteen-inch model from red cedar using tools from a local shop. Lincoln patented his invention a year later with the aid of Zenas C. Robbins, a patent lawyer from St. Louis. Although the model remains in the Smithsonian Institution's National Museum of American History, his invention was never manufactured. In this, Lincoln shared the fate of most patentees.

While the romance of the lone tinkerer buoyed many fantasies of American ingenuity, for the most part, a concentrated group of professional inventors made money off the patent system, mainly through persistence and strategy. These patentees aggressively managed their patent portfolios, selling and licensing patent rights and pursuing infringers in court. Models served these users as the materials for litigation, making technological objects into propertied ones.[25] Although the patent system may have been designed to relieve overburdened courts, patent litigation increased even more in the 1840s as businesses began to use patents as tools for business strategy. The effectiveness of patent protection as a profit-making strategy varied by industry. Machines that were hard to move or copy benefitted from patents, while smaller and more easily duplicated technologies did not. Likewise, processes that were easy to replicate with readily available materials benefitted less readily from patents.[26]

Although technical and logistical factors made patents suitable instruments for certain industries, as important are the different ways industries exploited patents. Patentees made rights into profits by licensing or assigning them to businesses, which in turn used them in a variety of ways. Railroads at first flouted patent claims, then formed cooperative organizations to work against them, prioritizing uniformity over innovation. Electrical suppliers, in contrast, recognized patents as tools for establishing monopoly control, acquiring scores of secondary

[24] Steven Lubar, "Representation and Power," *Technology and Culture* 36 (1995): (Supplement) S54–S81.
[25] Carolyn Cooper, "Thomas Blanchard's Patent Management," *Journal of Economic History* 47 (1987): 487–8 and "Social Construction of Invention through Patent Management: Thomas Blanchard's Woodworking Machinery," *Technology and Culture* 32 (1991): 960–98.
[26] Petra Moser, *Why Don't Inventors Patent?* (Cambridge, MA: National Bureau of Economic Research, 2007), http://papers.nber.org/papers/w13294.

patents to suppress alternative technologies.[27] In sum, the patent system did not so much encourage innovation as reflect the prevailing interests of manufacturers and statesmen. Patents became tools of business development.

Although the cost of assembling a model posed a barrier, their display made them available to other inventors and visitors to the Patent Office, at least partially to facilitate the spread of the innovation and increase the likelihood of licensing.[28] By contrast, diffusion in registration systems such as Britain and France tended to be underdeveloped. Nevertheless, we have limited evidence of the scale and effect of visits to the collection of patent models on the commercial circulation of inventions. Arguably these visits were performed pilgrimages by a small community of believers, working to shore up an American romance with innovation as an ideology.

The number of patent applications rose dramatically through the 1840s and spiked during the 1850s, before suffering a temporary decline during the Civil War. Afterwards, the dramatic increase resumed. Patents granted, in contrast, remained fairly level through the 1840s, and then rose along with applications in the 1850s, reflecting the success of patent solicitors in opposing examiners with overly rigid standards of novelty. At the helm of this pressure group was *Scientific American*, a mouthpiece for the patent firm Munn & Company. Patent agents made more money off the patent system than almost all inventors, overseeing an array of technical specifications including applications, caveats, extensions, and reissues.[29]

Meanwhile, the accommodation, preservation, and display of the ever-increasing stock of models presented an ongoing challenge to the funds and infrastructure of the early Patent Office. By 1835, there were about 7,000 models to some 10,000 patents issued. The Ruggles report emphasized the crowding, disorganization, and susceptibility to fire of models in the Patent Office. Models were kindling, and everyone knew it. And sure enough, they burned before the new building broke ground.

---

[27] Steve Usselman, "Patents Purloined: Railroads, Inventors, and the Diffusion of Innovation in Nineteenth-Century America," *Technology and Culture* 32 (1991): 1047–75. On patent management, see Carolyn Cooper, "Making Inventions Patent," *Technology and Culture* 32 (1991): 837–45.
[28] B. Khan, "An Economic History of Patent Institutions."
[29] Robert C. Post, "'Liberalizers' versus 'Scientific Men' in the Antebellum Patent Office," *Technology and Culture* 17 (1976): 24–54; *Physics, Patents, and Politics: A Biography of Charles Grafton Page* (New York: Science History Publications, 1976).

4.5   Restoration and Canonization

So it was that the commissioner of patents, Henry Ellsworth, inherited an empty building, which in subsequent years would become crowded with the handiwork of government science and bureaucracy. Almost immediately after the fire, Ellsworth set about securing appropriations to restore the lost models and specifications. The consumption, restoration, and ultimate sacralization of models marked their apotheosis from working documents to relics.

In Ellsworth's restoration project, the model's utility as a legal specification fused with its symbolic character as a specimen of ingenuity. The restoration project changed the context and purpose of the models and drawings recovered, powerfully shaping the meaning and function of those yet to be produced. Ellsworth appointed administrators to designate those models that were the "most important" and determine the compensation to be offered for them. He contacted inventors by means of notices in "almost all the papers in the union." Along with the recovery of models, Ellsworth produced a digest of patents issued by the federal government, along with an improved classification system in which the recovered models and drawings would be arranged. In a single year, he recovered 2,000 patents.[30]

Ellsworth noted the extensive difficulties facing the restoration project. Patentees would be unwilling to send their models until there were suitable accommodations for their display. Although patentees of some 10,000 had been addressed personally through the post offices where they resided when the patent was issued, many would have since moved.

Ellsworth was nevertheless optimistic in light of several restrictions in place, which ironically served to skew the corpus of recovered patents. No patent granted before the fire could be given in evidence without being first recorded anew. Ellsworth felt this restriction would "secure the return of the most important." Improvements on former patents would also require furnishing models of old inventions.[31] While this provision privileged patent holders intent on deriving profit from their inventions, it did not necessarily establish the importance of the technology in question. Use in infringement suits, too, would recover patents actively enforced by their owners without regard for the overall

---

[30] Annual Report of the Commissioner of Patents for 1838 (Washington, DC: US Gov. Print. Off., 1839).
[31] Annual Report of the Commissioner of Patents for 1837(Washington, DC: US Gov. Print. Off., 1838).

significance of the invention. That is, recovery indicated not so much the significance of a technology as its success as a legal instrument.

Ellsworth also made special efforts to recover patents for technologies he deemed important, creating a narrative of patented invention as success. These included the papers deposited by Robert Fulton, who had patented the first commercially successful steamboat years after John Fitch and James Rumsey's efforts fizzled. Fulton's drawings, unlike some others, "were executed by his own hand, and formed an interesting part of the records of American genius." While Ellsworth took care to hire skilled draftsmen to undertake the restored drawings for other patents, the standards and conventions of technical representations had changed considerably in the past fifty years.[32] The original patents represented a lost documentary style, which was much more fantastical and free-form than the specifications that succeeded it. Moreover, Ellsworth's restoration project did not represent the normative experience of inventors and patentees, which was one of failure and marginality rather than profit and achievement.

In addition to the patentees' hall of fame, Ellsworth solicited "unpatented models and specimens of manufactures," which he believed would increase the collection of the Patent Office such that none in Europe could rival it. He cited the "beautiful collections of manufactured articles" in temporary fairs or large cities as giving a hint of the "great gallery of arts and manufactures" that would be installed at the seat of government. "Interest and patriotism" would combine to multiply the articles deposited.[33]

As with his provisions regarding reissue and legal evidence, Ellsworth's efforts to court donations from manufacturers privileged already successful businesses. Businesses of means forwarded their machines gratis, grateful for the publicity. Here, the Patent Office functioned as an international exhibition. Manufacturers might take care not to send their latest and greatest machine for fear of piracy; but a well-established one would serve the same function. As the gallery in the new Patent Office building neared completion, Ellsworth reported that mechanics and manufacturers were taking the opportunity to present "the choicest contributions" for display in the Great Hall.[34]

Soon enough, the number of models outstripped the space available for display, and Ellsworth and his successors lobbied for the construction of additional wings of the Patent Office building. "The models of the

---

[32] Annual Report of the Commissioner of Patents for 1837, p. 3.   [33] Ibid., p. 4.
[34] Annual Report of the Commissioner of Patents for 1840 (Washington, DC: US Gov. Print. Off., 1841).

patented inventions are crowded so much as to prevent classification," Ellsworth wrote to Congress in 1844, "while models of the rejected applications, equally important for exhibition, to enable supposed inventors to settle doubts as to originality, are not exhibited at all."[35] His successors reiterated the embarrassments caused to the Office by the lack of space for classification and arrangement of models, until finally work on the west wing began in 1849.

Commissioners after Ellsworth retained his commitment to celebrating the history of American invention represented by the Patents Office. Thomas Ewbank added "historical notices on inventors and patentees" to the annual report, beginning with the Fitch–Rumsey steamboat controversy. The concerted effort to recover models had given the Patent Office a sense of historical mission, and the annual reports became a testament to its success on par with the exhibitions in the galleries. The restoration project was a success, and a revision of the patent system's work to date.

National boosterism and the promotion of the useful arts had never been mutually exclusive: indeed, they were of a piece. But the restoration and revision of early patents drastically altered the content available for subsequent analyses of the material relation between the two. In deciding where to focus his efforts, Ellsworth quite literally made history, recovering the evidence of inventions he could find, selecting the most significant, and presenting them in the halls and revised classifications of the Patent Office. The United States of America became the nation of Robert Fulton and the McCormick reaper. These were the heroes of invention to rival Britain's canonization of James Watt and George Stephenson.[36]

As space became ever more constrained due to the increased business of the US Patent Office, critics charged that the models requirement was an anachronism. Patent solicitors and popular trade publications intent on diversifying patenting activity in nonmechanical fields led the charge. Patents on chemical processes could not be specified by means of a model. To liberalizers of the patent system, this evidenced the restrictive limitation of the models requirement.

One writer for *Scientific American* claimed the model bore the same relation to patents "as does the pound or so of yellow wax which the English fasten to their patent document. The wax is of no use, neither is

---

[35] Annual Report of the Commissioner of Patents for 1844 (Washington, DC: US Gov. Print. Off., 1845), p. 2.

[36] Christine MacLeod, *Heroes of Invention: Technology, Liberalism and British Identity, 1750–1914* (Cambridge: Cambridge University Press, 2007).

the toy model, except that both tend to create an impression (literal and metaphorical) of useless formality." In an age of accurate drawings, cheap printing, and even photo engravings, models served no purpose for the diffusion of useful knowledge. "Models, as records, but poorly fulfil their purpose," the writer determined.[37]

When solicitors and industrialists committed themselves to exploiting patents for strategic advance in nonmechanical sectors, they succeeded. The widening enforcement of patent laws hastened the expansion and diversification of patenting activity across industries. Meanwhile, enforcement of patent laws facilitated protection of more products and processes, even those that were easily copied.[38]

Finally, the escalation in patent activity after the Civil War made the preservation and storage of models inconceivable. By 1876, the collection of some 175,000 had become so unwieldy that the acting commissioner of patents, William H. Doolittle, elected to bar the public from visitation. At the current rate of increase, Doolittle anticipated an additional 14,000 models a year.

Then, late at night on September 24, 1877, the Patent Office burned again. This time, employees carried all the records and models they could hold through every available exit. Nevertheless, it was a devastating loss. Even so, no matter how many models burned, there were far too many to be displayed; and their functions as instruments of demonstration or diffusion seemed unclear.

In 1908, Congress voted to sell all the models, giving the Smithsonian six months to select ones it deemed worthy of preservation. Of some 200,000, the Smithsonian selected 1,061. Once again, the selection canonized some technologies and marginalized others. The remaining lot was sold at auction. The pharmaceutical manufacturer, Sir Henry Wellcome, purchased somewhere between 125,000 and 175,000 models. Upon his death, Broadway producer Crosby Gaige purchased the collection and exhibited it to great fanfare at the Rockefeller Center during the late 1930s. Bankruptcy provoked another change of custody, this time to auctioneer O. Runclle Gilbert, who stored the models in a barn in Garrison, New York while preparing them for display and auction.[39]

---

[37] A. Graham Bell, "American Patent Office Models," *The Journal of the Society of Arts* 26 (1306) (November 30, 1877): 17–26, at 24.

[38] Petra Moser, "How Do Patent Laws Influence Innovation?" *American Economic Review* 95 (Sept. 2005): 1214–36.

[39] Donald W. Hogan, "Unwanted Treasures of the Patent Office," *American Heritage Magazine* 9, no. 2 (Feb. 1958): 16–19, 101–3; Ray and Ray, *The Art of Invention*, 14–27.

Models for patenting activity were vestiges of an increasingly ana-chronistic material conception of technical knowledge. As the physical embodiments of written patent specifications, they offered proof that property in ideas had a material form, a fantasy that all technical know-ledge could spring to life in three dimensions. This mechanical fantasy proved foolhardy as the rapid increase of patent applications created a crisis of storage, processing, and exhibition. By the 1870s, models seemed less a proof of American ingenuity than an outmoded attempt to represent knowledge, and a bureaucracy spinning out of control. As one commentator remarked in the wake of the latest fire, the models were but "an enormous mass of dry painted and varnished combustible matter, which burns like tinder."[40]

Yet, long past their utility as embodiments of technical knowledge, models survived as relics of Americana: visitors wondered at the rows of glass cases on the ground floor of the Patent Office building, the Smith-sonian National Museum of American History, or Rockefeller Center.[41] As the halls of the Patent Office became a shrine to Samuel Morse, Cyrus McCormick, Charles Goodyear, and Samuel Colt, the Patent Office's displays drew closer to those of international exhibitions for the promo-tion of industry than to working collections for examiners. Models became relics of the heroic inventors they represented, or the mass of hopeful tinkerers perpetuating fantasies of American ingenuity: more totems than privileges or rights.

Although cumbersome, restrictive, and destined for obsolescence, the US patent system's model requirement elevated a distinctively American culture of invention. The exhibition of models became an important instrument of publicity for the patent system, a proof of success to national and international observers. Specimens of ingenuity filled the halls of the Patent Office and international industrial exhibitions, a testament to the success of patent systems in promoting science and useful arts.

Their claims to represent a democracy of inventors belied the extent to which a select group of entrepreneurs had manipulated the system. If

---

[40] Bell, "American Patent Office Models," 24.
[41] Several catalogues of nineteenth-century patent models are: Cliff Peterson, *Catalogue of U.S. Patent Models* (Santa Monica, CA: Cliff Petersen Collection, 1980); *The Cooper-Hewitt's American Enterprise: Nineteenth-Century Patent Models* (Washington, DC: Smithsonian Institution Press, 1984); Barbara Suit Janssen, ed., *Icons of Invention: American Patent Models* (Washington, DC: National Museum of American History, Smithsonian Institution, 1990); Barbara Suit Janssen, ed., *Technology in Miniature: American Textile Patent Models, 1819–1840* (Washington, DC: Smithsonian Institution Press, 1988); Eugene Ferguson and Christopher Baer, *Little Machines: Patent Models in the Nineteenth Century* (Greenville, DE: Hagley Museum, 1979).

patents had become rights rather than privileges, it was chiefly through a sense of entitlement to the ownership of technical knowledge, the prerogative of a select group of entrepreneurs who turned the patent system to their advantage.

Meanwhile the model's gradual apotheosis from working document to relic signified the increasing abstraction of inventive rights and of property more broadly, first in relation to process and chemical patents in the nineteenth century, and then in relation to plants and biotechnology in the twentieth. The disassociation of patent rights from mechanical models enabled the ever-broader application of claims, both with respect to geography and patentable knowledge. Although governments studying the US system took heed of the model requirement's obsolescence and omitted it from their own statutes, they nevertheless aspired to the culture of patenting it had helped fashion: one encouraging ever more expansive efforts to profit through claims to property in knowledge.

5   Mexico and the Puzzle of Partial Harmonization
Nineteenth-Century Patent Law Reconsidered

Edward Beatty

5.1   Introduction

The national patent laws adopted by dozens of countries around the globe in the nineteenth century present an extraordinarily diverse institutional landscape. Within Europe itself we see an "unparalleled diversity of patent systems."[1] Although new patent laws in European colonies and former colonies often built on their imperial inheritance, we still see heterogeneity within, for instance, the British Empire as well as among the former Iberian colonies in the Americas.[2] Diversity among national patent systems has a long and resilient history, as many contributions in this volume show. Despite this global diversity, however, several factors have nudged national laws toward a more harmonized landscape over the past century and a half. Pressures to increasingly standardize patenting norms across countries came largely from the patent and technology exporters in North America and Western Europe. During periods of globalization in the late nineteenth century and again in the late twentieth, these efforts coalesced in major international conventions, from the Paris Convention of 1883, which highlights an era of global patent law reform that lasted until World War I, to the Trade-Related Aspects of Intellectual Property Rights (TRIPS) agreements of the 1990s. Pressures also appeared from within patent-importing countries. Local patent law reform movements argued for stronger, more standardized regimes but also typically sought to maintain regulatory limits on the rights of

---

[1] Eda Kranakis, "Patents and Power: European Patent System Integration in the Context of Globalization," *Technology and Culture* 48 (2007): 689–728.
[2] Lionel Bentley, "The 'Extraordinary Multiplicity' of Intellectual Property Laws in the British Colonies in the Nineteenth Century," *Theoretical Inquiries in Law* 12 (2011): 161–200; Edward Beatty, "Patents and Technological Change in Late Industrialization: Nineteenth Century Mexico in Comparative Perspective," *History of Technology* 24 (2002): 121–50.

patent holders, including (for example) compulsory working and licensing clauses.

In spite of international agreements and some convergence between the 1880s and the present across national systems, harmonization has never been complete. The heterogeneity of national patent systems persists, even within regions that otherwise share similar histories and interests, such as Brazil and Mexico.[3] Different colonial legacies do not fully explain persistent differences, given the diversity within colonial systems and many countries' divergence from their colonial inheritance. Nor do common sets of regional or economic interests among patent- and technology-importing nations fully explain divergent patterns, as we will see.

Mexico provides a particularly interesting case for exploring the puzzle of partial harmonization. The history of patent law and reform efforts in Mexico reveal many of the factors that over the past 150 years have pushed national laws toward convergence. But Mexico's history also reveals factors that have posed obstacles to harmonization, especially among the large set of relatively late-developing, patent- and technology-importing nations around the world. In the late nineteenth century as in the twentieth, the vast majority of patents came from a small handful of countries: the early industrializers around the North Atlantic, plus Japan. If patent law aims to balance the rights of patent holders with the interests of the public, we might expect countries that produce and export inventions, technologies, and patents to favor strong, unregulated rights, standardized across national borders. Generally, this has been the objective of international conventions from the 1880s to the present.

In contrast, we might expect countries that predominately import technologies and patents to accede to international norms that facilitate cross-border trade, but also to regulate patent rights in ways that promote the local use and diffusion of imported knowledge and expertise within their borders. This tendency has, in fact, also been embedded within international conventions, which have tended to standardize international norms of patentability and national treatment, while acknowledging the right of countries to require, for instance, the domestic working of patented inventions.

Mexico inherited the Spanish *ancien régime* system of patents-as-privileges at independence, joined the international harmonization trend in the wake of the Paris Convention, but then diverged from it by adopting a

---

[3] Kenneth C. Shadlen, "The Mexican Exception: Patents and Innovation Policy in a Nonconformist and Reluctant Middle Income Country," *European Journal of Development Research* 24 (2012): 300–18.

legal framework closely aligned with the United States' model, itself a global outlier. By 1903, Mexican law had shed the vestiges of its Spanish inheritance, strengthened protection for inventors and patent holders, joined the Paris Convention, and eliminated all regulatory provisions that might have favored local innovation by limiting patent holders' rights. The Mexican case offers a lens to view national patent cultures and the puzzle of partial harmonization from the perspective of a late-developing, patent-importing country – like those many outside the North Atlantic that pursued industrialization and economic growth (or "material progress," in typical nineteenth-century parlance) in the wake of the first industrial revolution. This chapter builds on and extends the author's previous work on the history of patenting and technology in Mexico.[4] It places Mexico's nineteenth-century history within a comparative global framework in order to highlight the role of colonial legacies, international economic and institutional contexts, and the ideas and interests of local actors in the changing landscape of national patent laws between 1870 and 1914.

5.2   The Emergence of Patent Cultures in Latin America

When the newly independent Latin American nations adopted their first patent laws in the nineteenth century, their Iberian heritage provided a common point of departure. This inheritance – embodied in early modern Spanish royal practice and in that country's first patent law of 1820 – did not, however, produce a monochrome landscape among Spain and Portugal's former colonies. Spanish monarchs had granted limited monopoly protection to new activities on an ad hoc basis as early as the fifteenth century, and royal policy carried the practice to Spain's American colonies over the next 300 years.[5] Spanish viceroys in the Americas conferred hundreds of vaguely defined and loosely regulated *privilegios* to a wide range of new techniques and activities. Following independence from Spain and Portugal in the 1820s, political and business leaders in Latin America typically viewed the acquisition of new

---

[4] Edward Beatty, *Institutions and Investment: The Political Basis of Industrialization in Mexico before 1911* (Stanford, CA: Stanford University Press, 2001), especially chapters 4 and 5; also "Patents and Technological Change"; and *Technology and the Search for Progress in Modern Mexico* (Berkeley: University of California Press, 2015).

[5] Manuel Márquez, "1573: The Oldest Patent Granted in Mexico and Latin America," *History of Technology* 31 (2012): 163–7; Ramón Sánchez Flores, *Historia de la tecnología y la invención en México: introducción a su estudio y documentos para los anales de la técnica* (Mexico: Fomento Cultural Banamex A.C., 1980); Patricio Sáiz, "The Spanish Patent System (1770–1907)," *History of Technology* 24 (2002): 45–80.

technologies from Europe as central to any vision of national progress. Consequently, the new nations gradually adopted their own patent legislation: Brazil in 1830, Mexico in 1832, Chile in 1840, Venezuela in 1842 and 1860, Paraguay in 1845, Colombia in 1848, Uruguay in 1853, Bolivia in 1858, Argentina in 1864, and Peru in 1869. Surviving colonial territories in Cuba and Puerto Rico remained under Spain's 1826 patent law, formally adopted on both islands in 1833.[6]

Until the last third of the century, however, vaguely specified laws, administrative frailty, and relatively weak domestic markets for technological innovation in the Latin American economies meant that patenting was infrequent, rarely exceeding a dozen or so grants a year in any country before the 1870s, often fewer. Many of these grants were closer to *ancien régime* economic monopolies than to novel inventions, reflecting their origin in older patents-as-privileges regimes.[7] However, the rising tide of Atlantic trade and investment began lifting Latin American economies after about 1870, dramatically increasing opportunities and incentives to import and adopt new technologies. As a result, governments in the region joined the emerging international movement to reform and strengthen patent legislation and to more vigorously promote stronger property rights in tradeable knowledge. Venezuela adopted a new patent law in 1878, Brazil in 1882, Uruguay in 1885, Mexico in 1890 and 1903, Colombia in 1902, Argentina in 1903, Bolivia in 1916, and Paraguay and Chile in 1925 (in the last case after several amendments throughout the 1880s and 1890s). Similarly, Peru introduced improvements to its 1869 patent law in 1896, while Cuba and Puerto Rico adopted the 1878 Spanish patent law two years later. Patent laws were adopted for the first time in Ecuador in 1880, Guatemala in 1886, Costa Rica in 1896, Nicaragua in 1899, the Dominican Republic in 1911, and Honduras and El Salvador in 1913. We do not yet have a coherent account of this regional history, but the nineteenth-century phases of initial patent law adoption (circa 1820s–50s) and subsequent reform (circa 1880s–1910s) are clear.

These new and revised laws comprised one part of a broader global move toward a set of international standards in the wake of the 1883 Paris Convention and its subsequent amendments. They tended to feature more transparent rights for original inventors, reciprocal treatment of

---

[6] Edward Beatty, Yovanna Pineda, and Patricio Sáiz, "Technology in Latin America's Past and Present: New Evidence from the Patent Records," *Latin American Research Review* 52(1) (2017): 138–49.

[7] Mario Biagioli, "Patent Republic: Representing Inventions, Constructing Rights and Authors," *Social Research* 73(4) (2006): 1129–72; Beatty, *Institutions*, chapter 4.

foreign patentees, a priority filing period following a first patent, no revocation for importing patented goods, and some leeway to regulate patent monopolies in order to promote domestic use. First and foremost, the Paris Convention sought to increase the security of those individuals and firms that traded new, patent-protected technologies across national borders, principally the patent and technology exporters of the North Atlantic.[8] The Paris Convention responded to the era's dramatic outward expansion of the Atlantic economy, and to rising levels of trade and investment in technologies and patents. Colonial legacies became increasingly less important and were sometimes overwritten by newly emerging international norms, themselves shaped by a dramatically new international economic context.

Patent applications in Latin American countries rose rapidly from the 1880s to at least 1914, driven by three factors: the rapidly increasing supply of new, patentable technologies from countries around the North Atlantic; rising local demand for technological innovation within the region; and a reformed (that is, stronger) institutional basis for patenting in many countries. Applications came increasingly from foreign inventors and firms, along with smaller numbers of local tinkerers, inventors, speculators, and companies. During this period Brazil conferred nearly 9,000 patents (1882–1914), Argentina nearly 12,000 (1866–1914), and Mexico about 13,500 (1872–1914). Over a longer period, Cuba awarded roughly 4,500 patents (1830–1914) – apparently independent of the Spanish imperial system even before 1898 – and Chile about 3,600 (1840–1911).[9] Throughout the region, nearly 70–80 percent of the dramatic increase in patenting after the 1870s came from North Atlantic patentees. The institutional reforms of the era, and the partial harmonization of global patent laws and the Paris Convention itself were, in other words, coterminous with rising levels of international patenting. This relationship was not necessarily causal: both were the result of expansion in the Atlantic economy.[10]

5.3   Mexico and the Transition from Colonial to National Patent Cultures

Mexico's patent history runs through two long stages in the nineteenth century. In the first (1820–90), national legislation reflected the legacy of

---

[8] Edith Tilton Penrose, *The Economics of the International Patent System* (Baltimore: The Johns Hopkins Press, 1951); Kranakis, "Patents and Power."

[9] Beatty, Pineda and Sáiz, "Technology in Latin America's Past."

[10] Beatty, *Institutions*, chapter 5; *Technology*, chapter 3.

the country's colonial inheritance. In the second (1890–1910s), new laws remade patent rights in a concerted effort to promote investment in the domestic economy, primarily by attracting new technologies to transportation, mining, commercial agriculture, and manufacturing. In this broad pattern, Mexico fell in line with the late-century global push toward partial harmonization, but with several crucial distinctions reflecting the resilient distinctiveness of national regimes.

Mexico inherited its first patent law from Spain at independence in 1821, modeled directly on the Spanish law of 1820. Subsequently, new legislation promoted by Lucas Alamán was adopted by the Mexican Congress in 1832 but did not substantially alter the nature of protection. Despite frequent critique and sporadic efforts at reform, the institutional regime created by the 1832 law remained in force until 1890.[11] Mexico's first patent law regime was more a continuation of colonial, *ancien régime* privileges in Bourbon Spain than the codification of modern intellectual property rights. It offered protection to inventors, but at the same time to anyone – inventor or third party – who was the "introducer of any branch of industry that, in the judgement of the general congress, is of great importance."[12] The law was not primarily concerned with the natural rights of inventors, but instead sought to encourage investment in new machines, processes, and novel economic activities. Vaguely worded, the law offered ten-year exclusive privileges on a discretionary basis as well as "patents of introduction" to third parties who could claim protection for activities new in Mexico, regardless of whether they were the original inventor. The 1832 law did not, in other words, represent an effective contract between inventor and the public to exchange temporary exclusivity for publically accessible knowledge.

Nor did Mexican patent law prior to 1890 contain transparent and consistent administrative procedures for conferring protection, defining and defending rights, and adjudicating disputes concerning infringement, nullification, or fraud. Mexico did not enact a national commercial code until 1884, and through the preceding decades responsibility for patent administration had shifted irregularly between the executive branch and the general Congress, resulting in "innumerable complications."[13] Complaints focused on the breadth of privileges and the

[11] For full discussion of Mexico's patent law history, see Beatty, *Institutions*, chapter 4.
[12] Manuel Dublán and José María Lozano, *Legislación mexicana; o, colección completa de las disposiciones legislativas expedidas desde la independencia de la república ... 1687–1910*, vol. 2 (Mexico: Imprenta de E. Dublán), 427–8.
[13] Mexico, Secretaría de Fomento, *Memoria* (Mexico City: Imprenta de la Secretaría de Fomento, 1877–82), 1:427–9; (1857), 104–5; (1876–7), 526; and (1883–5), 674–5; Sánchez Flores, *Historia de la tecnología*, 377–9; and Jorge A. Soberanis, "Catálogo de

discretionary nature of their conferral, and critics predictably charged that "some patents, by monopolizing certain branches of industry, extraordinarily prejudice the consumer, and are only beneficial to a certain number of persons."[14] But conferrals of exclusive privileges were scarce until well after mid-century, totaling under a hundred over the four decades after 1832.

Efforts at reforming the country's patent legislation began seriously in 1843, although this first effort yielded only the addition of a formal compulsory working clause. Congress passed procedural reforms in 1851 and 1852, but they were derided as improving little, while the creation in 1853 of the federal Development Ministry (Ministerio de Fomento) offered modest promise of more effective administration.[15]

Despite these reforms, the nature of patent protection remained little changed, complaints continued, and both applications and conferrals persisted at very low levels. Another effort to modify the law's provisions in the mid-1850s yielded nothing, and ten years of civil war and military occupation by French troops (1857–67) delayed further reform. Each of the annual *Memorias* published by the Development Ministry through the 1860s and 1870s noted the deficiencies of Mexico's existing legislation, highlighting inefficient bureaucratic processes, long delays, and low incentives for investors. Reformers launched a new effort in 1877 that sought (1) to clearly define patentability to only those objects that have novel industrial application; (2) to explicitly allow foreign patents, but only for the remaining term of their original patent; (3) to require domestic exploitation; (4) to establish moderate fees; (5) to divide the term of protection in fractions, extendible by the patentee; (6) to provide for the regular publication of applications and descriptions; (7) to specify penalties for falsification and infringement. The project represented a move toward more narrowly delimiting patent monopolies and the property rights they conferred, toward compensating the public with access to new knowledge, and toward making patents more accessible to the general public. First and foremost, however, this reform project – that gained momentum following ratification of the 1883 International Union for the Protection of Industrial Property in Paris – sought to increase the security of foreign patentees, though it balanced this security with a compulsory exploitation clause. It took nearly eight years to push the project through the Mexican Congress, and the resulting new patent

patentes de invención en México durante el siglo xix (1840 1900). Ensayo de interpretación sobre el proceso de industrialización del México decimonónico" (Tesis de Licenciatura, UNAM, 1989), 78–81, 141.
[14] Mexico, *Memoria*, 1857, 105.   [15] Sánchez Flores, *Historia de la tecnología*, 378.

legislation of 1890 contained only the provisions that supported foreign interests, and not those that regulated and limited them, such as the compulsory working clause.

Mexico's patent law of 1890 inaugurated an entirely new regime that in part conformed to the norms represented by the Paris Convention, but which also diverged from those norms in important ways.[16] New legislation followed in 1903 that extended but did not substantially alter the character of the 1890 law. The post-1890 regime limited patenting to the original inventor, substantially lowered patenting fees, established a patent office within the Development Ministry, detailed extensive procedures for the administration of patents and the adjudication of disputes, removed all vestiges of compulsory working provisions, and joined Mexico to the Paris Convention, assuring "national treatment" for foreign patentees. Seeking to enlarge the patent holders' ability to define and defend their rights in Mexico, the new patent legislation was intended to maximize returns from investment in patenting. It also required detailed specifications and claims, and called for their regular publication in journals.

While the new post-1890 patent regime offered stronger protection to all inventors and patentees, several aspects were particularly attractive to foreign applicants. First, the new legislation explicitly made foreign inventors eligible for patent protection, for the first time on equal terms with Mexican applicants – the "national treatment" stipulated by the Paris Convention. Second, foreign applicants no longer had to worry that their rights would be derogated for nonworking. In an era where large firms were beginning to systematically stake out potential markets across the globe, this was a critical benefit. The new legislation put aside the reforms proposed in the 1880s and again in 1903 that might have limited or regulated foreign patent rights using exploitation requirements, the ability of third parties to import patented goods, and requiring patentees to hire and train students from Mexican technical schools.[17] Proprietors of new technologies sought the freedom to stake out future markets and to develop – or not develop, as they chose – commercial projects at their own pace. The overwhelming majority of these new technologies originated in the countries of the North Atlantic, and those with an interest in the opportunities presented by technological innovation – the inventors, patent proprietors, and investors abroad and in Mexico – were the beneficiaries.

---

[16] Dublán and Lozano, *Legislación mexicana*, 20, 179–83.
[17] Mexico, *Memoria*, 1877–82, 1:435; 1901–4, cxxxvi; Sánchez Flores, *Historia de la tecnología*, 382.

Mexican patent applications rose sharply through these decades and, for Mexican officials, seemed to justify the institutional reforms embodied in the 1890 and 1903 legislation. As they watched annual patent solicitations climb tenfold from the 1880s to the 1900s, Mexican officials congratulated themselves on their accomplishments. Patents had become commonplace and valuable pieces of property. Thousands of Mexicans and foreigners invested in patent protection, and many hundreds bragged about their patents in advertising that littered the dozens of daily newspapers published in Mexico City and provincial capitals. Mexican patents were generally supported by the courts, where a variety of patent-related cases appeared regularly on the federal dockets. Reformed patent laws in Mexico provided one part of a broader institutional reform movement pursued by the 34-year government of Porfirio Díaz (1876–1911) in order to support rising investment in railroads, mining, commercial agriculture, and manufacturing.[18]

5.4   Mexico in Comparative Context

During the last third of the nineteenth century, dramatic growth in transnational, cross-Atlantic trade and investment provided the central incentive in countries like Mexico to consider harmonization of national patent laws. Rapidly falling overland and oceanic transportation and communication costs, the proliferation of international and national exhibitions, the emergence of new technology fields with ever greater proprietary interest in intellectual property (especially electricity, chemicals, and telecommunications), and generally rising levels of international trade and investment all combined to shift the incentives facing both *producers* and *users* of new technologies across the globe. This was, after all, a world starkly divided between technology (and patent) exporters in the North Atlantic and the rest, the relatively late industrializers and technology importers from Eastern Europe to Latin America who sought the wealth, and sometimes simply national survival, in a world they saw full of both opportunities and threats. For technology exporters, patent harmonization meant strengthening transnational protection of patent holders' rights in order to ensure that the intellectual property of North Atlantic inventors and firms would be protected in global markets, the primary motivating force behind the Paris Convention of 1883. Among technology importers, however, harmonization had different implications.

---

[18] Beatty, *Institutions*, chapter 2; *Technology*, chapter 3.

In the abstract, relatively late-developing, technology-importing nations around the world might craft a balance in patent law between the interests of patent holders and the public across a spectrum. This could range from strong, unregulated rights for original inventors and patent holders, on one end of the spectrum, to regulating those rights in ways that might maximize public use of new knowledge, on the other (through, for example, compulsory working clauses, limitations on patentability, the state's ability to abrogate in the public interest, and so forth). Most moved toward a place somewhere in the middle, adjusting their patent systems around the norms embodied in the Paris Convention and its successor agreements. This meant a rough standardization of protection for patent holders, sufficient to support rising levels of cross-border investment and trade in patented technologies. It also meant that many countries continued to regulate patent holders' rights by restricting patentability and by including compulsory working and licensing provisions, for example.

Mexico's history of patent law reform in this era of partial harmonization highlights two critical aspects of the broader story. First, as Mexico's policy makers considered new proposals and possibilities for what would become the laws of 1890 and 1903, they grappled with the same challenges that faced late-developing countries around the globe: how to balance the protection offered to original inventors, national or foreign, while at the same time regulating that protection in order to favor the diffusion and use of new knowledge, and to maximize the likelihood that the patent monopoly would not obstruct commercial adoption and diffusion. Strong rights to original inventors might incentivize investment in technology imports, they argued, while limits to those rights might support the diffusion of knowledge and open opportunities for local use and innovation. In considering this issue, Mexico's new laws ultimately diverged from international norms, and instead cleaved more closely to the "strong protection" end of the spectrum, modeled internationally by US patent law. Second, Mexico's history helps us better understand the factors that nudged late-developing countries toward harmonization, as well as those factors that pushed Mexico further than most toward the US model. New opportunities in the booming, post-1870s Atlantic economy loomed large, channeled through intermediaries in Mexico who argued that Mexico's best chance for "material progress" lay in offering strong and secure rights.

Three provisions of many nineteenth-century patent laws offered governments the ability to limit the rights of original inventors and to facilitate the diffusion of technical knowledge, products, and opportunities to society. First, some countries offered so-called patents of introduction, which allowed third parties to acquire patent protection for technologies not previously established within the country, even if they were not the original inventor. A direct legacy of early modern privileges, patents of introduction favored commercial innovation over the rights of inventors. However, these were uncommon, with Spain the most prominent.[19] Second and more commonly, many countries included compulsory working or licensing clauses in their patent systems. With the United States as a rare exception that did not, this clause threatened annulment unless the patented technology was worked in the country within a specified period, usually two or three years. However, enforcement was notoriously difficult and probably ineffective in many countries. Finally, countries sometimes sought additional ways to support the diffusion of knowledge over inventors' exclusive rights. These included, for instance, the right of governments to abrogate patents for the public interest, requirements of domestic sourcing, the employment of national workers, and hosting students from local technical schools. These issues were central parts of Mexican law or reform proposals prior to 1890, yet none were included in the post-1903 regime.

What factors pushed Mexican legislators to adopt a patent regime that, like its fellow late developers around the globe, moved toward the new norms embodied in the Paris Convention, but at the same time moved significantly further than others to strengthen the rights of original inventors and that excluded regulatory provisions that might favor local innovation and diffusion? An 1897 address to Mexico's foremost legal association, the Academy of Jurisprudence, offers one glimpse.

Trained as an engineer but devoted to a career in public service, Gilberto Crespo y Martínez offered his audience a vigorous and extended argument for patent law reform.[20] Like the dozen or so active patent agents in Mexico who represented both foreign and national applicants, Crespo y Martínez was an intermediary between the Mexican and North Atlantic interests, an agent in the transfer of knowledge and the diffusion of international norms. Patent law, he argued, constituted "one of those laws that most influence the material progress of the Republic" precisely because it sought to induce progress through "scientific discovery" and

[19] Patricio Sáiz, "Did Patents of Introduction Encourage Technology Transfer? Long-Term Evidence from the Spanish Innovation System," *Cliometrica* 8 (2014): 49–78.

[20] Gilberto Crespo y Martínez, *Las patentes de invención* (Mexico: Oficina Tip. de la Secretaría de Fomento, 1897). Crespo y Martínez was appointed Mexican ambassador to Cuba (1902–5), Austria-Hungary (1906–11), and after the collapse of the government of Porfirio Díaz in 1911, to the United States (1911–12) and again to Austria-Hungary (1912–16), before he died in Vienna in 1917, age 64. All quotations are from this unpaginated document unless otherwise noted, translated by the author.

the "invention of industrial applications." Like others in Mexico through the nineteenth century, he saw patent law in purely utilitarian terms, as a political tool to induce investment in new technologies within the Mexican economy rather than as a natural right. For Crespo y Martínez, the example of the industrializing nations of the North Atlantic – naming Germany, the United States, France, and England – provided the only viable model for achieving wealth, improving the welfare of workers, and ensuring national survival in the face of Darwinian international competition. Material progress had become the undisputed political and economic imperative in an era of growing international competition.[21] The origin of material progress in those countries lay in "the genius of man" and especially in those men "gifted with the ability to invent, the power to create novelty." Through the nineteenth century, Crespo y Martínez observed, it had been inventors who had pushed the North Atlantic countries "to the forefront of civilization through their superior capacity to know and their superior ability to execute."

Overlooking the quotidian, iterative, and cumulative aspects of technological change, he located "the passion to create, to discover, to perfect" in the "inexhaustible spirit" of a small number of extraordinary and exceptional men. The "universal desire" of every nation, in his view, was to stimulate this inventive spirit by allocating to inventors a proprietary right to their inventions: "the facility to acquire, the liberty to work, and the security to retain." Given the nonrival nature of intellectual creation (any and everyone can "examine … admire … and assimilate" the working of new machines and processes, he explained), inventors require the "legitimate hope that if others use the product of their efforts, they would receive just compensation." He bemoaned the anti-patent movements in England and Germany, and applauded the late-century reforms "in all civilized nations" to strengthen the rights of inventors through new legislation on industrial property, citing patent law reforms in Germany, England, and France, culminating in the Paris Convention's ongoing intent to "study, define, and adopt liberal reforms to industrial property law within a union of countries."

Crespo y Martínez made his case for patent law reform in Mexico, and laid out Mexico's interest in the strong protection of new knowledge in industrial property. After reviewing nineteenth-century debates about patents and monopolies, he argued that technological and industrial progress is the central character of the "modern epoch," and consequently argued that the protection of "those persons capable of discovery

---

[21] Richard Weiner, "Battle for Survival: Porfirian Views of the International Marketplace," *Journal of Latin American Studies* 32 (2000): 645–70.

and invention" is essential to ensure that progress. Given a Darwinian world marked by "economic struggle between nations," he asked rhetorically, what happens when patent law fails to provide "liberty and security?" Progress, he answered, is "constrained, improvements are discouraged, and industry languishes and dies." How can Mexico avoid this fate and keep pace with "the most advanced countries?" The answer is simple, he suggested: strengthen inventors' rights by lowering the barriers to patenting, free them to commercialize and work their inventions, and punish those who violate their rights. His recommendations included enhancing priority rights, standardizing patent terms at twenty years, allowing protection for chemical and pharmaceutical products, forbidding patents of introduction, allowing patentees to import protected products, and omitting obligatory use and licensing clauses. Strengthening inventors' rights, Crespo y Martínez argued, must be a national imperative.

Where did Mexico stand relative to these principles, in his view? Mexico's patent legislation of 1890 represented "a positive and considerable advance" relative to the original Mexican law of 1832, but its laws were not yet "in strict accordance with the progress of modern ideas." Mexico must work to further strengthen protection for inventors, increase punishment for infringers, and join the Paris Convention's Union for the Protection of Industrial Property. Only this would "elevate our legislation to the heights of the most advanced countries, stimulating the inventive ability of our citizens, *attracting to Mexico ... the capital and, more importantly, the intelligence and capacities of foreigners*" (italics added).

Did Mexicans possess inventive abilities themselves? Crespo y Martínez was pessimistic, suggesting that inventive abilities and the "spirit of invention" was not prevalent in Mexican society. But despite a "lack of knowledge and scarcity of models," he was cautiously optimistic, and saw in "our people" and "our workers" the seeds of imitation, of artistic and technical expertise, and, perhaps, of future inventiveness. The massive importation of new technologies to Mexico, from sewing machines to agricultural implements and new chemical processes, had dramatically expanded opportunities for technical learning among Mexican workers, but this had not been matched by an expansion in technical and mechanical training: "much remains to be done" he suggested, to expand opportunities for Mexican workers who faced the same kinds of challenges and opportunities as had English workers a century earlier, in that country's transition from artisanal workshops to large-scale industry.

For Crespo y Martínez, the dramatic expansion of the Atlantic economy after about 1870 and the "peace and security" imposed by the Díaz government offered Mexico the opportunity to begin this transition toward an industrial future. Nothing was more central to this development than access to new knowledge, to the "discoveries and inventions" of the era. Mexico's colonization and mining laws had liberalized access to land and subsoil rights, and the "new industries" law of 1890 aimed to "stimulate the spirit of enterprise and attract capital." Federal expansion of engineering programs and degrees within the reorganized National Engineering School would also support the "prosperity and growth of the Republic," he argued. However, the country still lacked crucial elements for development: effective secondary schooling, commercial institutes that could diffuse scientific and technical knowledge through business and commercial groups, industrial museums and exhibitions to spread an awareness of new advances and new techniques, and associations or institutes to promote and support the work of pure scientific research in physics, chemistry, and mechanics, to help inform "practical inventors." Forming these associations, enacting these laws and policies, and accomplishing the scientific, technical, and industrial advancement of the nation rested ultimately on the shoulders of his audience: "*los sabios,*" a wise and learned elite.

Like most of his contemporaries, Crespo y Martínez was profoundly optimistic about the potential of science, technology, and industry to "solve human problems." Also like most, however, he was pessimistic about the potential of most Mexicans to engage productively in inventive and innovative activity. The most he hoped for was a gradual process of learning through the "regularized, constant, and ennobling" labor of factory work. But first and foremost, he argued, Mexico must attract the latest technologies, as it found itself in the perfect situation to take advantage of the rapid and expanding scientific and industrial progress within the Atlantic economy. The government thus faced the imperative of embracing the very force that might otherwise threaten national sovereignty: the wave of trade, investment, and new technologies that swept outward from the North Atlantic over the last third of the century. Strengthening patent laws and harmonizing these with the norms and interests of technology exporters offered one part of this path to material progress. This aspect of his proposal became part of the 1903 legislation. In contrast, his proposals to support learning and diffusion received little attention, with significant long-term consequences.[22]

---

[22] Beatty, *Technology.*

5.5   Conclusions and Implications for the Twentieth Century

A century later, the Mexican patent system continues to occupy an outlier position in relation to its peers in the developing world. Mexican patent law at the end of the twentieth century persisted in defining relatively strong, lightly regulated rights, on paper, which contrasted with many systems around the globe that restricted and regulated patent rights in order to promote domestic innovation and diffusion.[23] Mexican law, in other words, has long diverged from the more common norm in technology-importing countries. In the late nineteenth century as in the late twentieth, countries around the world faced external and internal lobbying to harmonize their intellectual property systems. In both eras, technology exporters sought harmonization through international conventions that would strengthen patent holders' rights and facilitate their ability to capture and protect markets around the world. The rest, technology importers, were attracted by the opportunity to access new ideas and expertise embodied in this global technology trade. Most, however, were wary of granting the proprietors of foreign technologies strong and unregulated rights that might be used to close markets, protect imports, and create obstacles to local innovation and learning. As a result, many maintained provisions that regulated patent holders' rights in order to increase opportunities for local learning, diffusion, and innovation.

On one hand, Mexican law joined the global trend to offer uniform protection to foreign patentees in accord with the Paris Convention of 1883 and the TRIPS accords of the 1990s. Both these international conventions promoted uniform international standards in order to facilitate cross-border trade. On the other hand, Mexico went further than most of its peers by strengthening patent holders' rights *and* omitting regulatory provisions. Mexico's distinctive pattern likely derived in part from proximity to the United States and thus its relatively easy access to trade, investment, and technology spillovers from North Atlantic countries. It was also the product of a governing elite that, like Gilberto Crespo y Martínez, acted as intermediaries between local markets and international opportunities for trade and investment, who saw their own interests and their nation's as entwined, and who had little faith in the inventive and innovative potential of most of the country's population.

The results of Mexico's experiment have not been encouraging. Technological dependence on imported hardware and expertise has

---

[23] Shadlen, "Mexican Exception."

characterized the Mexican economy for more than a century, with only a few firm- and region-specific exceptions. Through the late nineteenth century and into the early twentieth, Mexico imported massive amounts of technological hardware and software without engendering widespread domestic processes of learning by local engineers, technicians, and workers.[24] This legacy of weak technological capabilities at the end of the nineteenth century meant that it would be more difficult for firms in the twentieth to become technologically creative. By the 1940s both industrialists and government officials expressed concerns not only about continued reliance on foreign technology, but also about the antiquated state of technology in many industrial sectors.[25] Mexico's patent regime itself lapsed into ineffectiveness through the middle of the twentieth century: applications did not regain 1910 levels for over half a century, and weak administrative capacity meant that only a small percentage of applications were processed and approved.[26]

By the 1960s, all this had attracted increasing concern among Mexican analysts who noted a continued "dependence" on imported technologies.[27] Echoing the concerns of mid-nineteenth-century observers, they noted that nearly two-thirds of Mexico's machinery needs continued to be satisfied by imports, capital goods still comprised well over a third of the country's total imports, and 90 percent of all machine tools in Mexico were imported.[28] Mexico's impressive experience of import-substituting growth in the 1940s and 1950s required massive technology imports without any substantial development of domestic technological capabilities. Since the 1980s, Mexican firms have continued to rely heavily on imported sources of innovation. They have frequently responded to new international pressures by relying on low-cost labor,

---

[24] Beatty, *Technology*.

[25] Marcelo G. Aramburu, "El desarrollo de las industrias de transformación en México," *Revista de Economía* IV(5) (1941).

[26] Juan Ignacio Campa Navarro, "Patentes en México en la época de la Industrialización por Sustitución de Importaciones" (PhD diss., Universitat Autònoma de Barcelona, 2016).

[27] Nacional Financiera, S.A., Comisión Económica para La América Latina, *La política industrial en el desarrollo económico de México* (Mexico: Nacional Financiera, 1971); Nacional Financiera, S.A., *México: Los bienes de capital en la situación económica presente* (Mexico: Nacional Financiera, S.A., 1985); Kurt Unger, "El desarrollo industrial y tecnológico mexicano: estado actual de la integración industrial y tecnológica," in *Aspectos tecnológicos de la modernización industrial de México*, ed. Pablo Mulás del Pozo (Mexico: Fondo de Cultura Económica, 1995), 44–80.

[28] Nacional Financiera, *Los bienes de capital*; Roger D. Hansen, *The Politics of Mexican Development* (Baltimore: The Johns Hopkins University Press, 1971); Juan Carlos Moreno-Brid and Jaime Ros, *Development and Growth in the Mexican Economy* (Oxford: Oxford University Press, 2009).

for example, and have generally invested only modest resources in research and development.[29] In the 1990s, two-thirds of Mexican contracts for technology rights had a US business partner and many businesses remained dependent on foreign licenses. Patents conferred on residents of Mexico averaged fewer than 600 yearly between 1991 and 2005, virtually the same absolute level as a century earlier, despite an almost tenfold increase in population.[30]

In both the late nineteenth and the late twentieth centuries, Mexican investors and officials pursued short-term incentives: it was cheaper to buy machines from abroad than to manufacture them at home, and cheaper to import expertise than to train it locally. In both eras, the specification of patent law was consistent with this objective, offering little direct support to local cultures of learning and innovation. The puzzle of partial harmonization is really not much of a puzzle at all. In the late nineteenth century, Mexico, like much of the rest of the world, was swept up in the patent law reform movement that followed the 1883 Paris Convention. Mexican officials and investors like Gilberto Crespo y Martínez generally joined voices with patent proponents in the North Atlantic to advocate for the adoption of new legislation that would strengthen patent rights. New laws in Mexico and elsewhere in the wake of the Paris Convention demonstrate some convergence toward a set of common norms. However, diversity proved persistent. The global history of inheriting, borrowing, adapting, and reforming national patent systems always occurred within a particular economic context and the contingent ways in which local political actors viewed the opportunities and threats they and their countries faced in the international market for knowledge. Mexico's patent system exhibited a set of contrasting characteristics during its mid-twentieth-century phase of rapid industrialization (circa 1940–70). On paper, the system offered strong, lightly regulated patent rights but in practice had little capacity to engage or incentivize domestic invention or even to effectively administer the growing wave of foreign applications. Despite the advocacy of men like Gilberto Crespo y Martínez, and although international pressures have achieved some convergence in patenting norms, harmonization remains as much a chimera as it was before the Paris Convention.

---

[29] Kurt Unger, "La globalización del sistema innovativo Mexicano: Empresas extranjeras y tecnología importada," Centro de Investigación y Docencia Económicas, Documento de Trabajo No. 175, 1999.

[30] Shadlen, "Puzzling Politics"; Patricia Graf, "Research and Development in Mexican-American Relations Post-NAFTA," *Journal für Entwicklunhspolitic.* 29 2 (2013): 11–30.

6 An Early Patent System in Latin America
The Chilean Case, 1840s–1910s

Bernardita Escobar Andrae

6.1 Introduction

Two complementary conceptions of patents in economic history and legal history are settling into a form of scholarly consensus. In the economic development theory domain it is assumed that the foundations of countries' long-term economic growth lies in the quality of their political and economic institutions, and in particular in the adequacy of protection granted to property rights, including intellectual property (IP) protection.[1] The second conception is grounded in legal history, and tells that the conception of IP evolved from being matter *awarded* by the sovereign into matter *belonging* to individuals before and during the nineteenth century.[2] Under the first point of view, the latter consensus provides a historical and doctrinarian account of the institutional changes that have taken place in contemporary developed countries, which were in the end responsible for letting them achieving their economic superiority in the contemporary

Early versions of this chapter were presented at the workshop "Rethinking Patent Cultures" at the University of Leeds (May 2014) and the Economic History workshop at University of Santiago and University of Valparaíso (May 2014). The author wishes to thank participants for their constructive comments and questions, especially to Graeme Gooday and Mario Biagioli. The author also wishes to thank Javier Núñez for commenting on drafts of the chapter. Kristina Pepe and Andrea Valenzuela assisted in the database construction work.

[1] See Douglass C. North, *Structure and Change in Economic History* (New York: W. W. Norton & Company, 1981); *Institutions, Institutional Change and Economic Performance* (Cambridge: Cambridge University Press, 1990); *Understanding the Process of Economic Change* (Princeton, NJ: Princeton University Press, 2005).

[2] For the UK, see Brad Sherman and Lionel Bently, *The Making of Modern Intellectual Property Law: The British Experience, 1760–1911* (Cambridge: Cambridge University Press, 1999); Lionel Bently, "The Making of Modern Trade Mark Law: The Construction of the Legal Concept of Trade Mark (1860–1880)," in *Trade Marks and Brands: An Interdisciplinary Critique*, ed. Lionel Bently, Jennifer Davis, and Jane C. Ginsburg (Cambridge: Cambridge University Press, 2008), 3–41; Sean Bottomley, ed., *The British Patent System during the Industrial Revolution, 1700–1852: From Privilege to Property* (Cambridge: Cambridge University Press, 2014); for the United States, see Mario Biagioli, "Patent Republic: Representing Inventions, Constructing Rights and Authors," *Social Research: An International Quarterly – Politics and Science: An Historical View* 73(4) (2006): 1129–72.

times. Yet, research in legal and economic domains focused on the emergence and evolution of IP has been mainly centered in developed countries of the "North." Therefore, the applicability to the process of economic development of developed countries remains conjectural. To date, little is known about the making, evolution, and actual usage of IP institutions in less developed countries during the nineteenth and early twentieth centuries. This chapter attempts to address this void by examining an early example of patent protection in a developing country through studying the first patent system established in Chile during the 1840s–1910s period.

Chile established its first republican IP protection system relatively early, both in terms of its own republican history and with respect to other developing countries. Its first IP protection system was enacted at a time when the best system for promoting and enhancing creativity and innovation was under debate within the developed world. The enlightenment provided by this debate supplied not only the opportunity, but also the means for the emergence of different rationales for explaining and supporting the development of IP institutions on both sides of the Atlantic.[3] During that debate Latin American nations were defining their own republican legal structures after gaining independence.[4] After the declaration of independence in 1818, Chile's 1833 Constitution became the first republican institution granting protection to authors and inventors over their productions. Its legal outcomes were the copyright law of 1834 and the patent law of 1840.

This chapter examines the genealogy and evolution of the first Chilean patent law by examining its main institutional features. In this effort, I try to single out the main actors and driving forces responsible for its enactment, and in particular identify its conception of two types of subject matter (introductions and inventions), as found in Mexican and Spanish laws during the nineteenth century. Second, I examine the actual use of the system, by examining data on patent grants for the 1840–1908 period and patent applications during the period 1877–1910. Data on patent grants are useful to identify the relative number of grants between the two types of patents while they coexisted, including the actual term of protection granted to them. The richer nature of the sources used regarding patent applications enables the identification of the origin of the applications (resident versus nonresident) and the different type of actors involved in the process (applicants, agents, examiners, and opponents). Together, the information on patent grants and patent applications

---

[3] Fritz Machlup and Edith Penrose, "The Patent Controversy in the Nineteenth Century," *The Journal of Economic History* 10(1) (1950): 1–29.
[4] For a broader view of how patent law developed in Latin American countries, see Chapter 5 in this volume.

allows for the identification of the level of importance posed in patents by economic actors and the actual degree of success of the patent application process throughout the period.

The chapter is organized in the following fashion: after this introduction, the next section analyzes the genealogy and evolution of Chilean patent law, with a special emphasis in identifying the factors, actors, and doctrines that led to the protection of introductions and inventions in tandem. The third section examines the degree of use of the patent system in Chile, and the final section contains my conclusions.

6.2   The Genealogy of the First Chilean Patent System

The origin of the first Chilean patent system can be traced back to three different sources: the colonial mining regulation, the 1833 Constitution, and the petitions made by individuals to Congress after the ratification of the Constitution and prior to the enactment of the patent law.

The 1783 Colonial Spanish mining regulation provided protection for inventions and for *introductions*. Protection was a perpetual exclusive privilege for both inventors (article 18)[5] and introducers (article 19)[6] of *useful and proven* inventions.[7] The rationales, the rationales for protecting the subject matter are utilitarian and natural rights doctrines.[8]

---

[5]   It read:

> Useful and approved inventions that after an overall assessment of its use for over a year shall be granted an exclusive privilege lasting the life of the author, so that nobody, without his consent, may use them without contributing a moderate part of the advantage and gain effectively resulting from the inventions [own translation].

[6]   It read:

> Any individual, who due to his own study, instruction or information received or due to travel to other regions, presents a machine, procedure or method used in other places and times, and it is approved and qualified as stated in article 17, has to be served and awarded in the same manner as if he were an inventor, because if his gratification may be less, his merit and work may be more and the public benefit shall always be equal where it is installed, either concerning an absolutely new invention or the transportation and application of an unknown practice [own translation].

[7]   This regulation dates from 1783 and included a mining tribunal that was implemented in 1787 in Chile. Although it has been claimed that the tribunal contributed to the promotion of inventions – Luz María Mendez Beltrán, "Prologo al Informe de Minería de Juan Egaña," in *Minería y Metalurjia Colonial en el Reino de Chile. Una visión a travez del informe de Don Juan Egaña al Real Tribunal de Minería en 1803*, ed. Gastón Fernandez Montero (Santiago: AGD, 2000) – there is little evidence of the claim. Juan Egaña, *Minería y Metalurjia Colonial en el Reino de Chile. Una visión a travez del informe de Don Juan Egaña al Real Tribunal de Minería en 1803* (Santiago: AGD, 1803) reported only one invention (made by Juan Francisco Herrera, in n90).

[8]   The reference to social utility is clearly coherent with Bentham's notion of establishing institutions that aim to achieve the highest social utility and perpetual protection is coherent with the natural rights doctrine.

6.2.1 The 1833 Constitution

The emergence of article 152 in the 1833 Constitution that granted IP protection in Republican Chile for the first time is closely linked to the role played by Mariano Egaña[9] in the Grand Constitutional Convention of 1831–3 that enacted the Constitution.[10] The only reference to this article is to be found in Egaña's "voto particular," his draft proposal for the Constitution.[11] The overall sources for Egaña's "voto particular" have been traced to the authoritarian Napoleonic and monarchical constitutional regimes of France and Brazil, and the Spanish Constitution of 1812.[12] His IP protection model that became article 152 had been rooted in article 26 of the 1824 Brazilian Constitution.[13] Articles 151 (establishing freedom of enterprise, also originating in Egaña's "voto particular") and 152 appear as a statement of Egaña's belief in the important role that individuals and business people have to play in enhancing society's welfare. There is prior evidence of his support for the development of the business community[14] and forms of IP protection[15] when he

---

[9] Mariano Egaña was a conservative politician who wrote a Constitutional draft that served as a template for part of the 1833 Constitution. It was his father Juan Egaña, a legal scholar and politician, who wrote the report on mining inventions in 1803.

[10] Article 152 of Chile's 1833 Constitution stated that every author or inventor should have the exclusive property right to their discoveries or productions for the time conceded by law, and should it require disclosure, a corresponding indemnity should be given to the author. The original Spanish text reads: "Todo autor ó inventor tendrá la propiedad exclusiva de su descubrimiento, ó producción por el tiempo que le concediere la ley, y si ésta exigiere su publicación, se dará al inventor la indemnización competente" [sic] .

[11] The compilation made by Valentín Letelier, *La Gran Convención de 1831–1833. Recopilación de Sesiones, Discursos, Proyectos y Artículos de Diarios Relativos a la Constitución de 1833* (Santiago: Imprenta Cervantes, 1901) contains this reference in n37 – complete notes of Mariano Egaña's "voto particular" – as article 177 (page 97); also as article 17 in the second and third drafts compiled (pages 100, 109). It appears as article 20 in the Bill for Constitution in n47 (page 160).

[12] Enrique Brahm García, "Mariano Egaña y La Constitución Política de 1833. Las fuentes del 'Voto Particular'," *Revista de Derecho de la Pontificia Universidad Católica de Valparaíso* XXV (2004): 65–91.

[13] Enrique Brahm García, "La estructuración del régimen de gobierno de el 'voto particular' de Mariano Egaña y sus fuentes," *Revista Chilena de Derecho* 31(2) (2004): 351–71.

[14] See for instance the tenor of the letters regarding the Anglo-Chilean Mining Association, the Chilean Mining Association, and the Chilean and Peruvian Mining Association. These letters are codified as no. 33 (December 17, 1824, 84–8), no. 47 (January 15, 1825, 107–10), no. 66 (July 20, 1825, 131–2) in Javier Gonzalez Echenique, *Documentos de la Mision de Don Mariano Egaña en Londres (1824–1829)* (Santiago: Ministerio de Relaciones Exteriores de Chile, 1984).

[15] This is revealed by his letter of support to the Chilean Government of Rudolph Ackermann's editing and distribution privileges petition in London in 1825. The letter stated that it "would be unfair to allow other foreign booksellers to introduce into the country original works that with so much fatigue and expense had been published by

channeled the business requests originating in Britain to the Chilean Government as the minister plenipotentiary in London (1824–9).

6.2.2   The Protection Petitions Made Prior to the Enactment of the Patent Law

Another source of the patent law can be found in legislative initiavies during the 1830s, in particular, to a series of petitions for exclusive privileges made by individuals. Perhaps grounded on colonial mining regulations that conceived protection for both introductions and inventions, many of these petitions requested protection for introductions, and confounded them with inventions. Congressional papers enable us to identify sixteen applications made by individuals asking for protection of their businesses to the government and the Congress, grounded on the Constitutional norm, prior to the enactment of the patent law. Table 6.1 identifies these petitions. One of the first republican antecedents for protecting introductions is found in Mr. Juan Quezada's petition for protection for a crystal and bottle factory in 1832 to President Prieto, who remanded it for consideration to the Congress:

Exclusive privileges are a well-known remedy to foster industrious men towards new discoveries, or to what is the same, to *new productions* [emphasis added]. They harm no one, because, not being created before granting protection, they cannot take away or harm non existing rights, and never would production be promoted if talents and risky anticipations were not fostered by such means, which will, in the short term, place society in the position to enjoy benefits that it did not formerly enjoy. The practice of all civilized nations, and more importantly, the liberal principles that in this regard are followed by the supreme government, agree with my request in all its parts.[16]

The presidential memorandum for this petition established at this early stage what would become a series of principles that would be shaped throughout the decade to be enacted in the 1840 patent law: (1) the introduction of a known but unexploited business was worth protecting; (2) these cases were useful to society as they increased its wealth; (3) exclusive privileges in these cases harmed future development of the industry and therefore the term of protection needed to be short.[17] Soon thereafter, the president sent a copyright protection bill to the Chamber

---

Mr. Ackermann." The letter is labeled as no. 93 and dated May 12, 1825 in Gonzalez Echenique, *Documentos de la Mision.*

[16] Own translation. See appendix no. 608 attached to the lower Chamber's session of September 3, 1832, in Valentín Letelier, *Sesiones de los Cuerpos Lejislativos de Chile* (Santiago: Imprenta Cervantes, 1899), 553–4.

[17] See appendix no. 607 in Letelier, *Sesiones*, 553.

Table 6.1 *Petitions to Congress for exclusive privileges, 1830–40***

No.	Year	Requester	Industry	No.	Year	Requester	Industry
1	1832	Juan de Quezada	Bottle and crystal factory	9	1834	José Antonio Silva	Exploitation of marble, jasper, and precious stones
2	1832*	Manuel Rojas	Mining invention	10	1835	Guillermo Wheelwright	Steam navigation
3	1832*	Onofre Bunster	Invention in silver mining foundry	11*	1835p	Andres Blest[d]	Rum factory
4	1833	Juan Lay and José Coupelon	Exploitation of marble, jasper, and precious stones	12	1836	Antonio Vásquez	Leather manufactures (*cabritillas i tafiletes*)
5	1833	Joaquín Pérez and Manuel Carrasco	Exploit of marble, jasper, and precious stones	13	1839*	José Vicente Larrain[d]	Introduction of unknown machine for oil extraction
6	1833	Carlos Thurn	Windmill in Valparaíso	14	1839*p	José Vicente Larrain[d]	New production method for stearin candles
7	1833	José Vicente Bustillos[d]	Sulfuric acid	15	1840p	José Luis Calle	Manufacture of spark plug from sebum
8	1834	Miguel Navas	Boot wax	16	1840	Guillermo Wheelwright	Steam navigation-extension

Notes: * = invention. p = redirected to 1840 patent law. d = deputy.
Source: own elaboration based on Congressional papers.
** Between Independence (1818) and 1830, only five exclusive privileges were published in the bulletin of Laws and Decrees: three factories and two mining privileges for British companies.

of Deputies in 1833, announcing that it was but the first half of an IP system designed to fulfill the regulation mandated by the Constitution. He also stated in the message that:

Industrial privileges, present in all advanced countries for the purpose of facilitating the operation of agriculture and the mechanical arts, were more limited than the rights granted for authors. The latter caused no harm to nations, but to the contrary, protected the orientation to the study and discovery of new truths, whereas industrial privileges, although extremely advantageous, could ruin a whole branch of industry at some point and benefit only the inventor.[18]

Soon thereafter, his perspective was also adopted by the Commission at the Chamber of Deputies arguing in favor of the copyright bill:

To declare that discovery or one's own labour is property and that it needs to be enjoyed for a limited time is to enact what is prescribed by justice and common interest, and it is also to concede a new enjoyment for the community, to whom in appearance it is denied, because otherwise it would never enjoy such benefits.[19]

Most of the petitions were granted rapidly following the criteria suggested in the former presidential memo, and three applications were remanded to the 1840 patent law sanction (petitions 13–15 in Table 6.1). Of these, two were finally granted soon after the new patent law came into effect and no information was found regarding the third application. It should be noted that, except for Wheelwright's petition, all were made by residents.[20] Among these petitions for protection, only four (25 percent) referred in some way to proper inventions (two falling under the mining colonial regulation) and the rest referred to introductions (of foreign innovations). The fact that the majority of these petitions referred to introductions, plus the colonial antecedent of equating protection for inventions and introductions in the mining sector, led the political actors to confound the strict spirit of the Constitutional norm (inventions) with an ampler set of situations worthy of protection, allegedly, under its umbrella. Below is a brief review of the discussions that gave birth to the protection of introductions in the patent law.

---

[18] See appendix no. 94 attached to the session of July 29, 1833 in the lower Chamber, Letelier, *Sesiones*. President Prieto's letter to Congress stated that "this Bill shall be considered the first part of the law that is referred by in Art. 152 of the Constitution, retaining for myself the privilege of presenting later another Bill regarding industrial privileges."

[19] See annex no. 104 in Letelier, *Sesiones*, 86.

[20] Petitions no. 4 and no. 5 in Table 6.1 were granted to nonnationals, but they had been residing in Chile for a long time when the application was made (see annex no. 8 and no. 9 in Letelier, *Sesiones*, 11 and annex no. 42 in Letelier, *Sesiones*, 34).

By early July 1840, the Senate received a new application (no. 15 in Table 6.1) from Vice President Tocornal for an exclusive privilege,[21] also requesting a provisional authorization for the presidential office to deal with these kinds of petitions until a general law regulating article 152 of the Constitution was passed. While a Senate commission drafted such a short-term bill, Senator Diego José Benavente drafted a bill of a general scope on his own account. During July both bills were discussed in the Senate, plus an extra one for privileges remanded by the lower Chamber (no. 13 in Table 6.1). In July the Senate approved Benavente's bill with only minor modifications.[22] During the following month both Chambers agreed on a definitive text; the law was promulgated on September 9, 1840.

Applicants and legislators became well-aware of the differences between introductions and inventions, but either they refused to acknowledge that the former fell outside the scope of article 152 of the Constitution,[23] or assumed an extremely weak understanding of "novelty," or simply surrendered the novelty principle to the utility principle. Among petitioners, the first assimilation of introductions to inventions was proposed in 1833 by applicants, labeled no. 4 in Table 6.1.[24] In 1834, applicant no. 8 simply cited the Constitutional norm to support the request for the exclusive privilege, and the Commission of Deputies could not overlook the fact that the subject matter asking for protection had no resemblance to an invention whatsoever. But the Commission could not simply turn down the application without a proper examination.[25] At this point, the lower Chamber was not only making it clear that the scope of the protected subject matter covered by the Constitution was restrictive, but it also introduced a standard of evaluation to qualify for protection. Conversely, at the same time the Senate had difficulty equating inventions to the introduction of a *new* industry when examining application no. 9 in Table 6.1, somehow diluting the principles set out by the lower Chamber, and even agreed to extend the term of protection beyond the term granted to similar privileges the previous year.[26]

---

[21] See appendix no. 216 in Valentín Letelier, *Sesiones de los Cuerpos Lejislativos de Chile* (Santiago: Imprenta Cervantes, 1906), 293.

[22] Amendments were introduced to articles 5, 7, 9 and 17 and article 15 was added.

[23] Jorge Huneeus Gana, *Los privilegios exclusivos en Chile: estudio de la legislación vigente y de la conveniencia de su reforma* (Santiago: Imprenta Cervantes, 1888) claimed the unconstitutionality of including introductions under the patent law in an celebrated law dissertation.

[24] See appendix no. 9 in Letelier, *Sesiones*, 1899, 11.

[25] See appendix no. 429 in Letelier, *Sesiones*, 1899, 361–2.

[26] See appendix no. 311 in Letelier, *Sesiones*, 1899, 194.

The distinctions between introductions and inventions that the lower Chamber was framing would eventually lead to an acknowledgment that the Constitutional norm would not allow granting exclusive privileges over introductions under the umbrella of article 152, and doing so would probably contravene article 151 of the Constitution. An invention would have to be equated to a standard of novelty much higher than national application of an art or manufacture. This conclusion posed a problem for the policy beliefs held by government and Congress. By 1839, the lower Chamber acknowledged this contradiction and surrendered the principle of novelty to the priority given to the principle of "public utility," when examining the application of fellow congressman Larraín (no. 13 in Table 6.1).[27]

The executive branch went through a similar process of initially ignoring the differences between inventions and introductions, merging them into one category, later acknowledging the differences but ignoring the consequences of the Constitutional tenor for greater good, and therefore extending the scope for protection explicitly beyond inventions. By 1833 the president was not yet alluding to introductions falling under article 152 when he discussed inventions in the presidential message for the copyright bill. But by 1835 the merging of inventions and introductions became noticeable in the Executive as well. The presidential memo concerning application no. 11 of Table 6.1 argued for the convenience of shortening the term of protection to "conciliate the encouragement that needs to be awarded to a new industry, with the general interest of society, which is always in contradiction to such privileges."[28] By 1836 the presidential memo presenting application no. 12 in Table 6.1 argued that because the subject matter was *not* an invention and the sector had the capability of expanding, the president advocated for a shorter term of protection, openly contradicting the claim of invention made by the applicant.[29] By 1839, the principle of *novelty* of introductions became subsumed to their usefulness. This merger was exemplified by the conclusions arrived at by the president and the Supreme Court official who dealt with application no. 15 of Table 6.1. The president argued for the usefulness for the country of the introduction of the *new* method to justify the granting of the privilege, whereas the Supreme Court officer had assured him that such method was not an invention made in the country and should not be granted a privilege under article

[27] See appendix no. 134 in Letelier, *Sesiones*, 1899, 109.

[28] See appendix no. 634 in Letelier, *Sesiones*, 1899, 433.

[29] See appendix no. 299 and no. 300 in Valentín Letelier, *Sesiones de los Cuerpos Lejislativos de Chile* (Santiago: Imprenta Cervantes, 1902), 280.

152 of the Constitution. However, the same officer argued that the usefulness of the introduction would be of such magnitude that this sole principle sufficed for granting the privilege.[30]

6.2.3   The 1840 Patent Law

According to the sources used for building Table 6.2, the first Chilean patent law emerged when only ten other countries worldwide had patent protection.[31] The law comprised seventeen articles and provided protection for inventions (products or processes) and for introductions (industries or technologies known abroad but not yet established in the country). From the extant patent systems, a similar dual subject matter model can be found in the 1826 Spanish patent law[32] and Mexican patent law, but not in countries of Italy before or after reunification.[33]

The features of the protection provided by the Chilean law are outlined in Table 6.3 and Table 6.4. It is clear from these tables that the protection granted for both families of innovations was almost identical, except for the term of protection provided to each one. Relative to the 1826 Spanish law model, Chile adopted a system that made both families of innovations much closer in terms of the protection provided, as introductions were allowed to obtain up to eight years relative to the three years granted under Spanish law. In this regard, the Chilean patent law appeared to be strongly influenced by colonial mining regulations, and therefore keeping the ambiguity of protection on grounds of an "*ancien régime*" of privileges and the new trend of recognizing the subject matter as property. Mexican law made no difference regarding the

---

[30] See appendix no. 216 and no.. 217 in Letelier, *Sesiones*, 1906, 293.

[31] Richard T. Rapp and Richard P. Rozek, "Benefits and Costs of Intellectual Property Protection in Developing Countries," *Journal of World Trade* 24(5) (1990): 75–102; *National Economic Research Associates Working Paper* 3 (1990). Holland repealed its patent law later. This source did not include the patent laws that existed within Italy before unification, as discussed by Nuvolari and Vasta in this volume (Chapter 7). Notably, this would place Chile later in the ranking.

[32] J. Patricio Sáiz González, *Las Patentes y la Economía Española (1826–1878)* (Madrid: Fundación Empresa Pública, 1996); "The Spanish Patent System (1770–1907)," *History of Technology* 24(1) (2002): 47–79; Edward Beatty, *Institutions and Investment: The Political Basis of Industrialization in Mexico before 1911* (Stanford, CA: Stanford University Press, 2001).

[33] The Spanish introductions remained in force until the mid-twentieth century. Article 21 of the Decree of May 7th of 1832 (Mexican patent law) provided for the protection of introductions, if government remanded to the Congress petitions for its assessment of the industry's degree of importance. Only those of great importance were eligible. For Italy, see Nuvolari and Vasta in this volume (Chapter 7).

Table 6.2 *Countries with patent laws prior to Chile's first patent law*

Country	First patent law	Region	Timing rank
UK	1624	Europe	1
USA	1790	Americas	2
France	1791	Europe	3
Netherlands	1809	Europe	4
Austria	1810	Europe	5
Russia	1812	Europe	6
Sweden	1819	Europe	7
Spain	1826–9	Europe	8
Brazil	1830	Americas	9
Mexico	1832	Americas	10
Chile	1840	Americas	11
Venezuela	1842	Americas	12

Source: Author's chart based on Rapp and Rozek's Appendix Table A1.[34]

Table 6.3 *Protected subject matter in Chile's first patent law*

Subject matter	Description	Term (Years)	Art.
Inventions	To the author or inventor of art, manufacture, machine, instrument, preparation of materials or any improvement of thereof	≤10	1, 3
Introductions	Introduction of arts, industries, or machines invented in other nations and unknown or not established or used in Chile	≤ 8	8

protection between introductions and inventions, except for the process of eligibility that the former needed to go through. Chile granted inventions a term of protection of up to ten years, whereas Spain provided protection for up to fifteen years.

Spain also granted privileges prior to the 1826 law, as exemplified in Chile by the cases disclosed in Table 6.1. However, Spain granted many more privileges than Chile prior to the enactment of the patent law.[35]

---

[34] Rapp and Rozek, "Benefits and Costs." The Venezuelan case is examined in Bernardino Herrera, *La expansión telegráfica en Venezuela: 1856–1936* (Caracas: Comisión de Estudios de Posgrado, Facultad de Humanidades y Educación, 2001).

[35] Sáiz González, *Las Patentes*, recorded seventy-nine privileges granted by the Crown between 1759 and 1826 in Spain. A revision of the Chilean Laws and Decrees Bulletins shows five privileges granted between 1822 and 1830, plus the sixteen privileges shown in Table 6.1 between 1830 and 1840. The Chilean Congress retained

Table 6.4 *Patent protection provided by Chile's first patent law*

Protection	Description	Article
Term for installation	Yes	14
Term of protection	Inventions up to ten years; introductions up to eight years	
Regional scope	Regionally, nationally	13
Term extension	Yes, in justified cases before six months of expiration	16
Infringement	Fine CL $100–$1,000	10
	Indemnity	
Property ownership	Transferable; sellable	9
	Need to be recorded before government	
Nullity	Yes	
	Fraud (regarding the inventor's identity/authorization, established industry, false testimony)	11
	Fine $100–$1,000	
	Imprisonment (3–12 months)	
	Competing privileges	12
	Arbitrage before three judges, not appealable	
Expiration, caducity	If not installed within installation period	15
	In case of abandonment for one year after installation	
	In case of degrading quality of products relative to level applied for	
Examination	Commission of external examiners (*experts*)	2
Publication	Not required for the subject matter during term of protection	2, 5, 6
Requirements	Originality (novelty)	2, 5
	Full disclosure to the examiners' commission	2, 5
	Registration fee $50	5
Registry	Yes	4

Notes: Money refers to nominal Chilean pesos.
Source: Own elaboration based on the 1840 Patent Law.

The first Chilean patent law not only treated introductions and inventions very similarly, but differed radically from the Spanish patent law, and to a lesser extent to Mexico's system by requiring a mandatory examination for patent applications. At the time of enactment of Chile's patent law, Nuvolari and Vasta (Chapter 7 in this volume) show that a similar approach was used in the *Regno di Sardegna* with a strict

the authority to grant exclusive privileges outside the scope of the 1840 patent law. The Congress's privileges were broadly granted during the nineteenth century as a means to build public infrastructure (roads, railroads, and so forth) through concessions to private individuals and corporations to exploit limited time monopolies in exchange for the private funding necessary to build such infrastructure.

examination procedure. However, the reform of 1855 eliminated it and the reunification of the 1860s extended the liberal approach to the rest of Italy. In Chile, originality was to be assessed by a commission of experts who were not required to be public officials, unlike the US examination system. In the Mexican system, examination was designed to assess whether the subject matter contravened public health, national security, or public morality, and not the utility or novelty of the inventions.

Like many other countries, Chile's law protected inventors. Protected subject matter was considered as a special type of property; it provided for the ability to dispose of it (transferable), but subject to approval and registration before government, subject to forfeiture and infringement remedies in case of disapproval. As to the remedies, infringement was punishable with fines, while fraud (whenever patents were obtained by individuals others than the inventors) was subject to similar fines plus imprisonment. Protection was subject to a working requirement valid throughout the entire term of protection, plus a keep-up-quality requirement.[36] The law was silent regarding priority of filing versus inventing, but any possible priority dispute was to be resolved by the judiciary.[37] The law was quite liberal in spirit, as it provided for no exceptions or exclusions, as found in existing patent systems elsewhere.[38]

In 1851, a significant new regulation was introduced, establishing the need for the examination report to clearly state the utility or inconvenience of granting the privilege; identification of the type of patent (invention or introduction), and also the relevant circumstances for establishing the term of protection and of installation. Five years later, another decree established a publication requirement for all applications regarding introductions while the right to opposition was openly stated.[39] These regulations aimed at filtering the set of subject matters worthy of receiving legal protection. In this regard, they aimed at fulfilling a utilitarian aim, not openly clear in the constitutional framework.

By 1872 introductions were repealed and in 1883 the term of protection for patents (inventions) was extended up to twenty years, based on

---

[36] The patent was subject to expiration or caducity in case of abandonment or lack of work for over one year after the completion of the term awarded to put it to work. Patents also expired when the product's quality diminished relative to the models or description provided in the application process.

[37] At first in a special court and later in the general judiciary system.

[38] For instance, the 1832 Mexican law prohibited the protection of inventions that were contrary to public health, morality, or national security.

[39] This feature of the early Chilean patent system is also commonly overlooked. See, for instance, table 4 in Josh Lerner, "150 Years of Patent Office Practice," *American Law and Economic Review* 7(1) (2005): 112–43.

the importance and nature of the invention.[40] By removing protection from *undeserving* subjects and by extending the term of protection to the *worthy* ones,[41] the Chilean patent system became more in concordance with the utilitarian and natural rights doctrines. In the next five years the government reorganized itself, and in doing so, secured the authority for internal examiners to conduct the examination of patent applications, retaining the ability to rely on external examiners, if it so decided. By 1909, the president relinquished the authority to award patents to the corresponding minister.

The 1895 regulation merely updated the 1856 regulation on opposition, examination, and publication. It was the 1905 regulation that significantly altered the functioning of the patent system: the working requirement was to be enforced. This regulation introduced teeth to the fulfillment of the implicit utilitarian aim of the law: to protect only deserving innovations.

Even though the utilitarian doctrine was not explicitly absent from the first patent law, this doctrine gained practical relevance in subsequent executive branch regulations.

6.3   The Patent System at Work in Chile

This analysis relied on two different type of sources to examine the patent system at work in Chile: information on patent grants and information on patent applications. A complete list of the patents granted under Chile's 1840 law was published as part of the centenary celebrations.[42] Each entry contained the name of the inventor, the term granted (protection and installation), and a succinct description of the patent. Since it did not disclose the type of patent, an effort was made to distinguish between the

---

[40] This fact is generally overlooked in the literature, and almost always ignored. Note the entries for Chile in table 2 in Josh Lerner, "150 Years of Patent Protection," *NBER Working Paper* 7478, 2000; "150 Years of Patent Protection," *The American Economic Review, Papers and Proceedings of the One Hundred Fourteenth Annual Meeting of the American Economic Association* 92(2) (2002): 221–5; Fred W. Barker, *Epitome of the World's Patent Laws and Statistics* (New York: The British and European Patent Agency, 1891), 11.

[41] The law amendments resulted after prior attempts to change patent protection. In 1864, Representative Manuel Antonio Tocornal introduced a bill for the comprehensive overhaul of the law, but did not succeed. In the 1880s, Congress was requested to grant an extension of the term of protection to an inventor, and decided to modify the general law after a heated discussion (see Official Gazette of September 2, 1882). By that time, a bill introduced by Deputy Felix Echeverría to radically modify the law was discussed and rejected.

[42] Arturo Montero, *Registro General de Patentes de Invención, 1840–1912*, (Santiago: Ministerio de Industria y Obras Públicas, 1913)

two types of grants, depending on whether the description contained the term "introduction" or "establishment" and did not contain terms referring to novelty ("modification," "improvement," or "perfection").[43]

I analyzed the patents protected by Chilean law during the 1840–1908 period and the term of protection granted to them. The evidence shows that during the period of coexistence of protection for introductions (1840–72) up to 30 percent of total patents were awarded to introductions. It is rather surprising to notice that introductions remained a minority among patent grants whilst protection for such innovations was in force, and even more surprising considering that minimal protection differences provided for both type of patents. Conversely, in Spain, 48 percent of Spain's patent grants during the 1826–50 period corresponded to introductions.[44]

Despite the small aggregate patent grant figures, there was a significant expansion in the number of grants both in absolute and in relative terms (relative to the population size), amounting by the turn of the century to four times the level reached by mid-century.

In spite of the extension of the term up to twenty years, the terms granted did not increase significantly after the 1880s, except for renewals and extensions. In fact, the term for renewals retracted by the turn of the century. On the other hand, extensions granted for the term for installing innovations experienced a significant expansion from the 1880s, more than tripling by the turn of the century. The evidence reflects that in the view of the examiners, inventions granted after 1883 that were susceptible to being awarded up to twenty years, contained no major inventive step, as they were very rarely awarded longer terms of protection.

The 1905 regulation that enforced the working requirement, rendered the majority of the 214 patents expirations decided during the period. While nearly 34 percent of the patent grants became ineffective to work within the prescribed term, the actual figure was nearly 25 percent since 9 percent of the patents were later reinstated. The extent of transfers of patent property reflects another dimension of their value and degree of economic use. Even though 6 percent of the patent grants were transferred at some point, the level of change of control of this property increased significantly by the turn of the century. What remained stable

---

[43] There were two types of errors that I needed to avoid with my method. First, to wrongly assign an invention as an introduction. Second, to fail at detecting introductions and treat such cases as inventions. The first type of error was assessed after derogation: the method merely identified seven "false-positive" introductions after derogation. I had no means for assessing the second type of error.

[44] See table 2 in Sáiz González, "Spanish Patent System."

throughout the period was the number of assignees and inventors per patent grant (one on average).

The *Official Gazette* was used as a source to build a dataset on patent applications for 1877–1910.[45] It contained petitions and oppositions letters made by applicants and third parties, government decrees regarding the application procedure (nomination of examiners, opposition summons), and government decisions (grant, extensions, and refusals). I was able to identify more than 3,600 patent applications, and from them, I could also identify resident from nonresident patent applications. The degree of objection that these applications were subject to is reflected by the exercise of the right of opposition to the patent applications. There was a larger number of patent applications made during the period relative to the number of patent grants analyzed earlier. Interestingly, the new evidence reveals that not only were patent applications on the rise since 1877, but also nonresident applications were growing faster than resident applications, exceeding 30 percent of the applications made by 1910. The data also show that nonresidents were significantly more successful in obtaining grants for their applications (I found evidence of grants for 64 percent of nonresident applications and merely 38 percent for resident applications). Partly, this finding is a reflection of the lesser resistance that nonresident applications were subject to from third parties, as I found evidence of oppositions in 12 percent of their applications, half the size of the oppositions made to resident applications. In addition, refusals were minimal for both resident and nonresident applications (2–3 percent of applications). Resident applications were more frequently challenged with oppositions than nonresident, but also the evidence suggests that they may have not completed the application process and got abandoned more frequently than nonresident applications. Two interpretations are coherent with this finding. First, residents were better informed regarding the businesses of fellow resident applicants that facilitated the making of objections. The other is that the inventive step of fellow resident applications was lower than that of applications originated abroad. No definitive judgment can be made on this issue based on the available information.

---

[45] I searched for patent applications in the online *Gazette* database after conducting a primary search using the words "privilejio," "invento," "industrial," and "patente." With that search system I retrieved pages from more than 4,114 issues. After building the dataset, missing information in each record was completed with specific searches with particular key words per record (names primarily). The process allowed me to gather vast and rich information, but the outcome is by no means the entirety of patent applications of the period, nor a full account of each application's individual history.

The data collected regarding the 3,605 patent applications allow identification of four types of roles performed by actors: applicants, opponents, examiners, and agents of applicants and opponents. Among these applications I identified 3,486 actors or individuals that performed alternative roles (applicant, opponent, examiner, or agent) in the application process. The origin of the application (resident versus nonresident) for which the actors performed such roles was used as a category to identify the actors. The evidence shows that they were highly segregated by the origin of the application, as 69 percent of the actors only dealt with resident applications (2,400), primarily performing as applicants. These interventions represented 72 percent of those made by such actors. The actors dealing with nonresident applications represented 26 percent of the total (902), but their interventions merely represented 18 percent of the interventions. The latter figure is coherent with the lesser propensity detected above for these applications to face oppositions. In fact, of the total number of interventions made by the actors dealing solely with nonresident applications, oppositions represented only 3 percent of their interventions. Finally, the 5 percent of actors (184) that dealt with resident and nonresident applications were largely agents, as 60 percent of their interventions were performed in that capacity. However dedicated to their job as agents (amounting to 66 percent of all agents' interventions), these actors were also active applicants and opponents, as their interventions made in those capacities represented 20 and 17 percent of their interventions, respectively. These figures show that there was a community of individuals involved in the patent system, either by acting as innovator, as objector, or as a representative of third parties in the system.

6.4   Conclusions

Chile enacted an early patent system in Latin America, becoming a peculiar one as it originated in the natural rights doctrine, but evolved systematically toward the utilitarian doctrine throughout the nineteenth century. The influence of specific actors during the enactment of the law appears to have been very significant. At the outset, Mariano Egaña was a decisive actor in drafting the norm in the 1833 Constitution that introduced the natural rights doctrinarian structure that defined the future patent regulation. Prior to the law enactment, utilitarian perspectives on IP protection emerged both from the Executive and the Congress. The inheritance of colonial institutions, and a weak definition of novelty and usefulness, seemed to have conspired for the inclusion of introductions as protectable subject matter in the first Chilean patent law. Diego

Benavente also became a significant figure as the drafter of the law in the Senate, and responsible for including an examination requirement. The analysis reveals that even though the protection for introductions had been in force for thirty years along with invention patents, granting protection for this subject matter did not alter in an obvious manner the capabilities to invent in Chile, by diminishing the potential number of invention patents while they were both in force. In spite of its distinct utilitarian features (exemplified by a strong examination system in place since 1840), the Chilean patent system systematically moved away from a model of a sovereign *granting* privileges into a model of the sovereign *acknowledging* property that *belonged* to individuals.

The data gathered on patent applications and patent grants reveal an economy that was very active in seeking patent protection, 70 percent originating in Chile, but not very successful in doing so. Only a third of the applications succeeded in the application process, and this outcome was the result of the proactive role played by opponents (in 15 percent of the applications), and probably mainly resulting from the fact of having an examination process in place from the outset. The actors of the Chilean patent system were multifaceted; the majority were applicants (70 percent) that acted as opponents or agents in some occasions. Similarly, agents represented 15 percent of the actors, and on occasion also opposed patent applications of third parties, and also applied for their own patents from time to time. Opponents who also represented 15 percent of the actors were patent applicants in most cases, and also agents, but on fewer occasions. In sum, the data gathered show an early patent system that was used reasonably widely by a group of national economic actors – a surprising result given Chile's relatively low level of economic development in the period covered by this chapter.

Part III

Southern Europe

7 The Italian Patent System during the Long Nineteenth Century
From Privileges to Property Rights in a Latecomer Industrializing Country

Alessandro Nuvolari and Michelangelo Vasta

7.1 Introduction

Following the 1789 Revolution, the French republic enacted a law that explicitly recognized intellectual property as a natural right of the individual. The main thrust of this reform was the shift from a notion of exclusive rights granted to inventors as "privileges" (that is, by virtue of a concession of the state) to that of exclusive "property" rights that were a reflection of the natural right of the individual to reap the fruits of his own ingenuity and efforts.[1] In the aftermath of the French and Napoleonic wars, the French revolutionary patent law became the template for many legislative initiatives in nineteenth-century Europe, including the "pre-unification" Italian states. This trend was not reversed by the Restoration. The aim of our chapter is to provide an account of the history of the Italian patent systems throughout the long nineteenth century.[2] We

We would like to thank Sara Pecchioli for outstanding research assistance and Michele Mannucci for granting us access to the historical library of Ufficio Tecnico Ing. A. Mannucci s.r.l. (Florence). A very preliminary version of this chapter was presented at the workshop "International Diversity in Patent Cultures: A Historical Perspective" (Leeds, 2014). We would like to thank the participants for helpful comments and suggestions. We are also grateful to Graeme Gooday and Steven Wilf for their helpful advice.

[1] G. Galvez-Behar, *La Republique des inventeurs. Propriete et organisation de l'innovation en France (1791–1922)* (Rennes: Presses Universitaires de Rennes, 2008).

[2] The early origins of patents in Italy can be traced back to the exclusive right granted for three years to Filippo Brunelleschi in 1421 for the special boat "Badalone," designed to transport marble stones on the Arno river for the construction of the Dome. See P. Long, "Invention, Authorship, 'Intellectual Property' and the Origins of Patents: Notes toward a Conceptual History," *Technology and Culture* 32 (1991): 846–84; F. Praeger and G. Scaglia, *Brunelleschi: Studies of His Technology and Inventions* (Cambridge, MA: MIT Press, 1970); M. Vasta, "Dal Badalone a Windows: la proprietà intellettuale e la tutela dell'innovazione," in *Nel mito di Prometeo. L'innovazione tecnologica dalla rivoluzione industriale ad oggi. Temi, inventori e protagonisti dall'ottocento al duemila*, ed. R. Giannetti (Florence: Ponte alle Grazie, 1996), 260–78. From this almost "mythical" beginning, the tradition of granting exclusive rights for new manufactures or technologies spread to other states in Italy and in Europe. These privileges or exclusive rights were substantially

shall interpret this epoch by means of a straightforward periodization in two stages. The first stage goes from the Restoration to the political unification of the country in 1861. The second stage (that Italian historians frequently refer to as the "Liberal Age") covers the period from 1861 to the Great War.

After this introduction, in Section 7.2 we describe the salient characteristics of the Italian pre-unitary states' patent systems. In Section 7.3, we discuss the Italian patent law of 1864 in comparative perspective (in particular in comparison with the English, French, and German models) and we provide a quantitative appraisal of the functioning of the Italian patent system. It is worth noting that the Italian patent law of 1864 remained substantially unchanged until the reforms of the Fascist period in the 1930s. In this Section, we shall also examine the implementation of the Paris Convention of 1883 in terms of legislative changes and also in terms of the activities of the Italian and foreign inventors in Italy. Section 7.4 draws conclusions.

7.2 The Italian "Pre-unitary" Patent Systems

With the Congress of Vienna, Italy was divided into five major political units: *Regno di Sardegna* (broadly corresponding to the regions of Piedmont, Liguria, and Sardinia) ruled by the House of Savoy, *Regno Lombardo-Veneto*, which was part of the Austrian Empire; *Granducato di Toscana* ruled by the House of Ausburg-Lorena (and in this way linked with the Austrian Empire); *Stato Ponitificio* (broadly corresponding to the regions of Latium, Marche, Umbria, and the southeast part of Emilia-Romagna) under the control of the Pope; *Regno delle Due Sicilie* (covering the southern part of Italy) under the rule of the House of Bourbons. In the center of Italy there were also some smaller political units linked by

---

granted on an ad hoc basis. In 1474, the Venetian Senate enacted a statute that recognized to inventors the rights to the protection of their inventions following a specific set of guidelines, rather than being subject to the discretion of the government. During the fifteenth and seventeenth centuries, the concessions of special prerogatives to inventors or importers of new technologies gained further momentum, becoming one of the key instruments of technology policy used by mercantilist states – C. Belfanti, "Between Mercantilism and Market: Privileges for Invention in Early Modern Europe," *Journal of Institutional Economics* 2 (2006): 319–38. These practices reveal both a growing awareness of European governments of the key role played by technological change in shaping the economic and military fortunes of the states and the understanding that the adoption and diffusion of new technologies in this period was tightly linked with the migration of skilled workers. See C. MacLeod and A. Nuvolari, "Technological Change," in *The Oxford Handbook of the Ancien Régime*, ed. W. Doyle (Oxford: Oxford University Press, 2012), 448–66.

means of dynastic connections to the Austrian Empire: *Ducato di Parma, Piacenza e Guastalla, Ducato di Modena,* and the *Ducato di Lucca.*

Overall, the legislation on patents and on privileges was not a major concern for the pre-unification states. During the Napoleonic period, at different moments in time, the French legislation of 1791 was extended to all the different areas of Italy. After the Restoration, somewhat paradoxically, most countries retained the main thrust of the French revolutionary law, introducing only minor adaptations and modifications.[3] The major exception to this pattern was Regno di Sardegna. This country, in various stages, adopted a reform that reestablished a fully *ancien régime* approach to privileges and patents. The Piedmont law established a strict examination process tightly controlled by the Academy of Science of Turin for the applications of privileges following the example of the French system before the revolution.[4] The law entrusted a relatively high discretionary power to the Academy in defining the final form of the patent protection granted in terms of scope and duration. The other country that prescribed a formal examination procedure was, between 1820 and 1832, Regno Lombardo-Veneto. In the Regno delle Due Sicilie, although the 1810 law did not explicitly prescribe an examination procedure for all patents, since the 1820s the Royal Institute for the Improvement of Natural Sciences was entrusted with the assessment of all patents' application. In this way, even in the absence of a change in the legislation, an *ancien régime* approach toward patenting matters was de facto restored.[5] Remarkably, Granducato di Toscana did not have any specific legislation concerning patents or privileges for the protection of inventions.

Table 7.1 provides a synthetic summary of the main features of the patent legislations existing in Italy before the unification.

In Figure 7.1 we report the patenting activity in Regno di Sardegna and Regno delle Due Sicilie, two of the major political units of pre-unitary Italy, using histograms. In general terms, in both cases there is a rather limited patenting activity, which confirms the impression that in the pre-unification Italian context, the issue of securing privileges or

---

[3] Also, the copyright laws of the pre-unitary states were characterized by a similar lack of harmonization. See M. Giorcelli and P. Moser, "Copyright and Creativity: Evidence from Italian Operas," Working Paper, Department of Economics, Stanford University, 2015.

[4] L. Hilaire-Perez, *L'invention technique au siècle des Lumieres* (Paris: Abin Michel, 2000).

[5] For the role of the Royal Institute for the Improvement of Natural Sciences in the monitoring process of patents applications, see M. Lupo, "L'innovazione tecnologica in un'area periferica: primi risultati di una ricerca sul Mezzogiorno preunitario (1810–1860)," *Rivista dell'Istituto di Storia dell'Europa Mediterranea* 4 (2010): 461–81. It is also worth noting that the selection process was quite strict since out of about 1,200 applications for the period 1810–60 only 364 patents were granted (ibid., 471).

Table 7.1 *Main characteristics of patent legislations in pre-unitary states*

Pre-unitary state	Year of main legislation	Notes	Examination	Working requirement	Duration in years
Ducato di Parma e Piacenza	1833	Before 1833 there was the French law of 1791	No prior-art examination	Invention must be put in practice within 2 years	5, 10, or 15 years
Regno Lombardo-Veneto	1820	Law modified in 1832 and 1852	From 1820 to 1832 examination by the Chamber of Commerce in Vienna; no examination after 1832	Invention must be put in practice within 1 year	From 1 to 15
Regno delle Due Sicilie	1810	Law modified in 1844	No prior-art examination; but examination for health and public safety	Invention must be put in practice within 1 year	5, 10, or 15
Regno di Sardegna (Piemonte)	1826	Privilege law of 1826, modified in 1829 and 1832	Examination by the Academy of Science of Turin	Yes, but discretionary	At the discretion of the government (usually 6, 8, or 10 years)
Stato Pontificio	1833	Law introduced by Gregorio XVI without modifications until the Unification	No examination	Invention must be put in practice within 1 year	Min 5, max 15 years

Ducato di Modena	1848	Adoption of Piedmont law also in 1854		Not specified
Granducato di Toscana		No specific patent or privilege law		
Ducato di Lucca	1807	Law modified 1819; in 1847 Lucca was absorbed into the Granducato di Toscana	Examination by an appointed committee	Not specified

Source: our own elaboration on R. Urlig, *The Law of Patents in Foreign Countries* (London: Simpkin, Marshall & Co., 1845); C. Loosey, *Collection of the Laws of Patent Privileges of All the Countries of Europe, the United States of North America and the Dutch West-Indies* (London: Weale, 1849); and A. Tolhausen, *A Synopsis of the Patent Laws in Various Countries* (London: Taylor & Francis, 1857).

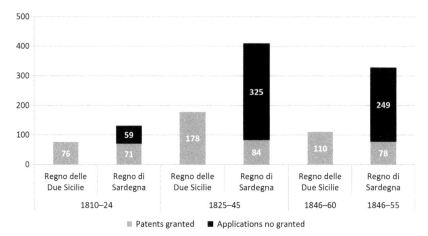

Figure 7.1 Innovative activities in Regno delle due Sicilie and Regno di Sardegna, 1810–60.
Sources: our own elaboration on Marchis, Dolza, and Vasta, *Privilegi*; and Lupo, "La filosofia del rotto?"

patents was probably not a major concern for potential inventors.[6] A revealing example is the case of Ascanio Sobrero, a professor of chemistry at the University of Turin. One of the most important technological breakthroughs attained in Italy during this period is his discovery of nitroglycerine. Sobrero made a demonstration of the synthesis of nitroglycerine at the Academy of Science of Turin in 1847, but did not apply for a privilege. Figure 7.1 also shows that the examination processes of the Academy were particularly exacting. Throughout the period considered, fewer than one-third of the applications were granted.

Also in Regno Lombardo-Veneto there was modest patent activity: between 1824 and 1845 fewer than thirty applications were filed per year.[7] Carletti suggests that this meager record in patenting was due to the preference of inventors for prizes and awards that were bestowed by

---

[6] For analyses of patent behavior in Regno delle Due Sicilie and Regno di Sardegna, see respectively M. Lupo, "La filosofia del rotto? Alcuni risultati di uno studio su brevetti, innovatori e innovazione tecnologica nel Mezzogiorno Preunitario," in *Crocevia Mediterranei: Società, Culture e Migrazioni nel Mediterraneo (secoli XIX–XX)*, ed. G. Biorciand and P. Castagneto (Cagliari: ISEM, 2010), 77–108; and V. Marchis, L. Dolza, and M. Vasta, *Privilegi industriali come specchio dell'innovazione nel Piemonte Preunitario* (Turin: La Rosa, 1992).

[7] C. Carletti, "Top-Down Legislation versus Local Traditions: Entrepreneurship and Innovation Strategies in the Lombardo-Veneto Kingdom," *Revue Economique* 64 (2013): 55–68, at 65.

many local societies for the encouragement of sciences and practical arts that were exerting a sort of "crowding-out" of the patent system.[8] Finally, it is worth remarking that these pre-unitary patent systems were not particularly attractive for foreign inventors. Lupo estimates that the patent share of foreign inventors in the Regno delle Due Sicilie was about 8.5 percent of the total (here foreign inventors comprises both inventors with residence in another Italian pre-unitary state and inventors with residence outside Italy).[9] According to Marchis, Dolza, and Vasta the share of foreign inventors in the applications for privileges in the Regno di Sardegna was limited until about the 1850s.[10] In the 1850s, they notice a significant growth and they estimate a patent share of foreign inventors of about 30 percent of the total (in this phase, foreign inventors were mostly French or English).

In 1855, a major reform was introduced in the Regno di Sardegna. This reform was prompted by Camillo Cavour (the prime minister of the kingdom) and carried out by Antonio Scialoja (a "liberal" patriot coming from the Regno delle due Sicilie and one of the most authoritative Italian economists of the time).[11] In preparation for this legislative reform, Scialoja undertook a major study of patent laws around the world. In the end, the model adopted was that of the French law of 1844.[12] In particular, the Piedmont law of 1855 (revised in 1859) followed the French model in prescribing a similar structure of patent fees and in using an application procedure based on registration and not on examination.[13] The major change, however, was in the rationale underlying the law. The law

[8] Ibid.   [9] Lupo, "La filosofia del rotto?," 98.
[10] Marchis, Dolza, and Vasta, *Privilegi*, 10.
[11] For a detailed account of the 1855 patent reform and the role played by Antonio Scialoja, see M. F. Gallifante, "Antonio Scialoja e le riforme legislative in Piemonte negli anni preunitari: la legge sulle privative industriali," *Il Risorgimento* 55 (2003): 367–404.
[12] For an account of the French law of 1844, see Galvez-Behar, *Republique*. For a useful comparative analysis of the English, French, and US patent systems in the eighteenth and nineteenth centuries, see Z. Khan, *The Democratization of Invention: Patents and Copyrights in American Economic Development, 1790–1920* (Cambridge: Cambridge University Press, 2005), chapter 2.
[13] Law March 12, 1855, n. 782 and Law October 30, 1859, n. 3731. The French system prescribed the payment of renewal fees at five, ten, and fifteen years. The 1855–9 laws established also a duration of fifteen years, but with a more flexible yearly fee structure. In this way, an inventor had the possibility of taking a patent for any duration between one and fifteen years. This higher degree of flexibility was deemed to be favorable to independent inventors with limited financial resources; see MAIC (Ministero di Agricoltura, Industria e Commercio), *Bollettino Industriale del Regno d'Italia* (Siena: Mucci, 1864), 21. The choice to avoid the strictures of examination process is in line with the strategy adopted by other southern European countries such as Greece and Spain. For an interesting case of the adoption of an examination system in a less developed country, see Chapter 6 on Chile by B. Escobar Andrae in this book.

established the principle that patents were granted to reward inventors for their efforts. Furthermore, they had to be understood as grounded in the natural rights of individuals to reap the fruits of their labors and as such they were not subjected to discretionary decisions of government and authorities. The parliamentary discussion of the law also established the notion that the patent system was an institutional device that allowed a suitable balance between incentive to innovative activities and the diffusion of knowledge.[14] Overall, both in terms of practical procedures and at the level of the perception of the system, the impact of the 1855–9 reform was extremely important. It definitely sanctioned in Italy the transition "from privilege to property" that some scholars have adopted to interpret the evolution of the patent systems of other countries during the eighteenth and nineteenth centuries.[15] In 1859, following the victory in the Second War of Independence against the Austrian Empire and the annexation of Lombardy, the patent law was extended also to this region. Finally, the law was extended, some years after unification, to the entire country in 1864 (Law n. 1657, January 31, 1864).

A particularly important feature of a patent system is the cost of the fees for taking and maintaining a patent alive. These fees determine the relative accessibility of the patent system for potential inventors and they can actually shape the functioning of the system in a major way.[16] In Table 7.2, we report the fees of different Italian states in 1857 and 1862. The source for 1857 is Tolhausen,[17] the author of an authoritative international handbook published for patent agents. Interestingly enough, in terms of fees, the majority of the pre-unitary patent systems were similar to the French model. The main exception was the Ducato di Parma e Piacenza that prescribed cheap fees in line with the US system.

---

[14] In Italy in the period 1840–60 there was a spirited discussion on the "patent question," mirroring the European debate studied by F. Machlup and E. Penrose, "The Patent Question in the Nineteenth Century," *Journal of Economic History* 10 (1950): 1–29. For an overview of the most authoritative positions in this debate in the Italian case, see V. Grembi, "La questione della proprietà intellettuale: il contributo degli economisti italiani al dibattito," in *La Scienze Economica in Parlamento, 1861–1922: Vol. 1*, ed. M. Augello and M. Guidi (Milano: Angeli, 2002), 267–94. Curiously enough, Scialoja in the early 1840s had an antipatent position (ibid.). See also Gallifante, "Antonio Scialoja."

[15] For a recent study of the institutional evolution of the English patent system using the interpretative notion "from privilege to property," see S. Bottomley, *The British Patent System during the Industrial Revolution 1700–1852: From Privilege to Property* (Cambridge: Cambridge University Press, 2014).

[16] Khan, *Democratization*.

[17] A. Tolhausen, *A Synopsis of the Patent Laws in Various Countries* (London: Taylor & Francis, 1857).

Table 7.2 *Patent fees in pre-unitary states, 1857–63*

Pre-unitary state	Patent fees for max duration (1857) in British pounds	Patent fees (1863) in Italian lire	Patent fees (1863) in British pounds
Ducato di Parma e Piacenza	6	150	5.92
Regno Lombardo Veneto	70	1,500	59.17
Regno delle due Sicilie	costs uncertain	85	3.35
Regno di Sardegna (Piemonte)	40	1,500	59.17
Stato Pontificio	30	808	31.87
Ducato di Modena	-	180	7.10
Granducato di Toscana	-	-	
Other countries			
United States	6 (US citizens); 60 (European citizens); 100 (British citizens)		
France	62.5		
England	175		

Source: Tolhausen, *Synopsis;* and MAIC, *Bollettino industriale del Regno d'Italia* (1864), 11–14. The 1863 data were converted from Italian lire to British pounds using data on exchange rates kindly provided by Giovanni Federico.

The source for the 1862 figures is MAIC,[18] a report that was describing the state-of-affairs of Italian patent laws right after the political unification (1861). At that time, the preexisting different patent laws were retained simply converting the fees in Italian lire.[19] As it is possible to see, the outcome of this hasty and incomplete harmonization created a situation with marked differentials in patent fees and in the related administrative procedures. In other words, right after the unification, different patent regulations coexisted creating a "virtual" and unwieldy patchwork. Rather than building a "real" patchwork, which would have required a long process of parliamentary negotiation leading to the formulation of new national law, full harmonization was achieved abruptly by means of the extension of the Piedmont law of 1855 to the entire country in 1864. In this way, the newly born Kingdom of Italy was endowed with a patent system that also from the point of view of costs was similar to the French one.

---

[18] MAIC, *Bollettino industriale del Regno d'Italia* (1864).
[19] Lombardy adopted the Piedmont law in 1859 after the Second War of Independence.

The rapid extension of the Piedmont law to the entire country allows us to study the possible existence of some long-term effects of the legislation of the pre-unitary states. This is done in Figure 7.2a and Figure 7.2b. Figure 7.2a shows the percentage shares of patents according to the pre-unitary borders in two benchmark years 1864–5 and in 1881. As one would have expected, in 1864–5 the share of Regno di Sardegna is more than 50 percent of the total. This probably reflects the familiarity of inventors in these regions with the Piedmont patent system. In 1881, this effect seem to have dissipated and the distribution of patents reflect substantially the economic geography of the country: the emergence of the so-called industrial triangle in the Northwest (more than 50 percent of patents in Regno di Sardegna and Regno Lombardo Veneto), the consolidation of Rome as capital and major administrative center, and the relative economic underdevelopment of the southern regions.[20] Figure 7.2b shows the distribution of patents per million inhabitants according to the pre-unitary borders. In this case, the most

(a)

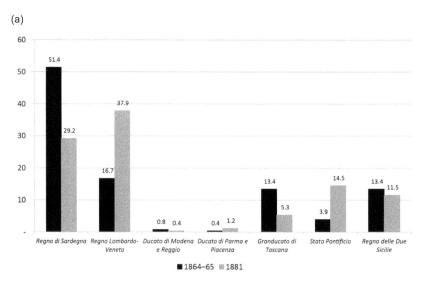

Figure 7.2a Distribution of number of patents (% shares) according to pre-unitary states borders, 1864–5 and 1881.

[20] E. Felice, *Perché il Sud è rimasto indietro* (Bologna: Il Mulino, 2011). A detailed study of the relationship between economic development and patenting activities in Italy during the second half of the nineteenth century is still missing. For a first exploration, see A. Nuvolari and M. Vasta, "The Geography of Innovation in Italy, 1861–1913: Evidence from Patent Data," *European Review of Economic History* 21 (2017): 326–56.

(b)

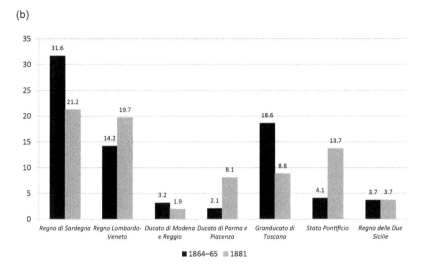

Figure 7.2b Distribution of patents per million population according to pre-unitary states borders, 1864–5 and 1881.
Sources: Authors' elaboration on MAIC, *Bollettino delle privative industriali del Regno d'Italia*, various years

remarkable finding is the high patent intensity of Granducato di Toscana (the only pre-unitary state that did not have a formal patent legislation) in 1864–5.[21]

7.3   The Italian Patent System during the Liberal Age (1861–1913)

The debate on the technological and economic performance of Italy during the so-called Liberal Age is still alive with no sign of imminent closure.[22] Since Italy, in the period in question, was a latecomer

---

[21] This finding is probably in line with the results of P. Moser, "How Do Patent Laws Influence Innovation? Evidence from Nineteenth Century World's Fairs," *American Economic Review* 95 (2005): 1214–36, who finds that countries without patent systems such as Denmark, Switzerland, and the Netherlands were characterized by a very intensive inventive activity. Another peculiarity of Granducato di Toscana is that it was the first country of the world to repeal the death penalty in 1786.

[22] See Nuvolari and Vasta, "The Geography," for a discussion focused on the issues of technology and innovation in Italy since unification. Among a huge literature, for an "optimistic" interpretation of Italian economic history in this period, see G. Federico, "Italy, 1860–1940: A Little-Known Success Story," *Economic History Review* 49 (1996): 764–86; for a "pessimistic" account, see P. Di Martino and M. Vasta, "Happy 150th Anniversary, Italy? Institutions and Economic Performance," *Enterprise and Society* 16

industrializer trying to catch up with the world technological frontier, it is clear that an assessment of the impact of the patent system is bound to be, to some extent, interconnected with a general appraisal of the effectiveness with which the country was able, in this historical phase, both to assimilate foreign technology and generate innovations. Furthermore, one would be called to assess to what degree the assimilation of technological knowledge and the generation of innovation prompted by the reformed patent system, enacted with the 1864 law, resulted in generalized productivity growth and contributed to the improvement of living standards. Here we shall simply sketch a suggested interpretation of how the system functioned with the assistance of some basic statistical data. As we can see, even if this approach does not provide a complete and precise assessment of the economic impact of the Italian patent system, it suggests an interesting interpretation in comparative perspective.

Our investigation of the total number of patents in international comparative perspective in the period 1861–1913 shows that Italy was characterized by a lower domestic patent activity when compared with countries such as the United States and the UK, France, and Germany.[23] Interestingly enough, Italy has throughout the period a higher patent intensity than Japan. It is also remarkable that throughout the period, Italy progressively converged toward the other countries. Patent fees also exerted a strong impact on patenting behavior, as is illustrated by the sharp increase in British patenting in 1883 (when the cost of patenting was drastically reduced). It is worth remarking that World War I caused a general decline in patenting activities in all the European countries coupled with a sharp increase in the United States. We investigated the total number of patents per million inhabitants in comparative perspective. By taking into account the different sizes of countries in terms of population, we gained insights on the relative "intensity" of patenting activities. The pattern is similar to the overall level of patenting, but with a more rapid convergence of Italy toward the other countries, especially Germany.

It would be misleading to speculate about the relative technological performance of countries on the basis of data presented from domestic patents, since these simply reveal patterns of patenting behavior. An international comparison of the number of patents granted in the United

---

(2015): 291–312. A very useful collection of essays is contained in G. Toniolo, ed. *The Oxford Handbook of the Italian Economy Since Unification* (Oxford: Oxford University Press, 2013).

[23] See A. Nuvolari and M. Vasta, "Independent Invention in Italy during the Liberal Age, 1861–1913," *Economic History Review* 68 (2015): 858–86.

States to citizens in the UK, France, Germany, Italy, and Japan per million inhabitants usefully compares the activities of inventors and firms of various countries with respect to a common patent legislation (taking as a reference point a large market of particular interest for all the countries).[24] Germany and the UK are clearly the two leading countries in this regard, with France lagging slightly behind. Italy is at a significantly lower level. However, the Italian series shows a slight amount of "catching up" throughout this historical phase, whereas Japan is consistently at the bottom of the rankings.[25] An extreme interpretation would be that of a technological race with leading countries such as the UK and Germany and followers such as Japan and Italy. In fact, even if the patterns emerging from this analysis are consistent with well-established narratives of nineteenth-century comparative industrialization, it must be taken into account that cultural factors, among others, were also likely to affect the behavior of patentees (including their decision to patent in foreign countries). For example, the high intensity of British patentees in the United States may be also due to the cultural proximity of the two countries; the high intensity of German patentees may reflect the strength of technical education in this country and the acquaintance of German patentees to the strictures of a formal examination system. In other words, differences in patent intensities across countries should be interpreted with particular care. For the purposes of this chapter, the salient point is that, since 1883, Italian inventors increasingly tried to exploit their inventions in US markets.

Table 7.3 documents the comparative "degree of openness" of various patent systems in the second half of the long nineteenth century. The degree of openness is computed as the share of patents granted to foreign residents in the total patents. The table shows clearly that the country with the lowest level of openness is the US system. This is probably

---

[24] The approach was originally introduced by L. Soete and S. Wyatt, "The Use of Foreign Patenting As an Internationally Comparable Science and Technology Output Indicator," *Scientometrics* 5 (1983): 31–54. Today, this is one of the most used indicators for assessing the relative performance of countries in the economics of innovation literature.

[25] Nuvolari and Vasta, "Independent Invention," 865–6. F. Barbiellini Amidei, J. Cantwell, and A. Spadavecchia, "Innovation and Foreign Technology," in *The Oxford Handbook of Italian Economy Since Unification*, ed. G. Toniolo (Oxford: Oxford University Press, 2013), 378–417 document that throughout this period the share of Italian patenting in other major European systems (the UK, France, Germany, Spain, and Switzerland) was also characterized by a growing trend. In fact, the estimates of industrial labor productivity by S. Broadberry, C. Giordano, and F. Zollino, "Productivity," in *The Oxford Handbook of Italian Economy Since Unification*, ed. G. Toniolo (Oxford: Oxford University Press, 2013), 187–226 indicate a modest catching up with the UK and widening gap with the United States and Germany.

Table 7.3 *Degree of openness (% of nonresidents on total patenting) of the patent systems, 1864–1922*

Countries	1864–5	1883	1901	1914	1922
France			51.4	50.8	40.6
Germany		31.1	37.1	30.1	25.5
Italy	50.7	63.8	64.9	61.5	56.0
United Kingdom			53.2		44.2
United States			13.3	11.5	11.6

Note: for United Kingdom, 1921 instead of 1922.
Sources: Authors' elaboration on WIPO, "Statistics database"; data for Italy from MAIC, *Bollettino delle privative industriali del Regno d'Italia*, 1864–85, 1886–93; MAIC, *Elenco degli attestati di privativa industriale*; MAIC, *Bollettino della proprietà intellettuale*.

accounted for by the low fees that resulted in a patent system that was particularly accessible and democratic for domestic inventors. The strong participation rate of domestic inventors overwhelmed the share of foreign inventors.[26] Italy is clearly the country with the most open system. In this respect it is worth noting that article 4 of the 1859 law established that inventions covered by patents taken in foreign countries could easily be granted an Italian patent, provided that the original foreign patent had not yet expired.[27] In practice, the system did not contain any form of discrimination against foreign patentees. This characteristic of the Italian patent system is probably due to the strong economic relations of some former pre-unitary states with foreign countries, such as Piedmont with France and Lombardy with Austria.[28]

It is also interesting to look for the possible impact of patent fees. In Table 7.2 we have shown the level of patent fees around 1862. Figure 7.3 provides more elaborated comparative estimates for the period of the 1880s. In Italy the system was extremely flexible: an inventor could register a patent for any duration from one to fifteen years according to his own choice. There was an initial fee that was proportional to the number of years for which the patent was requested (10 Italian lire for one year, 20 lire for two years, 150 lire for fifteen years). In addition, it was necessary to pay an annual renewal fee for keeping the patent alive. This fee increased over time: 40 lire for the first three years, 65 lire from the fourth to the sixth year, 90 lire for the seventh up to the ninth year, 115 lire for the tenth to the twelfth year and 140 lire for the last three years.

[26] Khan, *Democratization*.   [27] MAIC, *Bollettino industriale del Regno d'Italia* (1864), 1.
[28] L. Cafagna, *Dualismo e sviluppo nella storia d'Italia* (Venice: Marsilio, 1989).

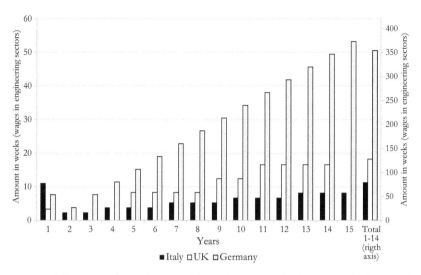

Figure 7.3 Annual renewal fees of patenting in Germany, the UK, and Italy, 1880s.

Accordingly, Figure 7.3 compares the structure of renewal fees in Italy, the UK, and Germany. The yearly fees have been measured in relation with the average weekly wages of workers in the engineering sector. Overall, this normalized measure confirms that, except for the initial year, the costs for keeping a patent alive was systematically lower in Italy than in Germany and the UK. The last three histograms on the right report the total amount of the fees paid throughout the patent life. Again, Italy appears to offer considerably cheaper fees in comparative perspective. Generally, it seems plausible to assume that the peculiar fee structure of the Italian system was an important factor in attracting foreign inventors.[29]

The historical evolution of the degree of openness in Italy over the period 1871–1922 starts from a level around 40 percent in 1871, exhibits an increasing trend up to the middle of the 1880s, and then remains relatively stable up to the eve of World War I (around 60 percent).[30]

---

[29] The estimates of Figure 7.3 are fully consistent with the estimates of J. Lerner, "150 Years of Patent Protection," National Bureau of Economic Research working paper n. 7478, 2000, table 3 for the year 1900.

[30] For a further discussion on the openness of the Italian patent system in the period 1855–72, see A. Nuvolari and M. Vasta, "Patenting the *Risorgimento*: Economic Integration and the Formation of the Italian Patent System (1855 1872), *Jahrbuch fur Wirtschaftsgeschichte* 60 (2019): 93–122. In the year 1862 the share of patents of foreign residents was about 58 percent (MAIC, *Bollettino industriale del Regno d'Italia* [1864], 19).

Table 7.4 *Number of patents by typologies*

	1891		1902		1911	
Typologies	No.	%	No.	%	No.	%
Patents	1,618	97.1	2,987	94.5	4,058	77.9
Imported and priority patents	49	2.9	175	5.5	1,151	22.1
Total	1,667	100.0	3,162	100.0	5,209	100.0

Source: Nuvolari and Vasta, "Independent Invention."

As one would have expected, World War I brought a sharp temporary decline in the degree of openness. We do not find any specific particular effect of the Paris Convention of 1883 on foreign patenting in Italy, even though the country was one of the first signatories of the Treaty.[31] The major tenets of the Paris Convention were concerned with "national treatment" and the "right of priority." National treatment is the right of foreign inventors to be treated on an equal footing with domestic inventors. As we have seen, the Italian patent system did not contain any particular discriminatory clause against foreign inventors, so this feature of the Paris convention did not represent a major discontinuity. The right of priority established that a foreign patentee had a period of six months from the date of the first application (the priority date) to file for patents in other countries. During this period, he would have still enjoyed protection against infringements.

Table 7.4 sheds light on the functioning of this condition of the Paris Convention in Italy. The table shows the total number of patents distinguishing from patents taken "originally" at the Italian patent office, either by domestic or foreign patentees, and the patents granted on the basis of the existence of a former patent in a foreign country following the Paris Convention ("imported" or "priority patents") in three benchmark years. Table 7.4 clearly indicates that, at least until 1902, the Paris Convention had a very limited impact. It is only in the last benchmark year (1911) that the number of priority patents represents a sizeable share of the total (22 percent).

It is useful to compare the characteristics of regular and "priority" patents. In patent systems characterized by a renewal scheme, as was the Italian one, the duration of the patent has been frequently used as an indicator for its economic significance. This intuition is relatively

---

[31] A useful discussion of the Paris Convention is in G. Dutfield and U. Suthersanen, *Global Intellectual Property Law* (Cheltenham: Edward Elgar, 2008), 22–44.

Table 7.5 *Foreign patents' average duration: scheduled versus real*

	1881	1891	1902	1911
Average "scheduled" duration				
Patents	7.1	8.4	7.6	6.7
Imported and priority patents	–	9.9	8.6	8.6
Total	**7.1**	**8.5**	**7.6**	**7.3**
Average "real" duration				
Patents	3.8	3.5	4.3	
Imported and priority patents	–	5.9	5.1	
Total	**3.8**	**3.6**	**4.4**	

Source: Nuvolari and Vasta, "Independent Invention."

straightforward. Inventors decide to maintain alive only the patents with relatively sound economic prospects.[32] Table 7.5 compares the duration of regular patents with that of priority patents. There are two possible measures of patent duration. The first is the duration chosen by the inventor at the time of the granting of the patent. This may be called "scheduled" patent duration and captures a sort of "*ex ante*" assessment of the economic potential of the patent in question. The second approach considers the duration of the patent from the granting date until the moment in which the inventor is no longer renewing the patent, by not paying the yearly fees. This can be called the "real" patent duration and provides an "*ex post*" assessment of the patent. Table 7.5 shows that the average durations of priority patents are higher than those of other patents. The data suggest that priority patents were typically covering inventions of a relatively higher economic impact.

Finally, we consider the distribution of patents across industries. Nuvolari and Vasta have proposed a classification of "high technology" sectors for the case of Italy in this historical period.[33] The taxonomy regards as high technology sectors those that have been characterized by a certain degree of technological sophistication, namely steam power, mechanical engineering, chemicals, electricity, and weapon systems. Table 7.6 shows that the share of priority patents was clearly more skewed toward high technology types of inventions than the regular

[32] M. Schankerman and A. Pakes, "Estimates of the Value of Patent Rights in European Countries during the Post-1950 Period," *Economic Journal* 96 (1986): 1052–76. For a more extensive discussion of the use of renewal rates in the Italian case, see Nuvolari and Vasta, "Independent Invention."
[33] Nuvolari and Vasta, "Independent Invention."

Table 7.6 *Share of hi-tech patents by typologies*

	1891	1902	1911
Patents	39.4	43.9	40.4
Imported and priority patents	57.1	45.7	52.5
Total	40.0	44.0	43.0

Source: Nuvolari and Vasta, "Independent Invention."

patents. Overall, the evidence of Table 7.5 and 7.6 suggests that priority patents, in the Italian context, were patents endowed with a substantial degree of economic and technological significance.

7.4　Conclusion

Our reappraisal of the Italian patent systems during the "long" nineteenth century indicates that Italy opted for a patent system without examination, with relatively cheap patent fees, and with no discrimination against foreign inventors. In a comparative context this made the system very attractive for foreign inventors. As a result, the openness of the Italian patent system was one of the highest of the world. In this way, the Italian patent system probably contributed to the transfer of technologies from abroad. However, we should also consider that, throughout the nineteenth century, patent systems were also designed to stimulate the domestic generation of new technologies. This was often attained with the use of discriminatory clauses of various sorts or by means of other de facto inhibitions against foreign patentees.[34] A particularly vivid illustration of the discriminatory treatment against foreign inventors is provided by the obstacles raised by the German patent office against US machine tool makers during the 1920s. These shadowy practices played a role in the development of the technological capabilities of German firms in the machine tool industry.[35]

To sum up, we would suggest that the Italian patent system during the nineteenth century can be characterized as an institution that was attractive for foreign inventors, possibly contributing to the technology transfer

[34] For example, the United States.
[35] R. Richter and J. Streb, "Catching Up and Falling Behind: Knowledge Spillover from American to German Machine Tool Makers," *Journal of Economic History* 71(2011): 1006–31.

from abroad. On the other hand, the modest innovative performance of the Italian innovation system in this historical phase raises the concern that the Italian patent system might have been less suited in stimulating the use of foreign technologies as a base for the development of genuine domestic innovative activities, which in Italy had a "ghostly" nature with only some sporadic appearances.[36]

---

[36] A. Nuvolari and M. Vasta, "The Ghost in the Attic? The Italian National Innovation System in Historical Perspective, 1861–2011," *Enterprise and Society* 16 (2015): 270–90.

8 Industrial "Property", Law, and the Politics of Invention in Greece, 1900–1940

Stathis Arapostathis

8.1 Introduction

Recent historical research has abandoned traditional assumptions that studying patenting activity can usefully measure a nation's past capacity for innovation.[1] Instead the focus is now on mapping at both state and transnational levels the coproduction of technical sciences and legal cultures, and the extent of national patent cultures' compliance with or resistance to international treaties.[2] In that vein this chapter unravels the co-construction of law and the culture of invention in Greece from 1900 to 1940. I look at the interrelation between the local legal and legislative culture, Greek politics, and innovation policies with the ideology of the propertization of knowledge and innovation emerging alongside, and due to, a technocratic ideology that permeated Greek public

I would like to thank for their comments the participants of the workshop "International Diversity in Patent Cultures: A Historical Perspective" in Leeds (2014) as well as those of the conference of the European Society for the History of Science in Lisbon (2014). I am grateful to the editors of the volume, Graeme Gooday and Steven Wilf, for their invaluable assistance and editorial guidance. Also, I am grateful to Mario Biagioli for comments and suggestions, as well as the participants of a seminar in UC Davis, Law School/ Science, Technology and Society (STS) studies where I presented aspects of the chapter's argument. The research was supported financially by a Fulbright Fellowship (2016).

[1] Jacob Schmookler, *Invention and Economic Growth* (Cambridge, MA: Harvard University Press, 1966); Kenneth Sokoloff, "Inventive Activity in Early Industrial America: Evidence from Patent Records, 1790–1846," *Journal of Economic History* 48(4) (1988): 813–50; Petra Moser, "Patents and Innovation: Evidence from Economic History," *Journal of Economic Perspectives* 27(1) (2013): 23–44; B. Zorina Khan and Kenneth L. Sokoloff, "Schemes of Practical Utility: Entrepreneurship and Innovation among 'Great Inventors' in the United States, 1790–1865," *Journal of Economic History* 53(2) (1993): 289–307; B. Zorina Khan and Kenneth L. Sokoloff, "Patent Institutions, Industrial Organization and Early Technological Change: Britain and the United States, 1790–1850," in *Technological Revolutions in Europe*, ed. M. Bergand and K. Bruland (Cheltenham: Edward Elgar, 1998), 292–313.

[2] Eda Kranakis, "Patents and Power: European Patent-System Integration in the Context of Globalization," *Technology and Culture* 48(4) (2007): 689–728; Pascal Griset, *The European Patent: A European Success Story for Innovation*, European Patent Office (EPO), 2013.

affairs. My narrative examines the transition of the Greek patent system from a system of privileges to a system of rights under pressure from a changing international context of patent cultures. I argue that by studying the changes in patenting I can unravel the social, institutional, and economic changes that occurred in Greece and that characterized the transformation of Greek capitalist state and society in the first half of the twentieth century.

Notwithstanding patent treaties and transnational agreements since the Paris Union of 1883,[3] and as emphasized by the editors of this volume in Chapter 1, diversity in patent practices can be identified both in industrial sectors and in different countries.[4] Moreover, in Greece, as in other national contexts, patents were only one of the options that political and industrial elites decided to develop in managing useful knowledge. Greece was not the only nation in which a resilient diversity of strategies in knowledge management was manifest in decisions to foster innovation either without formal intellectual property rights or at least with rather "soft" intellectual property legislation. Typically, the reasons for such innovation policies lay in local, regional, and national politics, as well as in local vested interests that influenced decision-making processes. It is in these processes that we see techno-scientific cultures coproduced notions of ownership together with legislation by socio-political processes of appropriation or through translational activities of individuals.[5] This chapter combines insights from these approaches with those from the perspective of transnational histories. It aims to provide an explanation about the tensions between the geopolitical pressures for international patent harmonization, and the quest for national sovereignty. The chapter studies the emergence of the Greek patent system within the geopolitical dynamics of the international scene of patent cultures.

8.2   The Politics of Invention and Patents as Privilege

In the first half of the twentieth century Greek debates and politics of intellectual property at the national or European level were linked with

---

[3] Kranakis, "Patents and Power."

[4] Stathis Arapostathis and Graham Dutfield, eds., *Knowledge Management and Intellectual Property: Concepts, Actors and Practices from the Past to the Present* (Cheltenham: Edward Elgar, 2013).

[5] K. Gavroglu, M. Patiniotis, Γ. Papanelopoulou, A. Simões, A. Carneiro, M. P. Diogo, R. Bertomeu-Sanchez, A. Garcia-Belmar, and A. Nieto-Galan, "Science and Technology in the European Periphery: Some Historiographical Reflections," *History of Science* 46 (2008): 153–75.

public discourses and emerging ideologies concerning national "progress" and "growth." Before 1920 when the first patent law was ratified, invention was viewed as an individualistic activity that should be protected by local and regional privileges. Such privileges were formally awarded only by a special Parliamentary Act by the Greek Kingdom.[6]

In fact, during the late nineteenth century there was no legislative framework in place regarding intellectual property rights in Greece, much to the disappointment of inventors and lawyers. While the former were seeking to secure ownership of their ideas and protect themselves from copying and misappropriation in a newly founded country that was interested in developing its industrial potential, the latter were seeking to expand their professional activities to new commercial and social activities. The lawyers were keen supporters of establishing a regime of patents as rights based on patterns of protection found abroad. The experience acquired from countries like France, England, and Germany where local inventors, technicians, and mechanics secured rights to their own discoveries led to the emergence of a strong rhetoric in support of ownership of the ideas and inventing activities.

One key figure in the late nineteenth-century Greek context was Kostantinos Fostiropoulos, a lawyer and representative of several foreign industrial concerns in the Greek legal market. He staunchly supported the French system of *brevet d'invention* as a simple and economical way to secure inventors' ownership of ideas and innovations. In his campaign in favor of proprietary knowledge management Fostiropoulos submitted to the Greek National Assembly a report in 1864 in which he not only described briefly the legal developments in other countries but also promoted the French system of protecting inventions. He argued that while the regime of privileges promoted favoritism and obscured relations between the interested parties, the system of privilege through the *brevet d'invention* would render transparent relations between state and inventors since it introduced documentation of proof of invention and ownership of the innovation. Fostiropoulos compared the privileges over an invention with those an artist should possess over his artistic creations. For Fostiropoulos, the institutionalization of a formal system of privileges would secure a social contract between society and groups of inventors, giving them the incentive to invest their human capital and inventive activities in the promotion of society. At the same time, as a side effect, the taxes and fees that inventors paid would increase state income. He thus supported a system of privileges as a necessary step toward progress

---

[6] A. M. Clark and W. Clark, *Patents, Designs and Trade Marks' Act, 1883, and the Patent Laws of All Foreign Countries and British Colonies* (London, 1884), 90–1.

that would elevate Greece to being an industrialized nation. Fostiropoulos dramatically stated that "two only kingdoms lack such a [patent] law, Greece and Turkey."[7]

Yet still it was understood that there remained a considerable difference between these two feudal countries. In the Ottoman Empire, the sultan had the legislative power to attribute privileges to inventors whenever they applied for them. In Greece, however, the lack of such legislation provided the setting for favoritism and nepotism on the part of the king and the royal family. The editors of *Melissa Athinon* (Μέλισσα Αθηνών), who published Fostiropoulos's report, took the opportunity to express their anti-Bavarian sentiments by drawing the distinction between the transparency of the Ottoman practice and the informal and highly feudal practice of the Greek royal family with their Bavarian origins. Fostiropoulos addressed his report to the Greek National Assembly and to a government that, years before, had dealt with several irregularities caused by the lack of any established legal procedure for the management of innovations. There were inventors – Kosonakos, for example, who invented a medical treatment – or industrialists – like Douroutis, owner of a textiles factory in Kalamata – who claimed compensation from the Greek kingdom for their losses from stolen ideas or pirated innovations. Their claims addressed the absence of suitable protection from the nascent Greek state while others like Lieutenant Koudoumas, an inventor of weaponry, asked the National Assembly to reimburse him for the cost of his patent application abroad since, as he argued, the country would profit from his invention.[8]

Fostiropoulos's 1864 report triggered public discussions. It initiated the political process that resulted in establishing a new legislative regime whereby Parliament awarded patent privileges. Any Member of Parliament could introduce a bill with respect to their own constituency and, if accepted, the bill would specify the time and regional limits of the exclusive privileges to the inventor.[9] This emphasis on locality reflected the understanding of invention as an activity pertinent, important, and socially relevant to the local economies and communities of the various regions. Inventors were often seen as local heroes rather than mere citizens. For example, in 1910 in Pyrgos, a village in rural southwest Peloponnese, renowned for its olives and sultanas, inventor Tassopoulos presented for the first time a new process for making sugar from sultanas. The Local Farming Association (Κτηματικός Σύνδεσμος Ηλείας) deemed it

[7] K. Fostiropoulos, "About the Law Providing Rights on Inventions," *Melissa Athinon* [Μέλισσα Αθηνών] 1(6) (1864): 188.
[8] Ibid., 186.   [9] Clark and Clark, *Patents, Designs and Trade Marks' Act, 1883*, 90–1.

appropriate to publicly support the invention and its inventor's privileges since it was an innovation that would contribute added value to their products. A local rally was organized to urge the local Member of Parliament to support Tassopoulos's privilege over his inventive activities. Tassopoulos became a hero of local farmers whilst at the same time he was using them as a pressure group to persuade the government to award him the much-sought privilege that would encourage him to release the information required to develop his innovation.[10]

8.3   Visioning Proprietary Regimes and Technocratic Roles

The dominance of localism resonated deeply with a political economy of technologies focused on local needs and local characteristics. Furthermore, the emerging role of engineers as technocrats who would control the state encouraged further support for stronger proprietary regimes of knowledge management. Industrial elites in the late nineteenth century pressed for changes in the legislation, by supporting a stronger intellectual property regime. By the early twentieth century, strong intellectual property rights for inventors were deemed *necessary* in order to secure viable industrial development.[11] Like in other national settings (for example, Mexico, Italy, or Spain)[12] patenting and a formal patent system were framed as the precondition for the transformation of Greece into a modern European country. Engineers, technocrats, and politicians often publicly promoted the view that innovation through patenting would result in "progress" and "development". Such was the case of Prokopios Zaharias, engineer, chemist, and inventor:

Through such laws the aim is the growth of industry and [increase] of national wealth and of employment through the encouragement of inventors and other entrepreneurs to introduce new industries and to continuously improve the existing ones. Fair competition is emerging among the forces that contribute to the industrial progress of the nation as its existence is impossible without rational protection of the industrial property of the workers of industrial progress and [without] their compensation for their services to the whole of the nation.[13]

The argument for progress and growth was further boosted by Zaharias's public intervention. He depicted Greece as lagging industrially due to the lack of strict, formal protection of inventive activities. According to

---

[10] *EMPROS* [*ΕΜΠΡΟΣ*], January 19, 1910, 3.
[11] P. Zaharias, "On the Protection of Inventions," *Archimedes* 4 (1912): 42–7.
[12] See Chapters 5, 7, and 9 in the present volume.
[13] Zaharias, "Protection of Inventions," 43.

Zaharias, lawless countries are condemned to fail since the lack of governance intensified intellectual and business piracy, which he deemed very dangerous to the national economy. While the Netherlands also had innovation without a patent system, Zaharias understood the Dutch and Greek paradigms to be irregularities in the context of European and capitalist countries that innovated successfully precisely because of the institutionalization of the patents. He believed that the Dutch abolition of the Netherlands patent system in 1865 prompted Greeks to move toward a formal legislative framework. According to Zaharias, systems of patent-free innovation based on copying and piracy were inappropriate and inefficient for securing the growth of a Western country such as Greece. Trying to boost the rhetoric for the appropriateness of a patent law he argued that such a law would promote the rights of working-class people, giving them the incentive to innovate and participate further in the economic life of the country. Furthermore, he played the "card" of patents as a vital means to inform public knowledge: an argument that since the mid-nineteenth century had been so prominently pertinent to supporters of patent laws in England and France.[14] Zaharias developed a clearly liberal argument based on the idea of a social contract between the country and the patentee and inventor. The inventive worker (always in this context an indigenous man) had the right to capitalize on his own capabilities and efforts in the promotion of his own interests while, at the same time, society also profited. Zaharias argued that the increase of Greece's national wealth should be conceived as the basis of social welfare, and therefore country and state should protect those individuals whose activities could boost that wealth further. Such individuals were the "captains of industry" and should be given the time and space to flourish by providing them with relevant rights for exclusive use and application of their inventions and ideas.

In his attempt to be a more effective public intellectual and technocrat, Zaharias provided a full draft of an industrial property law. His legislative proposal comprised twenty-two articles and regulated both the relations of the independent inventor with the state and those of the employed inventor and his employer. Patent would provide the inventor with the privilege of exclusive use of their invention for fifteen years and should be awarded for any new and original mechanical device, method of

---

[14] Christine MacLeod, "Concepts of Invention and the Patent Controversy in Victorian Britain," in *Technological Change: Methods and Themes in the History of Technology*, ed. Robert Fox (Amsterdam: Harwood Academic Publishers, 1996), 137 53; Christine MacLeod, *Heroes of Invention* (Cambridge: Cambridge University Press, 2008); Fritz Machlup and Edith Penrose, "The Patent Controversy in Nineteenth Century," *Journal of Economic History* 10 (1) (1950): 1–29.

production, or new application of an existing industrial method for the production of a new product or machinery. Zaharias proposed that the award system should be simple and inexpensive in order to reduce the burden of drafting patent specifications. The principle should be organizational minimalism as a means to promote the culture of invention rather than establishing yet another layer of bureaucracy. Zaharias's plan was permeated by liberal ideals, providing the individual not only the rights for the privileges on his invention but also granting him the agency to act as a moral subject who should guarantee the trustworthiness of his statements and his actions as the author of the specification.

To this end, Zaharias maintained that the Greek state could not and should not organize any new bureaucracy such as a fully operational patent office of the sort then commonplace in European capitals. As a pragmatist technocrat he knew the potential, the priorities, and the constraints of a state with no established borders, no stable political life, and continuous political turmoil. Hence, he promoted the idea that the inventor should be conceived as the author of the specification and should be required as a moral obligation to promote the diffusion of reliable information. While in other national patent systems the trustworthiness of a specification underpinned the obligation for completeness of the document that was important for the replication of the invention criteria, Zaharias introduced it instead to the Greek context as a means for reducing state bureaucracy. That the statements in the specification should be "clear" and "accurate" would be an essential requirement of an application for privileges over a newly introduced innovation.

It is therefore intriguing that in Article 20 Zaharias suggested severe punishment for those who might misappropriate an innovation and violate the law of patents. He went as far as to suggest the violator should be punished not only with a fine of up to 5,000 drachmas but also with the possibility of imprisonment for up to a year[15] – a unique and rather draconian way to promote the innovative activities of individuals and to secure the interests of the sole inventor. The state would profit both from the minimal application fee and also from the percentage that would be extracted from the profit of successful commercialization of the innovation. As already mentioned, Zaharias's suggestion took account of the complicated character of invention, particularly in the industrial context of a factory or a technical laboratory. In such situations, those inventions of the employee relevant to the industrial activities of the employer

[15] Zaharias, "Protection of Inventions," 47.

should be shared between the two and both should appear as patentees. In the case of a collective invention where many employees were involved he argued that the privileges should be granted to the employer. His technocratic vision was embedded in the liberal ideology that emphasized the rights over an innovation attributable to a sole subject or to a very small number of people.

A year later Zaharias returned to the same forum with a contribution on the "Protection of Industries," providing his views on how to maintain and secure the business sustainability of industrial sectors. He reiterated his approach to fashioning a stable legal system for patents as part of a national industrial policy. Yet this time, while supporting industrial property law as a state tool to boost innovation, he also argued that state policy should rely upon diverse factors such as:

a. The continuation of import taxes in order to secure the competitiveness of Greek products and local industrial sectors. The exception should be raw materials, different in each sector, but deemed appropriate to be tax free in order to support existing and planned industries. Importation taxes should be under continuous consideration and reconsideration according to the plans and the needs of the native economy.
b. The provision of cheap loans and capital in order to support new investments and entrepreneurial activities. The establishment of an Industrial Bank was deemed an important step in this direction.
c. The creation of a self-conscious working class with a distinct ethos, well-educated and productive. This would reduce the cost of production while at the same time contributing to the integration of new skills into Greek industries.[16]

It was commonly accepted among Greek industrial elites that local industry needed some kind of protection in order to be competitive in the global setting. A report by the Trade and Industrial Chamber of Athens suggested measures for the "Protection of the Industry" along the lines already expressed by Zaharias and others in the industrial sectors of the period. Established in 1909, the Chamber was a leading institution for the promotion of trade and industrial professional interests. In the report "protection" was firstly linked to measures to secure affordable capital for investments, cheap and easy procedures for the initiation of new businesses, and an inexpensive yet still well-skilled work force. For the latter, technical education of the working classes was emphasized, as well as

---

[16] P. Zaharias, "The Protection of Industry," *Archimedes* (1913): 99–102.

compulsory university education in chemistry, chemical engineering, and mechanical and electrical engineering for industrial scientists and engineers. The newly emerging industrial scientists were conceived as important actors in the industrial development of science-based industries such as the chemical and electrical industries. Specific proposals warned about the establishment of monopolies as a means of promoting technological progress. It was argued that:

> The proposal for the establishment of the exclusive rights within an industry (except for the state monopolies) is, in the opinion of the Chamber, not only unnecessary but also dangerous. The provision of exclusive rights within an industry or the provision of privileges to individuals or groups [of professionals] put barriers to competition and therefore to the most important factor of any progress since it triggers complaints from those who cannot acquire such an exclusive right and provides the setting for malpractice.[17]

While developing a polemic against monopolistic interests and activities, including an anti-patenting strategy, the Chamber understood that innovation and innovative activities needed moral and social bolstering. Support was required both for the diffusion of innovation and for the creation of spaces and institutions where attribution of credit would be both financially and symbolically possible. It was argued that alternative management of innovations, innovative industrial methods, and ideas could be implemented through awards and participation in industrial exhibitions. The organization of a Technical Museum would function as an institution for technical education and for the preservation of work by native innovators.[18]

Institutional actors representing the industrial elites of Greece understood innovation as an organized activity that involved structural reforms, educational investments, and technology transfer mechanisms. Nevertheless, there were individual actors from the engineering and legal community who promoted a linear approach of innovation that initiated with an invention and forged further with the necessary acquisition of monopoly rights over such an invention. Suggestions for a new patent law were linked to demands by local inventors and industrialists for a stable legislative environment that would ensure monopolist rights over ideas and innovations. In this way, Greek engineers and inventors aimed to secure their technocratic role in the Greek state and economy, which was under reconstruction, particularly following World War I. Yet such an emphasis on the importance of new legislation in promoting the

---

[17] *Bulletin of Commercial and Industrial Chamber of Athens* (May 1920), 283 [Δελτίον Εμπορικούκαι Βιομηχανικού Επιμελητηρίου Αθηνών (Μάιος 1920), 283].
[18] Ibid.

industrial production was not overwhelming since there were industrial elites that understood the much-sought protection of the industrial sector in a very different way.

8.4   The Patent Law and the Concepts of Invention in Interwar Greece

In an industrial culture with competing views about the measures necessary to protect native industry, it was external pressures that finally acted as the catalyst for legislative measures in Greece concerning the management of industrial property. During the Paris Peace Conference in 1919, it was made clear that:

Greece's reluctance to accept the globally acknowledged obligations in relation to the respect of commercial and industrial property is a set-back in the fulfilment of the international obligations of the Greek State and thus Greek alignment with the international Treaties of Paris, Brussels and Washington is essential...[19]

In late 1920 and 1921, pressure was exerted by the League of Nations; on November 19, 1920 an Extraordinary Economics Committee was established to report on necessary measures to secure fair competition. In this context the intensification of the existing agreements was suggested.[20] The quest for Greek compliance with international agreements and treaties regulating issues of the management of intellectual property, along with the technocratic pressure from engineering and scientific circles for new regulatory and legislative systems, reflected the liberal ideals of the centrist government of Eleftherios Venizelos. Internal and external pressures shared common ground: first, an emphasis on necessity for new legislation and, secondly, an emphasis on the rights of the individual to invent and to capitalize on their innovative ideas. Both priorities were at the center of Venizelos's political agenda. Greece's first patent law – the 2527 Law – came into force in 1920.[21] The new legal framework was part and parcel of the political and ideological strategy of the liberal government. The emphasis was on the importance for a "bourgeois modernization" of the state. New institutions were founded, and a new constitution was established with the intention of rationalizing

---

[19] "Greece's Ratification of the Paris–Brussels–Washington Agreement for 'The Establishment of a Union for the Protection of the Industrial Property'," *Bulletin of Commercial and Industrial Chamber of Athens* (1925): 653.
[20] G. Voudouris, "The International Interest for the Commercial and Industrial Fair Competition," *Official Bulletin of Industrial Property* 3 (1924): 41–4.
[21] Themidos Code [Κώδηξ Θέμιδος], 1920.

state affairs.[22] The values of the bourgeois classes of professionals influenced the novel institutional and legislative reforms. In this political and ideological context the establishment of patents as rights of individuals was deemed as an act of political liberalism.

The 2527 Patent Law was a pioneering attempt to approach patents as fundamentally the rights of individuals over their own ideas, innovative methods, or techniques. The Greek legislators proposed a patent as a fifteen-year monopoly whilst making provision for a period of three years as necessary for development and commercial exploitation of the invention.[23] While this new patent law gave the inventor rights over the potential monopoly that might be established, it did not provide rights over the property itself.[24] Emphasis was thus given not only to originality as a criterion for the award of a patent but also to the potential for transformation of the idea into an industrial application.[25] This law was also an initial attempt in Greece to define the term "invention" and to integrate it into the legislative system. It is significant that the geographic origin of the inventions was emphasized so that innovation and originality were defined in terms of territorial boundaries.

The new legislation's second article stated that: "Inventions will not be considered as new if, at the time of filing of the patent, they were well known in the Kingdom or there were already [public] descriptions or designs in [the region of] Greece that could result in their practical application by an expert."[26] The law's territorial emphasis reflected a governmental industrial policy strategy that aimed at combining establishing an attractive setting for foreign inventors and industrialists to invest in Greece with technology transfer from abroad by native inventors and innovators specifically through imitation. Article 4 of the law made

[22] G. Mavrogordatos, "Venizelos and Civic Modernization," in *Venizelos and Civic Modernization*, ed. G. Mavrogordatos and C. Hatziiosif (Crete: Crete University Press, 1988), 9–19; N. Alivizatos, "Eleftherios Venizelos and the Constitutional Reform of the Country," in ibid., 33–43; Christina Agriantoni, "Venizelos and Economic Policy," in *Eleftherios Venizelos: The Trials of Statesmanship*, ed. P. Kitromilides (Edinburgh: Edinburgh University Press, 2006), 284–318; S. Tzokas, *Eleftherios Venizelos and the Bourgeois Modernization Project 1928–1932: The Construction of a Bourgeois State* (Athens: Themelio, 2002) (in Greek); Mark Mazower, *Greece and the Inter-war Economic Crisis* (Oxford: Clarendon Press, 1991); Nikos Psiroukis, *Fascism and the 4th of August Regime* (Lefkosia: Aegean Publications, 1994) (in Greek); Th. Veremis and M. Mazower, "The Greek Economy 1922–1941," in *Aspects of Greece: The Metaxas Dictatorship*, ed. Th. Veremis and R. Higham (Athens: ELIAMEP-Vryonis Center, 1993), 111–30.
[23] Article 7 and Article 9, Themidos Code [Κώδηξ Θέμιδος], 1920.
[24] Chr. Agallopoulos, "The Protection of Inventions in Greece," *Official Bulletin of Industrial Property* 1 (1926): 1.
[25] Article 1, Themidos Code [Κώδηξ Θέμιδος], 1920.
[26] Article 2, Themidos Code [Κώδηξ Θέμιδος], 1920.

clear that the government should develop a pragmatic approach and institute a "first to file" patent system that would keep the necessary bureaucracy to a minimum and thus reduce cost to, and investment by, the Greek state.[27]

Greece's new patent system became part of an international intellectual property regime that originated in the 1883 Paris Treaty and was strengthened with the Washington Treaty in June 1911. On August 18, 1924, Greece applied to join the International Union of Industrial Property Protection:[28] a political decision that was deemed by native bureaucratic elites as a necessary step for the capitalist transformation of the country and its participation in the international political economy of innovation. Voudouris, head of the Hellenic Office of Industrial Property, argued that the quest to internationalize the Greek patent system should be seen as part and parcel of a regime of fair competition at an international scale. This argument for fairness in the competitive capitalist economy, enforced by international treaties, was the basis for wider arguments for social and political legitimization of the internationalist trend. Furthermore, Voudouris suggested practical advantages to the international integration of the Greek system. First, Greek industry would be more attractive to foreign industrial interests and inventors since with the ratification of international treaties they would feel more secure from misappropriations by local inventors and investors. Second, but equally importantly, with the new legislative measures and agreements Greek trademarks would secure their value and symbolic capital in the international setting, improving the position of Greek export businesses.[29]

By 1920 the Greek government had signed the Paris agreement for the establishment of the European Patent Office in Brussels.[30] This integration of the Greek patent system into the international regime of patent rights brought two important institutional changes to Greece. The first was the institutionalization of a unit of industrial property within the auspices of the Ministry of Finance and the second was the publication of the *Official Bulletin of Industrial Property* (Επίσημον Δελτίον Βιομηχανικής Ιδιοκτησίας) in which patents awarded would be registered.[31] Since the system did not provide for an examination process and encompassed an

---

[27] Article 4, Themidos Code [Κώδηξ Θέμιδος], 1920.
[28] Greece's official participation started on October 2, 1924.
[29] G. A. Voudouris, "International Union for the Protection of Industrial Property," *Official Bulletin of Industrial Property* 1 (1924): 1–2.
[30] The agreement had not been ratified until 1926. See Agallopoulos, "Protection of Inventions."
[31] Voudouris, "International Union for the Protection of Industrial Property," 1.

approach aimed at keeping bureaucracy to a minimum, the published information provided in the *Official Bulletin of Industrial Property* was restricted to only the inventor's name (or that of his agent), the invention's title, and the date the patent was granted.[32] The earliest patent specification available in the Hellenic Office of Industrial Property is for a "Manual Washing Machine" in 1920, and reads: "The [patent] in-hand is granted with no prior examination, and is the responsibility of the applicant and with no guarantee by the State for its real nature, neither for its originality nor for the value or the nature of the invention nor for its accuracy and its trustworthiness."[33] The inventor was thus configured both as author of the specification and as sole bearer of the responsibility for the trustworthiness of his claims and statements.

The Greek legislature created with this law the figure of a rational and moral inventor who, while having rights as an individual to capitalize on his innovations and ideas through a regime of exclusive use and monopolies, also bore the ethical duty of guaranteeing the complete publication of information. Within this legal and legislative framework provision was specifically made for the patenting of pharmaceuticals. In this respect, Greece was an outlier in the European setting since, in the early twentieth century, countries including England, Belgium, Germany, Bulgaria, Poland, and Russia excluded drugs of the pharmaceutical industry from patent protection.[34] While in other national regulatory cultures, an administrative regime would guarantee the public welfare, in Greece the emphasis was solely on individual inventors' rights. The establishment of a culture of publication and openness helped to avoid the pitfalls of secretive regimes in the chemical and pharmaceutical industries.

Yet soon the growing involvement of nonprofessional medical doctors and pharmacists in patenting increased the pressure from relevant professionals on the Greek state to change legislation. Thus, the state's concern about the applicability of patents to pharmaceuticals resulted initially in the partial abolition of such patents in 1926, with complete elimination following six years later. On June 8, 1926, the dictatorial regime of Theodore Pagkalos introduced the exception of drugs and

---

[32] *Official Bulletin of Industrial Property* 1 (October 1924) [Επίσημον Δελτίον Βιομηχανικής Ιδιοκτησίας 1 (Οκτώβριος 1924)].

[33] Ioannis Miltos and Konstantinos Krikos, "Manual Washing Machine," No. 4, Application Date December 4, 1920, in *The First Patents in Greece, Anniversary Edition 1920–1925*, Hellenic Office of Industrial Property, 5, www.obi.gr/OBI/Portals/0/ImagesAndFiles/Files/w_epetiaki_ekdosi.pdf (last accessed August 7, 2019).

[34] For a historical overview of the interrelation of law and pharmaceuticals in nineteenth- and twentieth-century Europe and the USA, see Graham Dutfield, *Intellectual Property Rights and the Life Science Industries: Past, Present and Future*, 2nd ed. (London: WorldScientific, 2009).

pharmaceutical products in Greek patent law. The changes introduced specified that all existing patents on drug innovations must be approved by the Ministry of Internal Affairs, more specifically by the Supreme Health and Safety Council.[35] The complete exclusion of pharmaceuticals from patenting was completed with the 5607 Act of 1932 that prohibited all drug patents for public health and anti-monopolist reasons.[36] Emphasis was placed on securing equal access to drugs rather than guaranteeing the right to invent and secure monopolies to individuals and companies.

By 1926 the Greek government introduced changes in patent law in order to secure fair competition and to prevent misappropriation of inventions. In the changes introduced in June 1926, the second article required that the patentee make clear that the application had not been subject to any state-approved examination process for the originality and the applicability of the invention.[37] Patent law, its use, and the effected changes were conceived by legislators and legal scholars as tools to regulate commercial and professional activities rather than as a law to attribute or restore appropriate awards and credit. In 1925, Thrasimvoulos Petmezas, professor of commercial law at the University of Athens, in his highly read handbook on commercial law, introduced an understanding of patents as protection of the industrial and commercial professions and of salaried work. He argued that patents were necessary as tools to regulate commercial and professional life and to secure healthy competition and protection of professional and business activities.[38] Petmezas understood industrial property legislation as a regulatory entity that combined the 2527 law of industrial property together with articles of the law of fair competition and articles of the penal code. The term "industrial property" referred to the protection of patentable inventions, trademarks, names of industrial and commercial products, names of geographic areas and regions of origin of specific products, industrial secrets (*secret de fabrication*), and professional secrecy.[39]

---

[35] "Alterations of the Provisions Relating to Patents and Unfair Competition," *Official Bulletin of Industrial Property* 8 (1926): 110 ["Περί τροποποιήσεως των περι ευρεσιτεχνίας και αθέμιτου ανταγωνισμού διάταξεων," Επίσημον Δελτίον Βιομηχανικής Ιδιοκτησίας 8 (1926): 110].

[36] Act 5607/August 27, 1932, Govermental Gazette, 300 issue A', September 5, 1932 [ΝΟΜΟΣ 5607/Αυγούστου 27, 1932, ΦΕΚ 300 τεύχος Α', Σεπτεμβρίου 5, 1932].

[37] G. A. Voudouris, "Comments on the Act for the Alterations in the Provisions Relating to Patents and Unfair Competition," *Official Bulletin of Industrial Property* 8 (1926): 109–10.

[38] Thrasimvoulos Petmezas, "Provisions for the Protection of the Trade Profession," *Official Bulletin of Industrial Property* 8 (1925), 164–8; 9 (1925), 179–84; 10 (1925), 200–3.

[39] Petmezas, 8 (1925), 165 and 168.

While Petmezas presented an instrumentalist approach in the development and function of the law regarding industrial property matters, a
dominant ideology developed through the public intervention of legal,
industrial, and engineering actors who viewed invention as a proprietary
right over innovations and ideas. Legal scholar Agallopoulos argued in
his essay on "The Protection of Inventions in Greece" that patents
should be viewed as a social contract between the inventor and society.
Industrial property was represented as a state tool rather than as a moral
right like intellectual property.[40] Yet Agallopoulos nevertheless acknowledged that the proprietary right was a peculiar right that would only be a
temporary means to guarantee potential financial credit and symbolic
capital to the inventor. After expiration, no mention of the inventor
would be required. Its knowledge should be circulated and freely used.
Agallopoulos approached the patent as a necessary monopoly to boost
entrepreneurial activities organized around inventions. In his public
statements he constructed a heroic image of the inventors whose
immense struggles to innovate were acknowledged even by the revolutionary communist regime of Russia.[41] The social and political legitimization of the patent system went in tandem with focusing upon the role
of individuals in driving the national economy.

Engineers and industrial scientists promoted this ideology through
their public interventions. For them the issue at stake in the interwar
period was the establishment of a stronger intellectual property regime
and its integration into in techno-scientific activities. It was a period of
emerging technocratic ideals where science and engineering appeared as
the forces that would change and transform Greek society and state.[42]
A strong legislative imposition would entrench the position and interests
of industrial scientists as critical to the country's economic life. Dimitrios
Zannos, an industrial scientist, argued that a strong and stable patent
system would regulate relations in the industrial sector by creating hierarchies and distributing economic and symbolic capital.[43] He argued that
patent rights were a necessary tool for the establishment of "science-
based" industries in the innovation system of the country and, more

---

[40] Chr. Agallopoulos, "Protection of Inventions in Greece," *Official Bulletin of Industrial Property* 11 (1925), 218–20; 12 (1925), 238–40; 1 (1926), 1–4.
[41] Agallopoulos 11 (1925), 218–20.
[42] Yiannis Antoniou, *Greek Engineers, Institutions and Ideas (1900–1940)* (Athens: VIVLIORAMA, 2006), 126–40, 150–64, and 181–93 (in Greek); Yiannis Antoniou and Vassilis Bogiatzis, "Technology and Totalitarian Ideas in Interwar Greece," *Journal of History of Science and Technology* 4 (2010): 50–61.
[43] Dimitrios Zannos, "Industry and Science," *Industrial Review [Βιομηχανική Επιθεώρηση]* (July 1939): 12.

generally, he stressed that patent rights would provide the government and the state with a tool to control and direct entrepreneurial and innovative activities and relations.

In 1938, E. Patrinos, a professional scientist-engineer, inventor, patent agent and representative of other patentees in Greece, went so far as to promote the idea of "Scientific Property" along the lines of "Industrial Property." His aim was the introduction of a regulatory system that would protect scientists' – more accurately "pure scientists'" – ideas and discoveries from illegal and immoral misappropriation.[44]

Three years later, in September 1941, the height of the Nazi occupation, Patrinos reported on the issue of Industrial Property to the Technical Chamber of Athens, the leading engineering institution in Greece and official advisor of the Greek state. He urged the Technical Chamber to take initiatives toward a stronger and stricter industrial property law. In the new legislative context, new and extended criteria of originality and applicability should be introduced. For Patrinos, the problems of the Greek patent system started with the fact that there was no examination process and thus no assessment of the innovativeness of invention. He supported a stronger patent law that would cover industrial designs and would also guarantee the protection of technologies and artifacts shown in national and international exhibitions. Furthermore, Patrinos suggested to the Technical Chamber the establishment of a Technical Council as an independent consultative and expert panel on issues of industrial property. He favored an institution similar to the French Comité Technique de la Propriete Industrielle (Technical Committee for the Industrial Property, 1920) and the Italian Consiglio Delle Privative Industriali e Dei Marchi (Council of Industrial Privileges and Trade Marks, 1934). His main argument emphasized the necessity of a new bureaucracy that would guarantee efficient examination of inventions and better cataloging, archiving, and systematization of information.[45] Patrinos's proposal resonated well with the technocratic ideals promoted by an exclusive circle of engineers who, during the Nazi occupation, were working closely with the National Bank of Greece and the Technical Chamber and masterminded the technological transformation of the country during and after the war. Patrinos's scheme fulfilled those ideals

---

[44] E. Patrinos, "The Proprietary Status of Scientific Discoveries," *Financial Postman* [Οικονομικός Ταχυδρόμος] (November 21, 1938): 1.

[45] E. Patrinos, "The Contribution of the Technical Chamber of Greece in Relation to the Institution of the Protection of Industrial Property," *Technical Chronicles* [Τεχνικά Χρονικά] (September 1–15, 1941): 218–22.

and encouraged new roles both for the individual engineers and for the Technical Chamber as an organization. Furthermore, there is no question that his professional expertise as a patent agent also influenced his proposals. The establishment of a strict system of examination would indeed bring social, professional, and epistemological validation to the profession of patent agent and industrial property consultant.

The lack of an examination process in Greek patent law was an issue of concern in industrial and engineering circles. In promoting the necessity of such a process, the important engineering journal 'Εργα (*Works*) reported the absurdity of the Greek patents and their inapplicability. Criticizing the transmission of legislative and regulatory regimes from other national contexts without a process of adjustment and critical appropriation, it was argued that the Greek patent system promoted patenting of wasteful, pointless, and trivial innovations.[46] The journal's editorial made clear that "[s]ometime we read patents for inventions that are irrational and call for the psychological examination" of their inventors, but it is "almost impossible to think that this would result in [useful] patents."[47] Satirically criticizing the Greek patent system, the leading industrial journal, Βιομηχανική Επιθεώρηση (*Industrial Transactions*), expressing the views of the Association of Greek Industrialists, published a series of humorous descriptions of Greek inventions. By 1950, 12,510 patents had been granted and the journal was writing about the "Nation of Inventions" and the "Walk in the garden of Greek patents – patents for all uses!" Patents for a method of typing by foot that would save the female manicure, or fighting methods exclusively for children, were described in order to criticize and condemn the existing situation and to press for a serious alteration of the system.[48] Despite the continuous pressures, a stronger intellectual property regime was enforced by the World Trade Organization and the European Commission in the mid-1980s. The new legislative changes were linked with the integration of the country in the European Commission and a further attempt for homogenization with the European legislative culture of the period.[49]

---

[46] *Works* 111 (January 15, 1930): 404 [Εργα 111 (Ιανουαρίου 15, 1930): 404].   [47] Ibid.
[48] F. P. Konstantinidis, "Walk in the Garden of Greek Inventions," *Industrial Review* 17 (1950): 23–4.
[49] Stathis Arapostathis, "Intellectual Property Law and Politics in 20th Century Greece," in Lifting Barriers to Empower the Future of Information Law and Ethics, Proceedings of the 6th International Conference of Information Law and Ethics, ed. M. Bottis, E. Alexandropoulou, and I. Iglezakis (Thessaloniki: University of Macedonia Press, 2016), 422–430.

8.5   Conclusion

In mapping the evolution of modern Greek patent law up to World War II, I have emphasized the coproductive nature of the legislative and political changes involved: legislative transformations went hand in hand with the country's political and economic transition. This development follows the pattern of Biagioli's diagnosis of Western patent laws shifting from an intellectual property regime of tradition of presentation of invention to one of its *re*presentation.[50] In the latter case, processes of political emancipation in Greece characteristically triggered (as elsewhere) a new thoroughly techno-scientific society. In the second decade of the twentieth century Greece's national patent law circumscribed the originality of an idea as needing to be demonstrable only within existing national borders. As with other emerging industrial nations, this enabled it to secure patents on prior innovations abroad and thus secure a knowledge transfer mechanism for innovation through mimesis.[51]

Taking a broader view beyond Greece's borders, however, we see that Greece could not entirely resist the broader global context of changing patent law conventions. Transnational pressures toward the homogenization of laws and of innovation policies functioned in a symbiotic way with the ongoing reconfiguration of Greece's place in the broader European political context. International treaties that directed innovation policies toward "strong" intellectual property systems thus obliged Greece to strengthen the implementation of its own patent laws with a new ideology of proprietary regimes of inventive knowledge that displaced traditional forms of nepotistic "privilege." During the interwar period then, emerging technocratic ideals adopted by a succession of Greek governments created new roles for industrial scientists and engineers in state and economic affairs that also forged a fully proprietary understanding of how patenting should be used in a capitalist system.

---

[50] M. Biagioli, "Patent Republic: Specifying Inventions, Constructing Authors and Rights," *Social Research* 73 (2006): 1129–72; M. Biagioli, "Patent Specification and Political Representation: How Patents Became Rights," in *Making and Unmaking Intellectual Property: Creative Production in Legal and Cultural Perspective*, ed. M. Biagioli, P. Jaszi, and M. Woodmansee (Chicago: Chicago University Press, 2011), 25–39.

[51] Kranakis, "Patents and Power," 693.

9   Mediation and Harmonization
Construction of the Spanish Patent System in the Twentieth Century

Ana Romero de Pablos

9.1   Introduction

Mediation and harmonization are two key words that aptly summarize the Spanish patent system of the twentieth century. Patents have served as intermediaries, and the manner of their regulation has generated complaints from both within and beyond Spain. To analyze this reality, I will compare two case studies that illustrate different patent cultures, subject to specific times and places: the introduction between 1948 and 1950 of the main patents to protect penicillin production processes in Spain under the law of 1929, and the 1988 market launch of the Spanish patent "An improved method for determining the nucleotide base sequence of a DNA molecule," under the 1986 law. Both cases highlight a significant issue within the processes of harmonization and mediation: the language in which a patent is written does not necessarily need to coincide with the language required by the legitimizing formalities. Patents are therefore subject to different mediations, and have been, and still are, points of conflict in attempts at international harmonization.

The first case study, the arrival in Spain of the first North American patents to protect penicillin production, illustrates this mediating role. The second, the market launch of a Spanish patent for a DNA polymerase, the product of research carried out in a Spanish laboratory and patented in the United States in 1988, demonstrates the effect of local regulations and the limitations of international harmonization.

Patents connected practices, languages, and interests from different Spanish and North American professional communities – clinical, industrial, and political – at the end of the 1940s, the beginning of the 1950s, and through the 1980s. While penicillin patents attracted US industry to the Spanish market – which was, as we will see, not highly competitive but fully able to incorporate new technologies – the polymerase patent had the opposite effect: a group of Spanish researchers, at the suggestion of an American university professor with links to the industry, protected their invention in the United States before doing so in Spain.

These two case studies demonstrate the multiplicity of actors who participate in the construction of inventions and patents[1] and bring to mind the concept that Carolyn C. Cooper has termed "patent management."[2] Patents are more than legal documents with technical descriptions; they are also interesting political instruments.[3] These cases present different patent cultures, each subject to a specific time and place:[4] they allow an analysis that goes beyond the local and national space, suggesting a redistribution of the places where knowledge is produced and challenge the use of terms such as transference and appropriation. A more suitable term, I would suggest, is circulation: a circulation always mediated by homogenizing logic and local cultures. The importance of local history lies in the local actors who incorporate and shape knowledge and practices. The cases studied here take on a greater significance in the framework of common networks of interaction woven by people, laboratories, tools, technologies, practices, and politics.[5]

The years 1929 and 1986 were crucial for patent legislation in contemporary Spain.[6] From the Estatuto de la Propiedad Industrial (Industrial Property Statute, EPI in its Spanish acronym) of 1929 until 1986, the year in which the Spanish Law on Patents (LP) was approved, important political, economic, and technical changes took place that had severe repercussions for social development.

The law of 1929 was created at a time of intense tension between the process of modernization, begun at the outset of the twentieth century, and the authoritarian political control of Primo de Rivera's dictatorship (1923-9). Antiquated authoritarian attempts to reduce social and political problems did not limit public works programs and the introduction of new technologies. These technologies – including electricity, the telephone, and an increased use of automobiles and other means of

---

[1] C. Bazerman, *The Languages of Edison's Light* (Cambridge, MA: MIT Press, 1999); A. Guagnini, "Patent, Agents, Legal Advisers, and Marconi's Breakthrough in Wireless Telegraphy," *History of Technology* 24 (2002): 171–201.

[2] Carolyn Cooper, "Social Construction of Invention through Patent Management: Thomas Blanchard's Woodworking Machinery," *Technology and Culture* 32 (1991): 960–88.

[3] S. Parthasarathy, "The Patent Is Political: The Consequences of Patenting the BRCA Genes in Britain," *Community Genet* 8 (2005): 235–42.

[4] G. Bowker, "What's in a Patent?" in *Shaping Technology/Building Society*, ed. Wiebe Bijker and John Law (Cambridge, MA: MIT Press, 1994), 53–74.

[5] D. Edgerton, "De la innovación al uso: diez tesis eclécticas," *Quaderns d'història de l'ingenieria* IV (2004): 1–23.

[6] Industrial Property Statute, approved by the Royal Decree-Law of June 26, 1929. Published in *La Gaceta* no. 127, May 7, 1930. The Law on Patents (*Ley de patentes de invención y modelos de utilidad* 11/1986). Published in the *Boletin Oficial del Estado* (*BOE*), March 26, 1986.

transport – had developed rapidly since the beginning of the twentieth century, making a reconsideration of patent policies imperative. In this context, a new type of patent was introduced: the Patent of Exploitation. This was added to the already existing Patent of Invention (twenty years) and Patent of Introduction (ten years), and was designed to cover objects already invented but not put into practice in Spain, to protect any kind of industrial development that had not previously existed, or that incorporated novel refinements of those already existing, over ten years, as long as they were in the interests of national industry.

Unlike Patents of Introduction, a Patent of Exploitation could continue beyond ten years, provided no new innovation had been added. Although this patent was in force for barely two months – it was repealed under the Royal Decree-Law of March 15, 1930 – it illustrates the attitude of the Spanish authorities: their willingness to encourage and support the introduction of new technologies, and recognition of the responsibility to fulfill international agreements. The speed with which the Patent of Exploitation was eliminated highlights two interesting issues I will address in this chapter: the conflict between local and transnational legislation, and the harmonization of patents required within a common regulatory space.[7]

The law of 1986 was enacted under very different circumstances. Since the law of 1929 the country had undergone a civil war (1936–9), the Franco dictatorship (1939–75), and on January 1, 1986, as a democratic country, Spain had joined the European Economic Community. Between 1939 and 1955 – the year in which Spain was accepted into the United Nations – the country had remained politically isolated.[8] It was not entirely commercially isolated, however, and Francoist autarkic policies were designed to favor native industrial development by imposing restrictions on foreign imports.[9] Despite having a negligible effect on industrial development for many years,[10] this protectionism did create

[7] J. P. Sáiz González, *Legislación histórica sobre propiedad industrial. España (1759–1929)* (Madrid: Oficina Española de Patentes y Marcas, 1996), 473.

[8] F. Portero, *Franco aislado La cuestión española (1945–1950)* (Madrid: Aguilar, 1989); J. Lleonart and F. Castiella, *España y la ONU: la cuestión española*, vols. I–VI (Madrid: CSIC, 1978–2002).

[9] S. López, *El saber tecnológico en la política industrial del primer franquismo* (Madrid: Universidad Complutense, 2002).

[10] J. Catalán, "Industrialización difusa y desarrollo económico: el retroceso de 1939–58," in *La cara oculta de la industrialización española. La modernización de los sectores no líderes (siglos XIX y XX)*, ed. Jordi Nadal and Jordi Catalán (Madrid: Alianza, 1994), 369–97; J. Catalán, *La economía española y la segunda guerra mundial* (Barcelona: Ariel, 1995); F. Guirao, "Naranjas y piritas: los embajadores de Franco en la inmediata segunda postguerra mundial," in *Economía y economistas españoles en la Guerra Civil*, vol. 2, ed. Enrique Fuentes Quintana and Francisco Comín (Barcelona: Galaxia Gutemberg/ Círculo de Lectores, 2009), 555–603.

the basis for the effective development of imports from the end of the autarkic period onwards.[11] Patents were the legal space where technologies could enter an economy like Spain's, which was centered on sectors such as agriculture, construction, and services.[12] There was even a proposal to modify the EPI, the most notable attempt being made between 1956 and 1966 by the Justice Section of the Institute for Policy Studies. No modifications were made, however, due to the lack of both political will and practical necessity.[13] It was entrance into the European Community that necessitated making Spanish patent legislation – as well as legislation in other areas – compatible with that of other member states. A draft law on patents dating to 1981 had content very similar to that later approved in 1986.[14]

Following Franco's death in November 1975, Spain experienced immense political, economic, and social change. For many historians the new Constitution of December 1978 ended the period known as the Transition, which began with the death of the dictator, and in which a series of political events transformed the Francoist regime into a social state with democratic rule of law, under the political form of a parliamentary monarchy.

Between 1929 and 1986, therefore, significant changes – political, social, economic, and industrial – favored the arrival of foreign patents, the creation of new spaces for research, and new opportunities for industry. Although it took time for these changes to be incorporated into Spanish legislation on industrial property, they had a significant effect on scientific, technological, and industrial practice.

The journey from one law to the other and the two cases outlined here, contain distinctive elements to reflect on patent culture in Spain. The political, social, and economic changes that protection systems demand differ from one place to another, and do not always coincide with voices calling for harmonization.

9.2   Penicillin Patents in Spain

The first patents granted in Spain to protect penicillin production were the subject and object of mediation: they connected researchers,

---

[11] M. Cebrián and S. López, "Economic Growth, Technology Transfer and Convergence in Spain, 1960–73," in *Technology and Human Capital in Historical Perspective*, ed. Jonas Ljungberg and Jan Pieter Smits (New York: Palgrave McMillan, 2004), 120–44.

[12] J. M. Ortiz Villajos, "International Patenting in Spain before the Civil War," *History of Technology* 24 (2002): 203–32.

[13] A. Bercovitz, *La nueva Ley de Patentes. Ideas introductorias y antecedentes* (Barcelona: Tecnos, 1986).

[14] Ibid., 89–100.

politicians, and healthcare authorities with procedures, instruments, and facilities; they brought politics and policies to industrial and research spaces; and they mediated in processes associated with training and practices. At the same time, the necessary translations, the obligatory changes in the way to state claims and in certification, the putting of these into practice, and the effective use of the content of patents, all turned them into objects of mediation.

In 1948, the Ministry of Industry declared the manufacturing of penicillin to be of "national interest." The decision to construct two plants to produce these antibiotics, under strict state control, was made public. At this time, Spanish doctors, pharmacists, and the general public were well aware of the therapeutic properties of this drug. The trip that Antonio Gallego took to the Merck plant in Rahway, New Jersey, at the beginning of 1949 – at the request of Spain's only industrial bank, Banco Urquijo – is a good example of the role played by doctors: the agreement signed by Merck and Banco Urquijo in January 1949 marked the initial step in the competition to install these factories or manufactory plants.[15]

In July of 1948, the first application for a patent to obtain penicillin was made to the Spanish Patents and Trademarks Office (Oficina Española de Patentes y Marcas, OEPM, in its Spanish acronym) by the Danish company, Lovens Kemische Fabrik. Alexander Fleming, regarded as the discoverer of penicillin, had been given a hero's welcome by the Spanish authorities when he visited Madrid and Barcelona a month earlier. This trip had been used politically to portray the Francoist regime as being on the side of progress and modernity.[16]

Compañía Española de Penicilinas y Antibióticos (CEPA) and Antibióticos S.A. were the companies created to compete for penicillin production within Spain. Although the Danish company was the first to apply for the patents, it was Merck and Schenley[17] that obtained the contracts. CEPA produced penicillin with patents from Merck; Antibióticos S.A. with those of Schenley.[18] The correspondence at the time – of the granting of the first patents, the notice of competition,

[15] M. J. Santesmases, *The Circulation of Penicillin in Spain: Health, Wealth and Authority* (London: Palgrave Macmillan, 2018).
[16] Ibid. Images from No-Do (Noticiarios y Documentales), a state-controlled series of newsreels and documentaries, which show Fleming's visit to Spain: 283 A Year VI, 284 B Year VI, 637 B Year XIII. Filmoteca Española Archive.
[17] Patents 184673, 187178, 187313, 187312, 187371, 187378, 188188, 188260, 190142, 190143, 193056, 194256. OEPM Archive, Madrid.
[18] A. Romero de Pablos, "Regulation and the Circulation of Knowledge: Penicillin Patents in Spain," *Dynamis* 31(2) (2011): 363–84.

and the allocation of plants – suggests a well-planned and carefully thought-out process.[19]

As such, a new area for the pharmaceutical industry was opened under a government that authorized and controlled the construction of a market to license patents.[20] Regulations were the connecting point between the scientific and the technological, the political and the institutional, between private initiative and society.[21] As we shall see, diverse practices and languages became homogenized due to patent regulations. Penicillin patents were more than just legal documents with technical descriptions: they became useful political tools for the Francoist government.[22]

The first problem faced by foreign companies was the impossibility of patenting drugs or pharmaceutical products in Spain. Political and economic concerns had led to this prohibition, particularly the beliefs that product patents could facilitate industrial secrecy, diminish incentives for industry to continue carrying out research, and encourage price fixing.[23] Therefore, what was patentable were the processes and equipment used to obtain products. For this reason, Merck and Schenley had to modify the wording of their claims, ensuring they referred to the processes not the products. Some claims were redrafted with more general headings, while others were completely removed from the final draft. The initial invention descriptions laid out the terms and limits the inventor wished to establish, and therefore, what he or she wanted to protect. The final text indicates how this knowledge was to be protected from then on. This is a good example of how patent specifications are subject to modifications and changes according to place and context.[24] Thus, regulations determined how the contents of patents were expressed, making patents both the object and subject of mediation processes.[25]

The Spanish tendency to import technologies, and the absence of technical examination in the EPI of 1929, have been cited by many as driving the interest of foreign industries in presenting patents for

---

[19] Decrees published, respectively, in the *BOE* of October 6, 1948 and in the *BOE* of August 11, 1949.

[20] N. Puig, "Networks of Innovation or Networks of Opportunity? The Making of the Spanish Antibiotics Industry," *Ambix* LI(2) (2004): 167–85.

[21] Bazerman, *Languages*; Guagnini, "Wireless Telegraphy"; S. Arapostathis, and G. Gooday, *Patently Contestable: Electrical Technologies and Inventor Identities on Trial in Britain* (Cambridge, MA: MIT Press, 2013).

[22] Parthasarathy, "Patent Is Political."

[23] A. Bercovitz, *La patentabilidad de las invenciones y la industria químico-farmacéutica* (Madrid: Montecorvo, 1978); C. Lema Devesa and A. Tato Plaza, *Patentes farmacéuticas y el tratado ADPIC* (Granada: Comares, 2008).

[24] Bowker, "What's in a Patent?"   [25] Romero de Pablos, "Regulation," 377.

penicillin production. But files kept in the OEPM archive show that the strategy used by North American companies in Spain was similar to that used in other countries: the applications made in Spain were made in other European countries at the same time.[26] The Spanish geopolitical situation, along with the fact that the pharmaceutical industry was mostly made up of small companies, explains the willingness to patent and produce penicillin in Spain. Nevertheless, the North American pharmaceutical companies' desire for expansion should not be forgotten.[27]

The 1929 law favored those Spanish industrial firms capable of taking advantage of imported technical developments. Patents have been considered some of the principal paths for technological appropriation,[28] but it is also necessary to state that part of the Spanish pharmaceutical industry was able to benefit from international technical improvements. The screening program for new antibiotics established by CEPA and Merck in Madrid in 1954 is a good example of this. This program – that opened a research laboratory inside a manufacturing space – incorporated techniques and tools, both physical and conceptual, originating from industrial production.[29]

By the mid-1960s, support for a revision of the ban on patenting pharmaceutical products had grown significantly and in 1986, when Spain joined the European Patent Convention (EPC), the prohibition was officially lifted. Lobbying by the pharmaceutical industry, however, succeeded in delaying implementation until October 7, 1992.[30]

9.3   The DNA Polymerase Patents

The second case I examine is the 1989 Spanish patent entitled "An improved method for determining the nucleotide base sequence of a DNA molecule." Research, techniques, and laboratory practices form part of this patent, but it also reflects the changes in Spanish economic, industrial, and scientific policies since the 1960s. These changes were in response to new realities and contributed to the formation of new cultures. The patent resulted from research carried out in the molecular

---

[26] Ibid., 377–8.

[27] Robert Bud, *Penicillin: Triumph and Tragedy* (Oxford: Oxford University Press, 2007).

[28] M. Cebrián, "¿Apropiación o mercado?: industria farmacéutica, patentes y poder de mercado," in *En torno a la propiedad: estudios en homenaje al profesor Ricardo Robledo*, ed. Salustiano de Dios, Javier Infante Miguel-Motta, and Eugenia Torijano Pérez (Salamanca, Spain: Ediciones Universidad de Salamanca, 2013), 179–90.

[29] M. J. Santesmases, The Circulation of Penicillin in Spain; M. J. Santesmases, "The Long Postwar and the Politics of Penicillin: Early Circulation and Smuggling in Spain, 1944–1954," *Medicina nei Secoli [Journal of History of Medicine]* 26(2) (2014): 615–38.

[30] Lema Devesa and Tato Plaza, *Patentes*.

biology laboratory of a public research center in Madrid, the Centro de Biología Molecular (Centre for Molecular Biology) at the Consejo Superior de Investigaciones Científicas (Spanish National Research Council, CSIC in its Spanish acronym). The developments introduced since the end of the 1950s – nuclear energy, biochemistry, and molecular biology are good examples – needed to be harmonized with policies, institutions, management styles, and legislation.[31] But this patent also shows how unusual patenting was for research scientists. Neither the work undertaken in the laboratory since the mid-1960s, nor the decisions made, indicates a consideration of possible industrial applications.

Following the Napoleonic invasion as it did, the law of 1929 had been strongly influenced by the French: the 1986 Law meant that, once again, Spanish legislation would be subject to Europeanization. It incorporated, almost literally, the decisions made at the Munich Convention on European patents in 1973 and the Luxembourg Convention of 1975 in relation to European community patents. The Treaty of Accession of Spain to the European Communities on June 12, 1985 (that came into force January 1, 1986) included Protocol No. 8 relating to Spanish patents. This established "the obligation of Spain to modify its patent legislation to be compatible with the free circulation of merchandise and with the level of protection of Industrial Property attained within the Community."[32] It was necessary to harmonize the Spanish system with that of the European Community.

One of the main consequences of harmonization with European regulations was elimination of the Patent of Introduction, considered incompatible with the level of protection for inventions within the European Community. This type of patent, present in Spanish legislation since 1811, was designed to encourage the introduction and exploitation of technologies proven abroad, although it had never been put to significant use.[33]

Modifications made to the admission process in 1986 were also in response to the need for harmonization with Europe. A technical examination and innovation registration were introduced as preliminary requirements.[34] Expectations for the patented innovation were then

---

[31] A. Romero de Pablos and J. M. Sánchez Ron, *Energía nuclear en España. De la JEN al CIEMAT* (Madrid: Doce Calles, 2001); M. J. Santesmases, "Peace Propaganda and Biomedical Experimentation: Radioisotopes in Endocrinology and Molecular Genetics, and Their Influence in Spain (1950–1971)," *Journal of the History of Biology* 39 (2006): 765–98; and also "From Prophylaxis to Atomic Cocktail: Circulation of Radioiodine," *Dynamis* 29 (2009): 337–64.
[32] Bercovitz, *Patentes*, 22.   [33] Ortiz Villajos, "International Patenting," 144–5.
[34] Chapter II, Articles 31–35.

made public, along with an invitation to anyone wishing to challenge certification. A report on the state of the technology was a necessary intermediate step toward a "strong" patent examination system, and an important condition for patents granted in Spain to have the same value as those legitimized by European processes. This strengthened the system, but took time to be incorporated: the system of granting patents subject to a technical examination was introduced only gradually, beginning in September 2001.[35]

In 1988, at a workshop of the European Molecular Biology Organization (EMBO) held in the Spanish city of Salamanca, Charles C. Richardson proposed possible industrial applications of the structure of the DNA polymerase of virus ø29. He was a researcher in the Department of Biological Chemistry and Molecular Pharmacology at Harvard Medical School and scientific advisor for the US start-up United States Biochemical Corporation (USB). Richardson, who at the time was working with another DNA polymerase virus, had been in contact with the Spanish laboratory and was aware of the work being carried out there.

The research being developed in this Spanish laboratory, and the similarities with work being carried out in the United States had attracted Richardson's attention. The first article referred to in the Spanish patent, in which a group of scientists led by Kary Mullis describe the PCR (Polymerase Chain Reaction) technique, dates to 1985. The PCR technique allows the action of a polymerase to be initiated and stopped at specific points on a DNA chain, and for a fragment of DNA to be amplified exponentially for identification and analysis. Improvement in this technique between 1985 and 1989 made it an extremely useful tool for biologists, and, in 1993, Kary Mullis was awarded the Nobel Prize in Chemistry.[36]

The scientific and industrial potential that interested Richardson and USB must also be understood in relation to the space opened up by the Bayh–Dole Act of 1980. Conceived in order for private companies to patent and license research carried out at universities,[37] this act had two

---

[35] Royal Decree 996/2001, *BOE* October 11, 2001, 34130–3.

[36] M. García-Sancho, *Biology, Computing, and the History of Molecular Sequencing: From Proteins to DNA, 1945–2000* (Basingstoke: Palgrave Macmillan, 2012), 160–2 and 200; P. Rabinow, *Making PCR: A Story of Biotechnology* (Chicago: Chicago University Press, 1996); K. Mullis, *Dancing Naked in the Mind Field* (New York: Vintage, 1998).

[37] D. C. Mowery, R. R. Nelson, B. N. Sampat, and A. Ziedonis, "The Growth of Patenting and Licensing by U.S. Universities: An Assessment of the Effects of the Bayh–Dole Act of 1980," *Research Policy* 30(1) (2001): 99–119.

clear consequences: it increased private research funding and resulted in a qualitative decline in academic patent applications.[38]

At this time, the Spanish R&D system did not take financial potential into account: research at universities and Spanish public research centers had been financed with public money since the 1986 Science Law. Additionally, the tendency in Spain has been to publish before patenting. For these reasons, the possibility of patenting played no part in the daily practices of Spanish researchers. USB's managers and researchers played a significant role in preparing the PCR technique patent application. In exchange, they were promised the license for commercial exploitation if the application was accepted. In this case, the mediating role of the patent limited the circulation of knowledge.

The assistance required by the technique's inventors, Luis Blanco, Antonio Bernard, and Margarita Salas, demonstrates how distant the culture of patents was from research laboratories, where priority was given to the presenting and publishing of results. The origin of these attitudes could be the weakness of protection provided by the law of 1929, although there was no custom of patenting in either biological research or biomedicine. Only industrial laboratories pursued patents. Another reason can be found in the organization of the Spanish R&D system: the first offices to transfer technology from universities and public research organizations were only established at the beginning of the 1990s.[39]

The first patent written, "Reactions of the synthesis of DNA (in vitro) that use modified phi29 DNA polymerase and a fragment of DNA that codifies said polymerase," was based on two achievements: the lengthening of a DNA fragment and the production of DNA molecules. Both procedures used the action of the phi29 DNA polymerase.

The patent was applied for at the United States Patent Office in 1988 and granted in March 1989. Blanco, Bernard, and Salas were listed as inventors, and CSIC as proprietor, reflecting the changes made to Spanish legislation since 1986 for job-related patents. The category of "job-related inventions" was designed to promote industrial research. Since the beginning of the twentieth century, various scientific policies

---

[38] B. N. Sampat, D. C. Mowery, and A. Ziedonis, "Changes in University Patent Quality after the Bayh–Dole Act: A Re-examination," *International Journal of Industrial Organization* 21(9) (2003): 1371–90.

[39] D. Represa, E. Castro, and I. Fernández de Lucio, *Promoción de la protección de los resultados de investigación pública española desde el Plan Nacional de I+D: balance de 10 años* (Madrid: OEI, Temas de Iberoamérica, 2003); M. Buesa, "Ciencia y tecnología en la España democrática: la formación de un sistema nacional de innovación," *ICE, 25 años de Constitución española* n° 811 (2003): 235–72.

had been initiated to change the way research in Spain was carried out and managed.[40] The inclusion of job-related inventions reflected a willingness to recognize research being carried out by Spanish firms (namely electrical and nuclear companies, and sugar confectioners), and the need to reconcile the interests of business owners with those of salaried inventors. However, this was not usual practice in state-controlled research centers.

Following approval of the Spanish group's patent, a request was made in March 1990 for it to be included in the worldwide PCT (Patent Corporation Treaty) system, the request being made public in October 1991. The PCT system was a North American initiative designed to quickly and cheaply protect the country's patents throughout the world. Signed in Washington in 1970 and managed by the World Intellectual Property Organization (WIPO), it is currently endorsed by more than 140 countries. Spain's entry into the PCT system came into force in November 1989. This system, which enables applications for "international" protection of inventions to be made without the need to present different national patent applications, has been widely used by public research centers and universities in Spain since the mid-1990s. It facilitates formalities and allows industry to view applications, enabling applicants to be aware of development and licensing possibilities. The actual granting of patents continues to be the responsibility of national offices. This agreement demonstrates, rather than resolves problems, resulting from the lack of harmonization and international uniformity.

The European patent, however, a project launched by the German patent office, simplifies formalities and lowers costs by having a single processing and licensing procedure, while at the same time strengthening European markets against those of North America.

The patent "An improved method for determining the nucleotide base sequence of a DNA molecule" was applied for at the European Patent Office in 1993 and granted in 1997. This is how it returned to Europe, the patent coming into force in Spain in August that year. Following a long journey, the outcome of research carried out in a Spanish laboratory returned to Spain, protected, normalized, and legitimized. The narrative of this patent is an interesting illustration of the dynamics of circulation.

---

[40] M. J. Santesmases and A. Romero de Pablos, *Radiactividad y biología: la física y las ciencias de la vida en el siglo XX* (Madrid: Universidad Autónoma de Madrid Consejo de Seguridad Nuclear, 2003).

9.4 Mediation of Language: A Problem for Harmonization

To be valid in Spain, the patent had to be translated into the Spanish language. The same was true for applications to protect penicillin production. In both cases, the original language had been English; and in both cases, at one moment or another, in one language or another, the mediation of translation was required for entry to the Spanish market. Both the EPI of 1929 and the LP of 1986 deemed that the originality and innovative advancement of the invention and claims had to be expressed in Castilian Spanish. The EPI of 1929 expressly states that: "The innovative advancement will be written in Castilian Spanish, without abbreviations, amendments or erasures, and without restrictive conditions or legal reserves of any type."[41] Clear and precise wording was also used in the claims section to avoid any potential confusion. In the LP of 1986 it is expressed in the same terms: "The application as well as the remaining documents that must be presented to the Industrial Property Registry [as of 1992 the Spanish Patents and Trademarks Office (OEPM)] must be written in Castilian Spanish."[42] Again, we have the patent as a limiting mediator, but for different reasons than in the case of penicillin.

Any patent application presented in Spain that did not meet this requirement had to be translated. For this, and the other formalities required for the presentation of an application, there existed industrial property agents and officially certified translators. The North American pharmaceutical companies, Merck and Schenley, and CSIC for the polymerase patent, used mediators and representatives from the office of Alberto de Elzaburu, founded in 1865 and renowned agents for industrial and intellectual property within Spain. The fact that the principal public organization for Spanish research operated in a manner similar to a foreign company, suggests not only that the patent came from abroad but also, as I have already mentioned, how distant the research laboratories were from the practices and mechanisms for protecting innovation.

The linguistic issue is an important part of the process, from the writing of the patent to possible litigation and other legal proceedings. Although the language problem has been present in diverse legislation matters and in practice (the different ways of carrying out translations and the variety of pricing schemes are just two examples), the search for consensus around a common language has been an important element in the international harmonization of procedures, above all in the desire to

---

[41] Chapter IV, Article 112, 3.   [42] Chapter I, Article 21, 4.

establish a European patent system.[43] At an intergovernmental conference held in May 1969 in Brussels, one of the most controversial issues
was deciding which languages to use in patent procedures. At this meeting they agreed on English, French, and German, a decision later ratified
by the Munich Diplomatic Conference in October 1973. To alleviate the
mistrust this choice aroused, the Munich agreement added the possibility
of requesting the patent holder provide a translation into any official
language of the state in which it sought to extend the application (Articles
65 and 57).

But the significance of language goes beyond legalities and procedures.
There are cultural, technological, and political issues that should also be
taken into account. For example, returning to the case of penicillin, the
translation of patents enabled access to various technologies (the manufacturing procedures) that would have been difficult to understand or
reproduce had the patents remained in their original language. Mediation by the translation and the agents who took responsibility for it was
culturally and politically important: the translation equalized two technologically and culturally different worlds, both interested in producing
and commercializing penicillin. Had the translation not mediated, the
consequences for the industry in both North America and Spain would
have been very different.

9.5   Conclusions

Legislation is an indication of realities, forming part of political, economic, and cultural interests. Spanish legislation dealing with industrial
property has reacted, on one hand, to a reality marked by political-
economic objectives, by opting to engage with countries that were technologically stronger in order to protect industrial production. On the
other hand, it has responded to political, social, and economic changes
that require the adaptation and development of specific protective
systems.

Although industrial property rights have been considered fundamental
for the promotion of innovation, in the cases shown here the status of the
patent as an essential requirement for encouraging "progress" in Spain is
ambiguous. For penicillin patents it is more relevant to speak about
political and business strategies – on the part of US industries as well
as the Spanish state – than about the protection of property rights on
inventions and technological advances: the duopoly that CEPA and

---

[43]   A. Elzaburu, *Languages Problems for Patenting in Europe* (Barcelona: AGESORPI, 1995).

Antibióticos S.A. enjoyed eliminated all competition. And in the case of the DNA polymerase patent, a patent was never the researchers' object- ive. Parts of the results were patented, but this was based on interests and strategies designed and originating from a space and culture of patents: from US research emerging from private companies and from a pursuit of financing quite different from that which existed in Spain.

The histories evoked by these patents increase their usefulness within the humanities, and challenge the perspective of considering patents as only developers and promoters of new knowledge.

The cases dealt with here forcefully demonstrate the important role played by patents in structuring the production and dissemination of knowledge, in the international transfer of technology, and in the forma- tion of politics. Patent application became attractive not only to scientists and industrialists, but also to politicians.

Both Bentley and Sherman, in their book on the origins of *Intellectual Property Law* in England, have discussed the artifice involved in the construction of "normality."[44] This is clear in the case studies outlined here. In the construction of the Spanish patent system, legal aspects and the demand for their harmonization have been as important as negoti- ation processes – mediation – between different actors such as polit- icians, lawyers, industrial property agents, scientists, clinicians, and the pharmaceutical and biotechnological industries. The penicillin and poly- merase patents demonstrate the influence of patents on – and the entanglement between – legal, economic, and scientific aspects within the research process. The combination of business and laboratory prac- tices, of politics and policies linked to specific times and spaces, provides a culture of normalization and control of knowledge that reconfigures, at least in the case of Spain, the narrations and discourses on the circulation of knowledge. The histories of these patents suggest a redistribution of the places of knowledge production and challenge the use of terms such as transference and appropriation. As I have suggested, circulation is a more appropriate term: a circulation always mediated by homogenizing logic and local cultures.

---

[44] L. Bentley and B. Sherman, *Intellectual Property Law* (Oxford: Oxford University Press, 2001).

Part IV

Central and Eastern Europe

10 The Struggle over "the Social Function of Intellectual Work in the Economy of Nations"
Engineers, Patent Law, and Enterprise Inventions in Germany and Their European Significance

Karl Hall

10.1 Introduction

International histories of patent systems in the nineteenth century tend to focus primarily on the significance of the French and Anglo-American models developed in the eighteenth century, with the German system treated as a later variant of the Anglo-American system. Such an approach understates, however, the novelty of the German system and the political ramifications emerging from its launch in 1877. Indeed, the rapid subsequent development of patent systems in Central, Northern, and Eastern Europe cannot be understood without reference to the success of the Germanic system in its variant forms. Partly this was due to the economic power of Germany. As in the Americas, neighboring nations tended to follow the patent model of the dominant regional state. It was also a matter of political alignment. The examination-free laissez-faire patent system of France did not suit governments that sought to keep state interests upper hand in managing the flourishing invention culture in a growing economy.

Yet while the German patent system did not explicitly grant a privileged status to inventors' rights as did the examination-centered American system, German patent theorists would continue to debate statutory rationales for patents as intellectual property for another fifty years. The variety of ideological interpretations to which the German system was susceptible was perhaps just one of the reasons for its influence. As one legal observer noted of the 1930s, where this chapter ends, German patent law was "very laconic and leaves considerable latitude for jurisdiction and government decrees." Of all the countries of the world, Germany undoubtedly possessed the "largest literature dealing with the theoretical aspects of patent law ... with typical German thoroughness the basic conceptions of patent law are dissected and followed up almost to a transcendental plane."[1] Much of this chapter will thus illustrate deep and prolonged debates on the abstract principles that should guide the legal frameworks of patenting practice.

10.2   Patents across the Deutscher Bund

Across the thirty-nine states of the economically cooperating Deutscher Bund, there was no single patent system prior to national unification in 1870–1, or indeed until the establishment of the Berlin Patent Office in 1877.[2] While the Hanseatic states did without patent laws entirely, Prussia adopted a form of patent law in the guise of a royal privilege statute of 1815 followed by Hessen (1820), Bavaria (1825), Württemberg (1828), Baden (1845), Hanover (1847), and Saxony (1853).[3] Engaging with French legal currents, it was the Habsburg lands, Württemberg, and Bavaria that adopted more complex patent system positions than Prussia in the middle decades of the nineteenth century.[4] Patent statutory variation was prevalent until the postunification debates leading to the 1877 law.

In attempting to explain the subsequent change that took place by 1877, the Czech patent attorney Jan Vojáček observed that the comparatively small number of patents taken out in these principalities in comparison to American and other European nations with patent laws was "out of proportion to the growing importance of German industry."[5] Nevertheless, the absence of patents and the imperatives of state unification are not sufficient to explain the shift to a unified national system. This was more likely made possible by the decline of the free-trade movement in the wake of the global depression beginning in 1873.[6]

---

[1] Jan Vojáček, *A Survey of the Principal National Patent Systems* (New York: Prentice-Hall, 1936), 149.

[2] For the early-modern history, Barbara Dölemeyer and Hans Mohnhaupt, eds., *Das Privileg im europäischen Vergleich*, vol. 2 (Frankfurt a.M.: Vittorio Klostermann, 1999).

[3] This remained largely undisturbed by the 1842 tariff union. Rudolf Klostermann, *Das geistige Eigenthum an Schriften, Kunstwerke und Erfindungen, nach preussischem und internationalem Rechte dargestellt*, vol. 1 (Berlin: I. Guttentag, 1867), 70; Otto von Gierke, *Deutsches Privatrecht*, vol. 1, Systematisches Handbuch der Deutschen Rechtswissenschaft (Leipzig: Duncker & Humblot, 1895), 852; Alfred Müller, *Die Entwicklung des Erfindungsschutzes und seiner Gesetzgebung in Deutschland* (Munich: J. Lindauer, 1898).

[4] Elmar Wadle, *Geistiges Eigentum: Bausteine zur Rechtsgeschichte*, vol. 2 (Munich: C. H. Beck, 2003), 28–34.

[5] Vojáček, *A Survey of the Principal National Patent Systems*, 144.

[6] Alfred Heggen, *Erfindungsschutz und Industrialisierung in Preussen: 1793–1877* (Göttingen: Vandenhoeck & Ruprecht, 1975); Peter Kurz, *Weltgeschichte des Erfindungsschutzes: Erfinder und Patente im Spiegel der Zeiten* (Cologne: Carl Heymanns Verlag, 2000), 361–84; Margrit Seckelmann, *Industrialisierung, Internationalisierung und Patentrecht im*

Prior to political unification, some patent advocates contended that a more informal harmonization could work simultaneously at the national and international level. For example, the Bohemian German patent advocate Franz Makowiczka (1811–90), argued in 1853 that German states could rally around patent law as a "politically harmless and economically important" means of overcoming isolation.[7] Yet even informally, there was no prospect among the Germanic states that French notions of intellectual property (*geistiges Eigentum*) as a natural right could have been the unifying principle, even after this idea was broached during the Frankfurt Parliament in 1848. For Carl von Savigny in Berlin, the state was incapable of protecting any such claim to a right. Using Roman law as a formal model for construction without invoking natural rights, the broader German *Pandektenwissenschaft* saw too much suspect metaphysics both in claims to patent rights and copyright motivated by Lockean theories of labor.[8] As an Austrian Polish law professor later put it, not entirely approvingly, patent privileges were nothing less than the state's "recognition of a will to appropriation" by the inventor.[9]

One determined German defense of patents as forms of intellectual property, however, stemmed from Rudolf Klostermann (1828–86) in 1869.[10] For him, the exclusivity of intellectual property rights stemmed from the property-related (*vermögensrechtliche*) use of "the mechanical duplication of a product of intellectual labor"; such rights would thus consist in the "unrestricted and exclusive authorization of the reproduction of this object."[11] Though subsequently marginalized in Germany as

Deutschen Reich, 1871–1914 (Frankfurt a.M.: Vittorio Klostermann, 2006), chapter 1; Kees Gispen, *Poems in Steel: National Socialism and the Politics of Inventing from Weimar to Bonn* (New York: Berghahn Books, 2002), 25–7. For the European economic debates for and against patenting, Fritz Machlup and Edith Penrose, "The Patent Controversy in the Nineteenth Century," *The Journal of Economic History* 10 (1950): 1–29.

[7] Franz Makowiczka, "Die österreichische Erfindungspatent-Gesetzgebung," *Archiv der politischen Oekonomie und Polizeiwissenschaft* 10 (1853): 314.

[8] Seckelmann, *Industrialisierung*, 131–2. On Lockean theories, Adam Moore, "Intellectual Property," in *The Stanford Encyclopedia of Philosophy*, ed. Edward N. Zalta, 2011, http://plato.stanford.edu/entries/intellectual-property.

[9] Friedrich Zoll, "Privatrechtliche Studien aus dem Patentrechte mit vornehmlicher Berücksichtigung des österreichischen Rechtes," *Zeitschrift für das Privat- und öffentliche Recht der Gegenwart* 21 (1894): 552–3.

[10] Klostermann, *Das geistige Eigenthum; Die Patentgesetzgebung aller Länder*, vol. 2, Das geistige Eigenthum an Schriften, Kunstwerke und Erfindungen, nach preussischem und internationalem Rechte dargestellt (Berlin: I. Guttentag, 1869).

[11] Ibid.1:113.

legal theory, his work nonetheless bears mention for several reasons.[12] First, and most obviously, it was the most comprehensive comparative treatment of patent law. Second, it had resonances outside German law, informing subsequent Austrian and Russian legal works. And finally, it reinforced a trend toward the more abstract nature of patent specification as a semantic assemblage standing in for the reification of the invention more commonly seen in the US model-centered patent system (see Chapter 4 in this volume, by Fullilove).[13]

When the 1871 German constitution granted the new unified state a species of authority in Article 4 over both patent inventions (item 5) and "the defence of intellectual property" (item 6), this meant that the former was not subsumed within the latter. Yet neither was any specific right articulated as the basis for Article 4, leaving much room for subsequent debate on intellectual property interpretations of patents. French law was not the default for this debate since its demarcation of intellectual property qua copyright from industrial property qua patent was not shared across the European continent.[14] In the German case such rights were understood monistically so that appeals to invention as an inherent personal right were rejected more firmly in principle. Nevertheless, many engineers and a provocative minority of legal scholars long continued to argue for the statutory utility of intellectual property.[15]

[12] Although contemporary reviews of Klostermann in law journals occasionally faulted his attitude toward "positive law," they were uniformly favorable and did not single out the issue of intellectual property per se.
[13] Mario Biagioli, "Patent Republic: Representing Inventions, Constructing Rights and Authors," *Social Research* 73 (2006): 1129–72; Brad Sherman and Lionel Bently, *The Making of Modern Intellectual Property Law: The British Experience, 1760–1911* (Cambridge: Cambridge University Press, 1999), 185–6; Alain Pottage and Brad Sherman, *Figures of Invention: A History of Modern Patent Law* (Oxford: Oxford University Press, 2010), 85–106.
[14] For histories of copyright, Benedict Atkinson and Brian Fitzgerald, *A Short History of Copyright: The Genie of Information* (Switzerland: Springer, 2014); Peter Baldwin, *The Copyright Wars: Three Centuries of Trans-Atlantic Battle* (Princeton, NJ: Princeton University Press, 2014); Michael Westren, "The Development and Debate over Copyright in Imperial Russia, 1828–1917," *Russian History* 30 (2003): 145–223; Ekaterina Pravilova, *A Public Empire: Property and the Quest for the Common Good in Imperial Russia* (Princeton, NJ: Princeton University Press, 2014); Leonard Górnicki, *Rozwój idei praw autorskich: od starożytności do II wojny światowej* (Wrocław: Prawnicza i Ekonomiczna Biblioteka Cyfrowa, 2013), www.bibliotekacyfrowa.pl/publication/41089; György Boytha, "A szerzői jog és az iparjogvédelem összefüggései," *Jogtudományi Közlöny*, NS, 23 (1968): 594–602.
[15] For example, Friedrich Ruppert, "Technisches geistiges Eigentum, Erfindung und Patentierung," *Zeitschrift des Vereines Deutscher Ingenieure* 48 (1904): 1686–9. As we shall see in Chapter 11, Austrian reform debates also broached the theme repeatedly. One notable advocate of the statutory system was Lorenz von Stein (1815–90): Lorenz von Stein, *System der Staatswissenschaft: Die Gesellschaftslehre*, vol. 2 (Stuttgart and Augsburg: J. G. Cotta, 1856), 185–203. Cf. vol. 5 (p. 4), and vol. 6 of *Die*

10.3 The 1877 Patent Law and the Growth of the Berlin Patent Office

Six years after the official inauguration of the second *Reich*, the first trans-Germanic patent law was instantiated on May 25, 1877, with the Imperial Patent Office opening in Berlin, on July 1, 1877. Such was the enthusiasm for the new patenting regime that the following day the first national patent was issued, a "production process for a red ultramarine color" granted to the color chemist Johann Zeltner of Nürnberger Ultramarin-Fabrik.[16]

The new German law was not only significant for the nascent nation-state, but also significant in the global context. It offered a new, robust, state-centered approach to the selective award of patents. In an unprecedented way, the law used both elements of the so-called Anglo-American system's check on the ambitions of aspiring patentees. These were the US Patent Office's formal examinations held by expert officials to determine the novelty and utility in a proposed patent, and the British system of opposition proceedings in which members of the public could challenge newly published provisional patent specifications with their own claims to priority. While each check worked separately to circumscribe the array of patents approved and sealed each year, their juxtaposition in the German system brought a new degree of challenge. A prospective patentee in Berlin had to pass through both the critical scrutiny of patent officials and also run the gamut of rival inventors who might wish to oppose the grant of the patent on any of a number of grounds. The German system was therefore the toughest patent law in the world, with the Berlin Patent Office empowered to deny patents more efficaciously than any other.

This was most startling for the aspiring French patentee who encountered neither form of check in Paris, where "every cobbler regards himself as an inventor and if he can pay for it, takes out a patent for his invention out of sheer vanity."[17] The French applicant in Berlin faced the prospect of hiring a dedicated patent agent to rewrite patent specifications to have any prospect of a French patent having a counterpart approved in Germany.[18] The challenges presented by scrutinizing

---

Verwaltungslehre, 8 vols. (Stuttgart: J. G. Cotta, 1868). Lorenz von Stein, *Handbuch der Verwaltungslehre und des Verwaltungsrechts* (Stuttgart: J. G. Cotta, 1870), 382–92.

[16] For a historical overview of the German Patent and Trade Mark Office, see www.dpma.de/english/our_office/about_us/history/index.html.

[17] "Politische Uebersicht," *Das Vaterland*, October 19, 1878.

[18] Guillaume Pataky, *Les Lois sur les brevets d'invention et marques de fabrique des principaux pays, et la procédure allemande en matière de contestations relatives aux brevets d'invention* (Paris, 1907).

officials at the Berlin Patent Office went unrivaled for decades, casting a procedural shadow well beyond the borders of the Reich. As William Phillips Thompson noted in the "Germany" section of the 1920 edition of his *Handbook of the Patent Law of All Countries*: "many inventions which would pass the United States examiners or a British Court as novel are refused because the principle of the invention is old, or the claims are mere combinations showing no new principle."[19]

The lower credence given to inventor's claims in the German system is readily understood by comparison with the French jurisprudential context, where notions of *propriété industrielle* were understood as purely economic rights, while the individual's moral right to copyright remained procedurally distinct.[20] Ascribing a personality-based right to the inventor in Germany invited tension, however, because German civil law sought to treat these domains monistically, and Roman-law conceptions of property were difficult to accommodate to an inventor's right. The seminal figure in the adoption of the 1877 statute, Werner Siemens, firmly rejected intellectual property conceptions.[21] That statute famously avoided defining invention, because it was enacted not for the sake of granting inventors patent rights but instead for the state to encourage inventors to disclose trade secrets.[22] The imperial patent office thus quickly acquired immense bureaucratic authority in its adjudication of patents. If three-quarters of patent applications were approved in the early years, it was taken as a sign of the office's effectiveness that the acceptance rate dropped to less than a third by the end of the century – prompting the kind of comparative observation made by Thompson.[23] This high rejection rate resulted in part from the ever greater body of staff

---

[19] William Phillips Thompson, *Handbook of the Patent Law of All Countries* (London: Stevens & Sons, 1920), 95.

[20] Thomas Dreier, "How Much 'Property' Is There in Intellectual Property? The German Civil Law Perspective," in *Concepts of Property in Intellectual Property Law*, ed. Helena Howe and Jonathan Griffiths (Cambridge: Cambridge University Press, 2013), 116–36.

[21] Carl Pieper, *Der Erfinderschutz und die Reform der Patentgesetze* (Dresden, 1873); Ludwig Fischer, "Werner Siemens und der Schutz der Erfindungen," *Wissenschaftliche Veröffentlichungen aus dem Siemens-Konzern* 2 (1922): 1–69; Heggen, *Erfindungsschutz*, 111–16; Alexander K. Schmidt, *Erfinderprinzip und Erfinderpersönlichkeitsrecht im deutschen Patentrecht von 1877 bis 1936* (Tübingen: Mohr Siebeck, 2009); David Gilgen, "Creating the Invisible Hand: The Construction of Property Rights and the Promotion of Economic Growth between State and Interest Groups in the First German Patent Law of 1877," *Historical Social Research* 36, no. 3 (2011): 99–111.

[22] Gispen, *Poems in Steel*, 27–30; Seckelmann, *Industrialisierung*, 19.

[23] The total number of patents awarded since 1877 had surpassed 150,000 by 1904. "'Die Entwickelung des deutschen Patentwesens und dessen Einwirkung auf die Industrie," *Dinglers Polytechnisches Journal* 275 (1890): 463–73; Felix Damme, *Das Deutsche Patentrecht: Ein Handbuch für Praxis und Studium* (Berlin: Verlag von Otto Liebmann, 1906), 107–8; A. Du Bois-Reymond, *Erfindung und Erfinder* (Berlin: Springer, 1906),

employed to exercise their substantial degree of scrutiny. By the early years of the twentieth century, the patent office employed more than seven hundred people, including a hundred engineers and more than a dozen lawyers in addition to several hundred civil servants and support personnel.[24] The number continued to swell, making it the most expensive civilian agency in German, although it recouped a great deal in fees.[25] Even highly placed patent officials conceded that, from the outside, it could look like an "administrative archipelago."[26]

10.4   Technicians or Jurists? Patenting Professionals versus Patent Officials

In response to the enormous power of the Imperial Patent Office, engineers and chemists demanded a greater role in the adjudication of patents. In 1891 the German statute was updated in part to accommodate them. Kees Gispen has described the frustrated professional aspirations of German engineers in a conservative political setting where inventor-ownership remained an elusive goal amid rapid industrial expansion; by contrast other salaried employees continued to enjoyed privileges based on preindustrial social relations.[27] In Margrit Seckelmann's complementary account it is the legal and bureaucratic tension between efficiency and rule of law that remains central to evolving German debates over patenting practices.[28] For present purposes, we emphasize that this was more than a clash of specialist competencies with engineers and jurists each appealing to their own strictly Weberian formal-rationalist authority.

Few German lawyers saw themselves as engaged in what the American jurist Roscoe Pound derided as "mechanical jurisprudence," an understanding of law as *scientific* only insofar as it limited "the personal equation in judicial administration," while binding the jurist to rote implementation of rules.[29] In systems with prior examination there were generally fewer court cases, but higher demands on the participants, and

---

31. Of that total less than one fifth remained active in 1904, whether due to simple expiration, neglect of fees, or renunciation.

[24] Julius Ephraim, *Deutsches Patentrecht für Chemiker* (Halle: Wilhelm Knapp, 1907), 197.

[25] Damme, *Das Deutsche Patentrecht*, 76; Kees Gispen, *New Profession, Old Order: Engineers and German Society, 1815–1914* (Cambridge: Cambridge University Press, 1989), 266. Most of that expense was offset by rather high patenting fees.

[26] Felix Damme, "Veränderungen in der Kompetenz des Patentamts?" *Deutsche Juristen-Zeitung* 19, no. 6 (1914): 395.

[27] Gispen, *New Profession, Old Order; Poems in Steel.*

[28] Seckelmann, *Industrialisierung*, chap. 4.

[29] Roscoe Pound, "Mechanical Jurisprudence," *Columbia Law Review* 8, no. 8 (1908): 605–23.

German reform debates often revolved around what sorts of technical qualifications Patent Office jurists ought to possess in order to pass judgment on specifications submitted for their scrutiny. Did the courts need more generalist technicians or specialist jurists?[30] Did patent attorneys require formal qualifications?[31] Were they in fact tradesmen, inconveniently blurring the lines between intellectual and manual labor?[32] Should chemists and engineers receive instruction in patent law as part of their training?[33]

Among German jurists Paul Laband (1838–1918) was the chief figure sustaining the view of patenting as administrative act, a position enshrined in his *Das Staatsrecht des deutschen Reiches* (1876, with later editions through 1911).[34] Although Laband saw patents as a species of intellectual property, for him the legal incoherence of *geistiges Eigentum* meant that, like Klostermann, the granting of patents gave no constitutive right to an inventor. Even as engineers and entrepreneurs argued about the organization and social nature of invention processes, they both tended to insist that jurists did not have the intellectual authority to say why an invention counted as an invention. Yet the trained engineer was not always mollified when the patent attorney stepped in to claim that his own role was subtly transformative, and never merely procedural. As the man who led the Siemens patent office for more than three decades put it:

If the invention itself is a perfectly rational, conceptually specifiable entity, this is not to say that the path that leads from the mere problem or functional idea to the invention is given unambiguously and rationally … these constraints include something irrational, indefinable; something that we are not able grasp clearly, to treat scientifically, to weigh and influence directly.[35]

---

[30] Gustav Rauter, "Aufgaben und Stellung des Patentanwaltes," *Archiv für öffentliches Recht* 22 (1907): 481; Albert Bolze, "Technische Sondergerichte?" *Deutsche Juristen-Zeitung* 12, no. 22 (1907): 1232–3; Julius Ephraim, "Techniker und Jurist," *Zeitschrift für angewandte Chemie* 21 (1908): 94–150; Fritz Rathenau, *Sondergerichtshöfe für gewerblichen Rechtsschutz* (Berlin: Sonderabdruck aus den Verhandlungen des XXX. Deutschen Juristentages, 1910).

[31] Franz Wirth, "Der Entwurf eines Gesetzes betr. die Patentanwälte," *Deutsche Juristen-Zeitung* 4, no. 8 (1899): 169–71; Felix Damme, "Das Reichsgesetz betreffend die Patentanwälte vom 21. Mai 1900," *Deutsche Juristen-Zeitung* 5 (1900): 406–9.

[32] Damme, *Das Deutsche Patentrecht*, 120–1.

[33] Carl Bülow, "Unterricht in Theorie und Praxis des Patentgesetzes für Chemiker und Ingenieure auf deutschen Hochschulen," *Zeitschrift für Industrierecht* 1 (1906): 25–8; L. Max Wohlgemuth, "Unterricht in Theorie und Praxis des Patentgesetzes für Chemiker und Ingenieure auf deutschen Hochschulen," *Zeitschrift für angewandte Chemie* 19 (1906): 569–71.

[34] Paul Laband, *Das Staatsrecht des deutschen Reiches*, 3rd ed., vol. 2 (Freiburg and Leipzig: J. C. B. Mohr, 1895), 208–28.

[35] Ludwig Fischer, *Betriebserfindungen* (Berlin: Carl Heymanns Verlag, 1921), 9.

In Ludwig Fischer's view, the patent attorney was uniquely qualified to give the invention legal reality via an act of judgment. If the engineer in turn suspected the courts lacked sufficient technical competencies and thus rendered judgments that, while not arbitrary, offended the engineer's own sense of rational procedure, jurists further countered that the law, too, was *Technik* mastered through long experience.[36] Specialist expertise was thus not something fully fungible.

Yet the "penetration of technology in all relationships of modern life" meant that the courts would eventually have to adjust to this more demanding state of affairs.[37] Senior patent officer Felix Damme lamented that legal training was not keeping up with the expansion of technical domains, and the convenient fiction that jurist and technical consultant were "expert" in the same sense only contributed to the average judge's temptation to elevate technical reports to the status of legal ruling without proper deliberation.[38] A Freiburg attorney with an engineering degree saw practical constraints on Damme's ambition to transform expertise in the courtroom, pointing out that one could not have chemist consultants evaluating bridge design elements, and so forth.[39] The domains of expertise were simply too diverse. It was not possible for the Imperial Patent Office to maintain a stable of civil servants capable of covering every conceivable subject, much less for state courts to do so.

While the German patent system had come to enjoy a massive scale advantage over much of Europe, by the early twentieth century it was actually becoming bureaucratically burdensome, and it further remained open to principled challenge. In 1908 the Reichstag passed a *Hilfsmitgliedgesetz* that allowed the Imperial Patent Office to hire provisional technical aid for patent examination, but because the number of applications continued to increase, individual examiners seemed in practice to be enjoying too much discretionary power, undermining the formal and rational aspects of examination. Engineer Carl Pieper complained about a bureaucratic dynamic where "each person at the Patent Office does everything, so each is everyone's enemy."[40] Adopting the comparatively lax American examination procedures did not appeal to Germans,

---

[36] Arno Kloess, "Technische Juristen oder Justizingenieure?" *Zeitschrift für Industrierecht* 3, no. 16 (1908): 181–3.
[37] Felix Damme, "Sachverständige Gerichte oder gerichtliche Sachverständige?" *Deutsche Juristen-Zeitung* 13 (1908): 399.
[38] Ibid.
[39] [Gustav] Runkel-Langsdorf, "Der sachverständige Richter," *Zeitschrift für Industrierecht* 3, no. 12 (1908): 133–5.
[40] Quoted in Seckelmann, *Industrialisierung*, 291.

however, with Damme commenting that if everything that was patented in America were to be patented in Germany, "a cry of disgust would go through German industry, because here one thinks more abstractly."[41] However, that level of abstraction did not mean that jurists and engineers reconciled their differences at the higher plane of *Wissenschaft*.

10.5   Josef Kohler's Defense of the Right to Intangible Goods

The German consensus around the inventor's right as fundamentally a private right rather than a property right was legally formidable but socially unstable in the early years of the twentieth century. The chief instigator of renewed debates among jurists was Berlin law professor Josef Kohler (1849–1919), perhaps the only German mandarin more prolific than psychologist Wilhelm Wundt. Surveying the pre-1877 state of affairs in 1908, he complained that "[t]he fruitful doctrine of intellectual property was crushed in schoolmasterly fashion without putting anything in its place," and the "goods of the intellect were left defenceless."[42]

Careful to distance himself from Klostermann's half measures, Kohler had begun laying out his theory of the right to intangible goods (*Immaterialgüterrecht*) in the 1870s, incorporating it into widely used textbooks of patent law.[43] He argued that legal scholars should accept the adventitious nature of the industry-driven concept of patent rights handed to jurists by the 1877 statute and get down to the business of developing the juridical science to accommodate and sharpen it. What set Kohler apart from his rivals were his systematic international appeals to comparative law. Keenly aware that French and American jurisprudence had little interest for German formalists, Kohler actually appealed to the US Supreme Court's decision in *Seymour* v. *Osborne* (1870) as evidence that a property-like construal was warranted.[44] Moreover, he invoked both British and French law as helpful models in recognizing the prior

---

[41] Felix Damme, "Die Reform des Patentrechts im Reichstage," *Deutsche Juristen-Zeitung* 10, no. 8 (1905): 379.

[42] Josef Kohler, *Lehrbuch des Patentrechts* (Mannheim: Bensheimer, 1908), 10.

[43] Josef Kohler, *Deutsches Patentrecht: systematisch bearbeitet unter vergleichender Berücksichtigung des französischen Patentrechts* (Mannheim: Bensheimer, 1878); "Autor-, Patent- und Industrierecht," *Archiv für Theorie und Praxis des allgemeinen deutschen Handels- und Wechselrechts* 22 (1887): 167–213, 327–66; *Forschungen aus dem Patentrecht* (Mannheim: Bensheimer, 1888); *Handbuch des deutschen Patentrechts in rechtsvergleichender Darstellung* (Mannheim: Bensheimer, 1900); *Lehrbuch des Patentrechts*; "Einfluss der Erfindungen auf die Rechtsentwicklung," *Deutsche Juristen-Zeitung* 17 (1912): 25–31.

[44] Kohler, *Handbuch des deutschen Patentrechts in rechtsvergleichender Darstellung*, 56. Regarding a contested patent the Supreme Court had concluded, "Inventions secured by letters patent are property in the holder of the patent, and as such are as much entitled

existence of prevalent general concepts and devoting effort to piecemeal legal improvements, rather than disqualifying them on abstract grounds.[45] Kohler also contributed to the further abstraction of patent specification, citing American practice that "what is patented is not an individual representational form, but a technical construction which is manifested in the individual representational form."[46] When the Imperial Court upheld an infringement case on behalf of the German patent for the Faure lead-acid battery assembly, it affirmed that nominally distinct characteristic components of two inventions that ultimately shared the same operating principles in their overall assembly could not deflect the infringement charge. Kohler was gratified that the court specifically cited his reasoning for how to compare equivalences in intangible goods.[47]

Kohler contended that intellectual property was not a strictly personal right, but rather an absolute right that lay outside the person and could be temporally restricted for pragmatic reasons. This was, however, eventually rejected in favor of Otto von Gierke's notion of the inventor's right as an inalienable right to a "personality good" (*Persönlichkeitsgut*).[48] Ultimately Kohler's theory only helped clarify the "material" aspects of invention and not the rights of the inventor qua person, since he did not show how to connect the defense of the intellectual creator to the market valuation of the invention.[49] Yet the German rejection of a split between private right and public right partly served to magnify the heuristic value of the Kohler-inspired intellectual property debates for those Austro-Hungarian and Russian observers who felt that the state should be playing a greater role structuring the obligations that bound the inventor to society and made the patent at once a public good and a creative right.[50]

to protection as any other property consisting of a franchise during the term for which the franchise or the exclusive right is granted."

[45] Kohler indeed believed that if one was not unduly distracted by the history of English copyright law, one would come to appreciate that a general notion of intellectual property remained the driving factor in the formation of English patent law. Josef Kohler, "Die Idee des geistigen Eigenthums," *Archiv für die civilistische Praxis* 82 (1894): 200.

[46] Kohler, *Forschungen aus dem Patentrecht*, 55.

[47] "Gerichtliche Entscheidungen. Reichsgericht, 9. December 1893. Verletzung des Patentes Nr. 19026," *Patentblatt* 18 (1894): 121–6; Kohler, "Die Idee des geistigen Eigenthums," 209.

[48] Gierke, *Deutsches Privatrecht*, 1:858.

[49] Boytha, "A szerzői jog és az iparjogvédelem összefüggései," 597; Volker Jänich, *Geistiges Eigentum: eine Komplementärerscheinung zum Sacheigentum?* (Tübingen: Mohr Siebeck, 2002), 90–102. Cf. Schmidt on how Kohler subtly changed tactics after Gierke's position prevailed, *Erfinderprinzip*, 33–6.

[50] Joseph Ludwig Brunstein, *Zur Reform des Erfinderrechtes: Vortrag gehalten im Niederösterr. Gewerbeverein am 10. April 1885* (Vienna: Manz, 1885); Ernst Bettelheim, *Das Recht des*

10.6   Reasserting the Historical Inventor

On the eve of World War I, engineers sought to move German patent law away from the administratively convenient first-to-file system to a more historically just "first-to-invent" system, as precedented in contemporary US practice.[51] However, new patent laws drafted to further clarify the relation between legal and technical members of the higher patent court only highlighted in the eyes of engineers that jurists still regarded the acquisition of ancillary technical skills as merely incidental.[52] Stimulated by the way that the 1897 Austrian law had taken modest steps to protect the historically defined "true inventor," German engineers also pressed for stronger guarantees.[53] Gispen has carefully analyzed the competing interests of industrialists and engineers in this process, but we would highlight in addition how the ongoing Taylorization of invention served to dilute the intellectual claims of engineers.[54]

In 1914 one analyst attuned to political economy, G. W. Häberlein, wrote that "great confusion has already arisen in German patent law doctrine." This was because "intellectual authorship has been far too overestimated in technical invention. The inventor has both feet on the shoulders of his predecessor, and it is a long path from the inventive idea to the practically useful invention. In particular, we have ignored the real contrast between the act of invention, the luminous flash of thought, and

---

Erfinders in Österreich nach dem Gesetze vom 11. Januar 1897 (Vienna: Manz, 1901); Béla Lévy, *A magyar szabadalmi jog rendszere* (Budapest: Márkus Samu, 1898); Oszkár Fazekas, "A szellemi tulajdon jogbölcseletéhez," in *Nagy Ference emlékkönyve* (Budapest: Athenaeum, 1906), 175; Zoll, "Privatrechtliche Studien,"; Karel Herrmann, "Právo z vynálezu v rakouském zákonu patentním," *Sborník věd právních a státních* 3 (1903): 215–35; A. A. Pilenko, *Pravo izobretatelia: Privilegiia na izobreteniia i ikh zashchita v russkom i mezhdunarodnom prave*, vol. 2 (St. Petersburg: M. M. Stasiulevich, 1903). While most of these writers (especially Zoll) disagree at some level with Kohler, they all sustain the discourse of intellectual property and intangible goods in part through engagement with his work.

[51] Julius Ephraim, "Das Verfahren der Patentprüfung nach dem Patentgesetzentwurf," *Zeitschrift für angewandte Chemie* 27 (1914): 447–55; W. Karsten, "Der Entwurf des Patentgesetzes," *Zeitschrift für angewandte Chemie* 27 (1914): 185–92; Th. Diehl, "Das Erfinderrecht des Patentgesetzentwurfs und die Angestellten-Erfindung," *Zeitschrift für angewandte Chemie* 27 (1914): 477–83; Emil Bierreth, "Kritische Betrachtungen zu den Entwürfen für das neue Patent-, Gebrauchsmuster- und Warenzeichengesetz," *Dinglers Polytechnisches Journal* 329 (1914): 465–8, 501–6.

[52] Gerhard Zeyen, "Betrachtungen zum Neuentwurf des Patentgesetzes," *Dinglers Polytechnisches Journal* 329 (1914): 129–33.

[53] Bettelheim, *Das Recht des Erfinders in Österreich*, 8, 57.

[54] Gispen, *New Profession, Old Order*, 255–87.

the patentable invention."[55] In the legal setting the threat to the auteur picture of invention sparked real misgivings about patent systems. There might come a time, warned patent attorney Hermann Kändler, when the interest of the state in protecting patents would diverge from the interest of the individual in enjoying such rights.[56]

Gierke's mainstream legal framework fed into this problem in one subtle respect: the statute's provision for so-called coinventor rights, when multiple individuals collectively create an invention. His influence stemmed in part from his extensive historical knowledge of medieval German texts that he employed as collectivist precedents for modern civil law. This carried over into his picture of coinvention, because his sense of what constituted that collective effort was entirely defined by the "bodies" (Organen) whose activity gave rise to the invention in their "joint life" (Verbandsleben), in a manner consistent with their ancient constitution.[57] Such an argument was conveniently historicist and not a little patriotic. It also was shaded by guild sensibilities that somewhat problematically supported German engineers' own understandings of their intellectual labor. Nor did it leave much room for the complex labor hierarchies of industrial laboratories.[58] Here was a collateral motive for casting invention as an increasingly scientific endeavor, bound to norms from domains other than the "joint life" of the enterprise.

Damme famously encouraged the reward theory of patenting as a social good by adopting the trope of "the inventor as teacher of the nation."[59] Some even recognized in this an echo of Friedrich List's normative claims about the modern individual's obligations to the general well-being.[60] Far more than industrial promotion or incentives to disclosure, this view of patenting suited the predilections of engineers and scientists, not least because it sat well with an understanding of

---

[55] G. W. Häberlein, "Erfinderrecht und Volkswirtschaft," *Dinglers Polytechnisches Journal* 329 (1914): 257; *Erfinderrecht und Volkswirtschaft: Mahnworte für die deutsche Industrie* (Berlin: Springer, 1913).

[56] Hermann Kändler, *Der staatliche Erfindungsschutz im Lichte moderner Nationalökonomie* (Berlin: Verlag von Franz Vahlen, 1914), 100; Gispen, *New Profession, Old Order*, 327.

[57] Gierke, *Deutsches Privatrecht*, 1:869. Cf. Otto von Gierke, *Die Genossenschaftstheorie und die deutsche Rechtsprechung* (Berlin: Weidmann, 1887).

[58] Notwithstanding differences in the American legal and employment context, there are compelling parallels in the exemplary work of Catherine L. Fisk, "Removing the 'Fuel of Interest' from the 'Fire of Genius': Law and the Employee-Inventor, 1830–1930," *University of Chicago Law Review* 65 (1998): 1127–98; *Working Knowledge: Employee Innovation and the Rise of Corporate Intellectual Property, 1800–1930* (Chapel Hill: University of North Carolina Press, 2009).

[59] Damme, *Das Deutsche Patentrecht*, v.

[60] Friedrich List, *Das Nationale der politischen Oekonomie*, vol. 1 (Stuttgart and Tübingen: J. G. Cotta, 1841), 289; Häberlein, *Erfinderrecht und Volkswirtschaft*, 1913, 40.

invention rights as a "personality good" tied to acts of intellectual creation.[61] Austrian patent attorney Emanuel Adler bemusedly asked how to recast the inventor's role in recent cultural development – Germany had finally joined the Paris Union treaty in 1903 – once he "appears no longer only as teacher of a single nation [*Nation*], but as teacher of the contractually bound peoples [*Völker*]."[62] Harmonization as a nominal ideal could also exacerbate domestic disagreements about how best to order patent systems. Germany nonetheless generally benefitted from these new international protections for domestic patents, for the Union signatories could now be imagined as "a single economic area, a single large state," and Kohler declared that there were no credible grounds to fear bureaucratic juggernauts set in motion for all countries by the dissolution of a patent in any single country.[63]

This was still far from the ideal of a "world patent" however, and the German chemical industry in particular retained modest concerns that the German law's provision for processes but not products might put the German applicant at a priority disadvantage compared to his French counterpart.[64] A stronger test came in 1907 when Britain, heretofore comparatively liberal in its provisions toward foreign applicants, enacted a fairly strict provision for compulsory working of patents domestically in its new statute.[65] The British provision, as well as Justice Parker's pragmatic decision to place the burden of proof on complainants against foreign importers of patents, excited much discussion at Union meetings.[66] Though it was cast as endangering the spirit of the Paris Convention, calmer voices drew attention to long-standing German strictures directed at foreigners, as well as its strategy of concluding bilateral agreements that freed it from compulsory working provisions, to the

---

[61] Gierke, *Deutsches Privatrecht*, 1:858.

[62] Emanuel Adler, "Review of Damme, *Das deutsche Patentrecht*," *Kritische Vierteljahresschrift für Gesetzgebung und Rechtswissenschaft* 48 (1909): 40.

[63] Damme, *Das Deutsche Patentrecht*, 213–20; Kohler, *Lehrbuch des Patentrechts*, 220–6. On the broader context of the Paris accord, Eda Kranakis, "Patents and Power: European Patent-System Integration in the Context of Globalization," *Technology and Culture* 48 (2007): 689–728; Stephen P. Ladas, *Patents, Trademarks, and Related Rights: National and International Protection* (Cambridge, MA: Harvard University Press, 1975), 1616–74; Kurz, *Weltgeschichte des Erfindungsschutzes*, 467–505.

[64] E. Kloeppel, "Der Anschluß des Deutschen Reiches an die Internationale Union für gewerblichen Rechtsschutz," *Zeitschrift für angewandte Chemie* 16, no. 30 (1903): 713–18. See also the announcement of the patent office in appendix 13 of Damme, *Das deutsche Patentrecht*.

[65] See Stathis Arapostathis and Graeme Gooday, *Patently Contestable* (London: MIT Press, 2013).

[66] *Jahrbuch der Internationalen Vereinigung für Gewerblichen Rechtsschutz: Dreizehnter Jahrgang 1909* (Berlin: Carl Heymanns Verlag, 1911), 11–21, 99–121.

possible disadvantage of third countries. The German chemical industry obviously preferred a reading in which a patent worked in any signatory should count as worked in every other Union country.

10.7 World War I and Its Aftermath

The Great War was the greatest threat to global patent law harmonization since the Paris Union came into being in 1883. Yet even as the commitment to international pacts withered during that horrific conflict, it was not unusual to encounter earnest wartime reminders of internationalist ideas such as "[p]atenting and design registration are among the basic concepts of public life."[67] To one of the most prominent German advocates of intellectual property the war initially seemed merely an episode, after which "the peaceful cultural development of the nations must take its further course."[68] But as the war progressed Germany found itself vulnerable "in the patent-law threads that draw all nations together net-like in our time", for other nations could not bear its dominant patent-holding position.[69] When England annulled some 11,000 patents held by Austrian and German citizens early in the war, this naturally aggravated Axis owners and raised awareness that 25 percent of German patents were held by English and French citizens.[70] As the hostilities dragged on, a leading trade journal began offering regular updates on changes to patent protection.[71] Eventually the German Defence Ministry declared that patents would not be published in the usual fashion, and the patenting process would be more tightly controlled for the duration of hostilities, though apparently only patents with potential military applications were seized.[72]

---

[67] Johannes Neuberg, "Der Krieg und sein Einfluß auf das gewerbliche Urheberrecht," *Weltwirtschaftliches Archiv* 11 (1917): 537.

[68] Albert Osterrieth, "Der Krieg und die internationalen Verträge über gewerbliches und geistiges Eigentum," *Deutsche Juristen-Zeitung* 19, no. 16–18 (1914): 1072–5.

[69] A. Binz, "Der Kampf der Völker um die Industrie," *Zeitschrift für angewandte Chemie* 37 (1924): 121; "Chemie, Technik und Weltgeschichte," *Zeitschrift für angewandte Chemie* 40 (1927): 449–55. Binz (1868–1943), who taught at the Berlin Agricultural Hochschule, was also publisher of the journal. The racist aspect of his reasoning is especially apparent in the latter essay.

[70] "Patentnachrichten. Ungültigkeitserklärung der österreichischen und deutschen Patente in England," *Elektrotechnik und Maschinenbau Anhang: Industrielle und Wirtschaftliche Nachrichten*, Bettelheim 36 (1914): 455; "Volkswirtschaftliche Nachrichten: Der Krieg und die Patente," *Pester Lloyd*, September 19, 1914; Mil [sic] Richter, "Die englische Kriegführung gegen den Erfinderschutz," *Pester Lloyd*, January 14, 1916.

[71] See the continuing series "Der gewerbliche Rechtschutz und der Krieg," *Elektrotechnik und Maschinenbau Anhang: Industrielle und Wirtschaftliche Nachrichten* (1915–1917).

[72] "Der gewerbliche Rechtschutz und der Krieg," *Elektrotechnik und Maschinenbau Anhang: Industrielle und Wirtschaftliche Nachrichten*, no. 22 (1916): 103–4; Richard Lutter and

Fritz Rathenau, the Berlin judge and *Regierungsrat*, saw the war as a test of public commitment to the social discipline of patenting:

[D]oing this systematic work is not for everyone, and not a matter for every nation. It is striking and regrettable that in the very extensive literature on the war so little emphasis is put on the differences between the nations in this regard; it is certainly worth investigating the apparently trivial phenomenon, whether the difference in patent systems (registration system – examination system) in different countries can be explained in terms of *Völkerpsychologie*, and not just in technical-economic terms.[73]

More pointedly, Rathenau drew the lesson from England's readiness to cancel patent rights that military considerations could limit the claims of private property in the name of the general good. That private rights were being socialized may have been wartime exigency, but perhaps it was more than that. Indeed, "patent rights as private rights have become problematic."[74]

There were patent attorneys who took a more optimistic long view, since among the major combatants, only Russia – following its purported "half-Asiatic culture" – had gone so far as to nullify the patent privileges of foreign nationals, while England and the United States were at least making some legal semblance that their seizures and compulsory licensing would not stand in the way of restoring international agreements once hostilities ended.[75] "But in yet another regard perhaps the patent system offers the basis for a certain clarification of conditions after the war, perhaps even for a new worldview," suggested a Berlin patent attorney:

[I]t is precisely the patent system that offers the technician a completely general way of bringing the factual-visual manner of thinking of the scientist, if not to victory, then to its proper scope, instead of or in addition to the kind of juridical-philological manner of thinking that alone remains valid in the world. The patent system namely is the best at giving the technician the necessary training and education for logical thinking, thus imparting to him indisputable advantages over any other manner of thinking, whereby his sense of reality, instilled by relentless and yet so salutary *practice*, saves him from getting lost in its abyss. What share has this manner of thinking had in political life up to now?[76]

Felix Damme, "Kriegswirtschaftliche Massnahmen im Kaiserlichen Patentamt," *Deutsche Juristen-Zeitung* 22 (1917): 383–8.

[73] [Fritz] Rathenau, "Gewerbliche Schutzrechte während des Krieges," *Weltwirtschaftliches Archiv* 7 (1916): 58.

[74] Ibid., 71–2.

[75] Otto Ohnesorge, "Das Patentwesen im Kriege," *Zeitschrift für angewandte Chemie* 30 (1917): 129.

[76] Ibid., 132. Emphasis in original.

The Treaty of Versailles tried to draw "a veil of oblivion" over the patent seizures during the war, essentially resetting the clock to July 1914 while also rejecting patent reparations.[77] A large number of compulsory licenses issued to firms in allied and neutral nations for German patents were to be repaid via mediation, and it was generally felt that the sections of the Treaty pertaining to patents had not left Germany too disadvantaged.[78]

The Weimar constitution proclaimed the protection of "intellectual work" based on invention, but this did not lead to revision of the patent statute.[79] As for the chemical engineer who credited the 1877 law with bringing about "a new intellectual force" for the good of German industry:

The collective nature of intellectual work established thereby has lent German industry something of the impersonal, which forces every chemist to work more for the whole than for himself. That our chemists so willingly fulfill these demands is an outflow of a national peculiarity that one may characterize as intellectual mass discipline.[80]

For the nationalist the struggle was now about the connection between industry and science, and this was not a "purely commercial moment."[81]

In 1919 one of the founding figures of the German Society for Technical Physics was indeed Hans Gerdien, head of the Siemens Research Laboratory and the corporate face of many Siemens patents. By bringing together technical physicists and scientifically inclined engineers, the Society hoped "to control the damaging disconnection and specialization that techno-scientific life today has acquired."[82] It would be a mistake to cast this as frustrated emulation of the prerogatives of academic physicists, when men like Gerdien were much more intent on safeguarding new spaces of "scientific-technical research works" from the short-term thinking of the commercial spirit (*kaufmännischer Geist*).[83] Merely

---

[77] Paul Abel, "Der gewerbliche Rechtsschutz im Friedensvertrag," *Anzeiger für Elektrotechnik und Maschinenbau*, no. 1 (January 4, 1920): 1–2. See especially articles 307 and 308 of the treaty.

[78] Hermann Isay, *Die privaten Rechte und Interessen im Friedensvertrag*, 3rd ed. (Berlin: Vahlen, 1923), 362; C. Wiegand, "Die Patente und das Reichspatentamt in der Nachkriegszeit," *Zeitschrift für angewandte Chemie* 39 (1926): 1470–3.

[79] Schmidt, *Erfinderprinzip*, 147; Gispen, *Poems in Steel*.

[80] A. Binz, "Geist und Materie in der chemischen Industrie," *Zeitschrift für angewandte Chemie* 35 (1922): 387.

[81] Binz, "Der Kampf der Völker um die Industrie," 123.

[82] G. Gehlhoff, H. Rukop, and W. Hort, "Zur Einführung," *Zeitschrift für technische Physik* 1 (1920): 3.

[83] H. Gerdien, "Das Forschungslaboratorium der Siemens & Halske A.-G. und der Siemens-Schuckertwerke G.m.b.H. in Berlin-Siemensstadt," *Siemens-Zeitschrift*, no. 6 (1926): 413.

invoking "science" was not enough in itself to sustain a corporate identity (in both senses), because there were no clear distinctions between basic research, applied research, and development at the time.[84] "The era of the polymath even in the domain of scientific-technical research in industry is past," claimed Gerdien, "the specialist has triumphed, but the specialist with the best understanding for neighboring domains will always be the most valuable co-worker."[85] But how was one to dignify that mid-level gaze while the threshold of invention was subtly shifting from the traditional figure of the "person skilled in the art" to the "normally gifted specialist" in the modern corporate context?[86] The patent remained divisive because it drove new forms of market coordination but also ratified a form of belonging to a community of technical creators, a community whose boundaries remained unsettlingly porous by comparison with more traditional scholarly enclaves.

10.8   Conclusion: The Broader Significance of German Patent Law

From 1928 onward repeated attempts were made to introduce patent reform in the Reichstag. The provision long sought by engineers, that the patent must be assigned to the "true inventor," was vigorously opposed by large industrial concerns like Siemens, where Fischer remained the most prominent advocate of "company inventions" as the legal form best suited to the collective research dynamic of the modern business enterprise.[87] German engineers faced an increasing employment crisis as global economic depression set in, and staff cuts at the biggest companies opened new possibilities for legislative alliances favoring engineers as employee-inventors.[88] The Ministry of Justice signaled its support for the shift to the inventor's right in 1929, but the Patent Office itself

---

[84] Ulrich Marsch, *Zwischen Wissenschaft und Wirtschaft: Industrieforschung in Deutschland und Großbritannien 1880–1936*, vol. 47, Publications of the German Historical Institute (Paderborn: Ferdinand Schöningh, 2000), 26.

[85] H. Gerdien, "Ziele und Aufgaben technisch-physikalischer Forschungsinstitute in der Industrie," *Zeitschrift für technische Physik* 10 (1929): 218.

[86] Fischer, *Betriebserfindungen*, 9. In patent law, experts were those possessing "a special knowledge [*Spezialkenntnis*], meaning technically well-trained functionaries of the industry branch concerned, so that it does not involve just gauging here the knowledge and skill of ordinary artisans." Oscar Schanze, *Patentrechtliche Untersuchungen* (Jena: Gustav Fischer, 1901), 117.

[87] Fischer, *Betriebserfindungen*.

[88] The number of highly qualified staff at the Siemens research laboratory dropped by half between 1928 and 1932. Paul Erker, "Die Verwissenschaftlichung der Industrie. Zur Geschichte der Industrieforschung in den Europäischen und Amerikanischen Elektrokonzernen 1890–1930," *Zeitschrift für Unternehmensgeschichte* 35 (1990): 86.

remained opposed until summer 1933, when it finally conceded that the cause of the individual inventor was consistent "with the social goals of national uplift."[89] The timing is slightly misleading since the full draft brought to the floor of the parliament in April 1932 already contained the key provision, and only the frequent dissolution of the Reichstag had derailed this and earlier versions. When the Nazis eventually enacted a new Patent Code in 1936, it retained the "true inventor" and other pro-inventor features like easier appeals and lower fees, and dispensed with company inventions. Unlike the 1925 Austrian statute, however (see the next chapter), the German statute did not seek to clarify the status of the employee-inventor in terms of labor law, so the right of the "true inventor" remained ambiguous in practice.[90] Patent attorney Vojáček indeed argued that Austrian patent law outpaced the German system in its solicitude for individual inventors, since it counted the duration of patents from the date of publication rather than filing, offered more favorable terms for defrauded inventors to reclaim their patent rights, and extended an in-principle legal claim to contractual employee-inventors to share benefits of invention.[91] While the German law was consciously promulgated to empower individual inventors, however, it stopped short of addressing this aspect of the engineers' corporate striving for professional autonomy.[92]

Ironically, just as the old German patent system – as the third major world model – was being eclipsed, it was reaching its zenith as an international template. As of 1936 the German system had been adopted by Sweden, Norway, Denmark, Finland, Holland, and Italy (1934), with the Austrian system adopted in Czechoslovakia, and an adapted version without formal inspection for novelty adopted in Hungary and Yugoslavia. Even the 1924 Soviet statute mimicked the German one (only to be superseded in 1931; see Chapter 12 on Russia). And according to Vojáček, in 1907 and in 1919 Poland selectively adopted features from the current patent systems of Germany and of Austria, but with neither examination for novelty nor opposition proceedings![93]

The late apotheosis of the individual inventor in German patent law was highly contingent, as much a reformulation of the inventor's obligations to the nation as it was a liberation from the supposed yoke of large enterprises. The growing conviction that inventions in the modern era were dependent on new scales of capital investment and infrastructure

---

[89] Schmidt, *Erfinderprinzip*, 210.   [90] Gispen, *Poems in Steel*, chap. 6.
[91] Vojáček, *A Survey of the Principal National Patent Systems*, 150.
[92] Gispen, *Poems in Steel*, 145; Schmidt, *Erfinderprinzip*, 223.
[93] Vojáček, *A Survey of the Principal National Patent Systems*, 151–2.

meant that Germany's scale advantages would dominate any legal discussion of the relation of technical creativity and collective productivity in neighboring countries. Recurrent calls for patent reform in America, Central Europe, and Soviet Russia, wrote the Austrian-Swiss economist Stephan Bauer, would surely win acceptance due to "the social function of intellectual work in the economy of nations."[94] Distinctive sociopolitical understandings of intellectual labor in multinational states indeed dogged efforts to formulate competing (and compatible) patent laws in imperial and postimperial Romanov and Habsburg contexts. The German patent debates inevitably loomed large for these neighbors, often economically reliant on German technologies, but equally determined to foster indigenous patent cultures that would empower inventors and increase production. Their dilemmas will be the subject of the next two chapters.

---

[94] Stephan Bauer, "Das Los des Erfinders. Internationale Gestaltungen des Patentrechts des Angestellten," *Archiv für Sozialwissenschaft und Sozialpolitik* 57 (1927): 416.

11 Multiple Loyalties
Hybrid Patent Regimes in the Habsburg Empire and Its Successor States

Karl Hall

11.1 Introduction

In the early twentieth century, Lemberg (Lwów to Polish speakers, Lviv in present-day Ukraine) lay on the eastern reaches of the Habsburg Empire, some fifteen hours by train from Vienna. The Polish inventor Jan Szczepanik (1872–1926), who hailed from the Lemberg countryside, could hire a Vienna patent attorney to acquire a patent that would offer him full legal protections throughout the Habsburg lands. Yet that was not enough for an enterprising inventor like Szczepanik. To secure economic value for his patents across the empire and beyond, he needed to live in the imperial capital and cultivate the requisite legal, commercial, and press connections. The worth of a provincial invention was not automatically recognized, but by the same token the brainchildren of this Polish inventor eventually lost credit as *Polish* inventions once in German-speaking markets, as Szczepanik realized after his long sojourn in Vienna.[1]

Of course, to speak of "Polish" inventions before the dismantling of the Habsburg Empire in 1918 is to impose an anachronistic national frame on a domain in which provincial inventors were claimed by multiple constituencies with conflicting interests in national identity. At various times Szczepanik was labeled a Polish Edison,[2] a Galician Edison,[3] and an Austrian Edison,[4] or could also be construed simply as a "European" Edison.[5] This phenomenon reflects broader tensions and inequities in Habsburg politics. While Bohemian and Moravian elites sought advantage in federal prerogatives that did not benefit all Slavic

[1] Edmund Libański, "Z wystawy wynalazków polskich," *Kurjer Lwowski*, June 15, 1902.
[2] "Der polnische Edison," *Neue Freie Presse*, June 19, 1898.
[3] Edouard Bonnaffé, "Le tissage photo-électrique," *Le magasin pittoresque*, 2nd Series, 16 (1898): 306–7; X. Y., "Der Fernseher," *Neue Freie Presse*, March 20, 1898.
[4] "Die Schlachten der Zukunft," *Prager Tagblatt*, January 4, 1899.
[5] "Učitel na závidenie," *Národné noviny*, June 13, 1898; Peter Krass, *Ignorance, Confidence, and Filthy Rich Friends: The Business Adventures of Mark Twain, Chronic Speculator and Entrepreneur* (New York: John Wiley & Sons, 2007), 224.

constituencies equally, the Magyar aristocrats who dominated the Trans-leithanian half of Habsburg politics in turn rejected any federal measures that would diminish Hungarian prerogatives. Such intra-imperial tensions extended to patent law as well. Divergent national aspirations were nevertheless not obstacles to patent harmonization within the empire, nor did they forestall engagement with the Paris Union on Industrial Property. The multilayered imperial relations to Continental legal traditions provided durable shared frames for national patent reform debates before and after 1918. With the evolving German patent system as the dominant external reference point, within the Habsburg Empire plural legal traditions and intra-imperial intellectual traffic meant both gradual reform and robust debate at every stage. This chapter traces the formal devolution from imperial to national patent systems as well as the persistent legal and technocratic imperatives that ultimately drew these legacy systems closer to each other.

Within the Austrian territories of the Habsburg Empire, the General Austrian Civil Code of 1811 exhibited stronger French influences than in the German states. Deeply imbued with the Roman law tradition and its distinction between possession and ownership, the Austrian civil code dominated legal instruction and debate for half a century.[6] The first imperial decree on patent privileges in 1810 was "a strange conglomerate of principles," excluding agricultural implements, and extending protection to the entire Reich only in some cases, while limiting them to provinces or even districts in others.[7] It took an examination system as its basis, but the addition of Lombardy to the empire led to the enactment of a French-style system in 1820 that required only registration of patent claims.[8] At mid-century it was indeed plausible to treat the Habsburg Empire rather than Prussia as a pacesetter in central European patent regulation.[9] The Habsburg Empire adopted a modified privilege statute in 1852 that defined novelty somewhat more strictly and demanded greater documentary specification of the invention, and also brought a measure of consistency to its many territories. It signed a trade agreement with the German *Zollverein* in 1865 that expanded the scope of mutual patent protection.

---

[6] Jan Kuklík, *Czech Law in Historical Contexts* (Prague: Karolinum Press, 2015), 57.
[7] J. G. Ritt. v. Woerz, "Die materiellen Rechtsgrundsätze des österreichischen Privilegiengesetzes," *Gerichtshalle* (May 30, 1892): 192.
[8] Paul Beck von Mannagetta, *Das neue österreichische Patentrecht* (Vienna: Alfred Hölder, 1897), 11; Elmar Wadle, *Geistiges Eigentum: Bausteine zur Rechtsgeschichte*, vol. 2 (Munich: C. H. Beck, 2003).
[9] Franz Makowiczka, "Die österreichische Erfindungspatent-Gesetzgebung," *Archiv der politischen Oekonomie und Polizeiwissenschaft* 10 (1853): 313–56.

While the Austro-Hungarian Ministry of Trade succeeded in producing a fairly functional registration system, nondisclosure of patent specification was permitted at the applicant's request. Over time it became apparent that the Ministry's arbitration mechanisms for handling infringement or contested patents were woefully inadequate. Some cases dragged on for as much as a decade. The state penalized inadvertent infringers too harshly while letting genuine abusers off too easily, thus discrediting the invention process itself.[10] As the German economy took wing in the latter decades of the century, various figures in Austro-Hungary began to question its patent system and looked increasingly to the German model of 1877.

We begin the discussion with Austria – meaning the dominant Cisleithanian half of the empire rather than the future nation-state. While subsequent sections on Hungarian, Polish, and Czech debates naturally highlight national aspirations, each must be taken within its broader imperial context, rather than distinct from it, since the evolving statutes came to incorporate a complex mixture of reference points from Roman, German, French, and Anglo-American legal traditions.

11.2 Securing the Traffic in Intangible Goods in the Eastern Kingdom

It was at the international patent congress hosted by the 1873 world exhibition in Vienna that the Siemens brothers famously attempted to forge a consensus in favor of a unified German patent law.[11] That exhibition's general director, Baron Schwartz, had seen the London exhibitions of 1851 and 1862 and the Paris exhibitions of 1855 and 1867 as instigators of patent reform.[12] In preparation for the 1873 exhibition the chief Austrian proponent of patent reform, the mechanical engineer Wilhelm Franz Exner (1840–1931), edited two volumes on

---

[10] Dr. H. B., "Die Reform der Privilegien-Gesetzgebung," *Neue Freie Presse*, October 3, 1891; Otto Mayr, "Das neue Patentgesetz," *Österreichische Zeitschrift für Verwaltung* 31, no. 44 (November 3, 1898): 197–9.

[11] Carl Pieper, *Der Erfinderschutz und die Reform der Patentgesetze* (Dresden, 1873); Ludwig Fischer, "Werner Siemens und der Schutz der Erfindungen," *Wissenschaftliche Veröffentlichungen aus dem Siemens-Konzern* 2 (1922): 46–8; Alfred Heggen, *Erfindungsschutz und Industrialisierung in Preussen: 1793–1877* (Göttingen: Vandenhoeck & Ruprecht, 1975), 111–16.

[12] F. X. Neumann, "Rückblick auf den Patent-Congress," *Internationale Ausstellungs-Zeitung [Neue Freie Presse]*, August 12, 1873.

the history of Austrian invention.[13] For him the puzzle was why Austrian regulation of patent privileges had generated so few great inventions.[14] Exner concluded that it was time to drop the lenient French-based registration model and move to a more rigorous system of inspection of the kind proposed for the Germanic states.[15]

At the subsequent International Congress on International Property at Paris in 1878, Exner and his allies took a leading role for Austro-Hungary.[16] Yet little headway was made in practical legislation owing to the sheer expense of prior examinations and the concern that civil servants were incapable of judging the "causal nexus" that motivated inventions.[17] Besides, any proposals for a Viennese patent office could prompt Hungarian demands for a counterpart institution in Budapest. The interim consensus was that an improved registration system remained preferable, since prior examination was both expensive and led to a "confounding fiction of governmental omniscience in patent affairs."[18] A Frankfurt patent attorney cautioned Exner that it was difficult in practice to establish novelty, and that the less strict French registration and mixed British systems were not overloaded with bad patents, while the German patent office actually dealt with many complaints about incorrectly issued patents. His verdict: Exner the high-minded engineer needed to be more practical.[19]

As a Liberal Member of Parliament from 1882, Exner was convinced that having more engineers in higher office would improve Austria's position in this reformist dynamic. Early in 1883 he presented a draft bill on patents, trademarks, and designs to a special parliamentary committee, legislation that would create a patent office and ensure the intellectual property of Austrian industry with generous twenty-year

---

[13] Wilhelm Franz Exner, ed., *Beiträge zur Geschichte der Gewerbe und Erfindungen Oesterreiches von der Mitte des XVIII. Jahrhunderts bis zur Gegenwart*, 2 vols. (Vienna: Wilhelm Braumüller, 1873).

[14] "International Patent-Congress," *Internationale Ausstellungs-Zeitung [Neue Freie Presse]*, August 6, 1873.

[15] "Politische Uebersicht," *Das Vaterland*, October 19, 1878.

[16] "Internationaler Patent-Congress," *Die Presse*, September 10, 1878; Stephen P. Ladas, *Patents, Trademarks, and Related Rights: National and International Protection* (Cambridge, MA: Harvard University Press, 1975), 61.

[17] Mayr, "Das neue Patentgesetz," November 3, 1898.

[18] "Der österreichische Advocatentag und die Reform des österreichischen Patentrechtes," *Die Presse*, September 30, 1882.

[19] Franz Wirth, "Die Patentreform," *Neue Freie Presse*, April 11, 1883. For similar sentiments from a Hungarian attorney, Rezső Dell'Adami, "A szabadalmi jog szabályozásának alapelvei," *Jogtudományi Közlöny* 19, no. 45 (November 7, 1884): 353–5.

terms.[20] However, officials in the Ministry of Trade put the expert review process on the slow track, partly blaming their Hungarian counterparts for poor communication.[21] After repeated confrontations with Exner, a junior civil servant, jurist, and minor aristocrat named Paul Beck von Mannagetta (1851–1921) eventually won the support of the Ministry of Trade for Exner's legislation, and later became the first president of the new patent office. Yet this did not necessarily represent a victory for more technical forms of expertise in state administration.[22]

High court lawyer Joseph Ludwig Brunstein (1840–1916) served as the official examiner of Exner's patent reform commission. In 1885 he weighed in with a lengthy essay, arguing that the balance between material property and intellectual property was difficult to sustain in the world of commerce. In Brunstein's view, although intellectual property might not be the best juridical construction to satisfy *Erfinderehre*, the functional parallels with property were strong enough to warrant the exercise. The specification of the invention was valid as a "symbolic act of appropriation leading to legal acquisition."[23] The nature of that acquisition was crucial to the viability of intellectual property.

Brunstein's position was potentially compatible with the view held by the leading authority on Habsburg civil law, Bohemian aristocrat Anton (Antonín) von Randa (1834–1914), that property rights were circumscribed by considerations of the common good. Trade monopolies, copyright, and patent privileges could all be objects of possession in Randa's reading, but so long as the subjective ownership right was not formalized and temporal limitations applied, intellectual property as ownership remained shaky.[24] For Brunstein, the inventor's right, though a check on the commercial interests of third parties, nonetheless served to curb their legal ability to diminish the common good. Those who took Brunstein as arguing that patent law simply needed to keep up with the "economic metamorphoses" of modernization welcomed the passing of the old privilege system. Less charitable adherents of Randa complained

---

[20] "Die Exner'schen Gesetzentwürfe über Patent-, Muster- und Markenschutz," *Neue Freie Presse*, February 8, 1883.

[21] "Reform der Patentgesetzgebung," *Neue Freie Presse*, February 6, 1885.

[22] Exner, *Erlebnisse*, 200–2. Beck von Mannagetta lacked technical expertise. The judicial portion of the patent office staff would still include a high number of Ritters and Freiherrs. "Der Personalstand des neuen Patentamtes," *Neuigkeits Welt Blatt*, December 14, 1898.

[23] Joseph Ludwig Brunstein, *Zur Reform des Erfinderrechtes: Vortrag gehalten im Niederösterr. Gewerbeverein am 10. April 1885* (Vienna: Manz, 1885), 8.

[24] Anton von Randa, *Der Besitz nach österreichischem Rechte*, 4th ed. (Leipzig, 1895), 620, 661–2; Ernst Bettelheim, *Das Recht des Erfinders in Österreich nach dem Gesetze vom 11. Januar 1897* (Vienna: Manz, 1901), 92.

that the process by which the inventor's idea was objectivized did not lead to a "thing" that could be protected in civil law. What was missing in strictly legal terms was an account of how to bring the inventor's interests into concert with the *Rechtsstaat*.[25]

In 1891 the imperial government finally introduced its version of the patent legislation under pressure from Exner concerning the imminent end of the trade agreement with Hungary (see below).[26] The final statute was only formalized in January 1897.[27] By then there was a growing consensus that the "traffic in intangible goods" (*Immaterialgüterverkehr*) had grown to proportions that demanded new legal protections for the inventor.[28] Now a firm advocate of the modern statute, Beck von Mannagetta portentously proclaimed that "the entire progress of mankind can be traced back without exception to the revolutionary power of new inventions."[29] The new Austrian statute made stronger requirements to establish novelty and commercial utility, and patent holders were obliged to work the patent in Austria within three years of issuance or forfeit their rights. Inventors were also obliged to license to third parties for appropriate compensation: no monopolies were permissible. The new statute established a patent office in Vienna with a staff of around seventy-five lawyers, technical specialists, and civil service support staff, and a separate patent court was required to include three members with specialist technical backgrounds.[30]

Austrians took some pride in the stronger protection afforded to the original inventor than in German law, including modest default provisions for inventor-employees in the enterprise setting. However, von Randa's work meant that patents could not be classified as intellectual property: better to treat the inventor's right as a special category to be placed alongside private law, but not subsumed within its categories. As one early author on Austrian patent law wrote, this might perhaps constitute a right to quasi-things (*quasidingliches Recht*).[31] As might be expected, the Austrian and Hungarian halves of the empire were subsequently attentive to issues of mutual recognition, and for good measure an 1899 imperial decree asserted that new inventions valued by industry

[25] "Zur Reform des Erfinderrechtes," *Die Presse*, June 13, 1885.
[26] "Aus dem Abgeordnetenhause," *Prager Tagblatt*, April 24, 1891; "Reichsrath. 56. Sitzung des Abgeordnetenhauses," *Wiener Abendpost*, October 22, 1891.
[27] "Gesetz vom 11. Jänner 1897, betreffend den Schutz von Erfindungen (Patentgesetz)," *Reichsgesetzblatt*, no. 8 (1897): 35–56.
[28] Otto Mayr, "Das neue Patentgesetz," *Österreichische Zeitschrift für Verwaltung* 31, no. 45 (November 10, 1898): 201–3.
[29] Beck von Mannagetta, *Das neue österreichische Patentrecht*, 1.
[30] "Zehn Jahre Österreichisches Patentamt," *Österreichisches Patentblatt* 11 (1909): 47–50.
[31] Bettelheim, *Das Recht des Erfinders in Österreich*, 57, 87, 92, 95, 98.

would automatically enjoy protection in both territories, so long as they did not contradict any individual provisions of one of them.

The real Austrian concern in the first decades of the twentieth century was nonetheless focused on finding ways to ensure mutual recognition with German patent law.[32] While German engineers now detected a friendlier environment in Austria for the notion of intellectual property and appreciated the modest Austrian protections for inventor-employees, the most successful Austrian inventors invariably attuned their efforts to the overwhelming dominance of the German market.[33] Of the 5,812 Austrian patents awarded in 1913, 40 percent went to German applicants, while American, British, and French applicants claimed another fifth.[34] Germany joined the Paris Convention in 1903, yet Austria and Hungary waited another five years, not least because joining meant modifying the favorable bilateral trade agreement with Germany from 1891.[35] But the important provision that patent priority in any two Union countries would hold for both based on the earliest filing in either then provided an important incentive to join.[36]

The 1897 Austrian patent law as a "mixed" system nonetheless remained less disputed up through the end of the Eastern Kingdom than was the case in Germany, where engineers were more vocal politically but the statute gave less heed to inventor-employees.[37] Although World War I presented a threat to the function of intellectual property in Austria, since so many patent holders were foreigners, the state cautiously imposed restrictions largely in reciprocal fashion.[38] Rump Austria also

[32] Emanuel Adler, *Die Beziehungen der beiden Staatsgebiete der österreichisch-ungarischen Monarchie betreffend den Schutz der Erfindungen, Marken und Muster* (Vienna: Manzsche Verlag, 1906); "Közös szabadalmi jog Ausztria, Németország és Magyarország számára," *Szabadalmi Közlöny* 22 (1917): 257.
[33] Friedrich Ruppert, "Technisches geistiges Eigentum, Erfindung und Patentierung," *Zeitschrift des Vereines Deutscher Ingenieure* 48 (1904): 1686–9.
[34] "Ausztria 1913. évi szabadalom- és mintaügyi statisztikája," *Szabadalmi Közlöny* 19 (1914): 422–4.
[35] "Autriche. Nouveaux traités nécessités par l'entrée de l'Autriche et de la Hongrie dans l'Union internationale," *La Propriété Industrielle* 24, no. 12 (1908): 180. Austria had originally declared its intention to join in 1897 when it hosted the First Congress of the International Union for Industrial Property Rights. ma. [Mannagetta?], "Der erste Congress der internationalen Vereinigung für gewerblichen Rechtschutz," *Allgemeine österreichische Gerichts-Zeitung*, November 6, 1897.
[36] "Beitritt Oesterreichs zur Internationalen Union zum Schutze des gewerblichen Eigentums," *Neues Wiener Abendblatt*, November 26, 1908.
[37] Kees Gispen, *New Profession, Old Order: Engineers and German Society, 1815 1914* (Cambridge: Cambridge University Press, 1989).
[38] Paul Abel, "Der Krieg und der Schutz des gewerblichen und geistigen Eigentums in Österreich," *Allgemeine österreichische Gerichts-Zeitung*, September 26, 1914.

experienced no urgent need to reform its statute after 1918, since the nation-states formed in its wake tended to take it as their point of reference.[39] Because the Treaty of Versailles drew "a veil of oblivion" over the patent seizures during the war, Austrian procedures essentially resumed as before, though notably reduced in scale.[40]

Against a background of recurrent economic crises, the technocratic spirit of a new "age of organization" elevated the role of the patent office in the eyes of the interwar Austrian inventor who saw it as the protector of inventors now more likely to be enterprise employees. "The intellectual property of citizens is indeed one of the most important assets of the ideal property of Austria," proclaimed an official in the Austrian Inventors Association.[41] In Red Vienna a 1921 employment law gave inventor-employees more protections.[42] While a new patent statute was passed in 1925 that nominally strengthened inventor-employee patent rights, the practical instances in which they could claim such rights were now more restricted.[43] As Siemens patent lawyer Ludwig Fischer had been arguing to the dismay of engineers, the locus of invention was firmly shifting to patent pooling in which no single employee could lay claim to rights in a collective inventive endeavor.[44] Industrial research laboratories were quickly becoming *Erfindungsautomaten*, sites for impersonal, machine-like production of inventions.[45]

[39] "Erfindungsschutz in den Nationalstaaten," *Anzeiger für Elektrotechnik und Maschinenbau*, no. 49 (December 7, 1919): 193.

[40] Paul Abel, "Der gewerbliche Rechtsschutz im Friedensvertrag," *Anzeiger für Elektrotechnik und Maschinenbau*, no. 1 (January 4, 1920): 1–2.

[41] Hans Hugo Stiotta, "Aus der Werkstätte der Erfinder," *Wiener Zeitung*, April 19, 1924, Beilage edition; Ferdinand Arlt, *Das österreichische Patentgesetz in gemeinverständlicher Darstellung, nebst den wichtigsten Bestimmungen des internationalen Rechtes und einem Anhang über den Schutz von Marken und Mustern* (Vienna: Steyermühl Verlag, 1927), 7. At the end of his long career Exner likewise employed the term "intellectual property"; Exner, *Erlebnisse*, 200–2.

[42] Hermann Heindl, *Der Erfinderschutz der Angestellten in der Patentgesetznovelle 1925* (Vienna: Bund der Industrieangestellten Oesterreichs, 1926); Oskar Meister, "Arbeitsrechtliches im neuen Patentgesetze," *Allgemeine österreichische Gerichts-Zeitung*, February 15, 1926.

[43] Emanuel Adler and Richard Reik, *Das Österreichische Patentgesetz mit den einschlägigen Gesetzen, Verordnungen und Staatsvertäge und einer Übersicht über die Rectsprechung* (Vienna: Manzsche Verlag, 1926).

[44] Ludwig Fischer, *Betriebserfindungen* (Berlin: Carl Heymanns Verlag, 1921).

[45] Stephan Bauer, "Das Los des Erfinders. Internationale Gestaltungen des Patentrechts des Angestellten," *Archiv für Sozialwissenschaft und Sozialpolitik* 57 (1927): 413.

11.3 A Nation of Lawyers, but Not Patent Attorneys: The Struggle for Technical Expertise in the Hungarian Lands

Although the 1820 Austrian privilege statute was nominally enacted on Hungarian territory two years later, mutual recognition of patent rights between all the territories of the Habsburg Empire only came with an 1852 imperial decree.[46] A more explicit legal statute in the same vein became part of the tariff and trade agreement formalizing the Dualist compromise in 1867. When the Austrian patent reform debate got underway in the early 1880s, Hungarians sought the creation of their own patent office as part of the periodic renegotiations of the tariff and trade agreement that were eventually concluded in 1893. While both sides sought legal protection for intellectual property,[47] the Austrians gravitated toward the German examination system, and the Hungarians preferred a more limited registration system in the near term.[48] The Hungarian statute of 1895 resembled the British system, with a limited period of opposition proceedings in which interested parties could criticize or lay counter-claim to a provisional patent.[49] While the new Hungarian patent office performed a limited technical examination for industrial applicability nearer to the US than the UK model, no universal test for novelty was applied.[50]

Two striking features of the Hungarian debates are the recurrence of the intellectual property concept and the heightened tension between legal and engineering professions.[51] While Hungarian references to intellectual property (*szellemi tulajdon*) date back at least to 1840 in the copyright context,[52] the first hint of a broader legal meaning stems from

---

[46] Béla Lévy, *A magyar szabadalmi jog rendszere* (Budapest: Márkus Samu, 1898), 8; Zsigmond Kósa, *A magyar szabadalmi törvények magyarázata*, 2nd ed. (Debrecen: Politzer Zsigmond, 1911), 3–23.

[47] "Reform der Privilegien-Gesetzgebung."

[48] Izidor Deutsch, *A szabadalmi törvényjavaslat* (Budapest: Franklin Társulat, 1895); Gyula Kovács, "A találmányok védelme Németországon," *Budapesti Szemle* 42, no. 101 (1885): 303–10.

[49] "Aus dem Reichstage," *Pester Lloyd*, May 8, 1895, second supplement edition.

[50] László Török, *A találmányi szabadalom: A szabadalmi jog és gyakorlat, különös tekintettel Magyarországra* (Budapest: Rényi Károly, 1913), 21–2; Henrik Fenyő, "Szabadalmi intézményeink mai állapota," *Magyar Mérnök- és Építész-Egylet Közlönye* 48, no. 8 (1914): 138–42.

[51] Izidor Deutsch, "Az ipari szellemi tulajdon védelme," *Jogtudományi Közlöny* 29 (1894): 251–4, 260–2, 275–6, 281–3, 291–3, 310–11, 315–17, 325–7, 346; Gyula Wetzel, *A találmányi szabadalmakról szóló 1895. évi XXXVII. tc valamint az ennek életbeléptetésére vonatkozó rendeletek magyarázata és a találmányi szabadalmakra vonatkozó összes törvények és rendeletek egybeállítása* (Budapest: Pallas, 1898); "A képviselőház ülése. A szabadalmak törvénye," *Budapesti Hírlap*, May 8, 1895, 3–4.

[52] Ferencz Schedel, "Az irói tulajdonról," *Budapesti Szemle* 1 (1840): 214–15.

the 1861 Provisional Juridical Rules, which proclaim that "the creations of the intellect [*ész*] also constitute the kind of property that is under the protection of the law."[53] The term had a certain appeal amid Dualist debates about Hungarian economic development.[54] Yet for the liberal young attorney Rezső Dell'Adami (1850–88) the shortcoming of the property analogy lay in property law's reluctance to allow for workplace and capital to shape concepts of property law beyond older material notions.[55] Intellectual property did not have to be subsumed within material property's legal structure. Nor did it have to become a sovereign concept, but it could rather be a constructed one consistent with the new institutional interests of the age. Legal institutions, however, were slow to emerge.[56]

Part of the appeal of intellectual property for some Hungarian contemporaries lay in their desire to remove patenting matters from the hands of ministerial trade and tariff committees in Vienna and construct a secure legal context for foreign inventors distinct from the Austrian half of the empire.[57] The most astute observer was Dell'Adami, who did not live to see the adoption of the Hungarian statute in 1895. He penned a series of essays in response to the Exner initiative (see above) where he argued that full reciprocity with German and Austrian statutes would be a mistake.[58] Dell'Adami agreed with Exner that patent protection had to be formulated in more than terms of utilitarian regulation, but should speak to the essence of invention, which is a species of intellectual

---

[53] László Arany, "Az írói és művészi tulajdonjogról," *Budapesti Szemle* 10, no. 19–20 (1876): 225–40; Róbert Palágyi, "A tudományos tulajdonról (Propriété scientifique)," *Szabadalmi Közlöny* 32 (1927): 169; Thomas R. Ilosvay, "Scientific Property," *American Journal of Comparative Law* 2, no. 2 (1953): 178–97; György Boytha, "A szerzői jog és az iparjogvédelem összefüggései," *Jogtudományi Közlöny*, New Series, 23 (1968): 596.

[54] "A Bécsben 1873-ban tartandó világtárlatról," *Erdészeti Lapok* 10, no. 10 (1871): 430–5; Sándor Matlekovits, "Üzleti törekvések a versenyben," *Nemzetgazdasági Szemle* 13 (1889): 253–70.

[55] Rezső Dell'Adami, "Az írói és művészi jog," *Jogtudományi Közlöny* 19, no. 12 (1884): 89–90.

[56] Sándor Matlekovits, "A magyar kereskd. törvénykönyv tervezete," *Jogtudományi Közlöny* 8, no. 38 (1873): 291–2.

[57] János Frecskay, "A találmányok szabadalmazásának önállósitása," *Nemzetgazdasági Szemle* 4 (1886): 293–305.

[58] Rezső Dell'Adami, "A szabadalmi jog szabályozásának alapelvei," *Jogtudományi Közlöny* 19, no. 31 (August 1, 1884): 244–5. Cf. nos. 34, 38, 42, and 45 (where he argued that the German patent office actually had too much administrative leeway to withdraw patents). His account of the Exner draft is in "A szabadalmi jog szabályozásának alapelvei," *Jogtudományi Közlöny* 20, no. 11 (March 13, 1885): 82–3. For his part Frecskay solicited the opinions of Ernst Hartig and Josef Rosenthal regarding the Hungarian draft; they unsurprisingly argued for a greater role for prior examination. János Frecskay, "Két külföldi szakvélemény a szabadalmi törvényjavaslat felől," *Nemzetgazdasági Szemle* 11 (1887): 124–38.

property. In his view, the law should develop to allow similar kinds of protection for literary work, scientific conception, and industrial invention. That patent-as-property was subject to temporal limits did not trouble him: "From the point of view of social and cultural interests the negation of inheritance law in the new domain of intellectual property is like a legal-socialist vanguard which signals the potential restriction of the individual owner's material goods in a future legal order."[59] Yet when couched in those terms, it is not hard to imagine why the Hungarian political elite, dominated by aristocratic landowners, felt little urgency to implement his recommendations.

The question of whether Hungary could legitimately pursue its own patent system independently of Vienna was entangled in more complicated legal debates about how to ensure symmetries between the two halves of the Dual Monarchy while also locating a distinctive legal rationale for the Hungarian state.[60] The 1895 statute ensured that Hungary would have its own patent institutions, including a new guild of patent agents at the urging of Izidor Deutsch (a consistent advocate of intellectual property), but that alone proved insufficient.[61] As became apparent in the following decade, it would be a greater challenge to persuade established Hungarian inventors and especially firms with institutional ties in Vienna to shift their interests to Budapest.[62]

Those more closely involved in the Hungarian draft process were eager to ensure that the political authorities played no part in patenting procedures. The lawyer Gyula Jámbor (born 1853), who served as secretary of the Technical University, sought to remove patent procedure from the long arm of the legal guild and render it solely a matter of technical expertise.[63] Chemical engineer and patent attorney Zsigmond Bernauer subsequently became the most visible proponent of this view.[64] While Jámbor urged the importance of training new technically qualified cadres on the US and German models, Hungarian lawyers generally

[59] Rezső Dell'Adami, "A szabadalmi jog szabályozásának alapelvei," *Jogtudományi Közlöny* 20, no. 19 (May 8, 1885): 148.
[60] László Péter, *Hungary's Long Nineteenth Century: Constitutional and Democratic Traditions in a European Perspective*, ed. Miklos Lojkó (Leiden: Brill, 2012), 77–84.
[61] "Enquete über die Patent-Gesetzgebung," *Pester Lloyd*, July 6, 1894; Deutsch, "Az ipari szellemi tulajdon védelme."
[62] István Kelemen Manó, *A találmányi szabadalmakról szóló 1895. évi XXXVII. törvénycikk revisiója* (Budapest: Országos Iparegyesület, 1905).
[63] Gyula Jámbor, "Szabadalmi ügyünk reformjához," *Magyar Mérnök- és Épitész-Egylet Közlönye* 28 (1894): 138.
[64] Zsigmond Bernauer, *A találmányi szabadalmahról szóló törvényjavaslat olőadói torvoactónck ismertetése és birálata* (Budapest: A Pesti-Lloyd Társulat Nyomdája, 1909), 18; "Szakbírák és szakértők a szabadalmi jogszolgáltatásban," *Magyar Mérnök- és Épitész-Egylet Közlönye* 45, no. 4 (1911): 49–52.

opposed any grant of special authority to patent examiners.[65] Actual inventors like Donát Bánki (1859–1922), an early developer of the automobile carburetor,[66] were concerned that the modified registration system did not do enough to protect the intellectual property of the true inventor.[67] His concern for intellectual property seems to have had more to do with scholarly credit than economic benefit: engineering had to be seen as good science.[68] Even the most progressive business circles took little interest in patenting. Although Hungarian industry remained firmly invested in trade secrets, it lacked a mechanism to criminalize their misappropriation.[69]

Dilemmas of jurisdiction were exacerbated by the changing nature of invention itself. Trade lawyer Oszkár Fazekas saw the growing "dematerialization of production" as generating ever newer problems for patents and trademarks, and he called for a philosophy of intellectual property in response. The legal apparatus was too fixated on the material artifacts of technical production, when modern culture and the "emanations of the spirit" were fast outgrowing its cramped forms. Patents and trademarks were ill suited to the property categories of Roman law, and old-fashioned dualisms of body and soul were becoming irrelevant in the face of new economic goods consisting of "a sensible body and a kind of abstract substance that exists both in and outside the bodily object."[70] It was vital for the law "to devote attention to every existing and generative intellectual product (relation) which has value in terms of the tasks of social economy."[71] Codification of the law of intellectual goods, however

[65] "Die Patentreform in Ungarn," *Neue Freie Presse*, July 3, 1894, evening edition; "Aus dem Reichstage," *Pester Lloyd*, May 21, 1895.
[66] Though he is known to have perfected the device several years earlier, the carburetor patent claim was based on Bánki Donát and Csonka János, Automatikus csőgyújtás gáz- és petroleummótoroknál, Magy. Kir. Szabadalmi Hivatal 7159 (Budapest, issued April 25, 1896). (There were subsequent British, French, and Swiss patents as well.)
[67] Donát Bánki, "A Szabadalmi Bizottság jelentése és a szabadalmi törvényjavaslat," in *Találmányi szabadalmak és használati minták oltalma* (Budapest, 1894), 145–50, http://tortenet.sztnh.gov.hu/getdatac81c.html#289.
[68] A lecture on a patented dynamometer makes this clear; Donát Bánki, "Bánki Donát szabadalmazott erőmérője," *Magyar Mérnök- és Épitész-Egylet Közlönye* 20, no. 2 (1886): 161–70.
[69] Lajos Szente, "Levéltitok – üzleti titok," *Jogtudományi Közlöny* 40, no. 47 (1905): 386; Oszkár Fazekas, *A jogász és a műszaki elem a szabadalmi hatóságok szervezetében* (Budapest: Franklin-Társulat, 1917).
[70] Oszkár Fazekas, "A termelés immaterializálódása és a jogfejlődés," *Iparjogi Szemle* 1, no. 9–10 (1906): 299.
[71] Oszkár Fazekas, "A szellemi tulajdon jogbölcseletéhez," in *Nagy Ferenc emlékkönyve* (Budapest: Athenaeum, 1906), 175. This is perhaps an early instance of what Mario Biagioli sees as the dissolution of the distinction between tangible device and intangible knowledge in patent law; "Between Knowledge and Technology: Patenting Methods, Rethinking Materiality," *Anthropological Forum* 22, no. 3 (2012): 285–300.

slow it might advance, also served the purpose of diminishing the pernicious influence of German Pandectists and Austrians on Hungarian law.[72] In his view, by fostering harmonization with larger international contexts, the law of intellectual goods brought Hungary much desired regional autonomy.[73] The abstractions of intellectual property could thus serve pragmatic ends.

In the prewar years the number of patents awarded by the Hungarian patent office rose in not quite lock-step fashion from 3,277 in the first full year of operation to 4,261 in 1913.[74] The standard patent term was fifteen years, with annual fees starting at 40 crowns in the first year (roughly a month's wages for a day laborer) and rising dramatically to 500 crowns in the final year.[75] Less than 2 percent of patents were maintained for the full term, however, and in general barely one-quarter were in effect a mere four years after issuance. Two out of five patents in 1913 went to German applicants, with residents of Hungarian territory claiming just one in four. Austrians held 10 percent, and around 5 percent went to British, French, and American applicants.[76] As the number of patent applications grew, the dozen engineers employed at the Hungarian Patent Office were simply overwhelmed. Keenly aware that all the major players in this international game had recently reformed their patent laws or were debating serious revisions (as in the German case), Hungarian engineers pressed for a more prominent role.[77]

When he became president of the Hungarian Patent Office in 1914, Kolozsvár-trained lawyer Rudolf Schuster (1860–1941) was determined to move closer to the examination system, while acknowledging that Hungary was not yet in a position to support an analogous administrative apparatus.[78] The sheer number of patents then in existence meant that prior examination could no longer pretend to deliver judgments with an exhaustive global scope. Perhaps three-quarters of the patent office work was now thoroughly technical, and while Schuster loved the legal "art," he felt the system must "render unto the technician that which is the

---

[72] Oszkár Fazekas, "Review of Meszlény, A tisztességtelen versenyről szóló törvény magyarázata," *Jogtudományi Közlöny* 58, no. 16 (1923): 126–7.
[73] Oszkár Fazekas, "Az iparjogvédelmi törvények egységesítése," *Iparjogi Szemle* 19, no. 3 (1925): 9–10.
[74] Statistics compiled from *Szabadalmi közlöny* 19 (1914): 646.
[75] Modest provision was made for inventors who could not afford the initial fees.
[76] "A m. kir. Szabadalmi Hivatal 1913-ik évi statisztikája," *Szabadalmi Közlöny* 19 (1914): 532–6.
[77] Fenyő, "Szabadalmi intézményeink mai állapota."
[78] Rudolf Schuster, "Az iparijogvédelmi reform kérdéséhez," *Jogtudományi Közlöny* 49, no. 51 (1914): 514–16.

technician's."[79] He drafted a new patent law that posited greater symmetry between legal and technical expertise, raising hopes among engineers for a "completely modern patent law."[80] This nevertheless involved a certain rhetorical finesse to placate the lawyers' guild. The Patent Office would become the Patent Court, while the Patent Council would become the Upper Patent Court, adjudicating counterclaims. Thus the form of institutionalization was shifted from the initial bureaucratic statutory norms to a form that superficially deferred to the judicial sector; this kept local judges from being drawn into unproductive depositions by competing technical experts.[81] But what aroused opposition from the lawyers was that both the registration process and the Patent Court would feature majorities of technical experts. Only in the Upper Court would a 3:2 majority of judges over technical experts prevail.[82] As the debate dragged on, advocates also cast the new law as vital in preparing Hungary for the postwar competitive industrial order.[83]

Budapest lawyer Jakab Kohn opposed Schuster's draft law, not least because it did not sufficiently take into account the "freer ethical approach" of the patent attorneys coming primarily from engineering backgrounds. He believed that the engineers and their agents were not only usurping legal authority, but that they were poor epistemologists. Look around the world, said Kohn, from the most abstract to the most concrete phenomena, whether literary, philosophical, technical, commercial, manufacturing, sociological, or marine: what do you see? "[W]ith their ability to judge what is essential, lawyers prevail over experts, because just as organization is to matter and mass, in intellectuals this distinction [*disztinkció*, capacity for judgment] gives to the intellectually disciplined the power which, besides shedding light on skill,

[79] Rudolf Schuster, "Az új szabadalmi törvénytervezet ismertetése," *Szabadalmi Közlöny* 21 (1916): 174–85, at 182; "Der neue ungarische Patentgesetzentwurf," *Pester Lloyd*, March 10, 1918; "Előadás az új magyar szabadalmi törvénytervezetről," *Szabadalmi Közlöny* 23 (1918): 109–11.

[80] Zsigmond Bernauer, "A magyar szabadalmi jog reformjához," *Magyar Mérnök- és Építész-Egylet Közlönye* 50, no. 12 (1916): 64–5. Cf. Béla Lévy, "A szabadalmi törvényjavaslat előadói tervezete," *Jogtudományi Közlöny* 51 (1916): 333–5, 362–5, 373–5, 383–5.

[81] Zsigmond Bernauer, "Észrevételek az új szabadalmi törvénytervezethez," *Magyar Mérnök- és Építész-Egylet Közlönye* 51, no. 7 (1917): 60.

[82] Gyula Térfy, ed., "XXXV. törvénycikk a találmány szabadalmakról szóló 1895: XXXVII. törvénycikk egyes rendelkezéseinek módosításáról és kiegészítéséről," *Magyar törvénytár* 1920 (1921): 227–9.

[83] Ernő Meller, "A szabadalmi törvényjavaslat sürgössége, tekintettel a háborús viszonyokra," *Magyar Mérnök- és Építész-Egylet Közlönye* 50, no. 49 (1916): 299–300.

will find the ways and means for attaining the truth."[84] Civil and criminal law also had frequent recourse to expert testimony, but that did not mean that experts decided cases, for only the judge knew how to explain the outcomes properly. True knowledge required trained judgment as a superior supplement to technical procedure.[85]

Kohn's reasoning resonated with lawyers keen to maintain their generalist status vis-à-vis specialists like engineers, physicians, factory managers, and commercial traders. Only the lawyer could make the necessary distinctions (*disztingválni*) among diverse domains and form proper judgments. Yet it was becoming clear to some legal scholars that their training was falling behind the more demanding curricula of the engineers. As modern economic life grew more complex, lawyers would have to pay increasing heed to specialist opinions, while becoming better prepared in their own right to "pass them through the sieve of legal distinction [*distinkció*]."[86] In response to Kohn, patent attorney Bernauer countered that preparation of a patent application was not purely rational-procedural, it was in fact the first rhetorical volley in securing the specific legal claim of the inventor. Only the technically trained patent attorney was capable of representing both aspects at the highest level.

Hungary's new patent law was finally adopted in 1920, after formal introduction by MP and mechanical engineer Miksa Herrmann (1868–1944).[87] It contributed in limited fashion to a broader recognition of "intellectual products" of the kind advocated by Fazekas, and Roman law notions of property were gradually loosened to accommodate the plethora of new forms.[88] Whereas the 1895 statute had arguably depressed the number of patents by subjecting novelty claims to a universal test, the new law concerned itself only with publication or public working of the invention inside Hungary. Since Hungary had joined the

---

[84] Jakab Kohn, "A képviseleti kérdése a szabadalmi törvénytervezetben," *Jogtudományi Közlöny* 52, no. 2 (1917): 12. Although *disztinkció* was a neologism very nearly synonymous with *megkülönböztetés*, that its meaning was more closely associated with the legal profession can be seen, for example, in a 1914 trial defendant's statement that "I was only aiming at the concept of nation, at the nation which does not recognize scholarly distinctions [*megkülönböztetések*] and subtle legal distinctions [*disztinkciók*]." In *Budapesti Hírlap*, January 18, 1914.

[85] On trained judgment as a regulative ideal in this period, Lorraine Daston and Peter Galison, *Objectivity* (New York: Zone Books, 2007), 309–61.

[86] Miklós Mattyasovszky, "A jogászság hanyatlása," *Budapesti Hírlap*, February 15, 1914. The Hungarian lawyer's insistence on using the neologism "distinkció" signaled his conviction that this form of judgment was peculiar to his profession. Mattyasovszky was a docent on the law faculty at the University of Budapest.

[87] "A Nemzetgyülés 117. ülése," *Nemzetgyülési Napló*, no. 6 (October 26, 1920): 130–2.

[88] Antal Almási, *A dologi jog kézikönyve*, vol. 1 (Budapest: Tébe Kiadó, 1928), 76.

Paris Convention in the interim, its rules for bilateral agreements on priority applied as well. It remained the case – as in much of central Europe – that patents were not permitted for medicines, food and chemical products, and military technologies; related processes could, however, be patented. In general, the statute did not represent any political or social consensus between technical and industrial elites, now riven further by the tumultuous aftermath of the war.

In the last months of World War I, construction engineer Henrik Bauer (1855–1933) briefly became perhaps the most prominent advocate of greater social engagement by the engineering profession, though he was still respectable enough to be heard in the pages of the conservative central venue.[89] His final appeal for unity came when the Communists were ascendant, in March 1919, and the lengthy technocratic agenda he advocated included the need for "international central examination of inventions and the creation of internationally valid patent law."[90]

Yet the audience for such sentiments remained comparatively marginal in this volatile political setting. Kálmán Méhely, appointed state secretary for trade during the short-lived Republic formed at the end of 1918, was somewhat more representative. Keenly aware of the massive political challenges facing his government, he sought to reframe the perception of incipient political revolution by focusing attention on the economic shifts accelerated by the war.[91] At his behest the inaugural session of the National Labor Council was convened at the Technical University in February 1919. The rector welcomed the technocratic aspirations of the new government, for in his view the rigorous mode of thinking of the natural and engineering sciences was also "free from biases and well suited to democratic and social affairs." Méhely in turn cast revolution as a moment of renewal that had to be seized, because "we can only create now, when the linkage of routine, tradition, pompous official bureaucracy, and intertwined networks of interests that have hardened into concrete do not stand in the way of the creative urge."[92]

[89] Henrik Bauer, "Szociáltechnika," *Magyar Mérnök- és Építész-Egylet Közlönye* 51, no. 45 (1917): 397–8; "Népegészség és szociáltechnika," 51, no. 47 (1917): 413; "Szociáltechnikai problémák," 52, no. 8 (1918): 61; "Szociáltechnika, vagy politika?" 52, no. 32 (1918): 265; "Politika vagy szociáltechnika?" 52, no. 45 (1918): 369–70. Occasionally the editor would remind the readership that Bauer's position was opposed to the mainstream.
[90] Henrik Bauer, "Szózat a technikusokhoz," *Magyar Mérnök- és Építész-Egylet Közlönye* 53, no. 12 (1919): 89.
[91] Kálmán Méhely, "Ipari forradalom," *Magyar Gyáripar*, no. 10 (1918): 2–7.
[92] "Az Országos Munkaügyi Tanács alakuló ülése," *Magyar Mérnök- és Építész-Egylet Közlönye* 53, no. 7 (1919): 49–52.

Nevertheless, it proved difficult to find allies for this view of revolution. A few months later, in the chaotic days of the Hungarian People's Soviet, the chance to cast engineers as the best mediators of ambitious productivist initiatives was indeed alluring to some.[93] But the eventual backlash against "social engineers" would be thorough, leaving the bulk of politically quietist engineers vulnerable, and even less likely to join forces with traditional industrial interests.[94] In part because some engineers had been supporters of the Hungarian Soviet, the Horthy regime sought to exert greater control over the profession.[95] Several years later, when the National Association of Inventors was reconstituted, it was with a bevy of privy councilors and industry figures presiding, and not engineers.[96]

The insecurities of engineers in Hungarian politics were not unique. Many scholars also chafed at the continued dominance of the lawyers' guild in all walks of Hungarian life.[97] Nevertheless, there were politicians who linked the success of Hungarian businesses to the functioning of the patent courts. Even so, the comparative administrative autonomy established in the 1920 statute was nonetheless reduced later in the decade when Herrmann (now minister of trade) proposed to absorb the Upper Patent Court into the Curia, nominally as a budget-saving measure.[98] The pending retirement of Schuster made this worrisome to some, for the unity of the judicial process required a "whole person" with integrated legal and expert technical knowledge and daily oversight of the offices.[99] Though this marked a step back from the nominal parity won by engineers at the patent office, the "Lex Schuster" remained firmly in place and the connection between technical innovation and intellectual

---

[93] Albert Fonó, "A proletárdiktatúra és a mérnökség," *Magyar Mérnök- és Épitész-Egylet Közlönye* 53, no. 13 (1919): 97.

[94] Mihály Polányi, "Új szkepticismus," *Szabadgondolat* 9, no. 3 (February 1919): 53–6; Mária M. Kovács, *Liberal Professions and Illiberal Politics: Hungary from the Habsburgs to the Holocaust* (New York: Oxford University Press, 1994), 70–5.

[95] "A mérnöki rendtartás," *Belügyi Közlöny* 28, no. 17 (1923): 599–621.

[96] "Megalakult a Feltalálók Országos Egyesülete," *Szabadalmi Közlöny* 31 (1926): 371.

[97] Jakab Bleyer, "Jövőnk és a tudomány," *Budapesti Szemle* 174, no. 498 (1918): 457. Bleyer was a leading scholar of German language and literature and soon to be a corresponding member of the Academy.

[98] "Az országgyülés képviselőházának 62. ülése," *Képviselőházi Napló*, no. 5 (June 8, 1927): 148–9; "Néhány szó a szabadalmi felsőbíróság megszüntetése kérdéséhez," *Jogtudományi Közlöny* 62, no. 10 (1927): 85–6; Gyula Harausz, "A m. kir. Szabadalmi Felsőbíróság elnökének távozásához," *Jogtudományi Közlöny* 63, no. 13 (1928): 126–7; Pál Pesthy and Miksa Herrmann, "A m. kir. igazságügyminiszternek és a m. kir. kereskedelemügyi miniszternek 18.691/1928. I. M. számú rendelete," *Belügyi Közlöny* 33, no. 20 (1928): 402.

[99] See the parliamentary debate in "Az országgyülés felsőházának 17. ülése," *Felsőházi Napló*, no. 1 (July 4, 1927): 354–61.

property was taken for granted by his successor.[100] Hungary continued as a signatory to further modifications in the Paris Union, and although there were recurrent reform debates, there was not substantive change in the patent statute until the Communist takeover in 1949.[101]

11.4   Securing the Enterprise from Unfair Competition: Patents as Administrative Measures in the Polish Lands

What tsarist Russia called the Kingdom of Poland retained its own patent statutes well after the imperial partitions of the late eighteenth century. Poland issued letters (*listy przyznania*) on the French model for recognizing inventions, discoveries, and improvements in all domains of industry, with precedents from 1817 and 1831 culminating in a statute of 1836.[102] This held until the aftermath of the second Polish uprising, but from 1867 onward the Russian law of privileges prevailed (see the next chapter). In Habsburg Galicia and Prussian Posen respectively the general patent privilege statutes applied. Though Polish inventors and legal figures interested in patent rights can be found in all three domains, with Polish inventors playing no small role in Russia's incipient industrialization, generalizations are hard to make.

The chief Polish legal figure of the Habsburg era to write on patenting was the younger Fryderyk Zoll (1865–1948), a native of the Cracow intellectual elite. It was while working at the Ministry of Trade in Vienna in the 1890s that Zoll undertook a lengthy study of Austrian and German patent rights and their relationship to private law.[103] Zoll had already published a guide to German patent applicants filing in Austria, objecting that the formal utility requirement for imported patents was neither essential nor modern, and not ideal for a country in which most inventions were imported.[104] Taking Anton von Randa's civil code reading of property as his starting point, Zoll stressed that the grand

---

[100] Zoltán Schilling, "A szabadalmi jog és a technika fejlődésének párhuzama," *Szabadalmi Közlöny* 41, no. 14 (1936): 181–5.
[101] Márió Zoltán Mihály, "Feltalálói jogunk fejlődésének új útja," *Jogtudományi Közlöny*, New Series 4, no. 9–10 (1949): 186–93.
[102] Carl F. Loosey, "Królestwo Polskie," in *Sammlung der Gesetze für Erfindungs-Privilegien der sämmtlichen Staaten Europa's, der vereinigten Staaten von Nord-Amerika und Holländisch West-Indien* (Vienna, 1849), 314–20; *50 lat urzędu patentowego w Polsce* (Warsaw, 1969), 15–23; Michał du Vall, "Geneza i rozwój prawa patentowego" (Polish Patent Office, 2008), 6, www.uprp.pl.
[103] Friedrich Zoll, "Privatrechtliche Studien aus dem Patentrechte mit vornehmlicher Berücksichtigung des österreichischen Rechtes," *Zeitschrift für das Privat- und öffentliche Recht der Gegenwart* 21 (1894): 533–82, 641–88.
[104] Friedrich Zoll, *Ueber den Schutz der vom Auslande nach Oesterreich-Ungarn eingeführten Erfindungen* (Berlin: Internationale Verlags-Anstalt, 1892), 25.

codification efforts of the preceding century needed to be updated with new concepts suitable to the machine age. The legal objects of property had multiplied as forests, hunting, and fisheries were managed more systematically. Why had copyright, patent, and trademark not yet found their place within the system of private rights?[105] Though he was not intent on establishing intellectual property, Zoll consistently adopted Kohler's language of the right to intangible goods to sketch out what a future private law of patents might encompass. To Zoll's way of thinking contemporary patent law lacked the Roman distinction between possession and ownership: once that separation took place, patent law qua private law would be sustainable.[106] Zoll was contributing to the general imperial reform debate. A Polish statute would not be enacted until the collapse of the Habsburg Empire in 1918.

As the prospects for a revived Polish Republic improved at the end of the war, the most assiduous advocate of a new patent statute was the successful Berlin patent attorney Kazimierz Ossowski (1854–1924).[107] In addition to long experience representing Polish inventors in Germany, Ossowski also maintained an office in St. Petersburg. Ossowski presumed that patent law was a crucial means of supporting the young Republic's growth, and Poland was in the fortunate position to choose which system best suited its interests. His knowledge of the German examination system and the Russian model did not lead him to favor either. Indeed the Bolshevik abolition of patents was for him an opportunity "to show the world, following the release of the Russian yoke, that [Poland] has not fallen under the psychosis of slavery and not taken the Russian line."[108] In part because Ossowski detected an irreducible element of subjective judgment in the examiner's adjudication of novelty he argued instead for a simpler registration system that served the "Roman" countries satisfactorily.[109] The way that patent challenges in court frequently recapitulated the examination procedure suggested to Ossowski that the German system of prior examination was not significantly more efficient. In any case, postwar Poland could not afford to dedicate highly

---

[105] Zoll, "Privatrechtliche Studien," 535. Keep in mind Zoll was commenting primarily on the 1852 Austrian law.

[106] Ibid., 572–3, 660.

[107] Kazimierz Ossowski, "Wiadomości z Biura patentowego Kazimierza Ossowskiego w Berlinie," *Przegląd techniczny* 36, no. 16 (1898): 291–3; Bolesław Kasprowicz, *Byłem juniorem* (Gdynia: Wydawnictwo Morskie, 1965), 70.

[108] Kazimierz Ossowski, *Ochrona praw własności umysłowej w przemyśle* (Berlin: [nakładem autora], 1922), 6.

[109] Kazimierz Ossowski, "Jak ukształtuje się w Polsce kwestya ochrony wynalazków (I)," *Przegląd techniczny* 55, no. 17–18 (1917): 123–5.

qualified engineers to such a labor-intensive system of prior examination since they were needed elsewhere.

The debate about patent systems was indeed understood as part of a larger struggle to establish more technocratic forms of governance in Central and Eastern Europe.[110] Holding a law degree had been a nearly indispensable requirement for administrative advancement in Warsaw, Breslau, or Cracow, and Ossowski voiced strong support for the city of Warsaw's more recent readiness to appoint "practical people who are handling practical issues in a practical manner, and not helpless in the face of each case in different areas of the national economy, as often happens with officials who have one-sided legal-formalist educations."[111] Among Polish engineers there was a strong push in 1918 to organize a separate Ministry of Technical Affairs. The leading figure was Edwin Hauswald (1868–1942), a bilingual mechanical engineer and professor at the Lwów Polytechnic who participated in the drafting of an administrative-technical code.[112]

Ossowski reminded his readers that any adjudication of inventive novelty must be subject to spatial and temporal limitations, not least because of linguistic considerations. Even if the Warsaw patent office had somehow secured a complete reference library, it would be practically impossible to say whether a Japanese or Hungarian document offered a precedent for a patent under consideration; so for the time being, Poland would have to take novelty as something mediated through the major European languages. He further pressed for a statute that did not take a narrow view of industrial property so that it could include agricultural inventions. This also played into Ossowski's view that Poland should ultimately acknowledge the true inventor – a point not germane to pure registration systems. And since Polish industry was in its infancy, it could also justifiably demand compulsory working of patents, with measures to protect inventors who were not already in a position to fund development of their inventions.[113]

---

[110] Martin Kohlrausch, Katrin Steffen, and Stefan Wiederkehr, eds., *Expert Cultures in Central Eastern Europe: The Internationalization of Knowledge and the Transformation of Nation States since World War I*, vol. 23, Einzelveröffentlichungen des Deutschen Historischen Instituts Warschau (Osnabrück: fibre Verlag, 2010).

[111] Kazimierz Ossowski, "Jak ukształtuje się w Polsce kwestya ochrony wynalazków (II)," *Przegląd techniczny* 55, no. 19–20 (1917): 152.

[112] Mieczysław Rybczyński, "Zarys organizacyi ministerstwa spraw technicznych," *Czasopismo techniczne* 36, no. 8 (1918): 66–72.

[113] Kazimierz Ossowski, "Uwagi w sprawie projektu polskiego prawa patentowego," *Przegląd techniczny* 56, no. 1–4 (1918): 3–12. Ossowski assembled these articles and self-published them as *Projekty ustaw o ochronie praw własności przemysłowej w królestwie*

Poland could not of course fashion its patent institutions *ab novo*. Promptly after the declaration of the Polish Republic in 1918 a patent office was created in part by the Polish delegation's close cooperation with its French counterparts in Paris.[114] As a condition of joining the League of Nations in 1919 it had immediately adopted a law for the protection of industrial property consistent with the requirements of the Paris Union: a registration system with a waiting period in which objections could be filed.[115] A more deliberative approach followed under Fryderyk Zoll's watchful eye when he served on the Republic's Codification Commission, where he had already drafted the basis for Polish copyright law.[116] He served in a similar capacity during the lengthy drafting of the 1924 Polish patent law, which opted for a registration-only system in which only the true inventor had the right to apply, thus positioning itself somewhere between the French and American systems.[117] The updated 1924 statute adopted the standard fifteen-year term with steadily increasing fees in the later years of a patent's exercise, although ambiguous notions of intellectual labor remained.[118]

But it was Article 27 that aroused concern since anyone could thereby lodge a complaint at the Patent Office concerning the legitimate "exclusivity of the indicated patent." This seemed like an invitation to nuisance complaints and a "compromise of the inventor's interest."[119] Detecting an excess of (Germanic) "police spirit," Ossowski indeed took Zoll to task for drafting statutes more concerned with the state's custodial role over the invention than with the fate of inventors, prompting even

---

polskiem *(Patenty, wzory użytkowe, wzory gustowe i znaki towarowe)* (Warsaw: [nakładem autora], 1918).

[114] "Projekt międzynarodowej konwencji w sprawie rejestracji i ochrony wynalazków i patentów," 1919, Polska misja zakupów w Paryżu, sygn. 15, Archiwum Akt Novych.

[115] "Ochrona własności przemysłowej w Polsce," *Przegląd techniczny* 57, no. 17–20 (1919): 83–4.

[116] Fryderyk Zoll, *Prawo autorskie w projekcie* (Warsaw: Ministerstwo sztuki i kultury, 1920). On Zoll's influence, Leonard Górnicki, *Rozwój idei praw autorskich: od starożytności do II wojny światowej* (Wrocław: Prawnicza i Ekonomiczna Biblioteka Cyfrowa, 2013), 238, www.bibliotekacyfrowa.pl/publication/41089; Beata Giesen, "Własnościowy model prawa autorskiego – analiza koncepcji przyjętej w prawie polskim," *Ruch prawniczy, ekonomiczny i socjologiczny* 77, no. 2 (2015): 61–73.

[117] E. Trepka, "Polska Ustawa Patentowa," *Przegląd techniczny* 62, no. 41–42 (1924): 474–7.

[118] S. Wojciechowski et al., "Ustawa z dnia 5 lutego 1924 r. o ochronie wynalazków, wzorów i znaków towarowych," *Dziennik Ustaw*, no. 31 (1924): 430–45.

[119] Klemens Czempiński, "Ochrona praw autorskich na wynalazki w Polsce," *Przegląd techniczny* 66, no. 34–35 (1928): 679. The author was an engineer and patent attorney. The patent office claimed that the number of Article 27 requests was actually minimal.

Ossowski to concede their rights to intellectual property.[120] As an aspiring technocrat Hauswald nonetheless strongly advocated the new patent law, since he, like Zoll, was less interested in the legal grounding of the inventor's right than in the patent's administrative functions.[121] The simpler registration system was chosen for ease of use, with the "unreality" of some patents left for exposure in subsequent court proceedings. Further adjustments to the Polish patent statute took place in the wake of the 1925 Hague modifications to the Paris Union and in the context of Zoll's more ambitious strategy for regulating unfair competition in 1926.[122]

As a newly industrializing nation subject to great structural disadvantages in the European marketplace, Hauswald believed Poland required something more than old-fashioned tariff protectionism. Among other things, he sought to formalize the legal status of the enterprise as more than a collection of assets, but also as an abstract entity possessing intangible goods. In this fashion property law and personal law could be kept distinct, yet the laws affecting intangible goods could encompass more than individuals qua creators. In a sense, Zoll was demystifying the inventor as the representative of a particular kind of interest vis-à-vis those of industry or the nation, and attempting to create a level playing field for patent and trademark holders that recognized the ways in which some patent owners brought much stronger market advantages in their relations to other patent holders. Perhaps inventors, individual or otherwise, needed regulatory protection from other inventors. In later work on the codification of Polish property law, Zoll classified mining rights and patent rights as new kinds of rights unknown to Roman property law, functioning as a species of administratively created right under special statutes, so that "alongside the great, stylish constructions erected on Roman law foundations remain these diminutive structures designed for such institutions, which undoubtedly spoil the harmonious picture of contemporary property rights."[123]

While there could be no immediate reconciliation with a grand civil code, for pragmatic reasons the patent statute with its property-

---

[120] Ossowski, *Ochrona praw własności umysłowej w przemyśle*, 14.

[121] Edwin Hauswald, *Wynalazki i patenty* (Lwów: Gubrynowicz i Syn, 1924).

[122] "1918–1928," *Wiadomości Urzędu Patentowego* 5, no. 12 (1928): 835–7; Alfred Kraus and Fryderyk Zoll, *Polska ustawa o zwalczaniu nieuczciwej konkurencji* (Poznań: Wojewódzki Instytut Wydawniczy, 1929); Tomasz Dolata, "Polska ustawa o zwalczaniu nieuczciwej konkurencji z 1926 r., a inne regulacje z zakresu praw na dobrach niematerialnych," *Studia z Dziejów Państwa i Prawa Polskiego* 12 (2009): 265–76.

[123] Fryderyk Zoll, "Przedmiot praw rzeczowych," *Kwartalnik prawa prywatnego* 1 (1938): 240.

mimicking aspects would have to stay.[124] In its first decade, the Polish Patent Office distributed nearly 10,000 patents, with electric technology, chemical engineering, railways, and agriculture as the largest categories. Germans claimed a third of those patents, Poles a quarter, and about one in a dozen patents went to Austrian, French, and American applicants, respectively. Czechs took out five patents in Poland for every one taken out by a Pole in Czechoslovakia.[125] As of 1936, there were still twenty patents taken out in Germany for every patent issued in Poland.[126] Although macroeconomic factors – especially capital shortages throughout the interwar period – surely swamp other effects here, it is worth drawing attention to the persistent cultural difficulties in using patents to draw inventors, scientists, and industrialists into mutually beneficial alliances.

11.5 Czech Patenting between the Imperial and the Technocratic

Until 1919, Austrian patent law covered the Bohemian lands. Like his Polish counterpart Zoll, Czech jurist Karel Herrmann had felt that the inventor's right was still unsatisfactorily caught between personal and property law considerations in the imperial statute, but there was little debate before 1918.[127] The new Czechoslovak state adopted the Austrian statute wholesale, albeit with proceedings henceforth in Czech.[128] While patent holders from formerly Hungarian portions of Slovakia could retain their patents, any subsequent proceedings would follow the Austro-Czech statute. Since two-thirds of patents in the Czech lands before 1918 were held by foreigners (40 percent of them German), it would take a while for Czech patentees to predominate. Indeed, the patent office systematically transferred more than six thousand patents

---

[124] Fryderyk Zoll, "Wstęp," in *Polskie prawo patentowe: Komentarz*, by Adam Ponikło and Jan Gutowski (Warsaw: Gebethner i Wolff, 1935), 3–34.

[125] "Patenty na wynalazki," *Wiadomości Urzędu Patentowego* 5, no. 12 (1928): 838–40.

[126] Józef Piłatowicz, "Wynalazczość w Polsce międzywojennej," *Dzieje Najnowsze* 22, no. 1–2 (1990): 3–19.

[127] Karel Herrmann, "Právo z vynálezu v rakouském zákonu patentním," *Sborník věd právních a státních* 3 (1903): 215–35.

[128] "Erfindungsschutz in den Nationalstaaten"; "Csehország. A szabadalmi oltalom a cseh köztársaságban," *Szabadalmi Közlöny* 24 (1919): 51; Erwin Hüttner, *Die Gesetze zum Schutze des gewerblichen Eigentums*, 2nd ed., vol. 11, Stiepels Gesetz-Sammlung des Tschecho-Slowakischen Staates (Reichenberg: Verlag von Gebrüder Stiepel, 1923); František Vitáček, *Československý patentní zákon s příslušnými zákony, nařízeními, vyhláškami a státními smlouvami, jakož i s rozhodnutími od r. 1899 do doby přítomné* (Prague: V. Linhart, 1933).

from the Austro-Hungarians rolls during the early years, roughly a third of the total.[129]

The most famous Czech inventor of the early twentieth century was František Křižík (1847–1941), the "Czech Edison," who first made his name in the 1880s with the invention of a new arc lamp.[130] Though the Bohemian lands were among the most industrially developed in the Habsburg Empire, Křižík thrived as a businessman selling his patent rights to larger enterprises elsewhere in Europe.[131] During the early Republic he became an icon of the "Czech selfmademan" (*sic*), both for his social mobility and as a very particular sort of intellectual model. When Czech sugar industrialist Hanuš Karlík endowed a prize upon his passing in 1927, Křižík was among the first recipients of what was styled as a "Czech Nobel Prize." Coverage of the event in *Národní listy* pointed to British tradesmen who became members of the House of Lords, to businessmen like Rathenau and Krupp who were held in esteem that rivaled that of politicians, writers, and artists. The challenge was how to get the younger Czech generation to take Křižík as their inspiration.[132] It was in this ambivalent setting that many Czech engineers became some of the most fervent advocates of "technocratic internationalism" during the interwar period.[133]

Czechoslovakia joined the Paris Convention immediately in 1919. But pressing the international side of patenting and intellectual property (*duševní majetek*) as "utopian impulse" in the early Republic was no easy task, since the catastrophe of world war had made this possible in the first place.[134] While it was fine to defend patents as tools for increasing foreign trade and indirectly fostering a return to material prosperity in a tense European environment, this species of trade internationalism mostly benefitted the major economies.[135] As a Czech observer noted

---

[129] Ivan Jakubec, "Patents and Licences in Interwar Czechoslovakia (1918–1938)," *Archive internationales d'histoire des sciences* 50 (2000): 154.

[130] Irmler, "Elektrická svítilna Křižíkova," *Světozor* 16 (April 21, 1882): 204; "Križik-Lampe (Patent Piette-Križik)," *Der Bautechniker* 3, no. 35 (August 31, 1883): 387–8; "The Pilsen Electric Lamps," *The Electrical World* 3 (1884): 89–91, 104–6. The single biography I am aware of is Jiří Kottas, *František Křižík* (Prague: Horizont, 1987).

[131] "Patent Křižík verkauft," *Prager Tagblatt*, June 1, 1882.

[132] A. Pimper, "Ceskoslovenská Nobelova cena," *Národní listy*, March 24, 1927.

[133] Elisabeth van Meer, "The Transatlantic Pursuit of a World Engineering Federation: For the Profession, the Nation, and International Peace, 1918–48," *Technology and Culture* 53 (2012): 120–45.

[134] Jos. Schmidt, "Problém světového patentu a Československo," *Národní listy*, January 1, 1922.

[135] On interwar Austrian-Czechoslovak trade relations, Herbert Matis, *Österreich und die Tschechoslowakei 1918–1938: Die wirtschaftliche Neuordnung in Zentraleuropa in der Zwischenkriegszeit* (Vienna: Böhlau Verlag, 1996).

of the League of Nations Committee on Intellectual Cooperation in 1925, a nation whose material needs were satisfied was not necessarily a pacific nation. But that was all the more reason to coax Czech intellectuals into a more expansive understanding of their role in the pursuit of national cultural prestige. He approved the Committee's call "that intellectual property [duševní vlastnictví] be recognized by all states, without exception, in all three of its normal forms: literary, artistic, and scientific." Yet, at the same time, he noted that Czech political culture remained worrisomely suspicious of the kinds of experts who advocated such arrangements.[136]

This played into a larger debate about why Czechoslovakia did not have more figures like Křižík. Political economist František Fousek (born 1889) lamented that twice as many patents went to Germans as to Czechs and Slovaks, and asked what benefit the patent office really provided to the latter.[137] The cartographer and geodesist Jaroslav Pantoflíček, who held around a hundred patents, was too much the exception for Fousek: a broader institutional culture of invention had to be fostered, because invention now required systematic research in large firms, not the lone genius. Fousek urged his readers that this was more than a rationalized procedure, but something deeply personal: "[w]ithout genuine love and passion there is not and cannot be discoveries." Yet it was not until 1937 that Czechs and Slovaks approached the halfway point in total numbers of annual applications at the patent office.[138]

The continuity of the Czechoslovak statute with its Habsburg imperial predecessor suited the desire of all parties to restore a functioning system as soon as possible in the most industrialized portion of the former Habsburg lands. Though the Polish and Hungarian statutes underwent more substantial modifications, it was politically feasible for them to cast the continuity as pre-Habsburg, usually an affirmation of Roman law, while the moments of legal tension between modern patents and Roman property concepts could be reconciled with technocratic measures understood to be post-imperial and thus implicitly national, even when the Paris Union's 1925 Hague meeting was providing the dominant reference points. The more immediate postwar problem, shared by the new Austrian nation-state, was that once all the successor states had created their own patent offices, the number of local applications was

---

[136] Emanuel Siblík, "Mezinárodní cíle duševních pracovníků," Národní listy, February 12, 1925.
[137] F. Fousek, "Kde tkví příčiny nedostatku technické tvořivosti?," Národní listy, May 13, 1928.
[138] Viktor Srkal, "Patentní úřad dostává průměrně měsíčně přes 700 patentních přihlášek," Národní politika, August 8, 1937.

proportionally small as processing costs soared. Thus, in 1921 the old Austrian patent office operated on a budget twice the size of the fees generated by its patents.[139] "The dissolution of Österreich has led to the phenomenon that patents once upheld uniformly in their priority," wrote a Viennese patent attorney in 1919, "have now been split into a series of partial patents, identical in content, but restricted in their local effectiveness to the territory of individual nation states, whose legal fates are independent of one another."[140] While the Paris Union continued to provide the common reference point for all four of the new states, the drive toward economic autarky still put them at a massive disadvantage vis-à-vis the patent pooling practices of large American and German corporations. In the fraught conditions of postwar economic recovery, motivating inventor-employees via patent regulations had to be quite detached from "class struggle and politics."[141] Insofar such a struggle was negatively associated with international processes of legal and economic cooperation, as was often the case in Horthy's Hungary, Piłsudski's Poland, or outside Red Vienna, patents would have to retain their local social justifications alongside technocratic aspirations for immanent harmonization.

---

[139] "Der verteuerte Erfinderschutz," *Neues Wiener Journal*, February 27, 1922.

[140] Paul Abel, "Zur Behandlung des gewerblichen Rechtsschutzes in den auf dem Gebiete Österreichs entstandenen Nationalstaaten," *Allgemeine Österreichische Gerichts-Zeitung*, July 19, 1919, 226.

[141] Meister, "Arbeitsrechtliches im neuen Patentgesetze."

12   Patent Debates on Invention from Tsarist Russia to the Soviet Union

Karl Hall

12.1   Introduction

In 1896 Imperial Russia adopted a modern patent system for inventions that had strong connections to German precedent. The following year Russian engineer Peter Engelmeyer published *Inventions and Privileges: A Guide for Inventors*, which featured an introduction by Leo Tolstoy that fell well short of endorsement.[1] Whereas Engelmeyer vigorously defended the dignity of the invention process, Russia's greatest anti-modernist saw "foolishly directed mental abilities" in the frustrated inventors who visited the Tolstoy estate each year. To improve their lot, Engelmeyer nonetheless required intellectual proximity to figures like Tolstoy, because mere legal procedure and institutional support were never enough: the engineer wanted theories of the creative individual that would show how to channel inventors' mental abilities for the common good.[2] Yet Engelmeyer was struggling against the perception that Russian industry actually had a structural surplus of state-certified engineers, men who often associated inventions and patents with humbler technical vocations.[3] In legal, economic, and social terms Russian inventors faced many difficulties casting inventive activity in the common currency of creative endeavor. As a founder of the All-Russian Union of Inventors asked in 1900, if the Russian capacity for creativity had been

---

[1] P. K. Engel'meier, *Izobreteniia i privilegii: Rukovodstvo dlia izobretatelei so vstup. pis'mom gr. L. N. Tolstogo* (Moscow: Tip. E. Lissnera i Iu. Romana, 1897); Boris Velikhov, "Na vstrechu russkomu izobretateliu (Patentno-pravovoi ocherk)," *Initsiativa i izobretatel'nost'* 1 (1917): 220–4; V. G. Gorokhov, *Tekhnika i kul'tura: Vozniknovenie filosofii tekhniki i teorii tekhnicheskogo tvorchestva v Rossii i Germanii v kontse XIX – nachale XX stoletiia* (Moscow: Logos, 2009), chap. 1; Carl Mitcham, *Thinking through Technology: The Path between Engineering and Philosophy* (Chicago: University of Chicago Press, 1994), 24–9.

[2] P. K. Engel'meier, *Teoriia tvorchestva* (St. Petersburg: Obrazovanie, 1910).

[3] K. A. Skal'kovskii, *Sovremennaia Rossiia. Ocherki nashei gosudarstvennoi i obshchestvennoi zhizni*, 2nd ed., vol. 2 (St. Petersburg: A. S. Suvorin, 1890), 237 49; V. T. Sudeikin, *Zamechatel'naia epokha v istorii russkikh finansov: Ocherk ekon. i fin. politiki N. Kh. Bunge i I. A. Vyshnegradskogo* (St. Petersburg: Tip. Pravit. Senata, 1895), 62; M. O. Men'shikov, *Kriticheskie ocherki*, vol. 2 (St. Petersburg: Trud, 1902), 403–4.

firmly established by Pushkin, Tolstoy, Dostoevsky, and Chekhov in the arts or Mendeleev in the sciences, why was it that the "brilliant work" of Russian inventors perished in "waves of general indifference and inertia"?[4] From research laboratories to trade exhibitions to contacts with Russia's merchant class, he recognized factors in need of improvement. But to what extent were problems with Russia's patent system central to this catalog of inventors' woes?

The question of patents had narrower legal subtleties tied to Russia's tangled histories of property and copyright respectively. And the elaborate discourse of inventive creativity itself was caught up in classic Russian and Soviet intellectual debates about the relation of the individual to the collective. Invention and its legal institutions were thus often treated warily both by those favoring and opposing strong state controls. So long as invention was "above all a means of demonstrating one's talent and standing out from the impersonal crowd," as the dean of Russian patent law Aleksandr Pilenko put it, the image of the inventor would be shaped by strictures of Russian social politics and theories of social psychology.[5] That is why Engelmeyer lamented that inventors' acts of creativity would always suffer the inertial reaction of the masses.[6] For many of his contemporaries, empowering Russian inventors required that human consciousness, more than legal statutes, be reformed.[7]

If Russian and Soviet patent laws (1812, 1870, 1896, 1924, 1931) largely disappointed expectations for their role in economic development, it was not because they remained "premodern" or conceptually isolated. Instead, I attribute greater importance to the persistent unwillingness of jurist, inventor, and political authority alike to yield inventive labor over to the realm of the institutionally mundane. Both before and after the revolutions of 1917, this disposition obscured the evolving cooperative processes of invention and prevented the formation of functional alliances.[8] Eventually, the Soviets would hold up "worker inventiveness" as the vital quality that would thrive under new production

---

[4] [A. P. Fedorov], "Ob"iasnitel'naia zapiska," in *Ustav Obshchestva pod naimenovaniem "Vserossiiskii Soiuz Izobretatelei"* (Moscow: A. I. Mamontov & Co., 1900), 6.

[5] A. A. Pilenko, *Pravo izobretatelia: Privilegiia na izobreteniia i ikh zashchita v russkom i mezhdunarodnom prave*, vol. 1 (St. Petersburg: M. M. Stasiulevich, 1902), 47.

[6] P. K. Engel'meier, *Tvorcheskaia lichnost' i sreda v oblasti tekhnicheskikh izobretenii* (St. Petersburg: Obrazovanie, 1911).

[7] P. M. Jakobson, *Protsess tvorcheskoi raboty izobretatelia*, ed. Iu. K. Milonov (Moscow-Leningrad: Izd. TsS Vsesoiuz. Obshch. Izobretatelei, 1934), 46.

[8] In the case of law, B. A. Kistiakovskii, *Sotsial'nye nauki i pravo. Ocherki po metodologii sotsial'nykh nauk i prava* (Moscow: M. & S. Sabashnikov, 1916), 684–90; N. N. Alekseev, *Vvedenie v izuchenie prava* (Moscow: Moskovskaia prosvetitel'naia komissiia, 1918), 108–19.

relations so thoroughly just and rational as to render patents superfluous. Yet occasionally in the face of shortfalls and disorganization they could not resist treating inadequate worker inventiveness as the elusive quasi-biological cause (rather than consequence) of faltering inventive enterprises in industry, closer to a poorly developed instinct (rather than a failure of consciousness). While the 1924 patent law would be a pragmatic concession to European industrial politics, the 1931 statute would reassert the primacy of state enterprises over patent holders, but even this truly Soviet law continued to pay lip service to the durable concern for inventors' creative authorship.

12.2   Autocracy, Invention Privilege, and Legal Reform up to 1896

Before 1812 Russia maintained an early-modern (royal) privilege system for patents. In that year an imperial manifesto permitted the Ministry of Internal Affairs to regulate the issue of such privileges in the form of a legal decree.[9] The Ministry's certification duties were vague, however, and adjudication of novelty was not required. Even so, this certification went further than the French registration system, initiating a system of examination that arguably preempted the 1836 opening of the US Patent Office.[10] Monopoly terms of three, five, and ten years were available in the new Russian system, with substantial fees disproportionately higher for the longest term and conventionally payable in full upon receipt of the privilege. In the event of a patent being contested, the Ministry protocol was to summon "experienced people" in equal number for each side to help settle the dispute.[11]

Two decades later, the State Council concluded that the Ministry had been too ready to issue exclusive privileges, often tied to prior foreign patents, without broader benefit to Russian manufacturing. It introduced more extensive examination rules in 1833 to establish whether the invention would foster manufacturing in the direction favored by the Russian state. The state accordingly retained certain powers over the invention

---

[9] "Manifest o privillegiiakh na raznyia izobreteniia i otkrytiia v khudozhestvakh i remeslakh," in *Patentnyi zakon Rossii 1801–2001*, ed. N. B. Leonidov and N. V. Mikheeva (Moscow: Iuridicheskaia literatura, 2002), 30–3.

[10] Rudolf Klostermann, *Die Patentgesetzgebung aller Länder*, vol. 2, Das geistige Eigenthum an Schriften, Kunstwerke und Erfindungen, nach preussischem und internationalem Rechte dargestellt (Berlin: I. Guttentag, 1869), 339–44; V. D. Katkov, *O privilegiiakh (patentakh) na promyshlennye izobreteniia* (Kharkov: Pechatnoe Delo, 1902), 46.

[11] *Svod zakonov Rossiiskoi Imperii poveleniem gosudaria imperatora Nikolaia Pavlovicha sostavlennyi: Zakony Grazhdanskie*, vol. 10 (St. Petersburg, 1832), 559.

privilege that prevented from serving as a form of property. Although transferable between individuals, the privilege could not be transferred to a stockholding company without the state's permission.[12] As such, the Russian conception of the invention privilege as a one-off legislative act exclusive to an individual was not unique to Russia, since pre-1877 German law functioned in much the same way. Notwithstanding the tsar's autocratic prerogatives, the Russian invention privilege likewise found a principled legal defender in the son of a court musician, D. I. Meyer, who studied in Berlin and taught law in Kazan and St. Petersburg at mid-century. Not coincidentally, he was an early advocate of Roman law conceptions in modernizing the Russian legal curriculum.[13] In Meyer's interpretation of the Russian civil code, the royal granting of various forms of privilege was subtly acknowledged as an affront to "social consciousness." He optimistically encouraged a reading in which each successive ruler did not simply grant new privileges and dismiss those of his predecessor on a whim, but rather was legally obligated to issue or abolish any privilege only in a manner compatible with the common good. The invention privilege stood out as a form of privilege where greater legal consistency already applied, since the inventor's "mixed labor" clearly warranted compensation. Both moral and political considerations supported an exclusive right that encouraged citizens "to seek out discoveries and to adopt foreign inventions" for the utility of all of society. Meyer went even further, however, arguing that the invention privilege was "more a limited recognition of a right than a privilege." It was indeed limited-term property (*dostoianie*) that would eventually revert to society.[14] Though Meyer died prematurely, his students repeatedly published his lectures during the Great Reforms of the 1860s, ensuring their currency for an entire generation of lawyers and civil servants.

Native and foreign applicants alike put little faith in Russian invention privileges before 1870. Only a few dozen of these were issued in any given year, and in any case three out of every five privileges awarded would eventually be nullified because the patentee failed to put them into

[12] P. I. Makhin, *Ustavy o promyshlennosti fabrichnoi i remeslennyi* (Moscow: Izd. brat'ev Salaevykh, 1869), 22–9.
[13] Martin Avenarius, *Rezeption des römischen Rechts in Russland: Dmitrij Mejer, Nikolaj Djuvernua und Iosif Pokrovskij* (Göttingen: Wallstein Verlag, 2004); *Fremde Traditionen des römischen Rechts: Einfluss, Wahrnehmung und Argument des "rimskoe pravo" im russischen Zarenreich des 19. Jahrhunderts* (Göttingen: Wallstein Verlag GmbH, 2014).
[14] D. I. Meier, *Russkoe grazhdanskoe pravo*, ed. A. I. Vitsin, 4th ed. (St. Petersburg: N. Tiblen i Komp., 1868), 187–97.

industrial practice.[15] A further obstacle was that it was often unclear which branch of the Ministry was responsible for issuing the privilege. According to Pilenko, the administrative revision of the privilege law in 1870 actually represented a substantive advance, because it invested more formal responsibility in the Scientific Committee tasked with determining whether inventions met the criteria for patenting, thus bounding the arbitrariness of the privilege and stabilizing it as a legal document.[16] Even during the high tide of the anti-patent movement in Europe, Russia did not consider patent abolition (as in the Netherlands and Switzerland), but rather looked to speed up the examination procedure, reduce fees, and eliminate favoring foreigners, who were more easily granted privileges on the basis of existing patents abroad.[17]

The lingering puzzle for lawyer and civil servant V. I. Veshniakov was that no one in Russia was taking up the debate.[18] That he was prompted to reflect on this by leading international law scholar F. F. Martens in the first volume of the short-lived *Digest of State Sciences* hints at the nature of the problem. The Russian merchant class did not regard factories as sites of invention, though a small subset of resident foreigners were increasingly investing in imported technology in manufacture. Russian stock companies in the decades before the war helped drive remarkable economic growth, many floating their issues on the Paris and Berlin exchanges. Although it had been legal since 1836 to form such companies for purposes of importing inventions, few chose to organize for that purpose, and credit institutions lacked the expertise to structure such investment.[19] The motley social composition of Russian factory owners offered little opportunity for policy coordination with sustained collateral benefits for engineers, a state of affairs in which the Imperial government was often complicit. It would generally be civil servants like Veshniakov and scholars like Pilenko who would argue in favor of state support for innovation, including improved legal protections.[20]

---

[15] V. I. Veshniakov, "O nastoiashchem polozhenii voprosa otnositel'no unichtozheniia privilegii na izobreteniia i usovershenstvavaniia," *Zapiski Imperatorskago Russkago tekhnicheskago obshchestva* 4, no. 1 (1870): 67.
[16] Pilenko, *Pravo izobretatelia*, 1902, 1:137–81; A. P. Sergeev, *Pravo intellektual'noi sobstvennosti v Rossiiskoi Federatsii*, 2nd ed. (Moscow: Prospekt, 2003), 41.
[17] Veshniakov, "O nastoiashchem polozhenii," 37.
[18] V. I. Veshniakov, "Privilegii na izobreteniia," *Sbornik gosudarstvennykh znanii* 1 (1874): 291–308.
[19] Velikhov, "Na vstrechu russkomu izobretateliu (Patentno-pravovoi ocherk)."
[20] On the state centered nature of Russian industrialization, Peter Gatrell, "Reconceptualizing Russia's Industrial Revolution," in *Reconceptualizing the Industrial Revolution*, ed. Jeff Horn, Leonard N. Rosenband, and Merritt Roe Smith (Cambridge, MA: MIT Press, 2010), 229–49.

In the wake of the 1878 Paris Congress the Imperial Russian Technological Society (RTO) launched a modest patent reform initiative. N. N.
Salov presented initial proposals to his colleagues in the years that
followed, and a commission subsequently offered recommendations at
the August 1882 All-Russian Industrial Arts Exhibition in Moscow.
Salov foresaw a rational system of rewards that would give rise to "a
new, durable, in the highest sense useful, and completely sustainable
'aristocracy of talent and mental power'." More than that, "mental
creative ability" was best empowered by unitary autocracy, not the welter
of patent practices stemming from European legislative diversity.[21] He
went further than any of his contemporaries, arguing that the "intellec-
tually-real property" protecting the invention should be fully analogous
to material property.[22] That the individual inventor's privilege would
thus be permanent did not come at cost to the general welfare, however,
because in his view this was a misconceived dichotomy. The inventor
exploiting prior science was indebted, not to society but only to the
creators of the facts immediate to his own case. Salov imagined that
intellectual property eventually reverted to the Storehouse of Knowledge,
not unlike certain forms of material property could be escheated upon
the death of the owner. He maintained that it was the strength of the
property relationship between inventor and Storehouse of Knowledge
that would protect society from the profit-taking of weaker intellectual
property regimes, where the inventor was constantly subject to short-
term capitalist sensibilities.[23] While he and his allies did not yet secure a
central patent office on the German model, a decade later the RTO's
recommendations were implemented for longer patent terms, graduated
fees, and specifications that emphasized an invention's essence rather
than its mechanical description.[24]

Though the 1891 German reform likely dominated Russian government discussions, there was little public debate beyond the RTO.[25] Salov

[21] N. N. Salov, *Teoriia privilegii i podrobnyi otchet o dvizhenii etogo voprosa v Imperatorskom Russkom Tekhnicheskom Obshchestve* (St. Petersburg: I. P. Voshchinskii, 1882), 62–3.
[22] N. N. Salov, *Izobreteniia: Kak my smotrim na izobreteniia i kak dolzhny by na nikh smotret'* (St. Petersburg: Slav. pechatnia, 1877), 5.
[23] N. N. Salov, *Neskol'ko slov ob "umstvennoi sobstvennosti": K "teorii privilegii"* (St. Petersburg: I. P. Voshchinskii, 1882); *Obshchestvennoe i gosudarstvennoe znachenie privilegirovaniia umstvenno-tvorcheskikh proizvedenii* (St. Petersburg: K. K. Retter, 1881).
[24] M. I. Alisov, *O nedostatkakh zakonodatel'stva po privilegiiam na izobreteniia i o tekh merakh, kotoryia mogli by sluzhit' dlia ograzhdeniia interesov izobretatelia* (St. Petersburg: Imp. Russ. Tekh. Obshchestvo, 1882).
[25] Anneli Aer, *Patents in Imperial Russia: A History of the Russian Institution of Patent Privileges under the Old Regime* (Helsinki: Suomalainen Tiedeakatemia, 1995), 182.

was surely justified in his earlier fear that expert transparency in patent matters would be thwarted by the "ultrabureaucratic principle" of incontestable staff jurisdiction at the Finance Ministry.[26] An 1893 proposal for a twenty-year patent term with no restrictions on foreigners was sharply rebuked by an economist on the Finance Ministry's Scientific Committee for fostering "enslavement by foreigners."[27] But like Germany and the Habsburg Empire, Russia's Department of Trade and Manufactures of the Ministry of Finance did eventually issue a new patent statute in 1896.[28] The statute introduced a Committee on Technical Affairs as the sole adjudicator under more detailed procedures of examination and contestation: patents as individual legislative acts had finally become objects of strict juridical procedure.

That the language of privilege rather than patent remained in the statute was, in the view of many Russian experts, a minor irritant, because inventions were now effectively protected by "general-civil norms."[29] Indeed, later Western observers have taken this lexical archaism as evidence that Imperial Russia never had a modern patent system. Yet this runs counter to the semantic usage and manifest convictions of contemporary Russians.[30] While the privilege could not be sold or otherwise transferred until a year had passed from the date of publication, a publicly documented "privilege" that could legally change hands without the tsar's approval indeed functioned very much like a patent in the modern sense. To liberal St. Petersburg legal historian A. D. Gradovskii such shifts were all part of the incremental development of Russian concepts of legality since Peter the Great. "Personal freedom appears initially in the form of privilege, but these privileges are gradually

---

[26] Salov, *Izobreteniia*, 21.
[27] A. N. Gur'ev, *O privilegiiakh na izobreteniia. K reforme zakonodatel'stva* (St. Petersburg: V. Kirshbaum, 1894). A version of the essay appeared earlier in *Novoe vremia*.
[28] For the text of the 1896 statute, "Polozhenie o privilegiiakh na izobreteniia i usovershenstvovaniia," Leonidov and Mikheeva, *Patentnyi zakon Rossii*, 44–54.
[29] A. A. Pilenko, *Pravo izobretatelia: Privilegiia na izobreteniia i ikh zashchita v russkom i mezhdunarodnom prave*, vol. 2 (St. Petersburg: M. M. Stasiulevich, 1903), 338; V. I. Shteininger, *Zashchita izobreteniia v Rossii* (St. Petersburg, 1908), 10–11.
[30] Ia. A. Kantorovich, *Zakony o privilegiiakh na izobreteniia i usovershentstvovaniia v glavneishikh gosudarstvakh* (St. Petersburg: Ia. A. Kantorovich, 1900); [A. P. Fedorov], "Ob"iasnitel'naia zapiska"; Katkov, *O privilegiiakh (patentakh) na promyshlennye izobreteniia*; A. P. Skorodinskii, *Privilegii i patenty: Posobie dlia izobretatelei i promyshlennikov* (St. Petersburg: Shreder, 1904); I. T. Tarasov, *Lektsii po politseiskomu (administrativnomu) pravu*, vol. 3 (Moscow: A. I. Snegireva, 1913), 88–117; A. Kagan-Shabshai and Ia. Rozen, "Patentnoe pravo," *Entsiklopedicheskii slovar'* (Moscow: Granat, 1915); V. I. Shteininger, *Patenty na izobreteniia v Rossii* (Petrograd, 1915); L. A. Rozentsveig, *Sistematicheskii sbornik privilegii (patentov), vydannykh v Rossii za 16 1/2 let* (Petrograd: Gos. nauch. obshchetekhn. izd., 1917).

promulgated to other ranks of people as well and strive to become a general right."[31] Iu. S. Gambarov, another scholar invested in (modern) Roman law models for Russian codification, published a textbook on European civil law in 1911 that cautioned against dismissing administrative privileges as merely historically misbegotten, an affront to any general system of law. Though such legal privileges might remain irreducible prerogatives of a given state's legal system, Gambarov was optimistic that transport, communications, copyright, and patent laws were pressing all national systems in more cosmopolitan directions.[32] By 1900 the invention privilege was embraced as a general right by most imperial subjects who were vested in its functions. Yet this remained a tiny group largely limited to major urban centers, and ill-equipped to persuade the public that such privileges differed in kind from traditional aristocratic varieties.

The 1896 statute diminished utility and enhanced novelty as criteria for the Technical Committee to adjudicate in paper specifications that were increasingly expected to convey the "essence" of the invention rather than merely the rules for its construction.[33] As in the German, Austrian, and Hungarian cases, the fees increased over time, and initial costs were waived for poor inventors. Likewise, scientific discoveries were ruled unpatentable, as were chemical, pharmaceutical, or nutritive materials, and any inventions contrary to public morals. The Russian statute was closest to the Austrian one in the sense that it combined moderate prior examination with quite strict provisions penalizing first registrants for abusing their claims as presumed inventors. The privilege, once granted after examination, obligated the inventor to put it into practice within a generous five years – a more generous compulsory working rule than for many other countries. And this 1896 statute was still relatively friendly to foreigners: an applicant in Russia could not patent an invention for which a third party already held a patent abroad. In sum, the statute's provisions were aligned to existing Central European patent laws, and indeed to transnational patterns of patent rights: in both the Habsburg and Romanov Empires at this time more than two-thirds of patents were granted to foreigners, predominantly German citizens.

---

[31] A. D. Gradovskii, "Slavianofil'skaia teoriia gosudarstvennosti," in *Teoriia gosudarstva u slavianofilov: Sbornik statei* (St. Petersburg: A. Porokhovshchikov, 1898), 74.

[32] Iu. S. Gambarov, *Kurs grazhdanskago prava*, vol. 1 (St. Petersburg: M. M. Stasiulevich, 1911), 278–9, 442.

[33] Shteininger, *Patenty na izobreteniia v Rossii*, 25.

The institutions of Russian patenting were nonetheless distinctive in certain respects. Technical experts rather than lawyers dominated the Technical Committee, but unlike its German, Austrian, and Hungarian counterparts it did not benefit from increased centralization or the creation of a new cadre of civil servants. Though many of its members taught at the St. Petersburg Technological Institute, others were located in distant provinces and frequently they did not have immediate access to journals and other supporting documentation that would have enabled them to vet patent claims more efficiently. Though the prior examination standards were strong, they were nearly impossible to implement in a timely fashion, with the average patent applicant waiting three years. According to Russian law, the term of the patent could not extend longer than any existing foreign patent for the same invention, so this immediately diminished the international value for foreign enterprises. Among patent attorneys – whose status was fostered by the new statute – the main complaint was that there were contradictory definitions of who had the right to apply for a patent, which in turn made it extremely difficult for two inventors to contest priority, given the importance attached to the moment of registration.[34]

Having dismissed misconceptions about the absence of modern patenting in Russia, we should then ask whether the 1896 statute represented a step toward harmonization of patent laws in Central and Eastern Europe. During the Great Reforms, Russian civil and commercial law, as well as parts of criminal law, had adopted many statutes in 1864 that were deeply informed by common Continental (and to a lesser extent, British) legal practices.[35] But these did not come close to encompassing the full administrative reach of the state, and private (reformed) law remained largely segregated from public (traditional) jurisdictions. As in the German case, the tension between personal and property law definitions remained.[36] For his part, Pilenko preferred to think that "the inventor's right can be constructed outside the forms of property and still be a right."[37] He treated invention as both "the crystallization of the person" and the fruit of useful labor, leaving him not so far from the German Otto von Gierke's position.[38] Although Russia looks isolated from European debates, considerable optimism seemed warranted to

[34] Shteininger, *Zashchita izobreteniia v Rossii*, 14–16.
[35] Brian L. Levin-Stankevich, "The Transfer of Legal Technology and Culture: Law Professionals in Tsarist Russia," in *Russia's Missing Middle Class: The Professions in Russian History*, ed. Harley D. Balzer (Armonk, NY: M. E. Sharpe, 1996), 223–49.
[36] G. F. Shershenevich, *Uchebnik russkogo grazhdanskogo prava*, 11th ed. (Moscow: Izd. Br. Bashmakovykh, 1914), 451–83.
[37] Pilenko, *Pravo izobretatelia*, 1903, 2:270.   [38] Ibid., 2:312.

contemporaries, with the government occasionally signaling (1880, 1895, 1904) its readiness to join international patent conventions.[39] After Germany, Austria, and Hungary finally became signatories of the Paris Convention in the first decade of the twentieth century, patent attorney A. P. Skorodinskii, backed by a wide circle of inventors, expressed renewed confidence that Russia would soon join as well, and he bruited plans for St. Petersburg to host the 1911 congress of the international association for industrial property.[40] While neither Russian bureaucrats nor jurists ever treated international harmonization as a process involving adoption of identical statutes by all signatories, comparison and criticism of the practices of other states served important domestic ends, legitimizing constructions of patenting that could potentially satisfy both traditional and reform jurisdictions.[41]

12.3   The Bolshevik Abolition of Patents and Their Revival in 1924

In the decade after the enactment of the new invention privilege law in 1896, the Technical Committee received some 30,000 applications, of which just over a third were awarded patent protection. The majority of Russian patentees were non-Russians (mostly Germans), and the outbreak of European war in 1914 could only damage this dynamic. Early in World War I Russia took legal steps to hold nonmilitary German patents in abeyance for the duration of hostilities, even though this partly served to enforce its economic isolation from Western Europe.[42] Around a thousand German and Austrian patents with potential military utility were also declared property of the Russian state.[43] The wartime disarray led inventors and patent attorneys to join with military-industrial figures to call for the creation of a "central social organ" to counter the strength of German technology, though with no concrete results.[44]

---

[39] A. A. Pilenko, "Russland und die Pariser Convention," *Jahrbuch der Internationalen Vereinigung für Gewerblichen Rechtsschutz* 1 (1897): 469–70.

[40] A. Skorodinskii, "Russland," in *Jahrbuch der Internationalen Vereinigung für Gewerblichen Rechtsschutz: Dreizehnter Jahrgang 1909* (Berlin: Carl Heymanns Verlag, 1911), 85–6. Pilenko had represented Russia at the first such gathering in 1897.

[41] Gambarov, *Kurs grazhdanskago prava*, 1:278–9.

[42] *Voina i promyshlennost'* (*Khronika s 16-go iiulia po 30-e dekabria 1914 goda*) (Kharkov: Mirnyi trud, 1915).

[43] "Der gewerbliche Rechtsschutz und der Krieg," *Elektrotechnik und Maschinenbau Anhang: Industrielle und Wirtschaftliche Nachrichten*, no. 35 (1915): 179–80.

[44] "Pervyi vserossiiskii s"ezd po voprosam izobretenii v Moskve," *Initsiativa i izobretatel'nost'* 1 (1917): 230.

After the abdication of the tsar, the Provisional Government began preparing a new patent law that would align Russian practice more closely with its allies in the war, but the Bolshevik coup intervened before anything was enacted.[45] At least one of the Bolshevik leaders adopted German politician Gustav Stresemann's view that England had been prosecuting an economic war against Germany well before 1914, and cited the 1907 changes to British patent law as one of the main factors driving increased economic hostilities.[46] Consequently, after the Bolsheviks seized power, they treated patents as devices of wealth accumulation akin to foreign debts and treaties – all international institutions unilaterally abrogated by the new regime.[47] Vladimir Lenin's understanding of the political economy of cartel patent pooling further dictated the Bolshevik policy of patent abolition, announced late in 1918.[48] Only after the end of the civil war did the Bolsheviks reconsider their position, eventually instituting a new patent law in 1924, the year that the Union of Soviet Socialist Republics was officially constituted.

The research laboratories of large capitalist enterprises had become sites where inventors were essentially producing industrial secrets, at least if their work did not fit into a patent pooling strategy for a given market segment. Yet the Bolsheviks imagined that the removal of private interests in the form of patents, in concert with the application of science, would bring about an open Russian enterprise system in which a "work of genius" could not be monopolized.[49] One of the canniest Marxist economists, Mikhail Tugan-Baranovskii, went out of his way to argue that intellectual labor under socialism would not be collectively organized in such a way that it would quash individual creativity, but in so doing, he identified the nascent dilemma for Soviet inventors. Whether it

---

[45] "Szabadalomügyi reform Oroszországban," *Szabadalmi Közlöny* 22 (1917): 222.

[46] G. Zinoviev, *Angliia i Germaniia pered mirovoi voinoi. O prichinakh voiny 1914–1916 g.* (Petersburg: Priboi, 1917), 7. Zinoviev was referring to a well-known 1915 essay of Stresemann.

[47] For the initial decrees abolishing intellectual property: "Dekret Soveta Narodnykh Komissarov o priznanii nauchnykh, literaturnykh, muzykal'nykh i khudozhestvennykh proizvedenii gosudarstvennym dostoianiem," in *Sobranie uzakonenii i razporiazhenii Rabochego i Krest'ianskogo Pravitel'stva* no. 86 (December 8, 1918), 1091–2; *Dekret SNK ob izobreteniiakh,* in *Sobranie uzakonenii i razporiazhenii Rabochego i Krest'ianskogo Pravitel'stva* no. 34 (July 1, 1919), 487–8.

[48] V. I. Lenin, "Odna iz velikikh pobed tekhniki," in *Polnoe sobranie sochinenii,* 5th ed., vol. 23 (Moscow: Izd. politicheskoi literatury, 1973), 93–5; V. I. Lenin, "Imperializm, kak vysshaia stadiia kapitalizma," in *Polnoe sobranie sochinenii,* 5th ed., vol. 27 (Moscow: Izd. politicheskoi literatury, 1969), 397.

[49] N. Bukharin and E. Preobrazhenskii, *Azbuka kommunizma: Populiarnoe ob"iasnenie programmy Rossiiskoi kommunisticheskoi partii bol'shevikov* (Moscow: Gosizdat, 1920), §§ 86, 102; N. I. Bukharin, *Teoriia istoricheskogo materializma,* 4th ed. (Moscow-Leningrad: Gosizdat, 1925), 286.

yielded marvelous machines or weapons of destruction, claimed Tugan-Baranovskii, the true gauge of mental power could not be institutional structures. "A barbarian can build a machine, too; but only a person with a completely exceptional ability to perceive beauty can sculpt an Aphrodite of Melos."[50] How far removed was this from the view that the exceptional geniuses responsible for discoveries and inventions "must be surrounded by an entire army of technicians applying the obtained results to life"?[51] It is no wonder that I. Ia. Kheifets, the chief author of the reconstituted Soviet patent law, took the view that "the inventive act arises as a result of an internal creative need satisfying a spiritual thirst and expressing the aspiration of technical talent and genius."[52]

The Bolsheviks eventually reinstituted a patent law in 1924, having realized that failure to honor patents internationally would choke off access to much-needed technologies for postwar reconstruction.[53] Conversely, they also hoped that Soviet inventors could bring in hard currency for their foreign patents: this was an overly optimistic assessment, but as events would show, not an entirely implausible one. A Bolshevik commission on patent affairs was formed in the summer of 1921, and its mandate originally included preparations for Russia to join international conventions.[54] Its agendas were overshadowed by the contentious Bolshevik efforts at Genoa and Rapallo to rejoin the repudiated international system on their own terms. The dominant Marxist rationale for transitional embrace of international law, while cognizant of technical issues like communications or weights and measures, nonetheless neglected trade in general and patenting entirely.[55] It took more than two years of work before a draft statute was ready, not least because the new Soviet trade delegations in Europe were understaffed and distrusted by the central authorities, though they would serve as the primary legal representatives of Soviet patent interests abroad – Kheifets, for one, did a stint in Berlin.[56]

---

[50] M. I. Tugan-Baranovskii, *Sotsializm kak polozhitel'noe uchenie* (Petrograd: Izd. Kooperatsiia, 1918), 129.

[51] M. A. Blokh, *Tvorchestvo v nauke i tekhnike* (Petrograd, 1920), 9.

[52] I. Ia. Kheifets, *Osnovy patentnogo prava* (Leningrad: Nauchnoe Khimiko-Tekhnicheskoe Izdatel'stvo, 1925), 14.

[53] V. I. Afanas'eva, "Stanovlenie i razvitie sovetskogo izobretatel'skogo prava (1917–1924 gg.)," *Gosudarstvo i pravo*, no. 2 (2009): 88–92.

[54] B. S. Mal'tsman, "Dekret soveta narodnykh komissarov o patentnoi komissii pri VSNKh po voprosam ob ograzhdenii prav inostrannykh izobretatelei v SSSR i russkikh izobretatelei zagranitsei (Polozhenie)," in *Zakonodatel'stvo o promyshlennosti, torgovle, trude, i transporte: Sb. dektretov, postanovlenii, prikazov i instruktsii*, vol. 2, ed. B. S. Mal'tsman (Moscow: VSNKh, 1923), 817–18.

[55] E. A. Korovin, *Mezhdunarodnoe pravo perekhodnogo vremeni* (Moscow: Gosizdat, 1924).

[56] "Novyi zakonoproekt ob izobreteniiakh," *Izvestiia*, August 4, 1923.

Since the Soviet state arrogated a host of powers to itself in the name of the proletariat, some caution is necessary in discussing the case of patents, especially to avoid the Anglophone tendency to see the state's proper role as facilitating individual and industrial patent interests within a general context of free trade. In the early postwar period, Western governments introduced provisions (articles 307 and 308 of the Versailles Treaty; the December 23, 1919 British law) that ratified certain wartime seizures of intellectual property and also made it easier to force patent licensing in the name of state interests. To Soviet observers this smacked of hypocrisy, and further reinforced their conviction that under transitional conditions of state capitalism it was entirely appropriate that the new patent law should be dictated by the industrial needs of the state.[57] Yet the very scope of nationalization meant that state enterprises would effectively be competing against each other, and patents had to be reinstituted in such a fashion as to counter the "factory secrets" mentality and serve the common good. When "every word of science and technology could serve as a source of enrichment" under capitalism, it was no small challenge to defend the legal interests of the inventor without reproducing similar social motives.[58]

The new patent law was intended to function regardless of citizenship, and indeed more or less tracked existing German law.[59] It did, however, adopt a stronger presumption that the patent holder ought to be the true inventor – a point not recognized in German law until 1936. The Bolshevik notion of utility was also distinctly innovative. It was not about the general consilience of the invention with its declared functions, but whether it could be used effectively "in conditions of Soviet reality." Crucially for holders of pre-1919 patents, the statute included provision for applying to restore abolished patents (albeit only for the term remaining as of 1919), though this had the consequence that patent officials were buried by a backlog of applications from the very beginning.

---

[57] I. O. Mikhailovskii, "Patentno-pravovye otnosheniia v usloviiakh gosudarstvennogo kapitalizma," *Vestnik Komiteta po delam izobretenii* 1 (1924): 61–6; S. Raevich, *Ocherki istorii burzhuaznogo grazhdanskogo prava so vremeni imperialisticheskoi voiny* (Moscow-Leningrad: Gosizdat, 1927), 81–96.

[58] S. V. Aleksandrovskii, *Grazhdanskoe pravo R.S.F.S.R.* (Novo-Nikolaevsk: Sibirskoe obl. gos. izd., 1922), 95–9.

[59] "O patentakh na izobreteniia," *Sobranie zakonov i rasporiazhenii RKP SSSR*, no. 9 (October 6, 1924): 130–42; A. M. Kirzner and V. V. Petrovskii, *Patentnoe i avtorskoe pravo: Zakony o patentakh na izobretenniia, o promyshlennykh obraztsakh (risunkah i modeliakh), o tovarnykh znakakh i ob avtorskom prave* (Leningrad: Rabochii sud, 1927); Leonidov and Mikheeva, *Patentnyi zakon Rossii*, 56–70; S. Raevich, "Izobreteniia," in *Entsiklopediia gosudarstva i prava*, ed. P. Stuchka (Moscow: Izd. Kommunisticheskoi akademii, 1925–6).

12.4   Patents, Worker Inventiveness, and Collective Creativity in the Soviet Era

It is, in part, the making of the 1924 law, its imperfect implementation, as well as significant modifications in 1931, which bound scientists and engineers of all stripes together in a common legal framework with invention at its center. When Nikolai Bukharin proclaimed the coming "scientization" of engineering and "engineering" of science as central to the planning debates of the First Five-Year Plan, he was on the trailing edge rather than the leading edge: the legal process had long been reforming Soviet meanings of expertise with this kind of convergence as a collateral consequence.[60] The new statutes provided one of the concrete locales where the role of the expert was sanctified in Soviet terms, continuous with the prerevolutionary procedural connotations of expertise, but shorn (at least formally) of trade and class imprecations. Soviet enterprises were to help the worker inventor "overcome the difficulties that stand in the way of realizing his invention as a result of inadequate scientific and technical knowledge."[61] They were seldom equipped to do so, however, as top trade-union officials acknowledged.[62] It would nonetheless prove extremely difficult to dispel Lenin's early hostility to any measures that could elevate "technical experts, supervisors, consultants, or advisors" who had supposedly been complicit in the exploitation by old-regime owners.[63] Early postrevolutionary pleas by scientists to recognize the value of "knowledge capital" as a counterpart to monetary accumulations were consequently rejected after 1917.[64]

Soviet political leaders had somewhat naïve motives for reviving the patent system abolished in 1918. They were far more concerned about inventors than experts, and Soviet historical commentary suggests that Lenin's purported solicitude for working-class inventors became a convenient way to avoid talking about expertise.[65] It was a far more

---

[60] N. Bukharin, *Metodologiia i planirovanie nauki i tekhniki* (Moscow: Nauka, 1989).
[61] F. Dzerzhinskii and Katsnel'son, "O rabochem izobretatel'stve," in *Patentnyi zakon Rossii*, ed. Leonidov and Mikheeva, 75–7.
[62] M. P. Tomskii, "Itogi raboty i ocherednye zadachi profsoiuzov," in *XV konferentsiia Vsesoiuznoi Kommunisticheskoi Partii (b): 26 oktiabria - 3 noiabria 1926 g. Stenograficheskii otchet* (Moscow: Gosizdat, 1927), 279.
[63] V. I. Lenin, "Pervonachal'nyi variant stat'i 'Ocherednye zadachi sovetskoi vlasti,'" in *Polnoe sobranie sochinenii*, vol. 36 (Moscow: Politizdat, 1962), 138.
[64] See the April 1917 public address of chemist L. A. Chugaev in Svobodnaia Assotsiatsiia dlia razvitiia i rasprostraneniia polozhitel'nykh nauk, *Rechi i privetstviia, proiznesennyia na trekh publichnykh sobraniiakh* (Petrograd: Parus, 1917), 43.
[65] A. Poryvkin and V. Kliushnikov, *Izobretateliam ob izobreteliakh* (Saratov: Gosizdat, 1930); V. S. Poznanskii, "O razvitii massovogo rabochego izobretatel'stva i ratsionalizatorstva v SSSR," *Voprosy istorii*, no. 3 (1960): 138–53; V. S. Poznanskii,

appealing prospect to imagine that invention could be turned into a mass enterprise for the proletariat, an end-run around the suspected anti-Soviet resistance of "bourgeois" specialists.[66] In normative accounts the early Soviet inventor is shown to be at odds with the petty interests of the shop floor master craftsman, while also renouncing material rewards and proving that he is not being driven by any lust for fame.[67] The restoration of the patent system represented the state's acknowledgment that ex post facto rewards by state-owned enterprises were insufficient incentives: some form of licensing system to protect individual inventors had to be retained, even if the state retained its nominal right to expropriate.

But it was soon recognized that the fraught issue of compulsory licensing would raise many questions about how to evaluate fair compensation to patentees whose inventions were appropriated for licensing by others. Both monopoly and alienation mechanisms could ultimately claim industrial development as their positive rationale. Yet by the same token, both should leave the creative inventor free of the corrupting influence of the creditor, so the collective should not become proxy for that role when patents were appropriated.[68] The inherent tension in the process was that industrial research no longer favored the individual inventor, but rather the enterprise as an organization. For all the collectivist rhetoric, industry authorities and scientific experts alike were continually disappointed in their attempts to empower the shop floor workers they imagined would lead the Soviet invention dynamic.

The top Siemens patent attorney reported that when a Soviet delegation visited Berlin in 1930, they were taken aback to learn that any Siemens production worker was free to suggest improvements and acquire any resulting patents; significantly, however, the contractual limitations were imposed precisely on those specialized employees who had privileged access to the kinds of company resources that could systematically support significant inventions.[69] The Soviet statute only grudgingly acknowledged the white-collar employee as the more likely

---

"V. I. Lenin i sovetskoe izobretatel'stvo," *Voprosy istorii*, no. 4 (1962): 3–17; G. M. Alekseev, "Dvizhenie izobretatelei i ratsionalizatorov v SSSR," *Voprosy istorii*, no. 9 (1969): 30–48.

[66] B. Petrov, "Front izobretatel'stva," *Front nauki i tekhniki*, no. 10 (1932): 80–3. On early Soviet treatment of technical experts, Kendall E. Bailes, *Technology and Society under Lenin and Stalin* (Princeton, NJ: Princeton University Press, 1978).

[67] Poryvkin and Kliushnikov, *Izobretateliam ob izobretateliakh*, 40–7.

[68] A. Iasvoin, "Iz praktiki patentnogo prava," *Ezhenedel'nik sovetskoi iustitsii*, no. 37 (1925): 1208–11.

[69] L. Fischer, "Bericht über meine dienstliche Tätigkeit 1899–1934," Siemens-Archiv-Akte 12/Lp 839, pp. 161–2.

applicant for patent protection, and contractual obligations in the industrial setting remained poorly specified in Soviet law.

Kheifets sincerely hoped that factories would become for the inventor-technologist what science departments were for the researcher.[70] In the wake of the League of Nations debate about scientific property he became the chief Soviet advocate of similarities between scientific discovery and technical invention.[71] His audience included Abram Joffe, a senior Soviet physicist who held international patents that he used to help fund his institute's research, including several in collaboration with the Siemens Research Laboratory in Berlin.[72] Joffe took the position that the inventor's identification of novelty was merely "unorganized science," and his highly publicized engagement with Soviet industry evinced complete confidence that all technology was properly understood as applied science.[73] Engaged at any given time in fluid collaborations across multiple laboratories, this tireless researcher was in a certain sense emblematic of the Soviet obsession with collective creativity. As a Soviet engineer acidly put it, the headlong pace of industrialization drove a dynamic in which the absence of clear conceptions about how to organize and evaluate collective creativity repeatedly led to hasty attributions of authority to the first person who managed to make himself spokesman on behalf of a given collective.[74] Joffe masterfully harnessed this dynamic to expand the institutional scope of Soviet physics beyond its more academic confines, but he was primarily concerned with legitimizing modern physics more generally in a volatile political setting, and not with organizing industrial research laboratories or dignifying white-collar social functions therein. This made him a poor ally for Kheifets, who by 1930 was even prepared to argue that the white-collar inventor would henceforth dominate, though this resulted in uninvited coeditors and

[70] I. Ia. Kheifets, "Pravo predpriiatiia na izobretenie, sdelannoe sluzhashchim ili rabochim," *Ezhenedel'nik sovetskoi iustitsii*, no. 43 (1924): 1025.

[71] Kheifets, *Osnovy patentnogo prava*, 14, 28; "Okhrana nauchnogo otkrytiia," *Vestnik Komiteta po delam izobretenii*, no. 2 (1924): 59–68; James M. Swanson, *Scientific Discoveries and Soviet Law: A Sociohistorical Analysis* (Gainesville: University of Florida Press, 1984), 35. On the French-dominated debate, David Philip Miller, "Intellectual Property and Narratives of Discovery/Invention: The League of Nations' Draft Convention on 'Scientific Property' and Its Fate," *History of Science* 46 (2008): 299–342.

[72] "Vsesoiuznyi s"ezd fizikov (Vtoroi den')," *Krasnaia gazeta*, September 17, 1924; A. F. Ioffe, "O moei poslednei zagranichnoi poezdke," *Pravda*, February 5, 1928.

[73] A. F. Ioffe, "Puti izobretatel'stva," *Izobretatel'*, no. 1 (1929): 6–7; "Nauka i izobretatel'stvo," *Izvestiia*, April 10, 1931.

[74] K. N. Chekhovskii, "Kollektivnaia tekhnicheskaia mysl' u nas i v Soedinennykh Shtatakh," *Vestnik inzhenera*, no. 4 (1926): 201–3.

recantation in later editions of his work.[75] The Soviet legal system nonetheless long entertained the possibility that certain constructions of scientific "discovery" as "creative achievement" could be aligned with the technical novelty of the inventor.[76]

In the short run, however, the 1924 Soviet patent law institutionalized an important form of expertise as part of the patent review process, while ensuring its continued ambiguous status by acknowledging that the Soviet Union possessed neither qualified cadres nor patent literature sufficient to apply formal review to each and every patent application.[77] When qualified civil servants could not be found to render verdicts, many a scientist spent time on the side reviewing patent applications for a fee of ten rubles each.[78]

Even more worrisome, although inventors were notionally the lead figures in the larger process of rationalization of industry, Soviet propagandists were annoyed to realize that ill-educated dreamers with fantastic schemes were discrediting the idea of worker-inventors.[79] Of some 275 Soviet enterprises surveyed in 1928, not one could offer technical consultations on site to its would-be worker-inventors.[80] "Shock work, socialist competition, and worker inventiveness are becoming organic forms of labor organization," claimed a reformer of engineering curricula during the First Five-Year Plan, but the last of these three proved the hardest to implement as a mobilizing factor in industrialization.[81] The most vocal advocates of worker inventions proved reluctant to accept the

---

[75] I. Ia. Kheifets, *Promyshlennye prava i ikh khoziaistvennoe znachenie v Soiuze SSR i na Zapade* (Moscow: Gosudarstennoe iuridicheskoe izd. RSFSR, 1930). For the "errors," see I. Ia. Kheifets, *Osnovnye problemy izobretatel'stva. Patentnaia okhrana sovetskogo eksporta*, ed. Iu. O. Lengiel' and I. I. Matveev (Moscow-Leningrad: Vneshtorgizdat, 1935), 9; L. Riabinin, "Izobretenie i izobretatel'stvo," *Bol'shaia sovetskaia entsiklopediia* (Moscow-Leningrad, 1938), 658.

[76] Raevich, *Ocherki istorii*, 85; V. I. Serebrovskii, "Nauchnoe otkrytie kak ob"ekt prava," *Sovetskoe gosudarstvo i pravo*, no. 3 (1959): 47–55.

[77] A. P. Kolesnikov, "Ob istorii razrabotki patentnogo zakona 1924 g.," *Voprosy izobretatel'stva*, no. 8 (1989): 18–22.

[78] S. Usov, "Bumazhnaia triasina. Rezul'taty obsledovaniia RKI Komiteta po delam izobretenii v Leningrade," *Izvestiia*, July 7, 1928.

[79] V. E. L'vov, "Ob izobretateliakh i 'izobretateliakh'," *Vestnik znaniia* 4, no. 10 (1928): 516–19; "Rabochii-izobretatel' dolzhen byt v pervykh riadakh stroitelei i industrializatorov," *Izvestiia*, August 5, 1929; Bailes, *Technology and Society under Lenin and Stalin*, 361–6.

[80] "Den' v TsBRIZ," *Izvestiia*, July 7, 1928.

[81] Al. Beilin, "Sistema podgotovki inzhenerno-tekhnicheskikh kadrov dlia promyshlennosti," in *Puti podgotovki proizvodstvenno-tekhnicheskoi intelligentsii iz liudei rabochego klassa* (Moscow: ONTI, 1931), 22.

tremendous winnowing process between inventive ideas and working products.[82] It proved difficult indeed to dispel the popular perception that every invention had to be revolutionary.[83]

A 1929 monograph on the *Psychology of Technical Inventiveness* – summarized in the first issue of the magazine *The Inventor* – suggests an important reason why the discourse of the creative inventor proved so difficult to reconcile with an egalitarian politics.[84] Inspired by Engelmeyer, experimental psychologist A. P. Nechaev undertook to develop research criteria for the distinction between inventive discovery and mere finding. In addition to innate talent, knowledge, and ability, he saw strength of personality as an important factor. Beyond the procedures for technical evaluation of the invention, argued Nechaev, psychological evaluation of the inventor was also important in the Soviet setting. Confident that experimental psychology had advanced considerably since Engelmeyer first put forward his theory of creativity, Nechaev studied a group of twenty-nine engineers with varying levels of professional accomplishment. Whether in terms of education, memory, attention, judgment, and "speed of psychological work" (with ability to take dictation as the proxy), he found a clear hierarchy correlated to their relative success in invention.

Then came the elusive category of imagination, where Nechaev undertook a more elaborate experiment, distinguishing between "perceptive" and "contemplative" imagination. The top inventors remained clearly superior in the latter category. As he formulated his conclusions, Nechaev was at pains to insist that formal intellectual skills were not what marked them as more inventive, but rather "the general structure of their personality." If inventiveness depended on the "natural organization of the person," however, then this yielded a worrisome conclusion: "Technical creativity is above all a fortunate gift of nature."[85] Fostering inventiveness was thus not so much a question of shaping an environment as it was of finding the people who possessed the required gift. To that end Engelmeyer and Nechaev sought to organize a laboratory in Moscow for the study of inventive creativity, enlisting the prominent

---

[82] "Navstrechu rabochemu izobretateliu," *Izvestiia*, September 23, 1928; S. Kapitonov, "Izobretatel'stvo i rekonstruktsiia promyshlennosti," *Izvestiia*, August 5, 1929. Both mention rates of around 1.5 percent, probably not too far from the rate for commercially profitable patented inventions in market economies. The rhetoric of innovation of course seldom recognizes how many patents fail to find larger audiences.

[83] A. El'kishek, "Sovetskie izobretately," *Krasnaia gazeta*, April 14, 1936.

[84] A. P. Nechaev, "Psikhologiia tekhnicheskogo izobretatel'stva," *Izobretatel'*, no. 1 (1929): 35–6.

[85] A. P. Nechaev, *Psikhologiia tekhnicheskogo izobretatel'stva* (Moscow-Leningrad: Gosizdat, 1929), 80.

geneticist N. K. Kol'tsov in the enterprise. Kol'tsov did not shy away from claiming that his own laboratory could already produce "rat-inventors with a patent that they can yield inventor descendants" with superior maze-negotiation abilities. Humankind as well possessed inventors and noninventors, he suggested, and what distinguished them lay in the chemical composition of the blood and "in the inventive temperament."[86] In keeping with these ambitions the magazine *The Inventor* featured intelligence tests for inventors to help readers ascertain whether they possessed that "special cast."[87]

The Promethean understanding of the new Soviet man left little room for any theory of inventiveness that privileged nature over nurture. Engelmeyer and Kheifets were marginalized in the 1930s as "idealists."[88] The conventional Soviet Marxist view of invention held that the problem-solving and "concentration of talent" that yielded inventions resulted from the long heritage of division of labor, to be understood strictly in socioeconomic terms. Early Marxist social psychologists struggled to demonstrate the dependence between "the development of instinct as an internal apparatus of adaptation" and the material productive forces that made possible the "psychic labor" leading from simple reflexes to "the scientifically knowing and technically inventing mind."[89] A new proletarian generation needed to foster "creative intellectual automatism," in the unartful phrase of A. B. Zalkind, but his brand of mental labor hygiene was hardly propaedeutic to invention.[90] Even these Lamarckian strategies for connecting talent and labor failed to identify a Soviet sociology of invention that did not suffer from the same contradictions between culturalist and rationalist explanations found elsewhere.[91] As the great survivor of Soviet psychology S. L. Rubinshtein put it in an enduring textbook from the Stalin era, invention and scientific research surely required inspiration, but that could not be cast as a "gift" or "faculty" in opposition to the labor concept. "The creative activity of the scientist is creative labor."[92] Yet both scientist and inventor ideologue tended to treat inventions as nothing more than reifications of scientific concepts, blocking off insight into the potentially technologic

---

[86] "U rabotnikov po psikhotekhnike," *Izobretatel'*, no. 2 (1929): 59.

[87] K. Veigelin, "Psikhotekhnika izobretatelia," *Izobretatel'*, no. 4 (1929): 62–3.

[88] Riabinin, "Izobretenie i izobretatel'stvo."

[89] M. A. Reisner, *Problemy sotsial'noi psikhologii* (Rostov-Don: Burevestnik, 1925), 40.

[90] A. B. Zalkind, "O gigiene umstvennogo truda proletarskogo studenchestva," in *Revoliutiia i molodezh': sbornik statei* (Moscow: Izd. Kommunistich. un-ta im. Sverdlova, 1925), 100–40.

[91] David McGee, "Making Up Mind: The Early Sociology of Invention," *Technology and Culture* 36 (1995): 773–801.

[92] S. L. Rubinshtein, *Osnovy obshchei psikhologii*, vol. 2 (Moscow: Pedagogika, 1989), 59.

character of the vaunted acts of creativity that nominally bound epistemic processes to materials and equipment.[93]

The increasing recognition that the patent committee could not keep up with the influx of applications (peaking at more than 22,000 in 1929) led to calls for moving toward a registration system as early as 1928.[94] A scholar from the Communist Academy chafed at the overestimation of the individual and the continued protection of "the inventor's property in his idea," when more efficient incentives to connect inventors to producers could surely be found in the socialist setting.[95] During the First Five-Year Plan the central bodies entrusted with fostering invention and vetting patent applications suffered from a dozen arrests amid campaigns against specialist "wreckers," to the point that they were portrayed as "crematoria of inventions" at the sixteenth party congress in July 1930.[96] Though some had already read the 1924 law as rendering patent and copyright analogous,[97] in 1931 Soviet authorities introduced a new statute that moved patents closer to copyright in terms of authorial attribution, guaranteeing a schedule of monetary rewards, but also making it easiest to reap them by assigning the usage rights directly to the state.[98]

The statute's mixing of the senses of invention and discovery ensured that the image of invention would remain difficult to tie to the large-scale industrial enterprise. But this firmer institutionalization of modest rewards for creativity served to uncouple inventors from any forms of control over the disposition of their work, with evaluation of the worth of the invention determined, not by any differential benefit to the state enterprises that utilized them, but rather by invention bureaus charged with calculating general savings for entire economic sectors.[99] Inventors were required to indicate at the time of application whether they desired an author's certificate or a formal patent, with the system firmly favoring the former, since individuals could not acquire the resources to put the invention to practice on their own, and the author's certificate was a surer means of monetary return than licensing the patent to the government.

---

[93] Wolfgang Lefèvre, "Science as Labor," *Perspectives on Science* 13 (2005): 194–225.

[94] M. Shipov, "Novyi patentnyi zakon," *Izvestiia*, September 23, 1928.

[95] I. D. Markov, "Patentovanie izobretenii v SSSR," *Revoliutsiia prava*, no. 4 (1929): 114–28.

[96] *XVI s"ezd vsesoiuznoi kommunisticheskoi partii (b): Stenograficheskii otchet* (Moscow, 1930), 515.

[97] A. A. Zhizhilenko, *Prestupleniia protiv imushchestva i iskliuchitel'nykh prav* (Leningrad: Rabochii sud, 1928), 181.

[98] "Polozhenie ob izobreteniiakh i tekhnicheskikh usovershenstvovaniiakh (9 April 1931)," in Leonidov and Mikheeva, *Patentnyi zakon Rossii*, 77–103.

[99] Sergeev, *Pravo intellektual'noi sobstvennosti v Rossiiskoi Federatsii*, 45.

The statute also made it easier for the state to seize the patent in case of need, albeit with guarantees of compensation. The author certificate or patent was nonetheless transferable and heritable. These were welcome developments for Old Bolshevik and dean of Soviet jurisprudence Pyotr Stuchka, who regarded the 1924 statute as a temporary concession to the old privilege system, and he urged that inventive ideas not be conceived as the individual property of single persons (*individual'naia sobstvennost' otdel'nykh lits*).[100] But, as with copyright, he and his contemporaries struggled to define the public nature of the object of the patent.[101]

The invention bureaus fostered by the 1931 statute soon faltered for a variety of reasons. I think, paraphrasing David Shearer, that it is important not to see the socialization of worker inventiveness as leading inevitably to centralization of the state apparatus for patenting.[102] It was indeed the state's combination of solicitude toward inventiveness and suspicion of expertise that made it difficult for Soviet patenting institutions to benefit from bureaucratic economies of scale. The 1931 statute required that all the organs involved in invention, right down to the enterprise level, had to be equipped with cadres from among "inventors, shock workers, and specialists-social activists" (*spetsialisty-obshchestven-niki*), the last being that peculiarly Soviet nomenklatura whose political qualifications could potentially trump any expert claims. That Soviet industrial enterprises had hypertrophied and that the biggest scientific research institutes at the time were also located in the People's Commissariat of Heavy Industry did not imply that the largest enterprises would accumulate the most patents, nor that a corps of engineers dedicated to invention would be found there, since Lenin's imprecations against such combines remained operative.[103] In time the functions of the invention bureaus were largely taken over by the very enterprise chiefs and their subordinates who had every incentive to minimize outlays to certificate holders.[104] It was not that the legal protections were lacking – solid provisions against third-party violations were retained, and émigré patent agents still judged it worthwhile for foreigners to take out patents.[105] But

[100] P. Stuchka, *Kurs sovetskogo grazhdanskogo prava*, vol. 3 (Izd. Kommunisticheskoi akademii, 1931), 63.
[101] Ekaterina Pravilova, *A Public Empire: Property and the Quest for the Common Good in Imperial Russia* (Princeton, NJ: Princeton University Press, 2014), 277–89.
[102] David R. Shearer, *Industry, State, and Society in Stalin's Russia: 1926–1934* (Ithaca, NY: Cornell University Press, 1996), 10.
[103] "Lenin i tekhnika," *Istoriia tekhniki* 2 (1934): 7–9.
[104] Victor G. Olkhovsky, "The Principles of Soviet Patent Law and Social Organization of Inventions in the U.S.S.R.," *Journal of the Patent Office Society* 17 (1935): 577.
[105] John P. Nikonow, "Patents in the Soviet Russia," *Journal of the Patent Office Society* 17, no. 4 (1935): 339–41.

from this point forward Soviet jurisprudence declared its militant opposition to international patent politics, effectively dropped any steps toward harmonization, and did not join the Paris Union until 1965.[106]

12.5   Conclusion

This depiction of Russian and Soviet patent cultures admittedly offers little to the economic historian keen to explain modern Russia's comparatively modest experience in fostering the full invention cycle across economic sectors. Yet it advances a more nuanced account of the role of jurists, patent attorneys, engineers, and scientists in the institutions of invention. This account should moderate the temptation to rely solely on persistent caricatures (discredited in the previous sections) of an imperial Russian state inadequately committed to the improvement of industry, or of a Soviet state whose hostility to private property disempowered inventors and obviated serious discussion of patenting. In fact, indifference to patenting in the first instance, or hostility in the second, generally stemmed from more than economic reasoning. This was indeed an exceedingly modest but highly contested site for debating the obligations of the state to Russian society.

The answer to Veshniakov's early puzzlement about the lack of discussion during the Great Reforms is not that no Russian saw a need for patenting. Rather, it was that the few who did so invested it with too much, rather than too little, social potential. Under a regime permanently skittish about the legacy of the French Revolution, a mechanical engineer and educator could make a veiled reference to the ways in which the masses were gradually laying claim to the social sphere. Yet it is telling that he cautiously pointed first to patent offices in Paris, London, and Washington as early sites for this quiet transformation of public life. Moreover, he directly linked the political events "that spurred the inert mass of society" to the growing role of science "when it merges with the life of society in its applications, when it becomes the basis of development for the well-being of society."[107]

Humbler practitioners of the mechanical arts played little part in this, because the business of invention too quickly became the province of the rare polymath. K. A. Skalkovskii, who trained as a mining engineer and

[106] S. Raevich, *Politika izobretatel'stva i patentnoe pravo dvukh sistem v period obshchego krizisa kapitalizma* (Moscow-Leningrad: ONTI, 1934).
[107] Iv. Rachmaninov, "Neskol'ko slov o vvedenii v fiziko-matematicheskie fakul'tety prepodavaniia prikladnykh nauk," *Zhurnal ministerstva narodnago prosveshcheniia* 118, no. III (April 1863): 350–78. Ivan Ivanovich Rachmaninov (1826–97) was a professor of mechanics at Vladimir outside of Moscow.

spent much of his career advocating reforms in the industry, acerbically claimed that the Russian education system "amounts to reproducing Lomonosovs": seeking out geniuses and, no matter what their initial state, elevating them "to the level of academicians and luminaries of science."[108] In his view this had damaging collateral effects on the training of engineers, who as students were socialized to think of themselves as applied scientists, but due to persistent resource shortages too many of them were shuffled through the system without adequate exposure to the equipment and laboratory work ethic that could help them make good on that proposition. This then contributed to a mismatch between their social expectations and their job opportunities.

Scholars from the natural and social sciences were complicit in the distinctively Russian social psychological elevation of invention. As St. Petersburg social historian Aleksandr Lappo-Danilevskii put it in his *Theory of Historical Knowledge*, "the higher the individual creativity, the less it depends on circumstances and the more the masses need it, and not it the masses."[109] His Moscow counterpart Nikolai Kareev believed it was "not the natural course of things" that created the steam engine, gas motor, and electrical apparatuses, but "human inventiveness" – "the intervention of the human will in the natural order of nature to force its powers to serve human ends."[110] Marxist disdain for this celebration of agency over structure did not come as an antidote after 1917, because the early Soviet obsession with worker inventiveness – and not simply hostility to private property – worked against institutionalization of the expert routine of patenting. Even orthodox Soviet jurists equally impatient with appeals to creativity and genius as well as with standard European legal rationales for patenting could never quite reconcile themselves to post hoc constructions of the inventor's right. The shortcoming of the 1931 authorial reward model was precisely that it reinforced the image of psychological individualism without fostering enterprise-level control over the disposition of inventions.

Chemical engineer Vladimir Ipatieff was emblematic of these lingering contradictions. An imperial artillery officer and instructor as well as member of the Academy of Sciences, he opted to remain after the Bolshevik revolution, and helped to restore the viability of the Soviet

[108] Skal'kovskii, *Sovremennaia Rossiia*, 2:216.
[109] A. S. Lappo-Danilevskii, *Teoriia istoricheskago znaniia*, vol. 1, Metodologiia istorii (St. Petersburg: Izdanie Studencheskago Izd. Kom. pri Istoriko-Filologicheskom Fakul'tete, 1910), 273.
[110] N. Kareev, *Obshchie osnovy sotsiologii* (Petrograd: Nauka i shkola, 1919), 46; N. I. Kareev, *Vvedenie v izuchenie sotsiologii* (St. Petersburg: M. M. Stasiulevich, 1897), 290.

chemical industry. Fearing the anti-expert currents of the First Five-Year Plan, he emigrated in 1930, later claiming in his memoirs that he "neglected to take out patents on all my discoveries in science."[111] The choice of terms is symptomatic, though he was being slightly disingenuous, since he acquired at least four Soviet patents late in his career, mostly regarding more efficient methods to produce phosphates.[112] In fairness to Ipatieff, three out of four of these patents were awarded only after he had resolved to emigrate. The general pattern in the German case, commented Ipatieff, was that anything even distantly connected to industry was patented first, and only then was thought given to publication. A scientific worker in Germany who could not claim patented works was not a chemist but a "philosopher." Ipatieff faulted his compatriots for behaving too much like philosophers, implying that patents did not become a vehicle for distribution of scientific credit.[113]

Within the cross-currents of imperial and later Soviet law, "philosopher" jurists could also impede more mundane patent reforms out of adherence to higher principles. Yet the 1896 and 1924 patent statutes were surely evidence that the basic legal mechanics of Russian and Soviet patent culture was quite compatible with its various Northern European counterparts. It was the state's administrative opacity and the lingering appeal of the psychology of invention more than the letter of the law that were the markers of comparative disadvantage. Disentangling patents from the realm of autocratic privilege conversely implied arriving at a social consensus about whether inventions as artifacts of universal ideas could be temporarily removed from the Storehouse of Knowledge for private advantage. Neither the older figure of the inventor-supplicant at Tolstoy's estate nor the newer figure of the worker-inventor ever gained much standing in that Russian debate. By the same token, the various kinds of experts who might have functioned as gatekeepers to the Storehouse never arrived at any working consensus that regarded patenting as a vital piece of Russia's nascent *res publica*.

---

[111] V. Ipat'ev, *Zhizn' odnogo khimika. Vospominaniia*, vol. 2 (New York, 1945), 467.
[112] No. 10088 (awarded June 29, 1929); no. 13394 (March 31, 1930); no. 20076 (April 30, 1931); no. 20593 (April 30, 1931).
[113] Ipat'ev, *Zhizn' odnogo khimika. Vospominaniia*, 2:618.

Part V

Asia

13 Patent Policy in India under the British Raj
A Bittersweet Story of Empire and Innovation

Rajesh Sagar

13.1 Introduction

Despite having its own patent law since 1856, by the time of its independence in 1947 India was far behind technologically in comparison to other developed countries that had patent laws introduced contemporaneously. This chapter examines this issue by focusing on patent policy and policy making in colonial India and highlights how the restricted political and legislative freedom of the Government of India within its colonial framework had an adverse effect on choosing a patent policy conducive to India's national interest.

13.2 The Positive Aspects of the Act VI of 1856

Until the first half of the nineteenth century, India did not have any statute for granting patent rights to inventors.[1] The introduction of statutory protection for inventions in India was kept in abeyance for nearly two decades from 1834[2] to 1856 because of the uncertainty as to which authority has the power to regulate the grant of patents in India.[3] However, this did not deter potential patentees from petitioning the Government of India and East India Company to introduce such rights in India. It was primarily their interest and perseverance that resulted in the introduction of the first patent law in India in 1856.[4]

I would like to thank David Baldwin and Michael Moore for their invaluable comments and suggestions on the chapter.

[1] This statement is made only in relation to British India, a territory within the administrative control of the East India Company as the chapter focuses on the development of patent law in British India. The Act VI of 1856 is the first legislative act that established patent rights in India. See Indian patent office website, available at www.ipindia.nic.in/history-of-indian-patent-system.htm, last accessed on July 31, 2018.
[2] According to the documentary research undertaken by the author, the first reference to patent protection in India was in the year 1834.
[3] Rajesh Sagar, "Introduction of Exclusive Privileges in Colonial India: Why and for Whose Benefit," *Intellectual Property Quarterly* 2 (2007): 164–85.
[4] Sagar, "Introduction of Exclusive Privileges."

The Act VI of 1856, entitled "An Act for granting exclusive privileges to inventors" (the 1856 Act), was enacted on February 28, 1856[5] and allowed the Governor General in Council (GGIC) to grant exclusive privileges to inventors of new manufacture for a period of fourteen years for British India.[6]

Even though the 1856 Act was in operation for only a year,[7] it was significant for many reasons. It was the first law that protected inventions in India and regulated the grant of earliest known Indian patents. It also embodied the more progressive idea of an inventor being given exclusive privileges through the operation of law rather than by an act of the Crown.[8] A number of important concepts embodied within the 1856 Act are discussed below.[9]

13.2.1 Definition of Inventor and Novelty Assessment

The word "inventor" was defined broadly under the 1856 Act and included not only *an actual and bona fide* inventor, but also an importer of an invention into India.[10] An importer of an invention could obtain an exclusive privilege under the 1856 Act[11] subject to the condition of

---

[5] The 1856 Act was passed by the Legislative Council of India on February 23, 1856. It allowed the Governor-General of India in Council (GGIC) to grant exclusive privileges to inventors of new manufacture for a period of fourteen years for British India. The leave for grant of exclusive privilege was required to be presented in written or printed form on a stamped paper of 100 rupees. See Section XXXVI of the 1856 Act.

[6] Section XXXVI of the 1856 Act. Prior sanction of Her Majesty was required in accordance with the statute entitled "An Act to provide for the Government of India," also known as the Government of India Act, 1853.

[7] The 1856 Act remained in operation for only a year because it had been enacted without the sanction of Her Majesty, Queen Victoria.

[8] The inventor was granted exclusive privilege once certain requirements prescribed in the 1856 Act were fulfilled.

[9] For detailed discussion of the 1856 Act, please see Sagar, "Introduction of Exclusive Privileges."

[10] Section XVI of the 1856 Act.

[11] It is interesting to note that, during the first reading of the bill, the Select Committee was not in favor of granting exclusive privileges to importers of inventions. The Select Committee was of the opinion that due to the increase in scientific publications and existing facilities of communication between the two countries, it would be improbable that an important invention will not be known in India and, therefore, a person who simply imported the invention should not be entitled to the exclusive privilege. However, during the second reading, the Committee changed its stance and recommended including importers of inventions within the meaning of "inventor." The Committee thought that an importer's time and efforts in bringing inventions into India should be rewarded by means of exclusive privileges. The same principle was applicable in England, and there was no reason to depart from the English practice while enacting the law in India.

"essential working."[12] In the event that he or she failed to commercialize the invention within a two-year period, the exclusive privilege would cease and the invention would become public property.[13]

The invention was deemed new where it was not publicly used or had not been made publicly known in India through any printed publication.[14] Prior public use might only on rare occasions be used to defeat claims of novelty.[15]

The above policy measures were similar to those of contemporary patent laws of the time implemented in other countries. They allowed foreigners and Indians alike to import technology into India and protect it through the means of exclusive privileges. An essential working requirement was deployed to take into account the public interest.[16] The 1856 Act also protected bona fide users who may have imported the inventions from other countries, or were using the same inventions in India prior to the enactment of the 1856 Act.[17]

Moreover, the 1856 Act granted special rights (so-called prior rights) to British patentees, who were actual inventors (not the importers of inventions in Britain) and had obtained patents in the United Kingdom for their inventions.[18] They could secure exclusive privileges for their inventions in India within twelve months of obtaining patents in Britain.[19]

---

[12] Section XVI of the 1856 Act. It requires that the importer should either work the invention himself, or grant licenses to others within two years from the date of the grant of the exclusive privilege. However, this condition was not applicable to privileges granted to actual inventors.

[13] This was thought important because an importer might abstain from using the invention and could also prevent others from importing or using it by virtue of his exclusive privilege. Thus, it was intended to curb this negative effect. This provision was an improvement over English law as it did not have an equivalent provision.

[14] Section XVIII of the 1856 Act. Mere oral knowledge was not a ground to defeat the novelty of an invention. This provision was incorporated to provide certainty and protection to the inventors from unnecessary and expensive litigation.

[15] Section XVIII of the 1856 Act. The public use or knowledge of the invention prior to the application for leave to file a specification was not deemed to be public use if it was obtained by fraudulent or surreptitious means, or was communicated to any member of public either in fraud or in breach of confidence of the actual inventor, provided that he has not acquiesced to such public use and has applied for exclusive privilege within six calendar months after the commencement of such public use. This was indeed a material improvisation over the British patent law, because in Britain the inventor would lose the benefit of his invention under similar circumstances.

[16] Section XVI of the 1856 Act.

[17] The 1856 Act provided that no owner of any exclusive privilege shall preclude any person from using the invention, who, prior to July 7, 1855, used the same in India. See Section XX of the 1856 Act. The date was chosen as on this day the 1856 Act was read for the first time before the Legislative Council.

[18] Section XIX specifically uses the term "Actual Inventor."

[19] This would result in the cessation of any previously granted exclusive privilege for the same invention to an earlier importer of that invention in India.

Yet, they could only benefit from their prior rights provided that the invention was not publicly known or used in India before the petition was filed in Britain – notwithstanding that it may have been publicly known or used in India before the petition to the GGIC under the 1856 Act.[20] If they failed to secure protection for their inventions within a year, any third party could import and secure exclusive privileges for those inventions.

Since the prior rights were available to an actual British inventor (and not to an importer of an invention into Britain), the system for granting exclusive privileges in India in relation to imported inventions essentially worked on a first-come, first-served basis.

13.3   The Act V of 1859: Imperialism at Work

The Act V of 1859 (the 1859 Act) replaced the 1856 Act.[21] Whilst it retained the original scheme of the 1856 Act for the grant, refusal, and enforcement of exclusive privileges, it made significant departures in respect of the concepts of inventor, novelty, and the prior rights of British patentees much to the detriment of Indian interests as explained below.

13.3.1 *Importation, Novelty Assessment, and Prior Rights of British Patentees under the 1859 Act*

Under the 1859 Act, an importer of an invention within India was no longer deemed to be an inventor within the meaning of the statute.[22] In addition, an invention had to be novel in both India and Britain to be eligible for an exclusive privilege.[23]

---

[20] Section XIX of the 1856 Act.
[21] Her Majesty's law officers advised the board of directors of the Company that under the provisions of the Government of India Act, 1853, the Legislative Council of India was not competent to pass the 1856 Act without first obtaining the sanction of the Crown. The grant of patents or exclusive privileges in India was a prerogative of the Crown and, therefore, any law made by the Indian legislature for their regulation required prior sanction of the Crown or that of its duly authorized signatory according to the mandatory procedure laid down under the 1853 Act. Sagar, "Introduction of Exclusive Privileges." The 1856 Act was repealed through the Act IX of 1857. The reason for the repeal of the 1856 Act was not mentioned anywhere in the repealing act, but the details were subsequently included in the preamble of the 1859 Act, which repeated the 1856 Act.
[22] Section XVII of the 1859 Act.
[23] See Section XIX of the 1859 Act: An invention shall be deemed a new invention within the meaning of this Act if it shall not, before the time of applying for leave to file the specification, have been publicly used in India or in any part of the United Kingdom of Great Britain and Ireland, or been made publicly known in any part of India or of the United Kingdom by means of a publication, either printed or written or partly printed and partly written.

When the 1856 Act was debated by the Legislative Council, it considered that providing exclusive privileges to importers of inventions and having limited novelty assessment were the two most conducive ways of encouraging technology transfer and fostering innovation in India. However, notwithstanding the introduction of these procedures in the 1856 Act, India witnessed a very limited patenting activity in the following year and none of the patentees was an Indian native. This should have prompted the Council to maintain the status quo on these policy measures, particularly considering Britain's own pursuit of encouraging technology acquisition through these measures.[24] However, the Council made a complete reversal of its own legislative policy following a missive sent by Her Majesty's law officers. The law officers specifically requested the Government of India to broaden the assessment of novelty by including Britain.[25]

The 1859 Act also expanded the prior rights of British patentees. They could obtain exclusive privileges in India based on their prior rights irrespective of whether they were actual inventors or importers of inventions in Britain.[26]

13.3.2 Drawbacks of the 1859 Act in Facilitating Importation of Technology into India

Under the 1859 Act, the importation of technology into India became highly cumbersome and expensive. Since an importer of an invention within India was not regarded as an inventor for the purposes of the 1859 Act, there was no incentive for importing technology (at least directly) into India. The only route available to obtain exclusive privileges for imported technology in India was for an importer to first obtain *letters patent* in Britain and, thereafter, apply for an exclusive privilege in India under Section XX of the 1859 Act as a British patentee claiming prior rights under the act.

The broadening of the novelty assessment was another major impediment to importation of technology into India. This not only prevented Indians from obtaining inventions that could have been novel in India (being made without any knowledge of any prior British invention), but

---

[24] The assessment of novelty for grant of patents in Britain was still limited to the territorial boundary of the United Kingdom during 1859.

[25] See File IOR/V/9/3. This was recorded in the meeting of the Legislative Council held on May 9, 1857.

[26] Under the new and amended Section XX of the 1859 Act any British patentee, whether the actual inventor or the importer of an invention in Britain, could obtain exclusive privilege by claiming prior rights.

also impeded the importation of foreign technology. This was unjustified as India was technologically far behind Britain at that time.

These developments highlight the importance of economic and political independence in choosing a particular patent policy that sufficiently accounts for a country's domestic interests. An independent India would not have followed a legislative policy that could seriously undermine the objective of becoming self-reliant in technology and industry.[27]

13.3.3 Patenting Activity in India under the Earliest Legislations

Figure 13.1 shows the total number of exclusive privileges obtained by all inventors, whether resident in India or not, during the first two decades of the operation of patent laws in India.

Figure 13.2 gives the differential number of patents obtained by native and non-native inventors during the first twenty-three years of introduction of patent law in India. The chart shows a disparity between the number of patents obtained by native Indians and foreigners. The dominance of foreigners in obtaining patents may be attributed to a number of factors. First, they were more familiar and comfortable with the patent system, while it was a completely new and perhaps an alien concept for Indians. Second, Indians were far behind technologically compared to

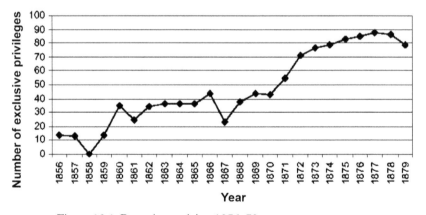

Figure 13.1 Patenting activity, 1856–79.

---

[27] This could be inferred from the fact that, as soon as India gained independence, a limited concept of novelty was adopted on the grounds of national interest. Novelty of invention was determined in reference to what was publicly used and known in India prior to the date of the patent application. India, *Patent Office Handbook* (Delhi: Manager of Publications, 1962).

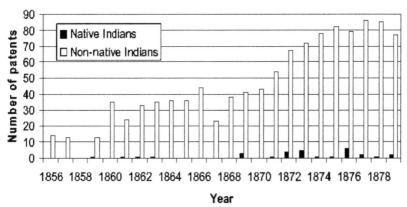

Total number of patents in twenty-three years: 1,138
Native Indians: 30 (2.63% of total)
Non-native Indians: 1,108 (97.37% of total)

Figure 13.2 Patenting activity by native Indians and non-natives, 1856–79.

their Western counterparts and, hence, the geographical broadening of novelty assessment prohibited them from taking advantage of the system. Third, native Indians could secure patents only for actual inventions under the 1859 Act, whereas the non-native patentees could obtain patents for actual as well as imported inventions. Fourth, the fee of 100 rupees to obtain a patent was considered to be very high and prohibitive for native Indian innovators to apply and obtain patents under the two Acts.

Analysis of the subject matter of the granted exclusive privileges also reveals interesting information. In the first few years of the operation of the two Acts, the native Indians mainly obtained patents in traditional industries and crafts like textiles and oil,[28] while the non-natives were dominant in securing exclusive privileges in new technological areas such as the telegraph, steam engines, arms, and railways. However, in the subsequent years and owing to their technological superiority and familiarity with the patent system, non-native inventors also became dominant in many traditional Indian sectors such as textiles, cotton, tea, and with respect to items of daily use such as *pankhah*.[29]

---

[28] There were one or two exceptions. See File IOR/V/25/600.
[29] A hand-held fan, which was of considerable interest to foreigners because of the hot weather in India. During that period, around ten to twelve patents were secured on the device.

13.4   Further Reflections on Pre-independence Patent Policy in India

> So discouraging do we find the present law that, although we have a patent, the original term of which will shortly expire, for a machine which is being generally accepted and the use of which is securing that faction of cultivators of India who at present use it, yearly benefits which in money alone amount to not less than one hundred and fifty lakh of rupees, and though, we believe, we can show that on grounds of equity and good policy an extension of the term may reasonably be asked for and granted, our recent experience shows us that the working and defence of such a patent under the existing law involves so much anxiety, disappointment and risk in proportion to the possible gain that we do not intend to prefer any application for an extension of its term.[30]

The above quotation sets the background for analyzing the appropriateness and effectiveness of the 1859 Act by assessing the concerns of the native and foreign patentees in obtaining and enforcing patents in India and by analyzing how those concerns were addressed within Indian patent policy until India's independence.

13.4.1   A Story of a Patent for a Sugar Mill

Since India was primarily an agrarian economy and sugar was one of the most important dietary and trade items during the nineteenth century,[31] it is not surprising that the first patent to be extensively commercialized in India related to a sugar mill.

At that time, the method of making sugar from cane juice in India was based on ancient practices rather than modern techniques. It involved using native mills called *Kolhu* mills that were animal-driven mortar and pestle mills sunk into the ground. The sugarcane pieces were dropped into the mortar, and the rotating pestle extracted the juice.[32] The juice was then collected, filtered, and boiled. The boiling allowed the sediments to settle down so that they could be dredged out; while the scum rose to the surface and was skimmed off. Then the juice was cooled to facilitate the formation of sugar crystals and any uncrystallized syrup was removed by centrifugation.

---

[30] Quotation from the memorial presented by Thomson and Mylne, Beheea, dated May 14, 1887 to Hon'ble A. R. Scoble, QC, who introduced the 1887 Patent Bill in the Legislative Council. See File IOR/L/PJ/5/49.

[31] H. H. Ghosh, *Sugar in India: Its Cultivation, Manufacture and Trade, etc.* (Calcutta: Industry Book Department, 1934).

[32] John Daniels and Christian Daniels, "The Origin of the Sugarcane Roller Mill," *Technology and Culture* 29, no. 3 (1988): 493–535.

Kolhu mills suffered from several disadvantages. The juice collector was difficult to clean as it was buried under the ground.[33] The inefficient extraction of juice resulted in the loss of approximately half of the value of the processed cane. Additional labor was required to cut the cane into smaller pieces. Despite these disadvantages, *Kolhu* mills were adopted and used extensively because of their low initial costs.

13.4.2   The Invention of Thomson and Mylne

The patentees Thomson and Mylne[34] obtained a patent for a sugar mill in the year 1874.[35] The patented invention (locally known as a *Beheea* mill) was significantly improved in comparison to the *Kolhu* mills. It included two rollers set in a wooden frame that squeezed the juice from the cane rather than grinding it.[36] The juice collector was above the ground and could be easily washed and cleaned.[37]

The *Beheea* mill was cost-effective and highly efficient. It could be operated with one bullock instead of two. It did not require the cane to be cut into small pieces.[38] Moreover, it was twice as efficient in extracting juice in comparison to the *Kolhu* mills.[39] The yearly gains per *Beheea* mill were thought to be at least 120 rupees when compared to the *Kolhu* mill.[40]

13.4.3   The Difficulties Faced by the Patentees

> The Beheea mill had to fight its way against the well-known ignorance and prejudices of the people the more so as it was the first aggressor, and

---

[33] The cleaning was necessary in order to prevent the juice from becoming foul due to active fermentation that affects the quality of *goor* or *raab*. *Raab* may be defined as cane juice concentrated to a solid or viscous stage without passing through any process of purification other than the addition of a small amount of alkali or other clarifying ingredient and the removal of scum.

[34] Thomson and Mylne were estate-owners in Bihar.

[35] The patent was obtained through their local agents and solicitors Messrs. Sanderson & Co., Calcutta.

[36] Ian Stone, *Canal Irrigation in British India: Perspectives on Technological Change in a Peasant Economy* (Cambridge: Cambridge University Press, 2002).

[37] Each mill had an iron roller, which was eight inches long and seven inches in diameter.

[38] This resulted in the savings of two rupees a day on average.

[39] The traditional *Kolhu* mill took about twenty days to grind an acre of sugarcane, the *Beheea* mill could crush the same amount in eleven to fourteen days. See Stone, *Canal Irrigation*.

[40] By 1887, the patentees had sold about 70,000 mills, and their use covered an area of 700,000 acres under cane cultivation. Therefore, the extent of their utilization and coverage area translated into a benefit of 8,400,000 rupees to those using the machines.

latterly, owing to the impossibility under the law of defending ourselves or the people against a multitude of infringers and makers of unreliable machines.[41]

Despite having a successful, efficient, and cheaper mill and a huge market for it, the patentees faced many difficulties in achieving widespread acceptance and sales of their mill. In Thomson and Mylne's own words: "The introduction of a patent in India is a long and tedious work, taking years, owing to the conservative nature and ignorance of the masses – a striking contrast to England."[42] They provided demonstrations to native Indians to convince them of the utility of the *Beheea* mill.[43] Moreover, the sugar industry was highly disorganized and scattered over large areas of different provinces and, on occasions, the patentees had to resort to the government's support.[44]

Despite the presence of a statutory law to regulate their grant and protection, patents were not effective means to reward an inventor and protect his or her capital investment in India at the time. This was mainly due to the peculiar circumstances and the legal lacunae encountered by patentees in their efforts to commercialize and enforce their patents as demonstrated by the *Beheea* mill case.

The patentees of the *Beheea* mill found it difficult to enforce their rights against *banias* (also known as traders).[45] The *banias*, after having found the utility of the *Beheea* mill, made cheaper versions of it and sold them either directly or through hawkers to the cane growers. Although cheaper in price, these mills were often inferior in quality and lacked any postsale service. As these machines did not yield the desired results, it made cane growers suspicious of the new technologies, thereby making the task of the patentees to sell genuine *Beheea* mills even more difficult.

---

[41] Memorial dated May 28, 1887 submitted by Thomson and Mylne, to the secretary to Government of India, Revenue and Agricultural Department. See File IOR/L/PJ/5/49.

[42] However, as per Kumar, these were not the only reasons responsible for the anathema of native cultivators toward adopting new technologies. The fear that the extra production could be taken by the landowners as taxes, was also responsible for unwillingness amongst the farmers to adopt new technologies. Deepak Kumar, *Science and the Raj 1857–1905* (Oxford: Oxford University Press, 1995).

[43] While outlining the history and growth of the sugar industry in India, Ghosh states that "many of our ancient crafts have resisted the rivalry of power industry because the products of the latter do not suit the simple tastes and slender means of our rustic folks." Ghosh, *Sugar in India*, 19–20.

[44] For example, the government of the North-West Frontier Province (NWFP) sanctioned advances to the cultivators to buy *Beheea* mills after being convinced of their advantages by the patentees.

[45] *Banias* are a class of people in India with primary interest in the trading of articles. Since they often travel around the country to find markets for their products, they are also referred to as "travelling dealers."

The patentees also encountered problems in obtaining and enforcing remedies against the *banias* for three main reasons. First, *Muffosil courts* (the lowest division of the Civil Court in British India) did not have any power to grant summary remedies such as confiscation or a temporary injunction to stop infringers. Second, the infringers would disappear immediately after carrying out an infringing activity making it difficult to locate them and pursue an infringement action. Third, even if a relief of damages was obtained against any *bania* after a prolonged trial, it was difficult to execute the judgment against them. The *banias* either did not hold any movable or immovable property within the territory where the infringement had occurred, or they would often transfer their properties to their relatives or friends through *benami transactions* (these are trans-actions carried out in the false name of another person)[46] making it extremely difficult to satisfy a judgment.

The judges also held hostile attitude toward patentees: "The judges viewed the patentee as a monopolist, and the native infringers as deserv-ing encouragement in their efforts in developing native industries."[47] The procedural rules for the conduct of infringement claims and judicial decisions were not helpful for patentees. There was no right to claim exemplary damages in addition to or in lieu of the regular rate of royalty. Furthermore, in the case of *Kinmond* v. *Jackson*,[48] the Calcutta High Court held that only one year of royalty payments could be claimed as damages.

The infringement proceedings in the district courts were dilatory and costly. In one instance, Thomson and Mylne spent 50,000 rupees over a period of ten years to obtain a favorable decision. In another case, they bore an expense of 8,600 rupees even though the proceedings were at an initial stage in a district in Punjab. Although the revenues from the *Beheea* mill were more than enough to offset such costs,[49] Thomson

---

[46] *Benami* transactions are transactions carried out in the false name of another person. That person does not pay the consideration but merely lends his name for registration of property, while the real title in the property vests in another person who actually purchased the property and is the beneficial owner. See the Introduction of Benami transaction (Prohibition) Act, 1988 (45 of 1988).

[47] Memorial dated May 28, 1887 submitted by Thomson and Mylne to the secretary to Government of India, Revenue and Agricultural Department. See File IOR/L/PJ/5/49.

[48] ILR 3 Cal 17 (1878).

[49] In order to commercialize their invention, the patentees appointed Fox and Aitchison and Renwick as their licensees for central India. They also commercialized the invention in Punjab and the upper districts of the NWFP through their manager, A. M. Eddis. Because of their combined efforts and the advantages of the invention, the sales of their mills soared to about 70,000 by 1886.

and Mylne found the general working of the 1859 Act and the judicial enforcement of the patents highly unsatisfactory.

The law and practice relating to the grant of patents were also not satisfactory. The novelty assessment was not carried out by professional assessors, and therefore subsequent patents were often granted for colorable imitations of an invention. This also happened in the case of the *Beheea* mill and Thomson and Mylne had to take multiple court actions against the grant of such patents.

13.5   Introduction of the 1888 Patent Bill in the Indian Legislative Council: Colonial Power Struggle at Play

The correspondence between the Government of India, the India Office,[50] and the Board of Trade (BoT)[51] on the subject of Indian copyright law in the early 1880s laid down the foundation for further amendments to Indian patent law.[52] When the Government of India wrote to the India Office expressing the need to amend Indian copyright law,[53] they also opined that when Indian patent law would be amended, a

---

[50] The India Office was established under the provisions of the Government of India Act, 1858. The act transferred the powers and functions of the East India Company to the Crown. The Indian Office was responsible to exercise the powers and carry out the functions on behalf of the Crown. See www.bl.uk/reshelp/findhelpregion/asia/india/indiaofficerecords/indiaofficescope/indiaofficehistoryscope.html, last accessed on January 10, 2008.

[51] The Board of Trade is a committee of enquiry originally set up by the Privy Council of the United Kingdom in the seventeenth century. During the nineteenth century, the Board advised the Crown on economic activity in Britain and its empire. During the second half of the nineteenth century it also dealt with legislation for patents, designs and trademarks, company regulation, labor and factories, merchant shipping, agriculture, transport, power, and so forth. For more information on the Board of Trade, see www.berr.gov.uk/aboutus/corporate/history/outlines/BT-1621-1970/page13919.html, last accessed on January 8, 2008.

[52] A review of the Indian copyright law was pending for more than two decades despite several representations made by Indian native citizens. The Indian citizens wanted copyright protection for their photographs. The delay was primarily on account of the British Government's inability to amend the British copyright law. When the first attempt was made to legislate on copyright law in India in 1877 (See Letter from the Government of India dated May 3, 1877, No. 15 to Lord Salisbury, secretary of state, India Office. File 2015: IOR/L/PJ/6/110), it was rejected by the India Office stating that the British Copyright Commission was yet to come up with its report and that the Government of India should await the proposals before legislating on copyright. See letter from Lord Salisbury, secretary of state, India Office dated July 5, 1877, No. 19: Judicial Despatch to the Government of India. See File 2015: IOR/L/PJ/6/110. An identical response was once again given when the Government of India raised the matter in the year 1884. See Letter by the India Office to the Government of India; see File 2245: IOR/L/PJ/6/165.

[53] See Government of India's letter dated October 22, 1883 to the India Office, No. 38 of 1883. See File 2015: IOR/L/PJ/6/110.

review of the design law should also be undertaken. The Secretary of State referred the letter to the BoT.[54]

In response, the BoT proposed that future patent laws in India should be assimilated and drawn fully along the lines of the British Patents, Trademarks and Designs Act of 1883.[55] It saw no objection in amending the laws relating to patents and designs in India, but emphasized that it was in favor of extending the British Patent Act to India, and that the Government of India should take an action accordingly.[56] The BoT wanted to harmonize patent laws throughout the British Empire.

However, the Government of India was quick to express its opposition to the BoT's suggestions.[57] It emphasized that patent law was introduced in India after due deliberation by the Legislative Council and after taking into account particular conditions existing in India. Consequently, the Indian patent law had incorporated substantive and procedural provisions that were materially different to the British patent law of the time.[58] The Government of India felt that the legislation had proved to be satisfactory for more than two decades and there were hardly any reasons to change it, especially when it had abided by most of the principles of British patent law. As a result, the Government of India suggested minor amendments rather than a complete overhaul of the law as demanded by the BoT.[59]

Once the India Office received the Government of India's reply and an outline of the proposed amendments to the law, it sent the papers to the BoT. The BoT refrained from making any observations.[60] The Indian Office interpreted the BoT's lack of response as expressing its unhappiness over the rejection of its proposals by the Government of

---

[54] See India Office's letter dated December 24, 1883 to the BoT, as included in File 2015: IOR/L/PJ/6/110.

[55] See Letter from the BoT to the India Office, No. 12600, dated January 28, 1884. See File 162: L/PJ/6/116.

[56] Letter from the BoT to the India Office, No. 12600, dated January 28, 1884. See File 162: L/PJ/6/116.

[57] Government of India's letter dated October 27, 1884, No. 36 of 1884 to Earl of Kimberley, secretary of state, India Office. See File 2290: IOR/L/PJ/6/139.

[58] For example, one such material variation was that under Indian patent law, a patent was a statutory right; whereas in the United Kingdom, a patent was granted by the Crown.

[59] As stated in the letter by the Government of India, "the difficulties which have been experienced are not of such a kind as to require in our opinion any alteration which would affect the main principles of the Act, or lead us to propose the closer assimilation of the provisions to those of the English law. We propose nothing more than the improvement of the act in minor details." Government of India's letter dated October 27, 1884, No. 36 of 1884 to Earl of Kimberley, secretary of state, India Office. See File 2290: IOR/L/PJ/6/139.

[60] The BoT letter dated January 24, 1885 No. 6942 to the secretary of state, India Office. See File 146: IOR/L/PJ/6/146.

India.[61] Nonetheless, the India Office approved the Government of India's suggestions with specific instruction that "no alteration is considered necessary which would affect the main principles on which it rests, nor its closer assimilation to the provision to those of English law proposed."[62] They also requested that the proposed bill should be sent to the India Office prior to its introduction before the Legislative Council of India.[63]

13.5.1   Positive Aspects of Patent Policy Making?

Patent policy making at this stage represented a significant change in comparison to 1856 when patent law was first introduced in India. At that time, the public, patentees, or business associations hardly provided any comments in response to the publication of the 1856 Patent Bill. However, this time the consultation carried out by the Government of India, both prior to and after the publication of the patent bill, elicited many highly critical and valuable comments.[64]

13.5.1.1   Fees for Obtaining Patents The fee of 100 rupees was considered to be a significant barrier in obtaining exclusive privileges by most of the native Indians.[65] However, Scoble, a Legislative Council member, did not give any consideration to this issue when he introduced

---

[61] See Minute paper attached to File 146: IOR/L/PJ/6/146.

[62] See the India Office's letter dated February 19, 1885 to the Government of India.

[63] India Office's letter dated February 19, 1885 to the Government of India.

[64] The responses received by the Government of India in response to the publication of the bill can be categorized into five groups: responses from government officials, responses from patentees, responses from patent agents, responses from business associations, and responses from the public. Some of the respondents expressed their concern about high fees and lack of priority rights in favor of Indian patentees. On the other hand, a large number of respondents held a passive view of the reforms being proposed in India, aptly summarized by the following quotation:

> [T]here can be little doubt as to the advantage of incorporating in the existing law in India the improvement suggested by experience of similar matters in England, the matter of course is not one in which the customs and circumstances of the Indian population would have to be considered, but is one in which what is good in England must apparently be good in India also.
>
> See Letter from G. M. Ogilview, deputy commissioner, Dera Ismail Khan, to the commissioner and superintendent, Derajat Division. See File IOR/L/PJ/5/49.

[65] Memorial from patent agents DePenning and DePenning, to secretary to Government of India, Legislative Department dated December 5, 1887, narrating the incident of a farmer who had invented a new machine, but was unable to secure a patent due to the high costs of obtaining a patent. See File IOR/L/PJ/5/49.

the 1887 Bill before the Legislative Council.[66] He simply took the British patent fees as a reference point[67] and used the then exchange rate applicable between the British pound and the Indian rupee to calculate the corresponding patent fees in rupees.[68] His proposal was criticized by most of the respondents.[69] H. H. Remfry, a patent agent based in Calcutta, stated that "300 applications is really small considering the vastness of the country and any legislation that would tend further to diminish this very small number would only tend to retard the development of the country."[70] The Select Committee acted on these representations and reduced the fees that ultimately formed the basis of the 1888 Patents Act.

13.5.1.2 Prior Rights for Native Indian Inventors Representations in response to the publication of the 1887 Bill also criticized the failure of the British Patent Act to provide prior rights to native Indian patentees when the Indian law gave equivalent rights to British inventors.[71] This prompted native Indian patentees to raise the issue not only

[66] The Select Committee was formed on January 14, 1887, while the bill was introduced a week before on January 7, 2009.
[67] The British Patents Amendment Act of 1853 had introduced a graded fees structure in Britain for obtaining and maintaining patents.
[68] See the 1887 Bill as framed and circulated by the Select Committee. The proposed bill sought to levy an initial application fee of 50 rupees, but increased the total cost of obtaining and maintaining a patent to 540 rupees for a period of fourteen years. This was considerably higher in comparison to the one-time initial fee of 100 rupees payable under the 1859 Act for the equivalent period of patent protection.
[69] However, not everyone was in favor of reducing the fees. The Committee of the Institute of Patent Agents (CIPA), an organization based in Britain, but with an active interest in colonial patents, advocated an increase in fees over what was proposed in the 1887 Bill. See Report of the Committee of the Fellows of the Institute of Patent Agents on the 1887 Bill of Patents and Inventions that is enclosed with the letter dated May 5, 1887 to the Government of India. See File 658 L/PJ/6/200. The Committee once again took British patent fees as reference and suggested that the initial fees should be increased to 150 rupees and further fees should be payable annually rather than at the intervals proposed in the bill. Such a demand from the CIPA was surprising since English inventors who were desirous of obtaining patents in India were critical of the total fees of £30 charged by the British patent agents for obtaining a patent in India when the official fees were considerably lower.
[70] He further stated that "any increase will have detrimental effect on the number of applications received by the government and instead of increasing the revenue, it will actually result in its decrease." See Memorial of H. H. Remfry dated March 10, 1887 to Hon'ble A. R. Scoble. The Madras Chambers of Commerce agreed with the views of Remfry. See the Letter from the Honourable S. R. Turnbill, chairman, Chambers of Commerce, Madras, to the chief secretary to government, Madras dated April 16, 1887. See File IOR/L/PJ/5/49.
[71] Letter from Cantwell & Co., Calcutta, to the secretary, Government of India, dated June 3, 1887. See File IOR/L/PJ/5/49. They also criticized the legislative scheme, where novelty for a patent to be granted in India was assessed in respect of both India and

with the Legislative Council, but also with the British and Foreign Patent Office (BFPO). The BFPO in turn wrote to the India Office and requested it to raise the matter with Her Majesty's Government for issuing an Order in the Council to this effect.[72] However, the India Office did not take any action on the pretext that Indian patent law was under the control of the Government of India, and advised the BFPO to raise the matter directly with the Government of India.[73] However, contrary to the practice followed by the India Office at that time especially in relation to the legislative issues,[74] it did not forward the papers to the Government of India for consideration.

13.5.1.3   Reevaluation of the 1887 Patent Bill in Response to Thomson and Mylne's Representations After the publication of the 1877 Patent Bill, Thomson and Mylne proposed several amendments based on their experience of commercializing and enforcing the *Beheea* mill patent. Their primary suggestions were that the law should provide:

(i)   summary reliefs, including summary injunction and destruction of infringing goods;
(ii) grant of exclusive licenses for each district that should be compulsorily registered; and
(iii) criminal sanctions and penal damages for patent infringement.[75]

Despite the fact that their own Agricultural Department was in favor of these proposals, the NWFP Government did not agree with them and asked the Government of India to ignore them.[76] While the Government of India was sympathetic to the idea of introducing penal damages and

---

Britain, whereas this was not the case for the patents granted in Britain. Such provision in Indian patent law was thought to be unjust and inequitable to Indian patentees.

[72] See File 1370: IOR/L/PJ/6/159. Letter from the BFPO, Liverpool, dated July 31, 1885, to the India Office.

[73] Such a suggestion on behalf of the India Office was not tenable, considering that the Orders in Council pertaining to intellectual property matters were issued by Her Majesty's Government upon receiving the suggestions from the Board of Trade. Therefore, the India Office in this case merely shrugged away from its responsibility rather than pursuing the matter with the BoT. See File 1370, IOR/L/PJ/6/159, Reply by the Indian Office to the British and Foreign Patent office, dated August 4, 1885.

[74] As a matter of practice, the India Office would send all the communications relating to India that were received from the organizations and people based in Britain to the Government of India. It would also issue an acknowledgment of such action to those organizations and people.

[75] From the director, Agricultural Department to the secretary to the Government of Bengal, November 11, 1887. See File IOR/L/PJ/5/49.

[76] See File IOR/L/PJ/5/49.

summary remedies against infringers, it did not agree with the proposal of imposing criminal sanctions against infringers.[77]

Due to the representations made by Thomson and Mylne, the Government of India asked all of the provincial governments to reconsider the bill and provide their comments on whether the new law could threaten or smother innovation in agriculture.[78]

13.5.2   Changes Introduced by the 1888 Act

The 1888 Act did not make any significant changes to the overall scheme of granting exclusive privileges, their enforcement and refusal.[79] However, it introduced some novel concepts such as the assignment of exclusive privileges for a particular territory in India;[80] a graded structure for the payment of fees;[81] grant of compulsory licenses by the GGIC in certain cases;[82] and different modes to pay fees.[83] The Agricultural

---

[77] The government was concerned that such a remedy could provide a tool to patentees to blackmail the public. See File IOR/L/PJ/5/49.

[78] Office Memorandum from the Revenue and Agricultural Department, Government of India to the Home Department of Government of India: August 18, 1887. See File IOR/L/PJ/5/49.

[79] The overall scheme relating to the grant of exclusive privileges and the definitions and scope of inventor, invention, manufacture, and so forth, was not amended. Some minor administrative changes were introduced in the 1888 Act, but they did not have any major effect on the grant of exclusive privileges.

[80] See Section 44 of the 1888 Act, which provided that "any person having any exclusive privilege or a share or interest in any exclusive privilege can assign the privilege or such share or interest for a particular area or a locality." This was thought to expedite commercial exploitation of an invention in remote parts of a vast country like India, as on occasions it may have not been feasible for an inventor to secure and guard his interest across the whole of India on his own.

[81] See Fourth Schedule of the 1888 Act, which provided that fees shall be payable at different stages. For example, 10 rupees: at the time of application for leave to file a specification; 20 rupees: to file a specification; 20 rupees: to extend the time for filing a specification; 50 rupees: to continue an exclusive privilege for each year of its operation until expiration of the eighth year from the date of filing of the specification; and 100 rupees: after the ninth year until the fourteenth year of operation. Thus, the total cost for keeping the patent alive for fourteen years increased five times, even though the initial cost was reduced.

[82] See Section 43 of the 1888 Act, which provided that

[W]here an exclusive privilege is not worked in British India; or the reasonable requirements of the public with respect to an invention cannot be supplied; or any person is prevented from working or using to the best advantage an invention which he is possessed, GGIC can order the inventor to grant a license on royalties, securities or otherwise as deemed fit by the GGIC.

[83] See Section 48 (3) of the 1888 Act, which provided that "the fees payable shall be collected by means of stamps or otherwise as the Governor General in Council directs." As per the notification issued under the 1888 Act, the fees were payable in cash instead of by means of stamps. The fees could also be tendered through post and checks provided

Department of the Government of India was made responsible for administering patent law in India.[84]

Due to rising British economic and political power in India, the 1888 Act was also extended with some modifications to other princely states such as Mysore (in 1894),[85] Hyderabad (1900),[86] and Marwar (modern name Jodhpur) in 1906.[87]

13.6   The Act No. II of 1911: Further Compromises

In 1907, British patent law underwent a significant change. The UK Patents and Designs Act, 1907 repealed all previous patent legislations, except the Statute of Monopolies. It introduced new provisions that dealt with adequacy of disclosure (for example, the power to require samples in support of chemical patent applications); prior rights; extension of patent

> that they were made payable at Calcutta and to the order of the secretary under the Inventions and Designs Act, 1888.
>
> [84] This measure was heavily criticized by some on the ground that since most of the patents granted in India related to agricultural sector, it was not advisable to give powers to accept or reject patent applications to a department that had direct interest in the subject matter. See File 1370, IOR/L/PJ/6/159, Reply by the Indian Office to the British and Foreign Patent office, dated August 4, 1885; Memorial of H. H. Remfry dated March 10, 1887 to Hon'ble A. R. Scoble.
>
> [85] The law was called "Regulation No. 11 of 1894." At present, Mysore is part of the Indian state known as Karnataka.
>
> [86] The law was called "Act No. 10 of 1899." At present, Hyderabad is part of the Indian state known as Telangana. Mysore and Hyderabad were not part of British India and were known as "Native Indian States." With the transfer of the East India Company's possessions in India to the British Crown in 1858, the country was divided into "two India's": (i) The "British India," which was under the direct authority and control of the Central Indian Executive and Legislature, and indirectly under that of the British Cabinet and the Parliament; and (ii) the India of the "Native States," which was not a British possession, and its inhabitants were not British subjects. Sidney Low, *The Indian States and Ruling Princes* (London: E. Benn Limited, 1929), 8. Some of these Native States were British protectorates bound by several political, commercial, and military ties through various treaties and engagements with Britain. Lee-Warner has defined the Native States with the following words: "A Native State is a political community, occupying a territory in India of defined boundaries, and subject to a common and responsible ruler who has actually enjoyed and exercised, as belonging to him in his own right duly recognized by the supreme authority of the British Government, any of the functions and attributes of internal sovereignty." See William Lee-Warner, *The Native States of India*, 2nd ed. (London: Macmillan & Co., 1910), 31.
>
> [87] The protection of inventions in Marwar was secured by the Inventions Act, 1906. Wallace Cranston Fairweather, *Foreign and Colonial Patent Laws* (New York: William S. Hein & Co., Inc., 2003). It is interesting to note that demands were made to extend British copyright law to other princely states due to the movement of pirated books from the latter to British India. See Letter from Publishers Association to the undersecretary of state, the India Office, dated May 31, 1902. File 1093: L/PJ/6/602. It is equally plausible that demands might have been made for the extension of patent laws to these states due to increasing trade opportunities between British India and the Native States.

term in cases of proven inadequate remuneration; compulsory licenses or revocation in the cases of non-working of patents in the United Kingdom; innocent infringement; and Crown use.[88] The Legislative Council of India introduced the Act No. II of 1911 (the 1911 Act), which followed the British Patents and Designs Act, 1907 as closely as possible.[89] Due to a marked increase in the number of patent applications,[90] it also established a separate Patent Office in Calcutta (now Kolkata) to handle the grant of patents. Most of the powers previously exercised by the GGIC were delegated to a Comptroller of Patents and Designs, who worked under the superintendence of the Government of India.[91] The term "exclusive privileges" was replaced by the term "patent."

13.6.1   The Principal Issue under the 1911 Act: Compulsory Local Working Clause

Another example of how the national interests of colonial India were sidelined by its rulers is demonstrated by the inclusion and modification of the clause relating to compulsory local working of patented inventions.[92] This was incorporated as Section 23 of the 1911 Act and is reproduced below:

(1) At any time not less than four years after the date of a patent granted under this act, any person may apply to the Governor General in Council for the revocation of the patent on the ground that the patented article or process is manufactured or carried on exclusively or mainly outside British India.

(2) The Governor General in Council shall consider the application, and, if after inquiry he is satisfied –
    (a) that the allegations contained therein are correct; and

---

[88] Stephen Adams, "Centenary of the Enactment of the United Kingdom's Patents and Designs Act 1907," *World Patent Information* 29, no. 4 (2007): 363–8.

[89] While introducing the bill to amend the patent law before the Legislative Council of India on March 23, 1910, Robertson stated as follows: "The Bill which is now to be introduced has therefore been drafted so as to follow the English Statute of 1907 as closely as possible, except in so far as material variations are necessitated by the different conditions prevailing in India." See File IOR 134 V/9/136–138.

[90] This can be seen from the fact that the receipts from fees had nearly doubled between 1900 and 1910.

[91] However, establishing the Patent Office in Calcutta (now Kolkata) did not provide easy access to the system for Indian inventors as each individual inventor had to either come in person to Calcutta to obtain patents or secure services of a patent agent based in Calcutta. Both these options involved significant investment of time and money.

[92] "Local working" means undertaking commercial exploitation of the invention embodied in a patent through local production and not importation.

> (b) that the applicant is prepared, and is in a position, to manufacture or carry on the patented article or process in British India; and
>
> (c) that the patentee refuses to grant a license on reasonable terms ...[93]

This clause was based on Section 27 of the British Patents and Designs Act, 1907, which was as follows:

> At any time no less than four years after the date of a patent, and not less than one year after the framing of the Act, any person may apply to the Controller for the revocation of the patent on the ground that the patented article or process is manufactured or carried on exclusively outside the UK.

Section 27 was derived from Article V of the Paris Convention for the Protection of Industrial Property of March 20, 1883:

> The introduction by the patentee into the country where the patent has been issued of objects manufactured in any of the States of the Union shall not entail forfeiture.
>
> Nevertheless, the patentee shall remain subject to the obligation to work his patent in conformity with the laws of the country into which he introduced the patented objects.

Section 27 was considered to have provided necessary impetus to industrial growth in Britain. Levinstein's speech at the annual dinner of the Society of Dyers and Colourists in Manchester on March 18, 1910 captured how important the clause was in strengthening the domestic industries in Britain:

> I consider this result, valuable though it undoubtedly is, to be a mere bagatelle compared with the enormous advantages which our manufacturers now possess in being able to secure licenses from foreign patentee on equitable and reasonable terms – terms which other competing countries enjoyed for many years prior to the passing of the Act in 1907.[94]

---

[93] Emphasis supplied.

[94] As quoted in the letter dated June 10, 1910 from the chairman, Indian Merchants Chamber and Bureau, Bombay, to the secretary to the Government of Bombay. See File 3237: L/PJ/6/1032 with 1148/10. The chairman further opined that

> The section refers to what is known as "compulsory working," which ensures the working of patents in the country from which they are taken, and thus become directly instrumental in opening new industries, getting work for many people and generally developing the industrial condition of the country. It is estimated that during two years which have elapsed since the passing of the patents act in England, about a million sterling have been invested there in land, building and plant by foreign patentees, thereby finding employment for some 8000 people.
>
> Similar views were expressed by other respondents such as Krishna Rao Phatak, a pleader in his letter dated April 3, 1909 and Dr. Denning, superintendent of industries, Bengal. See File IOR/L/PJ/5/82.

However, this compulsory local working clause was not included in the initial 1910 Indian patent bill that was circulated to the provincial governments by the Government of India despite the fact that it was based on the British Patents and Designs Act, 1907.[95] As many respondents were aware of Section 27,[96] they demanded its insertion in the Indian statute. The strongest support for its inclusion came from the Indian Merchants Chamber and Bureau, in Bombay (now Mumbai).[97] Similar thoughts were expressed by the acting principal of Victoria Jubilee Technical Institute, Byculla: "It is my opinion that there will be many patents and designs which will be patented in British India that can be manufactured in this country. May I suggest that any patent motion or design, which can be made in British India, must be made in this country."[98] However, the Calcutta Trades Association opposed adding a compulsory local working clause.[99]

Subba Rao, a native Indian member of the Legislative Council and the Select Committee, finally persuaded the Select Committee to amend the Indian patent bill to include this clause.[100] The clause was incorporated in the 1911 Act, but subject to two conditions (b) and (c) that were absent in Section 23. These conditions were included in the Indian law as a way of compromise between Rao and Robertson, the two members of the Select Committee who were primarily responsible for drafting the 1911 Act as explained below.

Many patentees, especially those with international patent portfolios, were not satisfied with the compulsory local working provisions included in the domestic legislation of a number of countries as they found these to be very onerous. Hence, they sought to amend Article V of the Paris Convention during the meeting of the Congress of the International Association for the Protection of Industrial Property held at Nancy in October 1909. After due deliberations, a resolution was passed to the effect that: "forfeiture should not be pronounced when the patentee can prove that he has sent to the manufacturers likely to be interested in the

---

[95] The first bill was prepared by the Select Committee in the year 1887.
[96] The act and the clause were formulated and introduced by Lloyd George, then president of the BoT.
[97] See Letter dated June 10, 1910 from the chairman, Indian Merchants Chamber and Bureau, Bombay, to the secretary to the Government of Bombay. See File 3237: L/PJ/6/1032 with 1148/10.
[98] See Letter No. C.219, dated June 7, 1910 from W. T. Pomfret, acting principal of Victoria Jubilee Technical Institute, Byculla, to the Government of India. See File IOR/L/PJ/5/82.
[99] Letter No. C.219, dated June 7, 1910. The Association thought that such measure was somewhat premature given India's poor technological capabilities at that time.
[100] See File IOR/V/9/136-138 for Legislative Council debates.

patent offers of a license on reasonable terms which they have not accepted."[101]

It was this resolution that formed the basis for a compromise between Rao and Robertson.[102] Although Rao succeeded in including the compulsory working clause within the Indian law as Section 23 of the 1911 Act, his minority status in the entire debate forced him to make a compromise by agreeing to incorporate condition (c) in the 1911 Act. This was despite the fact that the Government of India was not even a signatory to the Paris Convention of Industrial Property at that time.[103] Rao also acquiesced to condition (b) stated above in order to address the concerns of the Calcutta Trades Association. The inclusion of these conditions unfortunately diluted the effectiveness of Section 23. Thus, the patent law in India at this stage was not only "BRIT-compliant,"[104] but also had certain "BRIT-plus conditions."

13.7   Apathy Relating to Prior Rights for Indian Native Inventors: Reciprocal Arrangements and the 1920 Patent Amendment Act

In the 1880s, British patent law had provisions that enabled the British Government to enter into reciprocal arrangements with other national governments with a view to secure prior rights for British patentees in those countries and vice versa.[105] Section 103 of the British Patents and

---

[101] As provided in Article V of the Paris Convention for the Protection of Industrial Property of March 20, 1883.

[102] See File IOR/V/9/135-138.

[103] India was not a party to the Paris Convention of Industrial Property. See Letter dated October 13, 1884 of GGIC to Hon'ble Earl of Kimberley, secretary of state for India. File IOR/L/PJ/3/323. In 1884, the GGIC decided that India should not be a party to the Paris Convention when it was contacted by the secretary of state on the subject, arguing lack of appropriate trademark law protection in India. As all the signatory countries were supposed to have a proper trademark law as per the Convention's articles, absence of such a law in India did not fulfil this obligation.

[104] I have used the term "BRIT-compliant" to emphasize the fact noted by Vojáček, that the territories belonging to British Empire represented about one-half (63/140) of the total number of patent territories of the world (1935). Patent law in these territories was either an extension, or a close modification of British patent law. Jan Vojáček, *A Survey of the Principal National Patent Systems* (New York: Prentice-Hall, 1936).

[105] The grant of prior rights provided a grace period (usually of twelve months) to patentees within which they could secure their patent rights in different countries after filing an initial patent application in their country of residence. The prior rights were aimed at overcoming the issues a patentee had to face when filing simultaneous patent applications across different jurisdictions, and to reduce the risk of him losing his rights to third parties, who may acquire patent rights in other countries through importation of the invention.

Designs Act, 1907 provided that the patentees of signatory countries could secure prior rights provided their patent application in Britain was filed within a period of seven months from the date of filing of the national application.[106] Section 104 of the act made provisions for extending this benefit to British colonies and their inventors, provided that those colonies had already made appropriate arrangements for the grant and protection of patents within their territories. Despite the fact that India had enacted patent laws since 1856 and accorded prior rights to British patentees, the benefits of Sections 103 and 104 were never extended to Indian patentees.

The Government of India was apathetic to the issue of securing prior rights for Indian inventors in Britain. Even when the matter was brought to the notice of the India Office in the year 1887, the India Office shrugged off its responsibility on the entire matter as discussed above. The issue remained unresolved much to the detriment of Indian inventors until 1920, when the Indian patent law was amended and a provision was incorporated to allow "inter-imperial arrangements."[107] This provision finally enabled India to enter into reciprocal arrangements not only with Britain, but also with other dominions of Britain to secure overseas protection and prior rights for Indian patentees.

13.8   Patenting Activity until 1947

The total number of exclusive privileges/patents filed under various acts (including the number of applications filed by Indian nationals) is given in Table 13.1:[108]

These figures show a steady increase in the number of patents obtained by the native patentees, but in comparison to foreigners, their share was quite modest. Many of the factors responsible for this patenting trend emanated from the drawbacks in the legislative policy as explained earlier. However, in order to provide a better picture of patenting trends, one also has to look at the technical, educational, and industrial policies that influence innovation activity within a country.

---

[106] 46 & 47 *Vict. c.* 57.

[107] The section was entitled "*Section 78A: Reciprocal arrangements with the United Kingdom and other parts of His Majesty's Dominions*" and inserted by Section 2 of the Act XXIX of 1920.

[108] B. T. Chand, *Report of the Patents Enquiry Committee (1948–1950)* (Delhi: Government of India, 1950). These statistics were compiled from 1856 until the end of 1949.

Table 13.1 *Patenting activity under various Patent Acts enacted in India during the pre-independence period*

Act	Total no. of patents	Patents obtained by native Indians	Percentage share of native Indians (%)
The Act of 1856	33	Nil	Nil
The Act of 1859	3,417	234	6.8
The Act of 1888	11,727	1,131	9.6
The Act of 1911	42,498	5,899	13.9

13.9   Science, Technology, Industrial, and Educational Policies before Independence

> The Government of India is a mule as regards science ... It won't do anything unless driven.[109]

An emphasis on the Indian patent law to explain the reduced patenting activity undertaken by native Indian inventors during the pre-independence period would only present a partial view. The analysis would not be complete without evaluating the policies of the Government of India in the areas of science, education, research, and industrial development during this period. The marginalization of Indians from the scientific and technological research, industrial development, education, and job offerings also affected their inventive contribution and use of the patent system by limiting their technological knowledge and skills as explained in the following sections.

13.9.1   *Science, Technology, and Higher Education in India during the Pre-independence Period*

It was not only the Government of India's less than enthusiastic interest in establishing scientific institutions, but also the lack of administrative and economic freedom that held back scientific research in India.[110] MacLeod discusses the example of scientific research undertaken under the aegis of the Board of Scientific Advice (BSA) of the Government of

---

[109] See Ross to Manson, June 28, 1898, Ross Papers, Mss. 02/159 as quoted in Kumar, *Science and the Raj*.
[110] Kumar, *Science and the Raj*.

India to argue how the system was adverse to first-hand scientific research primarily due to the strong intervention by the Indian Advisory Committee (IAC) of the Royal Society in Britain.[111]

The universities in India were established not to impart scientific knowledge, but to prepare students for administrative posts.[112] The University of Roorkee (in the state of Uttarakhand) was established in 1847 with three faculty members. This number only rose to twenty after 100 years. This situation was unsatisfactory compared with other elite institutions established elsewhere around the globe.[113] The Government of India also exerted excessive control over research activities.[114] Moreover, general research funding was not available, while scholarships were withdrawn on one pretext or the other.[115] Students had to struggle with high fees in the absence of any scholarship or aid. The Government of India also did not provide systematic support for students to study abroad as opposed to other countries like Japan.[116] If any native Indian returned back after completing their foreign education, the Government provided little institutional support or job opportunities to them.

Not only was the institutional structure not conducive for local scientific research, but the natives were also discriminated against, or commonly given positions much below their caliber and educational qualification. For example, only 18 out of a total of 213 scientific personnel recruited by the Government of India were Indians.[117] These factors were responsible for "little or no scope for the professionalization of science in India," and thus the "culture of science was still struggling to be born in colonial India in the nineteenth century."[118]

[111] Roy M. MacLeod, "Scientific Advice for British India: Imperial Perceptions and Administrative Goals, 1898–1923," *Modern Asian Studies* 9, no. 3 (1975): 343–84.
[112] The main purpose of establishing universities in India can be traced back to the famous Macauley's "Minute of Education 1835": "We must at present do our best to form a class who may be interpreters between us and the millions whom we govern, a class of persons, Indian in blood and color but are English in taste, in opinions, in morals, and in intellect."
[113] For example, the Massachusetts Institute of Technology (MIT) was established in 1865 and had 306 lecturers by 1906. See Kumar, *Science and the Raj*.
[114] Kumar, *Science and the Raj*.   [115] Kumar, *Science and the Raj*.
[116] Ian Inkster, "Colonial and Neo-colonial Transfers of Technology: Perspectives on India before 1914," in *Technology and Industrialisation: Historical Case Studies and International Perspectives*, ed. Ian Inkster (Hampshire, UK: Ashgate, 1998), 25–51.
[117] V. V. Krishna, "Reflections on the Changing Side Status of Academic Science in India," *International Social Science Journal* 168 (2001): 231–46.
[118] Krishna, "Reflections on the Changing Side Status of Academic Science," 232.

13.9.2   Industrial Development, Private Enterprise, and Technical Projects

The industries in Britain were protected through tariff structures, financial aid, and monetary incentives; whereas in colonial India quite the opposite occurred. The Government of India allowed significant imports of textiles and other goods by lowering tariff barriers, thereby providing British industry unregulated access to the Indian market at the expense of the local industry. The Government of India also burdened local manufacturers with duties, tariffs, and taxes. Such policy measures were based on the ideology of "discriminating protection to selected industries plus preferences to British imports."[119] This principle remained the touchstone of British revenue policy and resulted in systematic distortion of Indian industry with a view to facilitate imports from Britain. Even after World War I, any imposition of tariffs by the Government of India to raise revenue was met with stiff resistance from the British Parliament on the grounds that it would harm Manchester, a key exporter of clothes to India.[120] Bagchi provides empirical evidence on how adverse government policies furthered British interests at the cost of local industry, which led to deindustrialization of Bihar, an eastern state of India.[121]

The British Empire looked at India as a supplier of raw material for its industries and had little or no interest in turning India into a strong manufacturing base. As a result, there was no institutional backing from the Government of India to develop industry in the country.

Even developmental projects such as railways and telegraph, which are commonly viewed as a means of technology transfer and capacity building, did not have the desired effect in India.[122] India did not gain any technological expertise through the development of other public works such as the Ganges Canal Project and the postal system. This was despite the fact that a Public Works Department was established in 1854 to execute these projects. These projects recruited a large pool of scientific personnel from abroad, consequently marginalizing Indians.[123] A notable example was railways. Even though India had the most important railway network in the whole of Asia in the early part of the twentieth

---

[119] Thomas D. Rider, "The Tariff Policy of the Government of India and Industrial Development, 1894–1934," *The Journal of Economic History* 30, no. 1 (1970): 278–81, at 279.
[120] Rider, "The Tariff Policy."
[121] Amiya Kumar Bagchi, "De-industrialization in India in the Nineteenth Century: Some Theoretical Implications," *Journal of Development Studies* 12, no. 2 (1976): 135–64.
[122] Inkster, "Colonial and Neo-colonial Transfers of Technology."
[123] Zaheer Baber, "Colonizing Nature: Scientific Knowledge, Colonial Power and the Incorporation of India into the Modern World-System," *The British Journal of Sociology* 52, no. 1 (2001): 37–58.

century, it did not have a single Indian occupying a senior management role. Technical know-how and machinery were all imported from Britain even though they could have been created in India. No efforts were undertaken to train or educate Indians on technical aspects.[124]

13.10   Conclusion

It was primarily the interests of British patentees that resulted in the first introduction and establishment of patent law or monopoly privileges in India in 1856. Their interest was very different from the justification for granting patents "as an incentive to innovate."[125] They sought patent protection to enable them to collect royalties for the use of their patented inventions in India or to protect their investment by preventing local competition.[126]

This chapter highlights how India was compelled to accede to British patent policies due to the lack of political and economic independence. Colonial India had to accept stronger standards of patentability requirements and a narrower utility of patent rights within its patent law in comparison to Britain due to its status as a colony. This in turn affected the ability to use patents as a policy lever to facilitate technology acquisition and foster domestic innovation.

The dominance of British patentees in the patent law debate (and the absence of native innovators), an emphasis on the British Patents Law Amendment Act, 1852, and a majority of non-natives within the Legislative Council responsible for framing Indian patent laws, led to the marginalization of interests of native innovators. The law prescribed high fees to obtain exclusive privileges, thereby affecting native patentees' ability to obtain protection for their inventions. It further disadvantaged native inventors by equating India and Britain at the same technological level for the purposes of assessing novelty for the grant of patents in India. The Indian patent law also accorded prior rights to British patentees to protect their inventions in India, but no corresponding rights were given to native patentees to secure patents in Britain for their inventions under British patent law. The patenting activity following the implementation of patent laws shows that the share of native Indians in the number of patents obtained in both the traditional and new technological areas

---

[124] Daniel Thorner, "The Pattern of Railway Development in India," *The Far Eastern Quarterly* 14, no. 2 (1955): 201 16.

[125] William Rodolph Cornish and David Llewelyn, *Intellectual Property: Patents, Copyright, Trade Marks and Allied Rights* (London: Sweet & Maxwell, 2003), 115.

[126] See Sagar, "Introduction of Exclusive Privileges."

fell as the time progressed; while foreigners continued to consolidate their position by obtaining exclusive privileges both in the traditional and new technology sectors.

The Indian experience seriously questions the expediency of introducing patent law in a country mainly based on extra-national trading interests. It also demonstrates that any curb on a country's freedom to choose its patent policies by disregarding its national interests and local conditions will have a significant negative impact on fostering domestic innovation and its technological status.

Ian Inkster has argued that the adoption, diffusion, and adaptation of technologies suffered in India due to the removal of effective sovereignty over decision making.[127] The analysis of Indian patent policy making, scientific, industrial, and educational policies, and the role of institutions such as the India Office undertaken in this chapter certainly supports Inkster's assertion.

As discussed, the development of Indian patent policy continued to be dominated by the interests of British patentees and British industries. The petition of Thomson and Mylne led the Government of India to consult the provincial governments and other government departments to address their concerns relating to implementation and enforcement of patent rights in India. The concerns of native patentees in relation to high patent application fees or reciprocal arrangements regarding the grant of prior rights to Indian inventors in Britain were largely ignored. Moreover, it was only in 1920 that the benefits of prior rights were accorded to Indian inventors.

Despite the positive effect of a "compulsory local working" clause on industrial development in Britain, there was reluctance within the Colonial Government to introduce it in Indian patent law. The existence of a large number of foreign patentees in India, many of whom were British, may have influenced the Government of India to refrain from incorporating such a clause as that would have been detrimental to the interests of British patentees. The incorporation of this clause would have forced them to establish industries in India, which would then be competing with British industries and British manufactured goods – a result undesirable at the time and contrary to the industrial policy undertaken by the British and the Colonial Government in relation to India. When the clause was finally incorporated in the 1911 Act, it was substantially watered down as explained above.

---

[127] This reduction of sovereignty was of greater importance than the supposed retardative impact of deeply held cultural traits. See Inkster, "Colonial and Neo-colonial Transfers of Technology."

Based on the discussion above, one can argue that although the patent system had become somewhat receptive to native patentees, the situation was far from perfect. Indian patent policy making had to struggle through the corridors of the "colonial-institutional" framework in which imperial interests were continuously given significant preference. This is discernible from the fact that major changes to Indian patent laws (both in 1888 and 1911) were undertaken as a result of the changes in the British patent laws, rather than based on domestic need. The correspondence between the Government of India and the India Office in the United Kingdom as outlined above also supports this conclusion. Further, a "BRIT-plus" Indian patent system, that is, a patent system based on the British law but containing more onerous conditions than British patent law, was a result of the British-dominated Legislative Council of India. Therefore, the lack of political and economic independence of the country resulted in a skewed patent policy. The lack of higher education and job opportunities as well as biased industrial and research policies resulted in little patenting activity by the native Indian inventors during the pre-independence period.[128]

---

[128] India's position with respect to those of its colonial masters has aptly been summarized by Tomlinson:

What is the purpose of British rule in India? ... the trend of their [Government of India] actions showed they did have an answer to it ... This lowest common denominator of official concern can be termed "India's imperial commitment": the irreducible minimum that the subcontinent was expected to perform in the imperial cause. The commitment was three fold: to provide a market for British goods, to pay interest on the sterling debt and other charges that fell due in London, and to maintain a large number of British troops from Indian revenues and make part of the local army available as an "imperial fire brigade."

B. R. Tomlinson, *The Economy of Modern India: 1860–1970* (Cambridge: Cambridge University Press, 1996), 125.

14 The India Twist to Patent Culture
Investigating Its History

Tania Sebastian

14.1 Introduction

Scholarly works on patents pertaining to public health are rapidly becoming more numerous[1] as are developments in international instruments to ensure the benevolent effects of patents for humanity.[2] These issues are especially important in relation to debates on the needs of developing countries to ensure equitable access to "life-saving"[3] patented drugs. Since the United States of America is pursuing a stringent protection regime for drugs marketed by US patentees, however, it becomes all the more essential to highlight such concerns among developing countries. Recently, Brazil, China, and India have individually been at the forefront of challenges to US patent policy; other countries such as Pakistan, Bangladesh, and Singapore are bound together in such campaigns by the colonial after-effects of the British Empire. This chapter considers the implications of the pricing of patented drugs for AIDS/HIV and cancer

---

[1] See generally, Frederick M. Abbott and Jerome H. Reichman, "The Doha Round's Public Health Legacy Strategies for the Production and Diffusion of Patented Medicines under the Amended TRIPs Provisions," *Journal of International Economic Law* 10 (4) (2007): 921–87; Frederick M. Abbott, "The WTO Medicines Decision: World Pharmaceutical Trade and the Protection of Public Health," *The American Journal of International Law* 99 (2005): 317–58; James Thuo Gathii, "The Legal Status of the Doha Declaration on TRIPs and Public Health under the Vienna Convention on the Law of Treaties," *Harvard Journal of Law & Technology* 2 (15) (2002): 292–317; Carlos M. Correa, *Implications of the Doha Declaration on the TRIPS Agreement and Public Health* (Geneva: WHO, 2002); Carlos M. Correa, *Guidelines for the Examination of Pharmaceutical Patents: Developing a Public Health Perspective* (ICTSD – UNCTAD – WHO, 2007).

[2] For example, and more specifically to this chapter, the November 2001 Doha Declaration on the TRIPS Agreement and Public Health.

[3] Also to include "life-enhancing." There is no differentiation for the purposes of this chapter between the two terms of "life-enhancing" and "life-saving" and they are used interchangeably, though the differentiation does find mention in the context of drugs for life-threatening diseases and the arguments in courts necessitating low drug price are structured around the fact of whether the drug saves the life of a person or is rather a mechanism to ease the pain and thereby increase the term of the life otherwise shortened by an incurable disease.

patients in developing countries, and argues that these should be considered in a distinct category of "positive discrimination." I explore how the boundaries on drug protection should be based on the urgency of procuring access to patented medicines so as to value each and every human life, not just those in industrially developed nations.

Concerns about such boundaries have arisen amid speculation about the fragmentation of the Group of 77 (G77) coalition of developing countries, and the apparent inability of India and Brazil to lead these developing countries after the fading away of the G77, among other developments.[4] After its inception in 1964, however, India and Brazil have seamlessly taken the lead in determining the optimum use of compulsory licensing measures to ensure that patented drugs are available to all. Thus, in addition to arguing for greater accessibility to essential medicines in developing countries, this chapter argues also for a robust imposition of compulsory licensing terms on patent-holding companies. That argument relates more broadly to balancing such companies' need for protection of intellectual property rights in developing new medicines against the humane imperative to make such medicines accessible to a broad public. In discussing attempts to achieve that balance, I look at the role of the relevant stakeholders: governments, civil society, and pharmaceutical companies.

14.2   Public Health: TRIPS and the Doha Declaration

A key issue of debate in establishing the socioeconomic rights claims to healthcare now made in most developing countries has been the flexibilities toward local conditions embedded in the 1994 Agreement on Trade-Related Aspects of Intellectual Property Rights (TRIPS).[5] As is well known, major differences soon emerged between the developed and developing countries on the appropriate implementation of TRIPS for healthcare. As drug patenting protection identical to that for industrialized countries was advocated in TRIPS, developing countries were quick

---

[4] Peter Drahos, "Developing Countries and International Intellectual Property Standard-Setting," *The Journal of World Intellectual Property* 5 (5) (2002): 765–89. See also Jerome H. Reichman, "Intellectual Property in the Twenty-First Century: Will the Developing Countries Lead or Follow?" *Houston Law Review* 46 (4) (2009): 1115–85.

[5] In India, these socioeconomic rights are enshrined in Part IV of the Indian Constitution. These socioeconomic rights are directives that enable the State to improve public goods. However, these directives are weak as they are not legally binding; the same is the case in Brazil. In the absence of an authority positioned to evaluate competing claims on state resources, these state "responsibilities" have a weak legal status. See, generally, Ellen F. M. 't Hoen, *Private Patents and Public Health: Changing Intellectual Property Rules for Access to Medicines* (The Netherlands: Health Action International, 2016).

to highlight its potentially deleterious impact on the health of their citizens. This debate was largely centered upon conditions of access to a series of generic drugs that had hitherto been produced cheaply in many developing countries. Before generic antiretroviral (ARV) drugs came onto the market, the price of Highly Active Antiretroviral Therapy (HAART) had ranged between US$10,000 to US$12,000 per person/ year. Obviously, this made prohibitive access to care for almost all AIDS sufferers in countries that had no state-financed health insurance scheme to support such a cost for each patient, while access to cheaper generic copies priced between US$200 and US$300 per person/year had partially mitigated this problem.[6] Yet a major new consequence of TRIPS-compliance for developing countries was that production of such generic copies was now outlawed. Hence drugs required for HIV/AIDS treatments could thereafter only be produced under license from the original patentee.[7] The high price of the treatments thus produced by patentee firms once again rendered their purchase in the developing countries almost impossible.

Nevertheless, flexibilities in TRIPS have permitted some negotiations on this issue. These flexibilities take the form of certain exceptions ranging from exclusive patent rights (article 30) to the provision for "Other Use without Authorization of the Right Holder" (article 31); an example of such flexibility would be the inclusion of compulsory licensing in the statutes of developing countries. Indeed the TRIPS Agreement allows signatory countries to authorize themselves or third parties to use the subject matter of a patent for reasons of public policy, without the

---

[6] For a better explanation, see, generally, Ravindra K. Gupta, Andrew Hill, Anthony W. Sawyer, et al., "Virological Monitoring and Resistance to First-Line Highly Active Antiretroviral Therapy in Adults Infected with HIV-1 Treated under WHO Guidelines: A Systematic Review and Meta-analysis," *Lancet Infectious Diseases* 9 (7) (July 2009): 409–17. See also F. Van Leth, S. Andrews, B. Grinsztejn, et al., "The Effect of Baseline CD4 Cell Count and HIV-1 Viral Load on the Efficacy and Safety of Nevirapine or Efavirenz-Based First-Line HAART," *AIDS* 19 (5) (2005): 463–71; Ellen F. M. 't Hoen, Jacquelyn Veraldi, Brigit Toebesc, and Hans V. Hogerzeila, "Medicine Procurement and the Use of Flexibilities in the Agreement on Trade-Related Aspects of Intellectual Property Rights, 2001–2016," *Bulletin of the World Health Organization* 96 (2018): 185–93, available at: www.who.int/bulletin/volumes/96/3/17-199364.pdf; Thomas Owen, "Twenty One Years of HIV/AIDS Medicines in the Newspaper: Patents, Protest and Philanthropy," *Media, Culture and Society* 40 (1) (2018): 75–93; Ambika Sahai and N. S. Kruthika, "The Need for Compulsory Licensing of Antiretroviral Drugs: The Indian Perspective," *Wake Forest Journal of Business and Intellectual Property Law* 16 (2) (2015): 241–61.
[7] The need for exclusive compulsory licenses over patents in pharmaceuticals began back in 1982 with the backing of a large group of developing countries. William Cornish, *Intellectual Property: Omnipresent, Distracting, Irrelevant?* (Oxford: Oxford University Press, 2004).

permission of the patent owner.[8] Although the scope of "public policy" is not expressly defined in the TRIPS Agreement, article 31b indicates that relevant considerations include "anti-competitive practices," "national emergency or other circumstances of extreme urgency," or "public non-commercial use." Moreover, article 31f for the grant of compulsory licenses includes the supply of patented products to the domestic market. In view of these considerations, joint efforts were initiated by African countries on access to drugs, especially in the context of application of TRIPS provisions for public health.[9] This eventually resulted in the adoption of the Doha Declaration on TRIPS and Public Health (hereinafter "Declaration") that maintained, inter alia, that "the TRIPS Agreement does not and should not prevent members from taking measures to protect public health."[10]

While various factors contributed toward the Declaration, the initial outcry in 1998 was precipitated by the lawsuit brought by the Pharmaceutical Industry Association and thirty-nine of its affiliated companies against the Government of South Africa;[11] an allegation was that this nation's Medicines and Related Substances Control Amendment Act (1997) had violated the TRIPS Agreement by its reduction of price rates.[12] The Pharmaceutical Industry Association's complaint was withdrawn subsequently due to adverse national and international public opinion. Nevertheless, the strong commercial pressure put upon them lent urgency to developing countries' negotiation of a bilateral agreement on the interpretation and application of the relevant provisions of the TRIPS Agreement. Its aim was to clarify the flexibilities to which Members were entitled, especially the "relationship between intellectual property rights and access to medicines."[13]

---

[8] Fabienne Orsi and Benjamin Coriat, "The New Role and Status of Intellectual Property Rights in Contemporary Capitalism," *Competition and Change* 10 (2) (2006): 162–79.

[9] E. K. Oke, "Patent Rights, Access to Medicines, and the Justiciability of the Right to Health in Kenya, South Africa and India," in *Justiciability of Human Rights Law in Domestic Jurisdictions*, ed. Alice Diver and Jacinta Miller (Switzerland: Springer International Publishing, 2016), 91–122.

[10] The fourth Ministerial Conference of the World Trade Organization in Doha adopted a Declaration on TRIPS and Public Health; see www.who.int/medicines/areas/policy/doha_declaration/en.

[11] See Steven Casper, *Between Free Market and Human Rights: Government Policy, the Pharmaceutical Industry and the HIV/AIDS Crisis*, 2011; see http://bit.ly/researchgatelink.

[12] Debora J. Halbert, "Moralized Discourses: South Africa's Intellectual Property Fight for Access to AIDS Medication," *Seattle Journal for Social Justice* 1 (2) (2002): 257–95. See also Amy Patterson, *The African State and the AIDS Crises* (London: Routledge, 2005).

[13] TRIPS Council Report, 2001. TRIPS: Council Discussion on Access to Medicines, "Developing Country Group's Paper," available at: www.wto.org/english/tratop_e/trips_e/paper_develop_w296_e.htm; Ahmed Abdel Latif, "Change and Continuity in the International Intellectual Property System: A Turbulent Decade in Perspective," *The WIPO Journal* 3 (1) (2011): 36–55.

In this campaign one major concern for enhanced access to patented medicines was the absence of a domestic drug manufacturing capacity in some developing nations. The original Declaration permitted governments to override patents only with domestically produced generic substitutes, but most countries that needed the drugs most urgently had no indigenous pharmaceutical industry. A campaign followed to allow the most desperate countries to override patents on expensive ARVs and order cheaper copies from generic manufacturers located in other countries. Although not formally recognized as having legal standing by the World Trade Organization (WTO), the Declaration affirmed the right of countries to interpret and apply TRIPS in the best way to protect public health.[14] So, after two years of negotiation, in August 2003, a document was approved by the TRIPS Council that spoke of "an expeditious solution" to concerns of those Members "with insufficient or no manufacturing capacities in the pharmaceutical sector in making effective use of compulsory licensing under the TRIPS Agreement." Under very precisely defined and restrictive conditions, the possibilities for least developed countries to import generic ARVs were set out.[15]

This addition to the Declaration has brought some respite even as debates continue on the effects of the high prices of patented medicines charged by the patent owners versus the limited resources to purchase the drug by the vast majority of developing economies. Brazil, for example, had secured access to ARVs under patent: indeed ARV procurement by importation by the Ministry of Health accounted for 63 percent of Brazil's federal budget in 2015. As no generic competitor was allowed to produce the new generation of ARVs, there emerged a huge

[14] The Declaration states that

> We agree that the TRIPS Agreement does not and should not prevent Members from taking measures to protect public health. Accordingly, while reiterating our commitment to the TRIPS Agreement, we affirm that the Agreement can and should be interpreted and implemented in a manner supportive of WTO Members' right to protect public health and, in particular, to promote access to medicines for all. (The Declaration, 2001, article 1)

> Thus the Declaration specifies notably that: "Each Member has the right to grant compulsory licenses and the freedom to determine the grounds upon which such licenses are granted" (The Declaration, article 5b); "Each Member has the right to determine what constitutes a national emergency or other circumstances of extreme urgency, it being understood that public health crises, including those relating to HIV/AIDS, tuberculosis, malaria and other epidemics, can represent a national emergency or other circumstances of extreme urgency" (The Declaration, article 5c).

[15] "Implementation of Paragraph 6 of the Doha Declaration on the TRIPS Agreement and Public Health" (the Decision). See, generally, Muhammad Z. Abbas and Shamreeza Riaz, "WTO 'Paragraph 6' System for Affordable Access to Medicines: Relief or Regulatory Ritualism," *The Journal of World Intellectual Property* 21 (2017): 32–51.

difference in the cost of first- and second-line treatments. Given the constant need for updating the HIV/AIDS treatment, "expeditious solutions" still have to be achieved to assure the sustainability of the treatments.

As of August 2005 developing countries were obliged to comply with the provisions of TRIPS within their legal systems. This deadline affected nations such as India and China since compliance severely hindered their previous customary access to low-price generic versions of ARVs and active pharmaceutical ingredients (APIs).[16] In India the affordable price structure of generic versions of HAART treatments (see above) crumbled after the Indian Patent Amendment Act, 2005, overrode the erstwhile domestic patent law that allowed generic drug manufacturers to freely make copies of branded medicines. Even more of concern was that generic versions of any new molecule or formulation produced under a patent could not now be produced by generic manufacturers. In health-care terms this severely affected access to patented versions of new ARVs employed in second- and third-line treatments for HIV/AIDS; access to these became essential due to growing resistance to first-line treatments, but could not now be available as generic equivalents.

The next major development in this story was the "TRIPS Plus" Agreement that developed new bilateral relations between developing countries and the United States in the field of public health. Signing this agreement nevertheless imposed more restrictive provisions on intellectual property rights (IPR) management whilst jeopardizing the conditions for access to treatment and care in the developing countries.[17] It is well documented that when the developing countries made an attempt to invoke flexibilities in TRIPS to mold their domestic laws more favorably for public access to patented medicines – for example, Brazil's compulsory licensing law[18] – strong-arm tactics were deployed by countries with substantial pharmaceutical patent industries, such as

---

[16] The mention of these two countries is crucial as they represent the largest international suppliers of APIs (in the case of China) and generic ARVs (in the case of India), and have strongly contributed to the procurement of medicines at reduced and affordable prices.

[17] Benjamin Coriat and Fabienne Orsi, "IPR, Innovation and Public Interest: Is the New IPR Regime Enforced Worldwide by the TRIPS Sustainable?" *Economica* 10 (2) (2008): 28–54.

[18] Anselm Kamperman Sanders, "The Development Agenda for Intellectual Property: Rational Humane Policy or 'Modern-Day Communism'?" in *Intellectual Property and Free Trade Agreements*, ed. Christopher Heats and Anselm Kamperman Sanders (England: Hart Publishing, 2007), 3–26 (describing the action brought [and subsequently withdrawn] against Brazil by the United States before the WTO [WT/DS199/1], based on the position that the Brazilian compulsory licensing provision for nonworking was in violation of article 27[1] of TRIPS).

the USA. Additionally, by virtue of sanctions under section 301, the minimum standards requirements were enlarged.[19] The negotiated transition periods for developing countries under TRIPS articles 65 and 66, which were to allow developing countries more time for compliance, were also bypassed.[20] This instantiates a broader pattern that even laws designed as concessions for the developing countries – for example, compulsory licensing provisions – can rarely be made to work to these countries' advantage. This is all the more so as TRIPS was forged in the context of an overdetermined relationship between the developed countries and their former colonies.[21]

14.3   Public Health and World Health Organization

The interest of the World Health Organization (WHO) in IPR issues began with the advent of the TRIPS agreement. With the adoption of a resolution on Revised Drug Strategy in 1996 by the World Health Assembly,[22] WTO Member States were encouraged to minimize the effects of patents on the availability of essential drugs by using the inbuilt flexibilities in TRIPS.[23] Though expressing initial opposition, the European Communities changed their position in light of the massive HIV/AIDS pandemic in Africa.[24]

---

[19] "Section 301" refers to unilateral action by the United States pursuant to the Trade Act of 1974. "Aimed at bolstering the leverage of U.S. trade negotiations, ... section 301 ... requires the United States Trade Representative to identify foreign countries that provide inadequate intellectual property protection or that deny American intellectual property goods fair or equitable market access" (citing 19 U.S.C. § 2242[a][1][A]). Though the sanction can be pursued only after the exhaustion of all actions permissible under the rules of the international trading body, section 301 is more correctly viewed as a technique of public shaming, which costs the infringing country political capital in the international trading system.

[20] Peter Drahos, "An Alternative Framework for the Global Regulation of Intellectual Property Rights," *Journal für Entwicklungspolitik* 21 (4) (2005): 44–68.

[21] Margaret Chon, "Intellectual Property and the Development Divide," *Cardozo Law Review* 27 (2006): 2821–912. See also Peter Drahos, "Negotiating Intellectual Property Rights: Between Coercion and Dialogue," in *Global Intellectual Property Rights*, ed. Peter Drahos and Ruth Mayne (London: Palgrave Macmillan, 2002), 161–82; 't Hoen, *Private Patents and Public Health*, 19.

[22] Revised Drug Strategy, World Health Assembly Res. WHA49.14, 2 (10) (May 1996).

[23] The guide was published as G. Velasquez and P. Boulet, *Globalization and Access to Drugs: Perspectives on the WTO/TRIPS Agreement*, rev. ed. 1999, WHOIDAP/98.9, available at: www.who.int/medicines/areas/policy/who-dap-98-9rev.pdf.

[24] See Laurence R. Helfer, "Regime Shifting: The TRIPs Agreement and New Dynamics of International Intellectual Property Lawmaking," *The Yale Journal of International Law* 29 (2004): 1–83.

Subsequently, the Commission on Intellectual Property Rights, Innovation and Public Health was established in February 2004 by the World Health Assembly (WHA):

to collect data and proposals from the different actors involved and produce an analysis of intellectual property rights, innovation, and public health, including the question of appropriate funding and incentive mechanisms for the creation of new medicines and other products against diseases that disproportionately affect developing countries.[25]

The final WHA report of 2006, however, sought both to construe how intellectual property issues affected public health and also to consider how "diseases which disproportionately affect developing countries could best be addressed, and to seek solutions."[26] This sent a proactive message that the protection of intellectual property rights was not an end in itself but should be seen as a means in the context of broader social aims. This Commission also challenged the presumed powers of the World Intellectual Property Organization (WIPO) in its contention that "intellectual property matters, particularly as they relate to innovation, are not an exclusive preserve of WIPO."[27] Indeed, the assumption was that allowing WHO to take up more responsibility in the intellectual property area, especially where it intersected with public health, would be beneficial.[28] With this in view, let us turn now to the case studies of Brazil, South Africa, and India.

14.4   Patents and Health – Investigating the Brazilian and South African Experiences

14.4.1   The Brazilian Experience

Attempts to generate low-cost drugs and advance the fulfillment of Brazil's national health objectives have created international controversies regarding the nation's intellectual property (IP) legislation. Two articles embodied in its Industrial Property Law, 1997 require specific mention in this regard. First, article 71 empowered the government to authorize production of generic drugs by local producers or to import the

---

[25] See details as given on the background of the establishment of the Commission at: www.who.int/intellectualproperty/background/en/.

[26] Available at: https://apps.who.int/medicinedocs/documents/s14146e/s14146e.pdf.

[27] Nirav Bhatt, "Who Quizzes WHO's Role in Solving the Influenza Pandemic Crisis: An Insight," IP Osgoode (2010), available at: www.iposgoode.ca/2010/02/who-quizzes-whos-role-in-solving-the-influenza-pandemic-crisis-an-insight/.

[28] Peter K. Yu, "A Tale of Two Development Agendas," *Ohio Northern University Law Review* 35 (2) (2009): 465–573.

drug from a generic producer in the event of a national health emergency; this then provided the authorization by the compulsory license route to drug manufacture in the case of national health emergencies. This article was understood to be consistent with TRIPS. Second, article 68 authorized compulsory licenses when manufactured goods are not produced locally within three years: the law will then authorize the Brazilian government to license local producers to produce the good, just as the current India law on compulsory licenses, again a TRIPS-compliant provision. The proposed implementation of these sections was challenged by the United States before the WTO panel in 2000 although the challenge was withdrawn in June 2001. That withdrawal, however, did not amount to a settling of the fundamental conflict since the United States has since threatened to reopen the case if Brazil ever implements articles 68 or 71.

While TRIPS did allow developing countries to some extent adjust their intellectual property laws to suit their national interests, the consequence of international power relationships in affecting the implementation of those laws reflects a broader pattern visible in the past behavior among developed countries. For example, the rise of the mighty German chemical industry brought about a change of the United Kingdom patent law before World War I that had previously prevented the patentability of chemical compounds.[29] The USA also had to deal with the exclusive patents held by the German companies in dyes during World War I, resulting in its import from Germany for the USA's coloring industry. It was within the time period of 1914–19 that both the United Kingdom and USA obtained free access to the German chemical plants (after the conclusion of the war and the confiscation of the plants).[30] The power of the German chemical companies grew as a result of the shortage of medicines and other chemical products during World War I, thereby enabling the German chemical companies to prosper as a result of strict patent protection. The absence of any legal mechanism to patent pharmaceutical products in Germany and the option to get a patent in the United Kingdom created an incentive for the German chemical companies to patent their products in the United Kingdom and USA. So the pre-World War I scenario of expensive and scarce medicines and chemical products in the United Kingdom as an outcome of German

---

[29] N. Rajagopala Ayyangar, *Report on the Revision of the Patents Law*, September 1959, available at: https://spicyip.com/wp-content/uploads/2013/10/ayyangar_committee_report.pdf.

[30] Michele Boldrin and David K. Levine, *Against Intellectual Monopoly* (Cambridge: Cambridge University Press, 2010), chap. 9.

companies holding most patents resulted in a change post-1919 with a modification of the English Patents Act, 1907, with the addition of section 38A introducing mandatory licenses for medicines.[31]

While these transnational concerns have emerged among developing countries too, it was the persistence of countries such Brazil in legislating domestic access to anti-AIDS drugs that has now enveloped other developing nations desperate for these drugs,[32] stating that compulsory licenses are required to achieve universal health coverage.[33] And, as Wade has rightly pointed out, the signal sent to other developing countries was that while emulating Brazil's program for distributing AIDS medicines is acceptable, emulating Brazil's efforts to use IPR policy as a tool of industrial strategy is not.[34]

14.4.2   The South African Experience

South Africa responded in 1997 to the HIV epidemic by proposing legislation that empowered the Ministry of Health to create "conditions for the supply of more affordable medicines … so as to protect the health of the public."[35] What transpired thereafter were consequences similar to the Brazilian experience in a dispute between the USA and South Africa on the specific question of compulsory licenses for pharmaceutical patents, and the broader question of developing countries' concerns toward equitable access to medicines.

As a developing nation, South Africa clearly could not afford to purchase life-saving drugs at the monopoly market price commanded by a patent-protected drug producer. Since attempts by the government to purchase these drugs at market price on a mass scale would place

---

[31] Ibid. See also Jeremy Howells and Ian Neary, *Intervention and Technological Innovation: Government and the Pharmaceutical Industry in the UK and Japan* (Basingstoke: Palgrave Macmillan, 1995).

[32] Joe Cohen, "Brazil – Ten Years Later," *Science* 313 (5786) (2006): 484–7, available at: https://science.sciencemag.org/content/313/5786/484.2. See also Samira Guennif, "Evaluating the Usefulness of Compulsory Licensing in Developing Countries: A Comparative Study of Thai and Brazilian Experiences Regarding Access to Aids Treatments," *Developing World Bioethics* 17 (2017): 90–9; Rochelle Cooper Dreyfuss and César Rodríguez-Garavito, *Balancing Wealth and Health: The Battle Over Intellectual Property and Access to Medicines in Latin America* (Oxford: Oxford University Press, 2014).

[33] Kyung-Bok Son, Chang-Yup Kim, and Tae-Jin Lee, "Understanding of for Whom, under What Conditions and How the Compulsory Licensing of Pharmaceuticals Works in Brazil and Thailand: A Realist Synthesis," *Global Public Health* 14 (1) (2019): 122–32.

[34] Robert Hunter Wade, "What Strategies Are Viable for Developing Countries Today? The World Trade Organization and the Shrinking of 'Development Space'," *Review of International Political Economy* 10 (4) (2003): 621–44.

[35] Medicines and Related Substances Control Amendment Act, 1997 (South Africa).

excessive strain on the already developing economy, it became apparent that a more community-specific regulatory mechanism was needed that embodied all state-individualistic and state-specific issues and concerns.[36] This could pave the way for a well-negotiated public-private partnership between the two as the balance amongst the private rights of inventors, individuals in need of treatment, and the public welfare obligations of governments could thus be collectively addressed.[37]

Nevertheless, the case of South Africa epitomizes the unresolved disagreements between the home governments of the pharmaceutical companies and the governments of the nations dependent on the drugs produced by these pharmaceutical companies.[38] In the long run, if not resolved, these high drug prices generally adversely affect the health of the populations of even the most progressive of the developing economies: this can result in interference in the prospects for economic development. It is in this context that we should see the advent of Indian Patent Amendment Act of 2005; a controversial provision is the one introducing product patents for pharmaceutical inventions.[39] In order to understand the significance of this, we need to examine the broader context of India's colonial past.

14.5   Colonialism: Effects and Aftereffects

The effects of colonization have played a key role in the intermingling, or often imposition, of various laws of the conquering nation into its colonies.[40] For example, as a Spanish colony, the Philippines' first patent laws originally borrowed from on Spanish patent law. After the USA established control over the islands, patent applications were assessed under US law. The Philippines largely followed US patent law up until 1997 when the Philippine Congress passed a new Intellectual Property

---

[36] Thomas J. Bollyky, "Balancing Private Rights and Public Obligations: Constitutionally Mandated Compulsory Licensing of HIV/AIDS Related Treatments in South Africa," *South African Journal on Human Rights* 18 (2002): 530–69.

[37] Ibid. The private sector is to supply pharmaceuticals and equipment to health service providers and to invest in research and technology to improve the diversity and quality of treatment options.

[38] Linda Muswaka, "The Impact of Patent Protection and Lack of Generic Competition on the Right of Access to Medicines in South Africa: Explicating Corporate Responsibilities for Human Rights," *Mediterranean Journal of Social Sciences* 5 (2) (January 2014): 229–35.

[39] Shamnad Basher, "'Policy Style' Reasoning at the Indian Patent Office," available at: www.researchgate.net/profile/Shamnad_Basheer/publication/228146700_%27Policy_Style %27_Reasoning_at_the_Indian_Patent_Office/links/02e7e5279f66e4d94c000000.pdf.

[40] For the Indian context, see Rajesh Sagar, Chapter 13 in this volume for the colonial power struggle that forms part of the 1888 Patent Bill in the Indian Legislative Council.

Code in order to comply with TRIPS. Many of the developing countries for most of their history have never exercised meaningful sovereignty over the setting of their own intellectual property standards. This becomes an important aspect for considerating the conflict when the erstwhile colonies tried to incorporate the TRIPS flexibilities to better suit their economies.

These trends can also be seen in the Korean patent regime that was affected by military conflict. The Japanese replaced Korean patent law with their patent law in 1910. In 1946, Korea acquired another patent law as a consequence of US military administration. In the 1980s, South Korea was among the first to have its intellectual property laws targeted under US trade laws. In discussing the pressure exerted by the United States on South Korea regarding intellectual property, the (then) ambassador to the United States, Mr. Kyung-Won Kim (in 1986) wrote:

Historically, Koreans have not viewed intellectual discoveries or scientific inventions as the private property of their discoverers or inventors ... Cultural esteem rather than material gain was the incentive for creativity.[41]

In essence Mr. Kim was suggesting that the set of intellectual property rights proposed by the United States and other OECD countries were illegitimate. In this assertion, he found the company of the likes of Brazil, India, Taiwan, Singapore, Mexico, China, and others. These sentiments are similarly expounded in various nations with a different cultural understanding of how IP should fit into their "community" and how to maintain the appropriate cultural standards.

International conventions indeed have accepted the central principle of allowing freedom to the Member States to attune their intellectual property protection system to their own needs and conditions. India's arguments about IP have promoted this central philosophy in implementing its patent legislation. Very specific concrete policies follow from the Indian position on the appropriateness of patenting to its culture: patents must be fully worked (or exploited) in the host country or forfeited, and that licensing of rights may be made compulsory for patentees. India's position finds support in developing countries on both developmental (economic) and moral (fairness) grounds.[42] The use of the Doha flexibilities in a few developing countries advances the argument of their usefulness, especially in issues relating to public health. Zimbabwe, for

[41] Kyung-Won Kim, "Business Forum; A High Cost to Developing Countries," *New York Times*, October 5, 1986, available at: www.nytimes.com/1986/10/05/business/business-forum-a-high-cost-to-developing-countries.html.
[42] See Richard T. Rapp and Richard P. Rozek, "Benefits and Costs of Intellectual Property Protection in Developing Countries," *Journal of World Trade* 24 (1990): 75–102.

example, allowed the government or a third party to use patented products for the service of the state, following the declaration of an emergency in 2002. Under the government-use license, a local producer could be authorized to manufacture and supply ARV medicines to government institutes.[43] In 2003, the Malaysian government permitted importation of generic ARV medicines from India for use in government hospitals by using the "government use" provision in its patent law.[44] The year 2004 was significant for Indonesia, Mozambique, and Zimbabwe. Local production in relation to patents of two ARVs for government use were authorized in Indonesia, and Mozambique and Zimbabwe made use of the compulsory licensing provisions for local production of ARVs.[45]

Other developing countries have at least partially utilized the Doha flexibilities allowed in the TRIPS, especially compulsory licenses. These include Kenya and South Africa.[46]

It has been suggested to make use of the experience of India in the working of patent law and use it for the benefit of other developing countries, for example in Bangladesh.[47]

In addition, one study has stated that:

[B]etween 2001 and 2007, 52 developing and least developed countries have issued post-Doha compulsory licenses for production or import of generic versions of patented medicines, given effect to government use provisions, and/or implemented the non-enforcement of patents. In addition, many countries have used the flexibilities as leverage in price negotiations with patent-holding pharmaceutical companies.[48]

Additionally, a few other developing countries including Malaysia, Mozambique, Thailand, Zambia, and Zimbabwe have made effective use of compulsory licensing.[49] Here the individual claims on intellectual property are subordinated to the more fundamental claims of social

---

[43] Sisule F. Musungu, "The Use of Flexibilities in TRIPs by Developing Countries: Can They Promote Access to Medicines?" Commission on IPRs, Innovation and Public Health, Study 4C, August 2005, available at: www.who.int/intellectualproperty/studies/TRIPSFLEXI.pdf.
[44] Ibid.   [45] Ibid.
[46] Carlos M. Correa, "Implication of the Doha Declaration on the TRIPS Agreement and Public Health," 2002, available at: www.who.int/medicines/areas/policy/WHO_EDM_PAR_2002.3.pdf.
[47] Monirul Azam, *Intellectual Property and Public Health in the Developing World* (Cambridge, UK: Open Book Publishers, 2016), 185.
[48] Ellen F. M. 't Hoen, *The Global Politics of Pharmaceutical Monopoly Power* (Diemen, The Netherlands: AMB Publishers, 2009), xvi, as cited in Abdel Latif, "Change and Continuity in the International Intellectual Property System."
[49] UNAIDS, WHO, and UNDP, "Using TRIPs Flexibilities to Improve Access to HIV Treatment," 2011, available at: www.unaids.org/en/resources/documents/2011/20110315_JC2049_PolicyBrief_TRIPS.

well-being. Unlike inalienable rights, intellectual property rights can be subordinated to greater interests; in this case the right of a people to livelihood. Further, intellectual property is primarily a form of common public property that may be permitted to take some limited private forms.

The "right to livelihood" and development takes precedence over other claims upon which property rights are based. Hence the food, pharmaceutical, and chemical sectors have been accorded a differential treatment in the patent laws of developing countries because of the critical nature of these sectors to their socioeconomic and public interests.[50]

14.6   The Indian Case

On the Indian subcontinent, national legislation was heavily influenced by the experience of British colonization, and patent laws were no exception.[51] Post-independence, a new law was implemented in 1970, which brought in substantial changes to the erstwhile 1911 Patents & Designs Act based on United Kingdom law. In the resultant Act of 1970, the Central Government of India was permitted to issue compulsory licenses for producing patented goods "in circumstances of national emergency or in circumstances of extreme urgency or in case of public non-commercial use."[52] Section 84 of the Indian Patent Act, 1970 provides grounds for the grant of a compulsory license by the authority.[53] This provision remained dormant until the *Natco* v. *Bayer* case discussed below. Two expert committees constituted after India's independence to

---

[50] Paul Steidlmeier, "The Moral Legitimacy of Intellectual Property Claims: American Business and Developing Country Perspectives," *Journal of Business Ethics* 122 (1993): 157–64.

[51] Cornish, *Intellectual Property*, 3. See also Lionel Bently, "The 'Extraordinary Multiplicity' of Intellectual Property Laws in the British Colonies in the Nineteenth Century," *Theoretical Inquiries in Law* 12 (1) (2011): 157–64.

[52] Section 92, Patents Act, 1970.

[53] Section 84. Compulsory licenses.—(1) At any time after the expiration of three years from the date of the grant of a patent, any person interested may make an application to the Controller for grant of compulsory licence on patent on any of the following grounds, namely:—

(a) that the reasonable requirements of the public with respect to the patented invention have not been satisfied, or

(b) that the patented invention is not available to the public at a reasonably affordable price, or

(c) that the patented invention is not worked in the territory of India.

review the preexisting Indian patent system[54] suggested radical changes keeping in mind the local conditions conducive for a nation with a low research and development base, a population including a larger poor-based segment, and medicine with high prices. Diverging from its British-based precursors, the Indian patent law of 1970 followed traditional German patent law in prohibiting patents of methods or processes for manufacturing drugs but not the patents for the drug themselves. Also, the duration of patent protection was varied for pharmaceuticals.[55]

At around the same time countries including Brazil, Argentina, and Mexico began to reform their patent laws along similar lines to weaken patent rights in pharmaceuticals. Such events threatened the Western-dominated pharmaceutical cartels, with developing nations increasingly "asking questions" about previously accepted notions of international standards of intellectual property thrust upon them in virtue of the Paris Convention and the Berne Convention. Most importantly, as Drahos asks: "[W]ere the international standards tilted too far towards the appropriation of knowledge rather than its diffusion?"[56] Developing countries unsuccessfully sought adjustments to both the international copyright regime and the international patent regime, the most vociferous of which were over the revisions of compulsory licensing clauses for the manufacture of patented technology.[57]

Four nations in particular – India, Brazil, Argentina, and Mexico – had shown that developing countries could lower standards of patent protection and yet still have a thriving generics industry. In sympathy with the aims of such developing nations, the European Court of Justice held[58] that in certain exceptional circumstances refusal to license an intellectual property right could result in violation of article 82 of the European

[54] Patents Enquiry Committee, 1948 (submitted its final report in 1950) and Shri Justice N. Rajagopala Ayyangar Committee, 1957 (submitted its report on patents law revision in September 1959).

[55] Patent protection for pharmaceuticals was only granted for seven years, as opposed to fourteen years for other inventions.

[56] Peter Drahos, "Developing Countries and International Intellectual Property Standard-Setting," *The Journal of World Intellectual Property* 5 (2002): 765–89.

[57] D. M. Mills, "Patents and the Exploitation of Technology Transferred to Developing Countries (in Particular, Those of Africa)," *Industrial Property* 24 (1985): 120–6. See also Peter Drahos, "Global Property Rights in Information: The Story TRIPS at the GATT," *Prometheus* 13 (1995): 6–19 and S. K. Sell, "Intellectual Property Protection and Antitrust in the Developing World: Crisis, Coercion, and Choice," *International Organization* 49 (1995): 315–49. Amy Kapczynski, "Harmonization and Its Discontents: A Case Study of TRIPS Implementation in India's Pharmaceutical Sector," *California Law Review* 97 (2009): 1571–649.

[58] *IMS Health GmbH & Co. OHG v. NDC Health GmbH & Co. KG*, Case C-418/01, Judgment of the Court (Fifth Chamber) of April 29, 2004.

Community Treaty.[59] Similarly, the European Commission of Human Rights observed that the grant under Dutch law of a compulsory license in a patented drug was not an interference in the patent holder's rights under article 1 of Protocol 1 of the European Convention of Human Rights and that the "compulsory licence was lawful and pursued a legitimate aim of encouraging technological and economic development."[60] Pointing out the World Bank's suggestion that development is about expanding the ability of people "to shape their own futures," we need to be concerned about the loss by developing countries of national sovereignty over standards that impact on sectors such as agriculture, food, environment, health, and education.[61]

What were the consequences of these developments for India? A compulsory license was granted for the first time in India in the case *Natco Pharma Limited* v. *Bayer Corporation.*[62] One of the reasons for March 2012 grant was on the grounds of nonaffordability of the drug "Sorafenib," used for treating advanced liver and kidney cancer, to a large segment of the patient population in India. Only a little over 2 percent of cancer patients there had been able to access the drug, the primary reason for which had been the very high price of the patented version: £2,730 per month. In the wake of the compulsory license award, Natco now plans to make the drug available at a cost 97 percent lower than Bayer, at £85 per month. Nevertheless with the Above Poverty Line income at £46.72 per month for urban areas and £38.16 per month for rural areas,[63] the drug is still inaccessible to the majority population of India. Hence, the judgment ordered that 600 needy and deserving Indian patients every year be given the drug free of cost. In 2014, the Supreme Court of India dismissed an appeal by Bayer Corp. against a Bombay High Court decision that had refused to revoke the compulsory license issued to Natco by the Intellectual Property Appellate Board (IPAB).

[59] Daniel Kanter, "IP and Compulsory Licensing on Both Sides of the Atlantic: An Appropriate Antitrust Remedy or a Cutback on Innovation?" *European Competition Law Review* 27 (7) (2006): 351–64.
[60] *Smith Kline and French Laboratories Ltd* v. *The Netherlands,* October 4, 1990, Application 12633/87. European Commission of Human Rights as cited in Peter Drahos, "The Universality of Intellectual Property Rights: Origins and Development," WIPO Panel Discussion on Intellectual Property and Human Rights, Geneva, November 9, 1998, www.wipo.int/edocs/mdocs/tk/en/wipo_unhchr_ip_pnl_98/wipo_unhchr_ip_pnl_98_1.pdf.
[61] World Bank, *The Quality of Growth* (Oxford: Oxford University Press, 2000), xxiii.
[62] MIPR 2013(2)97.
[63] Mihir Shah, "Understanding the Poverty Line," *The Hindu,* August 6, 2013, available at: www.thehindu.com/opinion/lead/understanding-the-poverty-line/article4989045.ece.

This outcome in India has been criticized on various fronts, and the American government has vociferously opposed the grant of the compulsory license. While one of the defenses of pharmaceutical companies against such compulsory licensing is on the grounds of their voluntary adoption of differential pricing, such a culturally sensitive policy was not in fact adopted by Bayer.

14.7   Conclusion

Following the ineffective moves of the G77 group in advocating equitable access to medicines, the subsequent initiatives of at least Brazil, South Africa, and India to take progressive steps have been significant. Moreover, the context of India and its contributions in a postcolonial intellectual property environment proved a stepping stone for other similarly situated countries engaged with similar political and economic complexities. The truncating of India's intellectual property regime, especially in the arena of compulsory licensing, has paved the way for adaptation and implementation in similarly placed developing economies struggling with exorbitantly placed price structures for medicines. This has been the case even when intellectual property rights have been undoubtedly the best way to promote innovation. The directives of many of the developing countries also put a responsibility on the state to perform certain duties for the betterment of their people in general. Though nonenforceable, these are supposed to find reflection in the states' actions; again, a reason life-saving drugs fall into a *positive discrimination* category, whereby they are associated with their availability to the public.

Developing countries will be better placed to take a lead in policy experimentation and innovations to improve their intellectual property regimes so as to offset the overly protectionist tendencies of the industrialized countries, with the added advantage of learning from the imperfections of the industrialized countries. The overall result will be to maintain the supply of global public goods in an emerging transnational system of innovation, especially those linked together by erstwhile similar colonial regimes such as the case of India discussed in this chapter.

15 The Life and Times of Patent No. 2,670

Industrial Property and Public Knowledge in Early Twentieth-Century Japan

Kjell Ericson

15.1 Introduction

In the aftermath of World War II, a Japanese children's book identified what its author, then a member of Japan's Diet, called "the two inventions that will lift up the homeland."[1] The book's cover presented two images, one of an automatic loom and another of a round pearl nestled inside an opened shellfish. At the time, each of these images served as an easy shorthand for the inventors whose faces did not appear alongside them: the loom maker Toyoda Sakichi (1867–1930), whose son had gone on to head the Toyota Motor Company, and the pearl cultivator Mikimoto Kōkichi (1858–1954). Toyoda and Mikimoto's reputations as dual exemplars of national invention, forged earlier in the twentieth century, were bound up with the patents they had controlled. Even so, the contrast between the inventions attributed to each of them is striking. In the background is a manufactured piece of textile machinery of the sort that, in a variety of places, has held a metonymic association with industrialization. In the foreground, there is a combination of fleshy bivalve and spherical pearl.

An overriding concern motivates this study: to elucidate how the cultivation of pearls in living shellfish entered an imperial industrial property rights regime that created opportunities to reward individual inventors for novel claims of artifice. Clues to this puzzle can be found by taking a closer look at Mikimoto Kōkichi's first pearl cultivation patent, the 2,670th issued by Japan's patent office upon its approval in 1896, and its relationship to the Japanese empire's changing early twentieth-century patent system.

To be sure, the movement of technical publications, apparatus, and skilled practitioners was a prominent feature of Tokugawa Japan's

---

[1] Toyosawa Toyoo, *Sokoku o okosu hatsumei futatsu: shinju to shinjidō shokki* (Tokyo: Gakushūsha bunko, 1948).

eighteenth- and nineteenth-century technological landscape.[2] But along with tacit and written "know-how" came legal mechanisms for authoring it, owning it, and controlling its spread. Following the Meiji government's 1885 implementation of a Napoleonic Code-inspired patent law and the 1888 restructuring of the law along American lines (including the adoption of full patent application examinations), one of those mechanisms was the patent system.[3]

For over a decade after 1885, Japan's patent system excluded anyone outside the Japanese empire from applying for a patent. As one condition for ending the extraterritorial rights granted under unequal commercial treaties signed with Japan from 1858 onward, Euro-American treaty signatories demanded the extension of Japanese patent rights to foreigners and insisted that Japan join the Paris Convention for the Protection of Industrial Property.[4] The substantial revision of Japan's treaty relationships and the end of extraterritoriality in 1899 thus coincided with new understandings of Japan's role in the international defense of industrial property and copyright.

Japan's post-1899 patent system reflected newfound Euro-American expectations that the Japanese state defend (foreign) industrial property and prosecute (domestic) patent infringement under imperial Japanese law. But, as this chapter shows, the spatial boundaries of invention were not predetermined. Paris Convention membership brought with it fundamental questions about how to map "new" knowledge, which in turn prompted fresh divisions between "domestic" and "foreign" invention. The fixing of Japan's place in an interlinked world of patent-protecting states was, moreover, accompanied by the emergence of patent-inspecting bureaucrats and patent-holding inventors who sought to define, police, defend, and promote internationally recognized industrial property rights *within* an expanding Japanese empire. It was this domestic

[2] See, for example, Thomas C. Smith, *Native Sources of Japanese Industrialization, 1750–1920* (Berkeley: University of California Press, 1988), 173–98; Tessa Morris-Suzuki, *The Technological Transformation of Japan: From the Seventeenth to the Twenty-First Century* (Cambridge: Cambridge University Press, 1994), especially chapter 4 on "Technology and the Meiji State, 1868–1912"; William Röhl, ed., *History of Law in Japan Since 1868* (Leiden: Brill, 2005), 402–543.

[3] Röhl, *History of Law*, 402–543; Tomita Tetsuo, "The Origin of the Patent System in Japan," *Japanese Studies in the History of Science* 3 (1964): 114–26; James R. Bartholomew, *The Formation of Science in Japan: Building a Research Tradition* (New Haven, CT: Yale University Press, 1989), 132.

[4] Prior to joining the Paris Convention for the Protection of Industrial Property in 1899, Japan entered into several bilateral patent protection agreements with Germany (in force from 1896), and the United States (1897), Great Britain (1897), and Denmark (1898). Röhl, *History of Law*, 426.

(and simultaneously imperial) culture of invention and patent protection, shaped by post-1885 patent law and reshaped by post-1899 international industrial property integration, that arose and transformed during the life of Mikimoto's 1896 patent for a step in the production of semi-spherical "culture pearls" inside living shellfish.

One narrative surrounding the introduction of formal patent systems in Europe and the United States is that of a slow, though by no means inexorable, transition from arbitrary royal or imperial privileges bestowed upon a chosen few to a bureaucratized system for granting legal rights to all who qualified.[5] Yet throughout Japan's early twentieth century, the distinction between the "open" disclosure of technical methods (from which derives the Latinate *patente* of "letters patent") and the *ancien régime* whiff of "special monopoly right" (a rendition of the patent office's original term for a legal patent right, or *senbai tokkyo ken* 専売特許権) was neither clear nor undisputed. Nowhere was this more apparent than with Mikimoto's first patent. "It is quite possible that nothing caused the patent office more trouble during the Meiji years [1868–1912] than pearl issues," wrote one Japanese zoologist in the 1920s.[6] Between 1908 and 1915, domestic opponents of Mikimoto's monopoly position brought more than ten suits against patent no. 2,670, resulting in dozens of rulings from Japan's patent office tribunal and other courts of appeal.[7] Records of this struggle survive in an array of sources, including patent office and higher court decisions, legal commentaries, case files, newspapers, and trade journals. Taken together, these accounts shed light upon what might be called Japan's first major patent conflict. They expose a range of often conflicting ideas about technical authorship and monopoly ownership in early twentieth-century Japan.

Two related questions of legal demarcation surrounded the highly contested life of patent no. 2,670, from Mikimoto's initial application to Japan's patent office in 1894 until the formal expiration of the patent's claims in 1921. The first question has to do with how patentees, patent examiners, and judges decided what was new, and what was not. What separated novel technical knowledge from previously known methods in the early twentieth-century Japanese empire? The second question focuses on the place of pearl oysters in a system of "industrial" property rights. On what grounds could processes that worked through the

---

[5] Mario Biagioli, "Patent Republic: Representing Invention, Constructing Rights and Authors," *Social Research* 73 (Winter 2006): 1129–72.
[6] Kawamura Tamiji, "Nihon no shinju," *Kaizō* (December 1927): 49.
[7] Kishi dōmonkai, ed., *Ko bengoshi hōgaku hakase Kishi Seiichi soshō kiroku shū, gyōseihen dai 3 gō* (Tokyo, 1935).

mediation of a living creature also count as industrial (and thus patentable) processes?

15.2   The Birth of Patent No. 2,670

From the late 1870s the young Mikimoto Kōkichi was, among other things, a buyer and seller of China-bound marine products. These marine products included pearls, which he bought from divers and fishers in the southern coasts of his native Mie Prefecture region of Shima. But when pearl supplies began to drop in the 1880s, Mikimoto the dryland pearl dealer became Mikimoto the saltwater pearl oyster farmer. Not long thereafter, Mikimoto made a public exhibition of living pearl oysters and their products in an aquarium hall built specially for Japan's 1890 national industrial exposition. There he met with the Johns Hopkins-trained Tokyo Imperial University zoologist Mitsukuri Kakichi and one of Mitsukuri's students, who were both acting as judges of a the aquatic creatures that Mikimoto and others had put on display in the exposition's temporary aquarium. Mitsukuri suggested methods for improving Mikimoto's nascent efforts at raising pearl oysters. Following the exposition Mikimoto traveled to the University's coastal zoological laboratory south of Yokohama at Misaki, where Mitsukuri and others tutored him on ways to propagate pearl oysters and hinted at methods for inducing them to produce pearls. Mikimoto returned to Shima to continue his experiments and applied for a patent in late 1894. He received patent 2,670 a little over a year later in January 1896.[8] Mikimoto's first patent was entitled "a method for causing the deposition of pearl nacre via human artifice."[9] It described an "improvement" to a process for crafting semi-spherical objects that would be placed along the inside edge of a living pearl oyster's shell. If all went well, over the next several years the inserted objects would be covered with nacre (also known as mother-of-pearl) secreted by the shellfish.

It is worth lingering for a moment on the route by which Mikimoto's method took the textual form of the claims in patent no. 2,670. Relatively little is known about the role of patent intermediaries and patent attorneys prior to Japan's 1899 adherence to the Paris Convention for the Protection of Industrial Property (and the subsequent formalization of patent attorney [*benrishi*] registration). What is clear, however, is that

---

[8] Mikimoto Kōkichi, "Shinju monogatari," *Kokoro no hana* 9 (April 1905): 53–6.
[9] "Jinkō shinju soshitsu hichakuhō" (人工真珠素質被着法), Japanese patent no. 2,670. Accessed via Industrial Property Digital Library (IPDL) www.ipdl.inpit.go.jp/.

go-betweens played a role in drafting patents before 1899.[10] According to a subsequent in-house Mikimoto company history, Mikimoto's help came in the form of one of Tokyo Imperial University zoologist Mitsukuri Kakichi's acquaintances: Hozumi Nobushige (1855–1926), who in 1882 had been the first and youngest Japanese professor appointed to Tokyo Imperial University's faculty of law.[11] A later challenge to patent no. 2,670 would reveal, moreover, that the initial wording of the 1894 patent had been rejected; Mikimoto (or perhaps Hozumi) submitted a reworded application in November 1895. While the division of labor during the drafting process is not known, Mikimoto appears not to have written his first patent or subsequent patents alone. Clearer still is that he did not defend his patent alone.

Patent no. 2,670 spelled out a key step in the production of the semispherical "culture pearls" for which Mikimoto would become famous at the turn of the twentieth century. It undergirded his entry into the full-time business of pearl cultivation for buyers not in China but increasingly in Europe and the United States. For over a decade, Mikimoto's patents (patent no. 2,670 and a subsequent one issued in 1902) remained the only industrial property rights related to pearl cultivation in Japan or, for that matter, anywhere else in the world.

15.3   The Origins of Dispute

One strand of domestic dispute over patent no. 2,670 can be traced to March 1908, when Mikimoto brought patent infringement charges against three nearby entrepreneurs whom Mikimoto claimed had made illegal use of his method.[12] Police in Mie Prefecture promptly arrested

[10] For an explanation of the post-1899 *benrishi* patent attorney system and a rare example of nineteenth-century archival correspondence between an entrepreneur and his patent counsel, see Tom Nicholas and Hiroshi Shimizu, "Intermediary Functions and the Role of Innovation in Meiji and Taishō Japan," *Business History Review* 87 (Spring 2013): 121–49.

[11] *Mikimoto shinju 100 nenshi* (Tokyo: Kabushikigaisha Mikimoto, 1994), 59. Hozumi pursued his legal studies at the University of London and later at Humboldt University in Berlin. See Byron K. Marshall, "Professors and Politics: The Meiji Academic Elite," *Journal of Japanese Studies* 3 (Winter 1977): 71–97. Mikimoto remained on close terms with the Hozumi family: Nobushige's daughter Utako recorded no fewer than fifteen house calls from Mikimoto between 1899 and 1906, the end of her published diaries. See Hozumi Shigeyuki, ed., *Hozumi Utako nikki: Meiji ichi-hōgakusha no shūhen, 1890–1906* (Tokyo: Misuzu shobō, 1989), 495–6, 534, 548, 552, 584, 599, 606, 616, 670, 686, 833, 841, 946–7.

[12] At the time, patent infringement was a criminal offense that carried a penalty of up to three years' imprisonment. Infringement covered the unlawful imitation of someone else's patented product or method, as well as the conscious use or sale of the imitated product or method. A number of European and American countries, including

the trio, which consisted of the merchant Nagatsuka Shichirō, his nephew and associate Kitamura Jūkichi, and Jūkichi's elder brother Kitamura Kōichirō.[13]

Nagatsuka and the Kitamura brothers wasted little time in countering Mikimoto's criminal patent infringement charges. Within two months of their arrests, they engaged the services of the Tokyo-based legal practitioner Matsumoto Takashi and brought two suits to the Japanese patent office.[14] They claimed that even though Mikimoto owned a patent over an "improved" process, the older method on which patent no. 2,670 was based consisted entirely of publicly available information. They said that they had only followed the older method. The trio asked the patent office to evaluate the patent's novelty, arguing that Mikimoto's "improved" method did not differ substantially from already-published ones.[15]

Each side in the dispute had a different story about how this flurry of litigation had come to pass. "The cornered rats are trying to bite the cat," said Mikimoto's legal counsel Kishi Seiichi. Kishi claimed that the trio had attacked Mikimoto because they were scrambling to avoid the pending criminal charge of patent infringement.[16] By contrast, the trio's counsel Matsumoto suggested that Mikimoto had never pressed infringement charges against them in the past, precisely because Mikimoto "had feared a patent invalidation suit" of the very same sort the trio had presently launched. What, then, had changed? For one thing, the trio saw the makings of a fishing rights grab around their pearl farms in Gokasho Bay, an inlet next door to Mikimoto's thousand-acre marine cultivation headquarters in Ago Bay. The trio's legal counsel suggested that Mikimoto coveted exclusive cultivation rights to the seafloor around their coastal plots and had decided to use patent infringement as a pretext to gain control of them.[17]

Argentina, Chile, Guatemala, Mexico, Portugal, Switzerland, Uruguay, and Venezuela, also treated infringement as a matter of criminal law as of 1905. William Phillips Thompson, *Handbook of Patent Law of All Countries*, 13th ed. (London: Stevens & Sons, 1905). Criminal prosecution of patent infringement is still possible under Japan's revised 1959 patent law, although (as in present day France and Germany) it is rarely enforced. Thomas F. Cotter, *Comparative Patent Remedies: A Legal and Economic Analysis* (Oxford: Oxford University Press, 2013), 302.

[13] *Ise shinbun*, March 19, 1908.

[14] Matsumoto registered as a patent attorney (*benrishi*) in 1904; Kishi did so shortly after the promulgation of the new registration requirement in 1899. See Nōshōmushō Tokkyokyoku, *Tokkyo benrishi meibo Meiji 44 nen 3 gatsu genzai* (Tokyo: Tokkyokyoku, 1911), 33, 43. Patents were only one part of Kishi's legal practice, as the collected papers from which I draw upon in this chapter make clear.

[15] Kishi dōmonkai, ed., *Ko bengoshi hōgaku hakase Kishi Seiichi soshō kiroku shū*.

[16] Ibid., 26.   [17] Ibid., 41.

15.4   The Making of a Japanese Public Domain

Well before patent no. 2,670 first went to a patent tribunal in April 1908, legal practitioners inside and outside the patent office had been wrestling with the meaning of *kōchi kōyō* 公知公用, a term derived from the clause of Japan's patent law that referred to processes and apparatus that were "publicly known and publicly used" – and thus, no longer patentable. Legal practitioners understood this term as shorthand for two kinds of wider familiarity with technical information: "knowledge" that came from published sources, including earlier patents, and the practical "use" of machines and methods irrespective of textual circulation. *Kōchi kōyō* was, in effect, a public domain of accessible (or already accessed) know-how of the sort that Anglo-American law would have termed "prior art."[18]

At the turn of the twentieth century, changes in Japan's international treaty structure propelled *kōchi kōyō* to the center of domestic patent debate. The 1899 ratification of revisions to the mid-nineteenth century's unequal treaties brought with it bilateral industrial property agreements and the stipulation of Japan's incorporation into the Paris and Berne international conventions for patent, copyright, trademark, and design protection. For the first time, foreigners could apply for patent protection in Japan (via Japanese patent agents). For the first time too, disputes could be appealed to Japan's highest court, the *Daishin'in*.[19]

Patent integration occurred alongside new questions about how far the geographic scope of novelty would extend under Japanese law. Foreign business interests and the Japanese legal practitioners who represented them expressed concern that some Japanese patentees under the pre-1899 patent regime had been able to receive patents for claims that seemed to duplicate machines and methods that had been previously published or even patented abroad. This issue reached provisional resolution in the years after 1903, when a key ruling by the *Daishin'in* civil court asserted that technical knowledge was "unknown" unless published evidence or active practitioners could be located *within the Japanese empire*.[20] Only when knowledge and practice reached Japan's

---

[18] Takeuchi Kakuji, "Tokkyo seraru beki hatsumei no yōken o ronzu," *Hōritsu shinbun* 879 (July 25, 1913): 27–8, and 886 (August 25, 1913): 178–80.

[19] Tokkyochō, ed., *Kōgyō shoyūken seido hyakunenshi*, vol. 1 (Tokyo: Hatsumei Kyōkai, 1984).

[20] Hanaoka Toshio, *Kosodewata seizōki tokkyo mukō shinketsu fufuku jōkoku jiken hyōron* (Tokyo: Yūhikaku, 1903). The 1903 ruling centered around a carding machine patented in Japan in 1892 (patent no. 1,601), but which was claimed to have been based on a machine already patented in Britain in the early 1870s.

shores would it fall under the rubric of "public knowledge and public use." In other words, Japanese courts ruled that the empire's public domain was a *Japanese* public domain, not a global one.[21]

Ensuring compliance with the terms of industrial property rights agreements underlay the formation of the Japanese Society for the Protection of Industrial Property in 1905. Officials affiliated with this institution leveled criticisms against domestic entrepreneurs who, they claimed, did not abide by the rules of Japan's patent system. In theory, limiting the scope of known information to "know-how that was in the Japanese empire" made easier the task of protecting patents and maintaining the international integrity of the patent system.

Japanese courts limited the scope of novelty to the empire, which included Taiwan after the first Sino-Japanese War of 1894–5 and the southern half of Sakhalin Island (known as Karafuto) after the Russo-Japanese War of 1904–5. But the patent system was itself inextricable from Japanese state efforts to project imperial power in East Asia. This was evident in an 1908 agreement by which the United States agreed to end the extraterritorial application of American industrial property law in the Korean peninsula (that had been under a Japanese protectorate since 1905) and instead accept Japanese patent, design, and trademark statutes.[22] To observers in Japan, a functioning patent system served both as a prerequisite for membership in a civilized world of nations and as a vital diplomatic bargaining chip, one that within a decade had contributed both to the end of extraterritorial privileges in Japan and their partial end in Korea, which Japan would formally annex in 1910. Patent protection within the Japanese empire was of a piece with a broader logic of protection as a shield for defending against Western extraterritorial privileges while, in other cases, serving as a spear for expanding the reach of internationally recognized imperial Japanese law to new territories. As a result, and in contrast to the pluralism evident in the imperial codification of distinct categories of local customary law in Korea and Taiwan, patent law looked essentially the same on paper from any vantage point in the Japanese empire – even from places, like Korea in 1908, that were not

[21] The precedent was officially incorporated into patent office examination procedure in 1909. See *Kōgyō shoyūken seido hyakunenshi*, vol. 1.
[22] Toyomi Asano, "Regionalism or Imperialism: Japan's Options toward a Protected Korea after the Russo-Japanese War, 1905–1910," in *Transnational Japan as History: Empire, Migration, and Social Movements* , ed. Pedro Iacobelli, Danton Leary, and Shinnosuke Takahashi (New York: Palgrave Macmillan, 2015), 21–46.

formal colonies.[23] The center of imperial Japanese patent law remained squarely in the Tokyo patent office.

The redefinition of an imperial-wide Japanese public domain in the wake of international patent integration also gave new resonance to the title of "Japanese inventor."[24] The Japanese Society for the Protection of Industrial Property soon redubbed itself the Imperial Invention Promotion Society. The society extended its purview beyond the suppression of patent piracy to the cultivation of wider participation in Japan's industrial property rights regime.[25] Publications provided step-by-step instructions for anyone looking to have their machines or methods patented. Hagiographical anecdotes of Japan's great inventors appeared in newspapers, magazines, and monograph compilations. Icons of invention began to appear in the patent office's on-site patent museum and in regional and national "patented product" (tokkyohin) exhibitions. Mikimoto and his "culture pearls" featured prominently in print and on display.[26]

15.5   The "Ancient Method" and the Prehistory of Patent No. 2,670

Judicial interpretations of a Japanese public domain shaped strategies in subsequent lawsuits against Mikimoto's patent. During the patent suits, Mikimoto's competitors claimed that a method for inducing shellfish to produce semi-spherical pearls had already been common knowledge in the Japanese empire prior to Mikimoto's well-publicized 1890 meetings with the Tokyo Imperial University zoologist Mitsukuri Kakichi and other Japanese fisheries boosters.

---

[23] Marie Seong-Hak Kim, *Law and Custom in Korea: Comparative Legal History* (Cambridge: Cambridge University Press, 2012); Edward I-te Chen, "The Attempt to Integrate the Empire: Legal Perspectives," in *The Japanese Colonial Empire, 1895–1945*, ed. Ramon H. Myers and Mark R. Peattie (Princeton, NJ: Princeton University Press, 1984), 258–9.

[24] For a different trajectory of "national" inventors in the nineteenth century see Christine MacLeod, *Heroes of Invention: Technology, Liberalism, and British Identity, 1750–1914* (Cambridge: Cambridge University Press, 2008).

[25] The extent to which formal integration enabled colonized subjects to obtain patents throughout the empire remains little researched. Jung Lee has shown that hundreds of "Korean Edisons" successfully applied for patents during the 1920s and 1930s, though it appears that local patent promotion was targeted mainly toward metropolitan Japanese settlers in the Korean peninsula. See Jung Lee, "Invention without Science: 'Korean Edisons' and the Changing Understanding of Technology in Colonial Korea," *Technology and Culture* 54 (October 2013): 782–814.

[26] Wakabayashi Seiya, ed., *Hatsumei hakurankai hōkoku* (Tokyo: Hatsumeihin hakurankai zanmu torishimari jimusho, 1909), 87.

As the trio's legal counsel Matsumoto Takashi argued, if pearl culture had a place of origin, it was surely in China. In 1908 and 1912, Matsumoto made two separate requests for over a dozen monographs and articles to be used as evidence in the trio's patent office suits. He referred to a number of 1880s Japanese journals and fisheries studies that pointed to a long-standing "Chinese method" of pearl culture.[27]

These sources all had links to mid-nineteenth-century descriptions of freshwater pearl cultivation in southern China.[28] In 1853, the Ningbo-based American missionary doctor Daniel Jerome MacGowan and the local British consul Patrick Hague each delivered reports compiled from accounts delivered to them by "an intelligent native" whom they had dispatched to survey several villages. Both reports introduced a supposedly hundreds of years old method for inducing freshwater mussels to yield shells studded with semi-spherical "artificial pearls" or mother-of-pearl-coated icons of the Buddha.[29] Throughout the nineteenth century, "Buddha shells" found their way into museums and private collectors' cabinets across Europe. The rapid European circulation and translation of reports on southern Chinese pearl culture and the up-close examination of "Buddha shell" specimens spurred research into the origins and physiological mechanisms of pearl formation in freshwater shellfish, particularly among German naturalists.[30]

In patent office tribunals, the trio's counsel Matsumoto pointed to published transcripts of fisheries lectures given to audiences in Tokyo, Shizuoka, and elsewhere in Japan. German-language publications of the MacGowan and Hague accounts and other offshoots had spread widely among Japanese fisheries boosters, particularly after the 1880 international fisheries exposition held in Berlin.[31] According to Mikimoto's

---

[27] Kishi dōmonkai, ed., *Ko bengoshi hōgaku hakase Kishi Seïichi soshō kiroku shū*, 3–8, 373–6.

[28] Although it did not come up in the trial, the Swedish polymath Carl Linnaeus had learned of a similar method over a century earlier from a fellow countryman who had traveled in China. The Swedish king granted Linnaeus a royal monopoly for his method in 1761. Shortly thereafter he sold the process to another Swedish entrepreneur, who appears to have made no further use of it. Lisbeth Koerner, *Linnaeus: Nature and Nation* (Cambridge, MA: Harvard University Press, 1999), 140–63.

[29] D. T. [*sic*] MacGowan, "Pearls and Pearl-Making in China," *Journal of the Society of Arts* 2 (November 1853–November 1854): 72–5; F. Hague, "On the Natural and Artificial Production of Pearls in China," *Journal of the Royal Asiatic Society of Great Britain and Ireland* 16 (1856): 280–4.

[30] See, for example, Karl August Möbius, *Die echten Perlen, ein Beitrag zur Luxus-, Handels- und Naturgeschichte derselben* (Hamburg: Meissner, 1857).

[31] An engraved image of such shells appears in a publication entitled *Kaisanron* 海産論 (On Marine Products), an 1881 translation of a German fisheries monograph undertaken by the Kaitakushi, the agency charged with the development of Hokkaidō.

competitors, these publications provided a mechanism of textual circulation whereby zoologists had seen the potential for extending methods of
Chinese freshwater pearl cultivation to locally abundant varieties of saltwater shellfish.

The "Chineseness" of previously circulating pearl culture methods –
rather than, as the text of patent no. 2,670 implied, their "ancientness" –
surely posed a problem for patent officials who were evaluating the legal
basis of Mikimoto's industrial property rights. For officials to say that
Mikimoto's method was no different from the "Chinese method" was
both to suggest the inadequacy of in-house Japanese patent office examination procedures (after all, there had been multiple Japanese-language
references to Chinese pearl culture in the decade before Mikimoto's
1894 patent application, all within easy reach of Tokyo-based patent
examiners at the time) and to imply that one of Japan's best-known early
twentieth-century inventions was not, in the end, a result of homegrown
ingenuity.

It was within this context that substantial textual evidence of a circulating "Chinese method" did not sway the patent office to rule against
Mikimoto. To the trio's dismay, patent office tribunals and the civil
section of Japan's highest court refused to allow outside publications to
be used as evidence in the first round of patent invalidation suits. The
patent office ruled that it was not possible to prove that all the publications had circulated within the Japanese empire before Mikimoto's
patent application. As for books and articles that had clearly been in
Japan before the application, the patent office stated that they described
something other than the specific improvements described in Mikimoto's
patent claims, and were thus inadmissible. Matsumoto's second request
in 1912 remedied the previous list by including only texts published prior
to Mikimoto's patent application in 1894.[32] However, the Patent Tribunal ruled that the new set of articles described something other than
Mikimoto's patented method.

Through the first months of 1912, the patent office's rulings consistently accepted the arguments put forth by Mikimoto's representative
Kishi, dismissing the appeals to public knowledge and public use that
had been brought to bear against patent no. 2,670. Tribunals and higher
courts affirmed that Mikimoto's patent represented something distinct
from any other "publicly known" methods.

---

[32] Kishi dōmonkai, ed., *Ko bengoshi hōgaku hakase Kishi Seiichi soshō kiroku shū*, 373–6. The
texts included the English-language entry for "Pearl" in the 1889 edition of the
Encyclopedia Britannica.

15.6   Laws of Nature and Laws of Industry

The novelty of Mikimoto's method was not the only issue in suits brought against his first patent. Debate arose over the question of whether a method that relied on living shellfish could itself be patented as "industrial" property under Japanese law.

Following then-director Takahashi Korekiyo's American-inspired 1888 overhaul of the 1885 industrial property law, Japan's patent office was one of the world's few patent-issuing bodies to examine every application it received. One of a post-1899 Japanese patent official's examination criteria was to determine the "industrial" (*kōgyōjō*) utility of any proposed machine or method.[33] Yet, as it stood in the early twentieth century, the patent office did not have a formal position regarding the industrial qualities of processes involving living plants, animals, or microorganisms. In 1892, the agricultural chemist and one-time patent official Takamine Jōkichi received a Japanese patent for an improved method to produce the *tane-kōji* mold starter cultures used in the brewing of *sake* and other grain alcohols.[34] But, in 1908, just two months after the trio's counsel Matsumoto Takashi unveiled his arguments against Mikimoto, the patent office denied a different patent request for a chicken-breeding improvement, ruling that "methods of raising chickens and the like are not industrial processes."[35]

The industrial issue turned on a crucial question: What, or *who*, actually made a pearl? The trio's legal representative Matsumoto questioned the place of human agency in pearl production. Matsumoto argued that pearl production depended first and foremost on living pearl oysters, not on human handiwork. He suggested that Mikimoto's "method for causing the deposition of pearl nacre via human artifice" was a misnomer. A living pearl oyster would be expected to continue secreting mother-of-pearl, "human artifice" or not. Matsumoto noted that aside from the patent's title, which implied an active (and "industrial") human role in the inducement of mother-of-pearl deposition, the patent's *written* claims did not explicitly cover the moment when

---

[33] This was, in fact, written into the very first clause of the 1899 patent law to put Japan in line with the *industrielle* of the Paris industrial property convention. Hōten kenkyūkai, ed., *Nihon roppō* (Tokyo, 1899), 228.

[34] Japanese patent no. 1,748. At the same time as the Nagatsuka/Kitamura trials, Takamine Jōkichi's patent for the isolation of the hormone adrenalin was prompting a landmark US court ruling over the patentability of "natural products" that has informed subsequent debate over the United States' so-called product of nature doctrine. Christopher Beauchamp, "Patenting Nature: A Problem of History," *Stanford Technology Law Review* 16 (Winter 2013): 257–312.

[35] *Meiji 41 nen Tokkyokyoku shinketsuroku* (Tokyo: Tokkyokyoku, 1909), 87–8.

someone actually inserted a semi-spherical nucleating object inside a shell of a living pearl oyster. In any event, Matsumoto pointed out that no Japanese patent had ever been issued for the farming of two of Japan's other major aquacultural products, edible oysters and salmon. Like salmon and edible oyster cultivation methods, went Matsumoto's reasoning, Mikimoto's pearl cultivation process was not "industrial" in the slightest.[36]

In response, Mikimoto's counsel Kishi Seiichi harkened to the fields of brewing and fermentation. Kishi insisted that if Mikimoto's pearl culture patent were invalidated because it made use of "natural laws" (*shizen no hōsoku* 自然の法則), so too should patents for the brewing of alcohol or soy sauce.[37] Kishi used an analogy: just as brewers added grains and fruit to yeast and *kōji* in order to produce alcoholic beverages, Mikimoto's technicians implanted objects into living shellfish in order to produce pearls. As Kishi claimed, "Both make use of artifice in order to aid nature's powers. It therefore goes without saying that both are industrial processes."[38]

Things were not as cut and dried as Mikimoto's legal counsel Kishi made them out to be. In fact, the wording of the two claims that constituted patent no. 2,670 mentioned only the processing of semi-spherical nucleating objects. That is to say, the claims only referred to (1) lopping off a portion of a round object and (2) polishing it with salt or dipping it in brine. Not a word concerning pearl oyster physiology, or the means by which the surgical procedure would take place in practice, appeared in the body of the patent's text itself. In spite of this, Mikimoto's counsel Kishi steered legal debate toward broader questions of the patentability of human interventions in natural processes, in particular where such processes involved living creatures. Intentionally or not, Kishi echoed the wording of Mikimoto's own publicity, which described the company's pearls to prospective foreign buyers as "A Successful Case of Science Applied in Aid of Nature."[39]

On the question of industry, as with the question of novelty, the patent office sided with Mikimoto's counsel Kishi and extended its reading of the patent's scope to the surgical manipulation of pearl oysters themselves. Japan's highest civil court concurred. The court's ruling stated that it was clear that the process "makes use of natural side effects

---

[36] Kishi dōmonkai, ed., *Ko bengoshi hōgaku hakase Kishi Seiichi soshō kiroku shū*, 16–18. It should be noted as well that early twentieth-century Japanese sericulturists do not appear to have patented methods of silkworm raising either.

[37] Ibid., 22.   [38] Ibid., 136.

[39] K. Mikimoto, *Japanese Culture Pearls: A Successful Case of Science Applied in Aid of Nature* (Tokyo: Mikimoto Pearl Company, 1907).

through human artifice."[40] Courts affirmed that Mikimoto's patent covered not just human interventions, but also the commingling of artifice with the "laws of nature."

15.7   Anti-Patent Office, Anti-Mikimoto, Pro-patent

Ongoing dispute over patent no. 2,670 dovetailed with other cultivators' attempts to patent additional methods of pearl oyster manipulation. Courts ruled time and again that novel methods of pearl culture fell within the bounds of patentable industrial activity in Japan. But who else could receive those patents?

Two men – one from a neighboring bay, the other Mikimoto's own son-in-law – tried to patent methods of their own. The first, a man named Mise Tatsuhei, applied to the patent office for a process of spherical pearl formation in May 1907. Not long after, Mikimoto's son-in-law, the zoologist Nishikawa Tōkichi, submitted a similar application. Mise and Nishikawa proposed methods to induce the formation of *spherical* pearls via processes that differed significantly from the *semispherical* pearl culture method described in the initial patent specification. Both patent applications described methods by which technicians would implant spherical objects *inside* the soft body of a shellfish, not along the edge of its shell as with Mikimoto's first patent. Spherical pearl methods required the step of grafting tissues from the exterior of the same oyster or from another recently killed oyster. These steps were designed to create an internal "pearl sac" that would fully envelop the implanted round nucleating object.[41]

Like Nagatsuka and the Kitamuras, Mise and Nishikawa had both experimented on pearl oysters in southern Mie Prefecture. After falling out with his father-in-law Mikimoto, Nishikawa continued to develop a method at his alma mater, Tokyo's Imperial University, and at his own farm in the Seto Inland Sea. Mise became a technical advisor at the Ōmura Bay Pearl Company, a major startup farm in Nagasaki Prefecture. However, the patent office put both applications on hold, citing overlaps in their claims. In the meantime, Mikimoto received a patent in 1908 for a method that, while neglecting to mention the "pearl sac," was intended to produce spherical pearls. Seeking to consolidate their claims and speed up patent approval, Mise and Nishikawa reached an agreement over their conflicting patent applications in 1908. Under the terms of

---

[40] Kishi dōmonkai, ed., *Ko bengoshi hōgaku hakase Kishi Seiichi soshō kiroku shū*, 217.
[41] *Mise Tatsuhei shuki* (1923), unpaginated manuscript copy, held at the Mie Prefecture Historical Archives.

their agreement, Nishikawa would gain sole title to the patent. Mise would obtain full rights to make use of the method – assuming that the patent office approved the patent. Yet, even after the thirty-four-year-old Nishikawa succumbed to stomach cancer in 1909, the combined patent application remained in limbo.[42]

In contrast, patent no. 2,670 gained a new lease on life when the Japanese patent office announced that it had granted Mikimoto's patent a ten-year extension, the first one ever authorized under a recent provision to the patent law.[43] Mise and other pearl cultivators across Japan agitated against the extension, which had come only months before the patent's scheduled expiration. Rumors circulated of favoritism and corruption; many would have known, for example, that Mikimoto and his council Kishi Seiichi were highly placed members of the Imperial Invention Promotion Society. Cultivators began to suspect that delays in the approval of competing patent applications was part of an institutional effort to protect Mikimoto's patent monopoly.[44] Trade publications appealed for fairer allocations of inventive credit, along the lines of what Stathis Arapostathis and Graeme Gooday have termed the "moral economy of invention."[45] The *Japan Watchseller and Watchmaker's Journal* summed up the situation in 1911:

The recent rise in the price of pearls has grabbed our average countryman's attention. There are a great many artificial pearl inventions. Word is that patent applicants continue to appear. But we have still not heard of the patent office granting a patent to anyone besides Mr. Mikimoto. The reason for this is said to be that the new applicants' methods overlap with Mikimoto's. From our perspective, the above-mentioned patented process is nothing more than an appropriated ancient method. In no way is it a superlative invention. The patent office has granted a patent only to a single individual. It has protected an unsophisticated method and stifled the development of this industry, which is truly a disgrace.[46]

Cultivator dissatisfaction with the patent system at times even bubbled over into violence. In one widely reported case, a rejected pearl patent sparked cultivator Kinoshita Yasujirō's decision to hurl a chair at

---

[42] *Mise Tatsuhei shuki.*
[43] Mikimoto took out newspaper advertisements to announce the extension. See, for example, *Asahi shinbun*, May 13, 1911, and *Yomiuri shinbun*, May 14, 1911. Contemporaneous Mikimoto inventor biographies also gave a prominent place to the extension. See Makino Terutoshi, ed., *Gendai hatsumeika den* (Tokyo: Teikoku Hatsumei Kyōkai, 1911), 100.
[44] *Mise Tatsuhei shuki.*
[45] Stathis Arapostathis and Graeme Gooday, *Patently Contestable: Electrical Technologies and Inventor Identities on Trial in Britain* (Cambridge, MA: MIT Press, 2013).
[46] "Shinju no kaisetsu," *Nihon tokei shōkōshi* (Tokyo: Kinseki tokei shōhōsha, 1911), 211.

Kawasaki Saijirō, then director of the patent office in late 1915. Kinoshita had made his way to the capital from Mie Prefecture in order to check on his seven-year-old pending patent application in person. He grew upset upon hearing that officials had made no effort to inform him of his application's rejection over a month earlier. By all accounts, Kinoshita's irritation turned to rage when Kawasaki retorted that "it is the height of insolence for someone in the position of a supplicant to face off against the director."[47] It was, as one article noted, a "most unusual occurrence."[48] True enough, but it was also part of an established pattern of patent-related criticism, fueled by pearl cultivators' perceptions of unequally distributed patent rights.

For cultivators, the moral economy of invention was nuanced. Pearl cultivation emerged in Japan alongside Mikimoto's first patent. Mikimoto quickly established himself as a cultivator rather than a buyer of pearls; disseminating cultivation techniques to all comers in order to purchase their wares was not part of his initial strategy. Even so, resistance to Mikimoto's patent monopoly did not mean resistance to pearl cultivation patents *in toto*. As early as 1912, the Ōmura Bay Pearl Company and other cultivators, including the chair-wielding patent applicant Kinoshita Yasujirō, launched their own suits challenging the scope and validity of patent no. 2,670.[49] The specter of a never-ending Mikimoto master patent thus brought the trio's demands for access to publicly known semi-spherical cultivation methods into conversation with wider efforts to persuade the patent office to approve new spherical pearl patents.

15.8   From Patent Holder to Patent Holders

Mikimoto never commented publicly on the ongoing dispute over patent no. 2,670 or the new round of spherical pearl patent applications. He did, however, proclaim himself the prime candidate to farm round pearls two months after the July 1912 death of the Meiji emperor Mutsuhito. A memorial published under Mikimoto's name recalled his well-publicized 1905 audience with the emperor near Mie Prefecture's Ise shrine. The memorial linked Mikimoto's personal imperial connections to the project of cultivating spherical pearls by mentioning that he had donated a select number of round pearls to the emperor in 1908. "[Round pearls] are not yet ready to be put on the market as products for sale, but I have plans to cultivate more and more of them," read the

[47] *Jiji shinpō*, September 9, 1915.   [48] *Yomiuri shinbun*, October 3, 1915.
[49] Kishi dōmonkai, ed., *Ko bengoshi hōgaku hakase Kishi Seiichi sosho kiroku shū*.

memorial. "Together with scientists [*gakusha*] I plan to pour all my energies toward the advancement of research. If it takes off, I will make a great many spherical pearls that can be exported widely, even overseas, as an imperial Japanese product [*teikoku kokusan*]."[50] Out of court, Mikimoto sidestepped thorny questions of patent priority by claiming priority of imperial favor. At the same time, he pushed the date of the new method's practical, large-scale fruition farther into the future. In so doing, he implied that continued imperial support would make the cultivation of an exportable "imperial Japanese product" possible.

Mikimoto in fact *never* lost any of the many patent tribunal and civil court challenges to his first patent. Rulings stated over and over that processes involving living pearl oysters were subject to protection by "industrial" property rights. What Mikimoto did lose was his criminal patent infringement case against his trio of competitors. This reversal came about when *criminal* courts decided to accept published evidence of "publicly known" cultivation methods – precisely the materials that had been ruled inadmissible in the *civil* trials. In June 1912, the Nagoya regional appeals court overturned an earlier criminal infringement conviction that had been handed down to Nagatsuka and the Kitamuras by a Mie Prefecture district court – though not before the trio had served several months in jail. The Japanese high court's criminal division upheld the appeal ruling and threw out the infringement case against the trio in November. The high court noted that it was "clear based on the court's gathered evidence and evidence submitted by the lawyers" that a method for the cultivation of artificial pearls had been publicly known and publicly used prior to Mikimoto's patent. In its ruling the court claimed it was not bound by earlier patent office decisions. In any case, it suggested a fundamental flaw in previous opinions, noting that "one must always look beyond the scope of a patent right in order to determine what parts of it are publicly known and publicly used."[51]

The weakened position of patent no. 2,670 was on full display when Mikimoto and two Japanese competitors exhibited pearls at San Francisco's 1915 Panama-Pacific International Exposition. One of those competitors, the Ōmura Bay Pearl Company, noted its own "painstaking application and investigation as to the improvement of the old Chinese method of pearl culture."[52] In December that same year, Mikimoto

---

[50] Mikimoto Kōkichi, "Sentei no ōmigokoro ni soitatematsuran to no negai," *Shimin* 7 (September 1912): 84.

[51] "Meiji 45 nen (re) dai 1572 go," in *Daishin'in keiji hanketsuroku dai 18 shu, dai 23 han* (Tokyo: 1912), 1331–2.

[52] Hakurankwai Kyokwai [Hakurankai Kyōkai], ed., *Japan and Her Exhibits at the Panama-Pacific International Exposition* (Tokyo: 1915), 196–7.

broke patent no. 2,670 into two component claims, one for the "partially cut" nucleus and the other for a salt processing step. Both were set apart from an "ancient method."[53]

The rejection of Mikimoto's infringement claims did not end practices of pearl cultivation patenting. To the contrary, resolution of dispute over the *semi-spherical* pearl culture method described by patent 2,670 was nearly coterminous with the approval of patents for *spherical* pearl cultivation.[54] In 1916, more than eight years after Mise Tatsuhei's first patent application, the patent office gave approval for three spherical pearl process patents in Nishikawa Tōkichi's name – though not before issuing to Mikimoto a patent for a spherical pearl induction process a month before.[55] Dozens of patents followed for Mikimoto and others.[56] With these and subsequent industrial property rights, Mikimoto's competitors ceased their public campaigns against Mikimoto's first patent and the institutions that appeared to support it.

A new set of concerns emerged. As long as Japanese patentees held industrial property rights over spherical pearl methods, cultivators had little choice but to legally distinguish their own processes or else find space under someone else's patent umbrella. Mikimoto did not sell access to his methods, but other patent holders licensed patents for spherical pearl cultivation and instructed licensees in how to cut into a living shellfish without killing it. This came at a hefty price. Under the first licensing agreements for the "Nishikawa method," payments could exceed one-third of a licensee's future revenues.[57]

The proliferation of patents did not stop efforts to gain other kinds of competitive advantage. Craft secrecy and public patents went hand in hand. As one Mikimoto employee who joined the company in the 1930s later put it, "the operating room worked on the principle of complete secrecy."[58] Another Nagasaki-based cultivator noted of the pearl industry prior to World War II that "it was unthinkable to share your own techniques with outsiders."[59]

---

[53] Honjō Osamu, *Shinju yōshoku ni kan suru hōritsu kankei* (Nagoya: Nagoya Kōsoin, 1935).
[54] *Mise Tatsuhei shuki.*
[55] Mikimoto received patent no. 29,409 on May 5, 1916; Nishikawa's patents nos. 29,628, 29,629, and 29,630 were granted on June 16, 1916.
[56] One 1935 pamphlet listed fifty pearl-related patents covering methods of pearl induction and other implements like the cages used in the raising of pearl oysters. See *Shinju yōshoku ni kan suru hōritsu kankei.*
[57] Nishikawa entered into technical licensing agreements as early as 1908, well before the patent was issued. See Kuru Tarō, *Shinju no hatsumeisha wa dare ka?: Nishikawa Tōkichi to Tōdai purojekuto* (Tokyo: Keisō shobō, 1987), 327–8.
[58] Kuru, *Shinju no hatsumeisha wa dare ka?*, 153.
[59] *Shin'en shinju nanajūnen* (Tokyo: Shinju shinbunsha, 1978), 130.

Infringement claims, moreover, remained difficult to pursue. As one zoologist at the time commented, "with objects such as pearls, where secret surgical methods are used in their production, it is very difficult to enforce claims of infringement."[60] Smoking-gun evidence was bound to be scarce when one attempted to evaluate subtly differing procedures, each one performed by cagey technicians who hid themselves and their techniques behind the walls of enclosed surgical operating rooms and under the shells of living pearl oysters.

Finally, cultivator-led organizations became a locus of negotiation, not tribunals and courts. No legal battles remotely approaching the length or vitriol of the dispute over patent no. 2,670 would reach a courtroom or tribunal during the active lives of the first generation spherical pearl patents, which lasted until 1936. Until that time, calls for extra-judicial technical self-policing *among* a growing number of spherical pearl cultivators brought the issue of cultivator coordination to the fore.[61] Even so, the boundaries of subsequent pearl cultivator communities, of which one 1928 Mikimoto-led instantiation became known informally as the "patent control association" (*tokkyo tōsei kumiai*), were themselves shaped fundamentally by state-authorized industrial property rights.[62]

Several kinds of interpretive ambiguity stemmed from the trials over patent no. 2,670 and their aftermaths. To Mikimoto's competitors, patent dispute freed access to an "ancient" semi-spherical pearl culture method and, with the granting of a new round of patents to applicants besides Mikimoto, allowed for broader-based access to methods of *spherical* pearl culture. For his part, Mikimoto began to treat patent no. 2,670 and other semi-spherical methods as distant technological precursors, not claims that had laid the groundwork for his continued reputation as an inventor. Mikimoto stopped basing his claims of inventive priority and industry leadership on a single, decisive patent, preferring instead to present images of pearl cultivation to audiences of patrons – whether retail customers, foreign zoologists, or the Japanese imperial household – as a story of progressive innovation that underlay a consistently branded "Mikimoto method." Mikimoto's aquatic production and promotional focus turned toward the techniques of spherical pearl cultivation for which his company became widely known abroad after World War I, even as multiple pearl cultivation patents protected multiple inventors within the Japanese empire.

[60] Kawamura Tamiji, "Nihon no shinju," *Kaizō* (December 1927): 49.
[61] Koseki Nobuaki, "Senzen ni okeru shinju dantai no hensen," *Suisan jihō, shinju tokushū* (1958): 12–28.
[62] *Shin'en shinju nanajūnen*, 49.

If nothing else, the substantially weakened claims that constituted patent no. 2,670 were, following their ten-year extension, the longest-lived industrial property rights ever issued in Japan upon their unheralded expiration in 1921. But the patent's effects continued to be felt. Mikimoto Kōkichi's chroniclers later suggested, perhaps apocryphally, that patent examiners had once informed Mikimoto in 1894 that his semi-spherical method was the first patent application they had ever seen to involve a "living creature" (*seibutsu*).[63] Other Japanese legal commentators from the 1920s onward identified rulings on Mikimoto's first patent as a precedent for the patentability of agricultural and aquacultural processes that involved living creatures – including the very *spherical* pearl culture processes that Mikimoto and his competitors had come to patent for themselves.[64]

15.9   Conclusion: The Afterlife of Patent No. 2,670

The legal status of invention changed several times between Mikimoto's first patent application in 1894 and the sweeping postwar (and post-imperial) overhaul of Japan's patent law in 1959 that, with a number of modifications, remains in effect.[65] Examiners examined Mikimoto's 1894 application under the 1889 law's specification of a "novel and profitable industrial method, machine, manufactured good, or synthetic object."[66] Judges judged patent no. 2,670 under the 1899 law's specification of "a first and original invention of any industrial article or process."[67] By contrast, their post-1959 counterparts evaluated whether

[63] Mamada Takashi, *Yōshoku shinju no hatsumeisha Mikimoto Kōkichi* (Tokyo: Nihon Shuppansha, 1942), 215; Ototake Iwazō, *Denki Mikimoto Kōkichi* (Tokyo, 1950), 78–9.

[64] The jurist Kiyose Ichirō cited the July 26, 1910 Patent Tribunal appeal ruling 612 against Nagatsuka and the Kitamuras' patent invalidation claims in the patent law standard *Tokkyohō genri* (Tokyo: Chūō shoten, 1922), 89. A discussion of the 1909 patent office ruling on patent no. 2,670, seemingly gleaned from a translation of Kiyose's writings, found itself in a lengthy (and uncited) footnote in Stephen A. Bent et al., *Intellectual Property Rights in Biotechnology Worldwide* (London: Macmillan, 1987), 73–4. For an early discussion of "living creature" patents that refers to spherical pearl patents, see also Murayama Toshizō, *Senbai tokkyo to wa: saishin tokkyo hō to jitsuyō shin'an hō* (Tokyo: 1942), 48–9.

[65] As of 2005 there had been twenty-five revisions to the 1959 law, including Japan's 1980 signing of the Budapest Treaty on the International Recognition of the Deposit of Microorganisms for the Purposes of Patent Procedure. See Röhl, *History of Law*, 409–10.

[66] Suzuki Hikoto, *Hatsumei tokkyohō annai* (Tokyo: 1890), 51.

[67] *Laws of Japan: Patent Law, Patent Rules, Trade-Mark Law, Trade-Mark Rules, Design Law, Law of Registration Tax* (Yokohama: Japan Mail Office, 1899), 1; *Nihon roppō* (Tokyo, 1899), 228.

incoming applications exhibited the "highly advanced creation of technical ideas utilizing natural laws."[68]

When it came time to work through post-1959 relationships among patent law, natural laws, and living creatures, some latter-day Japanese officials looked to patent no. 2,670. Upon being asked in 1963 about the possibility of granting plant patents under Japanese law, leading patent office appeals official Yoshifuji Kōsaku replied as follows:

A patent invalidation suit was once brought against the production method for the cultured pearl, Mr. Mikimoto's world-class invention, on the grounds that it did not fit within the idea of an industrial invention ... . However, the [patent office] ruling rejected the invalidation claims by taking the line of reasoning that, in the sense that a so-called industrial step [kōteki na shudan] had been added, it was industrial. The Daishin'in high court also supported this way of thinking. This does not apply only to the fisheries industry, but also to agricultural inventions. As long as they include an industrial step and it is deemed that they should be patented, plant patents would of course be accepted as well. However, the plant patents I speak of here are not for plants themselves, but rather for methods of raising plants or other cultivation methods along the lines of cultured pearl production methods.[69]

To be sure, patent no. 2,670 does not undergird contemporary debates over biopatenting in Japan or elsewhere. Nor is this *process* patent cited in ongoing dispute over the possibility of making exclusive claims on "*products* of nature." The patentability of modifications to pearl oysters (rather than claims over new varieties of shellfish) was, after all, the focus of the original cases.[70] Nevertheless, patent no. 2,670 came to be seen as an early example of the incorporation of living creatures into Japan's system of industrial property rights.[71]

Patent no. 2,670 was one of a larger subset of industrial property claims in the late nineteenth and early twentieth-century world that made living creatures a part of inventive claims.[72] What makes patent no. 2,670 stand out among its global contemporaries is the extent to which it became embroiled in dispute. Crucially, the notion that the patent

---

[68] Teruo Doi, *The Intellectual Property Law of Japan* (Alphen aan den Rijn, The Netherlands: Sijthoff & Noordhoff, 1980), 9.

[69] "Tokkyohō seminaa," *Jurisuto* 286 (November 15, 1963): 31.

[70] See Beauchamp, "Patenting Nature."

[71] Mark Janus points out that along with the United States, "the practice of issuing utility patents on plants now appears to be well-established in Japan, South Korea, and Australia." He notes that "no definitive judicial decision has been rendered to date, but the Examination Guidelines of the Japan Patent Office (JPO) assume that plants can constitute patent-eligible subject matter." Mark D. Janus, "Patenting Plants: A Comparative Synthesis," in *Patent Law in Global Perspective*, ed. Ruth L. Okediji and Margo A. Bagley (Oxford: Oxford University Press, 2014), 217–18.

[72] Beauchamp, "Patenting Nature."

extended to living creatures only emerged after the patent went on trial. If criminal court rulings crippled Mikimoto's claims in particular, civil courts, patent tribunals, and patent officials used the patent to affirm the patentability of methods that aided "nature's laws" in general. This was not the victory that Mikimoto or his attorneys wanted; legal battles rendered the patent incapable of supporting a pearl cultivation monopoly. Instead, patent no. 2,670 exists as part of an alternative genealogy of agricultural and aquacultural biopatenting, one that begins with heretofore understudied ways of defending "industrial" applications of living creatures at a late nineteenth and early twentieth-century inter-section of global patent system integration, imperial patent protection, and national invention promotion.

Part VI

Epilogue

16   Postscript

Steven Wilf and Graeme Gooday

Harmonization has long been a prominent historical narrative of international patent law. Yet patent, like copyright, began historically without any such narrative, manifested as a disparate collection of fragmented territorial regimes with bespoke schemes for governing rights over technological inventions. Early patent law was thus metropolitan in scope, simply operating within a country's geographic boundaries. While there was nothing initially to harmonize the diverse territorially specific patent laws of nations, from the late eighteenth century onwards our contributors have shown how some degree of commonality from two sources. One route was via the imperialist project, through which colonizing European powers typically imposed some version of their own native patent system upon their subordinated territories. Conversely, we have seen how independent nation-states (including newly liberated colonies) across Latin America, Central Europe, and India, looked to the developed industrial powers to find the most appropriate patent system to adopt and adapt for their particular economic and political circumstances. Thus, variants and hybrid forms of the Anglo-American, French, and latterly German patent systems had proliferated to some extent by the time that the Paris Convention for the Protection of Industrial Property (1883) was launched to enable the newly important activity of transnational patenting.

While some scholars portray the Paris Convention as the start of an incremental move to greater international harmonization in patent law, this book's contributors have explored instead the resilient diversity among national systems that this convention was designed to accommodate and mediate between. We have seen that this involved divergent approaches to balancing the patent bargain (or social contract), the distinctive rights of inventors, the economic and political interests of the state, and the benefit of the domestic public. Only in the strongly inventor-centered US system, informed by natural rights theory, was there any resilient long-term commitment to the notion that patentees directly owned their inventions as forms of intellectual property. By contrast, strongly interventionist governments, as found in Germany and Central-Eastern Europe, gave inventors rights only as expedient for the broader interests of the state and, secondarily, for the benefit of the public. In that context ownership of intellectual property lay by default with the state, not the patentee – who was only allowed to monopolize an invention under very specific conditions.

Such variation in the operation of patent law entailed that it was no easy matter for an inventor to secure global patent rights. For the many nations that did not initially subscribe to the Paris Convention, the services of an international patent attorney with knowledge of such local particularities was thus indispensable. Then again, as we have seen, some European nations such as Greece resisted formalizing the bureaucracy of an open patenting system until after World War I, and China resisted much longer. This highlights how patenting has tended to be a feature that has emerged symbiotically with Euro-American forms of business-capitalism and with other more collectivist or privilege-centered under-standings of how inventions should be managed actually lasting well into the twentieth century. Even nations that did eventually adopt patenting systems under pressure from global business were not compelled thereby to use them for globalizing purposes. Certain patent systems even sought to reward those who introduced new inventions and methods developed abroad without any compensation for the foreign inventors. In an overtly nationalist vein, some countries unambiguously favored their own citizens in the patent process, and refused patents – or heavily restricted patenting rights – to noncitizens. Patenting could thus be as liberal or illiberal a tool as the political culture in which it was embedded.

Ironically, the effect of establishing international institutions of intellectual property governance has been to highlight the limits to which harmonization has been or could be accomplished. It indeed has been difficult to follow up the major achievements of harmonization such as the Patent Cooperation Treaty (1970) that simplified patent filing. While harmonization over formal rules such as registration was comparatively straightforward, deeper harmonization concerning the operating of patent offices and courts, remedies, and the divergent policy agenda of different industrial economies often proved elusive. Political gridlock in Geneva increasingly prompted the emergence of alternative routes to harmonization such as multilateral treaties. The 1995 Agreement on Trade-Related Aspects of Intellectual Property Rights (TRIPS) set minimum standards for national patent systems. Significantly, it linked enforcement to trade and provided for a compliance mechanism through the World Trade Organization (WTO).

Long before TRIPS, already in the mid-1960s, there was a growing disenchantment with international patent governance. Multinational corporations as rights holders and Northern hemisphere countries often engaged in asymmetrical market exchanges with less well-to-do trading partners. The World Intellectual Property Organization (WIPO) imposed legal norms from the outside that often proved disadvantageous to developing economies. Following the broader trends in post-colonial political mobilization, academics and activists articulated a broad critique of harmonization. It was perceived as an institution of legislative colonization whereby wealthy countries imposed norms that extracted wealth from less fortunate countries. In that regard, TRIPS actually had the effect of galvanizing *opposition* to the plan to achieve harmonization by the tightening of enforcement standards. After all, the threat of potential trade sanctions for transgressing TRIPS effectively brought about a contraction in the policy space allotted to signatory nations, and reduced their flexibility to shape domestic patent systems that reflected their own domestic needs.

The contention over harmonization has resulted in renewed attention to the possibilities of national diversity. In 2014, the Max Planck Institute of Innovation and Competition: Declaration on Patent Protection – Regulatory Sovereignty under TRIPS[1] urged that states be provided with greater discretion in implementing intellectual property rules. The basic idea behind patent sovereignty is that sovereign states should retain the discretion to adopt a patent system that best suits their technological capabilities as well as their social, cultural, and economic needs and priorities. Yet even those most strongly asserting patent sovereignty acknowledge that national patent systems must remain within the compass of global patent norms. In other words, sovereignty and harmonization should work in a kind of dynamic equilibrium – not with an inevitable journey to global uniformity.

Recognizing this ongoing dynamic, our book has sought to surface the historical varieties of national patent cultures at the moment when the boundaries between global and sovereign patent systems remain uncertain. Patent diversity has been remarkably resilient in the face of harmonization. In the age of empires, colonial patent cultures on the periphery diverged from those of the metropole. In the post-colonial period, newly independent nations envisioned patents as a strategic means to achieve economic traction by promising security to foreign investors, as a form of inventors' property to satisfy the demands of political circles promoting technology or, quite simply, as a signaling of progress.

What future directions might be seen over the horizon? Our current global patent system is in flux. Regional blocs are constructing their own

---

[1] www.mpg.de/8132986/Patent-Declaration.pdf.

patent norms. A patchwork of multilateral treaties challenge the hegemony of broad universal conventions such as the Paris Convention and international governance institutions such as WIPO. Domestic patent systems are under immense political pressure from a variety of stakeholders. The burden of an enormous number of patent filings has overwhelmed the examination process, and weak patents have passed through the usual gatekeeping mechanisms that prevent the granting of monopolies to marginal inventions. Patent thickets have emerged creating a kind of anti-commons, and nonpracticing entities or patent trolls threaten the underpinnings of the patent system as a mechanism for promoting innovation. Facing these challenges, architects of patent law have sought to carve out policy-making space at the national level.

Neither national nor international patent governance has proved capable of responding as effectively as had been hoped to these challenges. In many ways, the old debate about the efficacy of harmonization has become less significant. Large corporations through a variety of private ordering mechanisms have erased the very borders upon which official patent systems are grounded. Patent pledges – whereby companies release a limited amount of proprietary material in order to foster the production of apps or other add-ons – is just one example. Open-source and open-access arrangements might be granted with limitations. Industry groups setting technical interoperability standards is another. Indeed, private ordering has increasingly rested on trade secrets rather than patent because of its flexibility. In 2016, the passage of the European Union Directive on the Protection of Trade Secrets and the United States legislating the first comprehensive civil law statute protecting trade secrets, the Defend Trade Secrets Act, has opened up new avenues to establishing proprietary rights in inventions. Using trade secrets with technological security measures, such as encryption, might substitute for the acquisition of patents.

Private ordering does more than simply add another layer of complexity to an already bewildering amount of variation in the intellectual property protection of scientific and technical innovation. It threatens to erase the very territorial boundaries upon which both national patent diversity and harmonization are grounded. What does pervasive patent diversity mean for harmonization? Will international governance mechanisms develop that can accommodate variation in patent norms? And how willing might domestic patent systems be to experiment within their own patent cultures? This volume presents a portrait of creative, often innovative variants in how invention can be encouraged through patent. Might the master historical narrative of patent law not be harmonization – but resilient heterogeneity?

Index

Titles in the Series (formerly known as Cambridge Studies in Intellectual Property Rights)

For EU product safety concerns, contact us at Calle de José Abascal, 56–1°,
28003 Madrid, Spain or eugpsr@cambridge.org.

www.ingramcontent.com/pod-product-compliance
Ingram Content Group UK Ltd.
Pitfield, Milton Keynes, MK11 3LW, UK
UKHW020402140625
459647UK00020B/2604